Past and Present Publications

French Society and the Revolution

Past and Present Publications

Past and Present Publications will comprise books similar in character to the articles in the journal *Past and Present*. Whether the volumes in the series are collections of essays — some previously published, others new studies — or monographs, they will encompass a wide variety of scholarly and original works primarily concerned with social, economic and cultural changes, and their causes and consequences. They will appeal to both specialists and non-specialists and will endeavour to communicate the results of historical and allied research in readable and lively form. This new series continues and expands in its aims the volumes previously published elsewhere.

The first volumes to be published in the series by Cambridge University Press are:

Family and Inheritance: Rural Society in Western Europe 1200-1800, edited by Jack Goody, Joan Thirsk and E. P. Thompson

French Society and the Revolution, edited by Douglas Johnson

Peasants, Knights and Heretics: Studies in Medieval English Social History, edited by R. H. Hilton

Volumes previously published with Routledge & Kegan Paul are:

Crisis in Europe 1560-1660, edited by Trevor Aston

Studies in Ancient Society, edited by M. I. Finley

The Intellectual Revolution of the Seventeenth Century, edited by Charles Webster

French Society and the Revolution

edited by
DOUGLAS JOHNSON
Professor of French History, University of London

CAMBRIDGE UNIVERSITY PRESS
Cambridge
London · New York · Melbourne

Published by the Syndics of the Cambridge University Press
The Pitt Building, Trumpington Street, Cambridge CB2 IRP
Bentley House, 200 Euston Road, London NW1 2DB
32 East 57th Street, New York, NY 10022, USA
296 Beaconsfield Parade, Middle Park, Melbourne 3206, Australia

© Past and Present Society 1967, 1971, 1972, 1973, 1974, 1976

First published in this form 1976

Printed in Great Britain
at the
University Printing House, Cambridge
(Harry Myers, University Printer)

Library of Congress Cataloguing in Publication Data

Main entry under title:

French society and the Revolution.

(Past and present publications)

Articles originally published in the journal Past and present.

Includes index.

1. France – History – Revolution, 1789–1799 – Addresses, essays,
lectures. 2. France – History – Revolution, 1789–1799 – Causes
and character – Addresses, essays, lectures. I. Johnson, Douglas
W. J. II. Past & present.

DC142.F7 944.04 76–1136

ISBN 0 521 21275 8

Contents

Introduction   1
DOUGLAS JOHNSON, *Professor of French History,*
University of London

1 Was There an Aristocratic Reaction in Pre-Revolutionary
France? (No. 57, November 1972)   3
WILLIAM DOYLE, *Lecturer in Modern History,*
University of York, England

2 The Revolution and the Rural Community in Eighteenth-
Century Brittany (No. 62, February 1974)   29
T. J. A. LE GOFF, *Associate Professor of History,*
York University, Ontario, and
D. M. G. SUTHERLAND, *Associate Professor of History,*
Brock University, Ontario

3 The High Enlightenment and the Low-Life of Literature
in Pre-Revolutionary France (No. 51, May 1971)   53
ROBERT DARNTON, *Professor of History, Princeton*
University

4 Nobles, Bourgeois and the Origins of the French
Revolution (No. 60, August 1973)   88
COLIN LUCAS, *Fellow of Balliol College, Oxford*

5 The Survival of the Nobility During the French Revolution
(No. 37, July 1967)   132
ROBERT FORSTER, *Professor of History, Johns Hopkins*
University

6 Women in Revolution, 1789-1796 (No. 53, November 1971)   148
OLWEN HUFTON, *Professor of Modern History, Univer-*
sity of Reading

7 The Justices of the Peace of Revolutionary Paris,
September 1792–November 1794 (Frimaire Year III)
(No. 52, August 1971)   167
RICHARD M. ANDREWS, *Professor of History, John Jay*
College, City University of New York

8 The Condition of the Poor in Revolutionary Bordeaux
(No. 59, May 1973)   217
ALAN FORREST, *Lecturer in French History, University of*
Manchester

9 Resistance to the Revolution in Western France
(No. 63, May 1974)   248
  HARVEY MITCHELL, *Professor of History, University of
  British Columbia*

10 The White Terror of 1815 in the Department of the Gard
(No. 58, February 1973)   286
  GWYNN LEWIS, *Senior Lecturer in History, University
  of Warwick*

Index   314

Introduction

DOUGLAS JOHNSON

THE FOLLOWING ARTICLES HAVE ALL APPEARED IN *PAST AND PRESENT*. They do not include all the articles which this periodical has published relevant to the history of the Ancien Régime and the French Revolution, and it is unfortunate that for reasons of space, certain have had to be omitted.[1] But they do suggest some of the aspects of French history in this period which have most interested British and North American researchers. At a time when we have recently been reminded that every year French scholars publish more books and articles on the Revolution than on the sixteenth, seventeenth and eighteenth centuries put together,[2] and that there is enough information available to invalidate any impressionistic generalization whilst being too much for systematic analysis, it has also been pointed out that the *Annales: Économies, Sociétés, Civilisations* (to which *Past and Present* has often been compared) has tended to neglect the history of the French Revolution.[3] If "l'école des *Annales*" admits that it might have shied away from a subject which, in terms of syllabus, dating and concept, fitted too easily into the "histoire événementielle" which "l'école des *Annales*" was only too eager to avoid, then it could be that this is an argument for believing that British and North American historians have a distinct contribution to make to the debate on the French Revolution. It has been claimed that in the past this was because of their lack of imagination or mental effort;[4] but it can now be claimed that historians who are not French, writing on the French Revolution, avoid the only too obvious schools and cliques into which many French historians seem easily, naturally and perhaps inevitably, to fall, and that they address themselves more directly towards the major problems of the period.[5] It could be too that they have less hesitation in approaching and developing certain themes than do their French colleagues. Professor

[1] For example, Albert Soboul, "Robespierre and the Popular Movement of 1793-4", *Past and Present*, No. 5; "The French Rural Community in the Eighteenth and Nineteenth Centuries", *ibid.*, No. 10; Clive H. Church, "The Social Basis of the French Central Bureaucracy under the Directory", *ibid.*, No. 36.

[2] Norman Hampson, *The French Revolution: A Concise History* (London, 1975), p. 6.

[3] François Furet, "Ancien Régime et Révolution: Réinterprétations", *Annales, E.S.C.*, xxix (1974), p. 3.

[4] See Richard Cobb's review of Hedua Ben-Israel, *English Historians on the French Revolution*, 1968, in *Tour de France* (London, 1976), pp. 35 ff.

[5] Douglas Johnson, "From Below and Above: French History, Anglo-Saxon Attitudes", *Encounter* (January 1976), pp. 47 ff.

Olwen Hufton, commenting on the importance of violence in the social life of the Ancien Régime (such as emerged from the study by T. Le Goff and D. Sutherland, reproduced in this volume), has suggested that historians may have shunned a close analysis of violence because they thought that in some way it detracted from the essential worthiness of those destined to win the ultimate political crown.[6] A French historian, commenting with some cynicism on the controversy whereby the class struggle as the motivating force which brought the Ancien Régime to an end was replaced by the importance of "ceux qui constitue l'élite", whether of wealth, culture, or ability, has said that all this discussion would simply remain as an example of the ideological discussions which were taking place within French historiography within the 1960s.[7]

This is not the place to try to define the "état actuel des questions", concerning the end of the Ancien Régime and the Revolution. A number of historians have written interesting and important articles, in which they have tried to put together the social and political elements,[8] or in which they have surveyed a particular problem, for example that of the exclusivity of the nobility,[9] or the role of the State in the Ancien Régime.[10] But whatever the details of the research, or the nature of the assumptions, there is one viewpoint from which much else stems. And that is the largely dominant French view that the French Revolution was the outstanding bourgeois revolution, that it was the culmination of a long economic and social evolution, that it marked the emergence of a bourgeois, capitalist society in France. But it is the achievement of British and North American scholars to have highlighted the complex reality of late eighteenth-century French society, and the essays which follow consider the problems of change in ways which are particularly relevant and perceptive.

[6] Olwen Hufton, *The Poor of Eighteenth Century France* (Oxford, 1975), pp. 360-1.
[7] Michel Vovelle, "L'Élite ou le mensonge des mots", *Annales, E.S.C.,* xxix (1974), p. 49.
[8] C. Mazauric, "Voies nouvelles pour l'histoire de la Révolution française: histoire politique", *Annales historiques de la Révolution française,* xlv (1975), pp. 159 ff.
[9] G. Lemarchand, "Sur la société française en 1789", *Revue d'histoire moderne et contemporaine,* January-March 1972; David Bien, "La réaction aristocratique avant 1789: l'exemple de l'armée", *Annales historiques,* xlv (1975), pp. 23 ff. and pp. 505 ff.
[10] Régine Robin, "La nature de l'état à la fin de l'ancien régime", *Dialectiques,* No. 1-2 (1974), pp. 31 ff.

1. Was There an Aristocratic Reaction in Pre-Revolutionary France?*

WILLIAM DOYLE

AMID THE TURMOIL OF DEBATE WHICH HAS CHARACTERIZED THE STUDY of the French Revolution and its origins in recent years, it might seem that no aspect could escape renewed and critical scutiny. Yet this impression is deceptive. The history of the Revolution continues to be charted with reference to many landmarks seemingly so well-established that historians take them for granted. One such landmark is the "aristocratic reaction" of the last years of the old régime. Emphases differ, and some historians use the idea in a far broader sense than others. But it finds its place in most of the standard works,[1] and writers of monographs feel equally obliged to take account of it. Most descriptions of the aristocratic reaction comprise one or more of four elements:

1. *Political* reaction. This was the campaign of the nobility, beginning in 1715 and culminating in the "noble revolt" of 1787-8, to recover the political power it had lost under Louis XIV. The main vehicles of the movement were the parlements, which became the spearhead of all noble pretentions over the century.[2]

2. *Ideological* reaction.[3] This was exemplified by the works of such writers as Saint-Simon, Fénelon, Boulainvilliers and Montes-

* I am grateful for the critical comments of Professor Douglas Johnson and the members of his seminar, before whom an early draft of this paper was read. I am also indebted to Professor Norman Hampson for many helpful suggestions.

[1] E.g. R. R. Palmer, *The Age of the Democratic Revolution*, 2 vols. (Princeton, N.J., 1959), i, pp. 458-60; A. Goodwin, *The French Revolution* (London, 1959), pp. 24-5; N. Hampson, *A Social History of the French Revolution* (London, 1963), pp. 2-13; M. J. Sydenham, *The French Revolution* (London, 1969), pp. 25-6; F. Furet and D. Richet, *The French Revolution* (London, 1970), p. 23; G. Lefebvre, *The Coming of the French Revolution* (New York, 1947), pp. 14-19; A. Mathiez, *La Révolution Française*, 3 vols. (Paris, 1922-4), i, pp. 8-9, 17; A. Soboul, *La France à la veille de la Révolution : Economie et Société* (Paris, 1966), pp. 79-86.
[2] The classic statements of this case are J. Egret, "L'Opposition aristocratique en France au XVIIIᵉ siècle", *L'Information Historique*, x (1949), pp. 181-5; and F. L. Ford, *Robe and Sword: the Regrouping of the French Aristocracy after Louis XIV* (Cambridge, Mass., 1953), *passim*.
[3] Well summarized in Ford, *op. cit.*, chaps. ix, x, xii; and more briefly in Soboul, *La France à la veille*, pp. 79-82.

3

quieu; and the remonstrances of the parlements, all of which were manifestoes for noble control of the state.

3. *Social* reaction, "caste spirit" or "noble exclusivism".[4] This refers to the aristocracy of Louis XVI's ministers, the noble monopoly of high ecclesiastical positions, the exclusion of commoners from the parlements, and is most classically exemplified by the famous Ségur ordinance of 1781, excluding non-nobles from the officer corps of the army.

4. *Feudal* or *seigneurial* reaction. This means the reconstruction by aristocratic landlords of their terriers, and the revival of obsolete or moribund rights and dues, which took place in the last two decades of the old order, and so incensed the peasantry in 1789.

Some historians only stress some of these aspects, others attempt to synthesize them all into one great movement. But however it is used, the idea of a reaction helps to dramatize the Revolution's break with aristocracy and all it stood for; it emphasizes the difference between the incorrigible old order and the radical new.

Recently indeed some doubts have been raised. Miss Vivian Gruder has used the conclusions of her work on eighteenth-century intendants as a departure point for a critique of the idea of a social reaction, while in France M. François Furet has raised a whole series of terminological doubts.[5] But *clichés* die hard. Others who have come within intellectual striking distance of questioning the concept of a reaction have preferred to use their conclusions to add nuances to the old picture instead.[6] Yet if such doubts are well founded, we shall sooner or later be compelled to revise our whole view of the origins of the Revolution. Important theses on broader topics, which attach some weight to the reaction, might also be undermined.[7] So the question is perhaps worth pursuing. Was the aristocratic reaction an illusion? Even if we cannot reply definitively, we can at

[4] The terms are Soboul's, *op. cit.*, p. 83.

[5] V. R. Gruder, *The Royal Provincial Intendants: a governing elite in eighteenth century France* (Ithaca, N.Y., 1968), ch. viii, *passim*, and pp. 219-24; F. Furet, "Le catéchisme révolutionnaire", *Annales, E.S.C.*, xxvi (1971), pp. 255-89.

[6] A. Goodwin, "The Social Origins and Privileged Status of the French Eighteenth-Century Nobility", *Bull. of the John Rylands Library*, xlvii (1964-5), pp. 393-4, comes close to questioning it but does not follow his conclusions through, although in "The recent historiography of the French Revolution" in *Historical Studies, VI*, ed. T. W. Moody (London, 1968), pp. 132-3, he goes somewhat further. A. Cobban, *The Social Interpretation of the French Revolution* (Cambridge, 1964), p. 52, prefers to question the nature of the "feudal" reaction rather than the thing itself. F. Furet, *loc. cit.*, pp. 263-9, takes this line too.

[7] E.g. C. Brinton, *The Anatomy of Revolution* (New York, 1965), pp. 36-7; Barrington Moore, Jr., *Social Origins of Dictatorship and Democracy* (London, 1969), pp. 63-6; Palmer, *The Age of the Democratic Revolution*, i, ch. iii.

least review some of the evidence which suggests that it was; and in
so doing we can perhaps indicate where further research might prove
more conclusive.

I

Much of the argument about a political reaction turns not upon
what we know of the eighteenth century, but upon what we know of
the seventeenth. The eighteenth-century evidence which gave rise
to the idea is not open to question; what is in doubt is the singularity
of that evidence. If the policies of Louis XIV were not anti-
aristocratic, and if under him the nobility were not stripped of all
power, then what has looked like a new set of developments in the
eighteenth century may turn out to have been far less important.
Had the nobility lost so much that it took a century to recapture?
A clear view of the reign of Louis XVI, from this point of view,
depends on an accurate knowledge of that of Louis XIV.

There can be little doubt that Louis XIV was not hostile to
aristocracy as such. His whole way of life, surrounding himself at
Versailles with the cream of the nobility, and upholding their
privileges and social standing, shows how profoundly he accepted it
and its values.[8] The search after false nobles of which some
historians still make so much,[9] far from being anti-aristocratic, was
directed against those who adulterated nobility and usurped its
privileges. Many legitimate nobles welcomed it.[10] The expansion
of the nobility's ranks through the sale of venal ennobling offices
was a fiscal expedient, not a hostile policy.[11] Arguably it
strengthened rather than weakened the position of the nobility in
society by making noble status a constantly attainable aspiration.[12]
The campaign to strengthen the law of derogation (*dérogeance*),
shocking as it may have been to the commercial noblemen of
Brittany, can only with perversity be described as anti-noble.[13]

---

[8] See P. Goubert, *L'Ancien Régime*, 2 vols. (Paris, 1969-73), i, p. 155;
R. Mandrou, *La France aux XVIIe et XVIIIe siècles* (Paris, 1967), pp. 149-50;
G. Pagès, *La Monarchie d'Ancien Régime en France* (Paris, 1928), pp. 178, 191;
J. B. Wolf, *Louis XIV* (New York, 1968), p. 271; and Ford, *Robe and Sword*,
pp. 9-18.
[9] E.g. P. Goubert, *Louis XIV et vingt millions de Français* (Paris, 1966),
pp. 66-7.
[10] See Mandrou, *op. cit.*, p. 93; P. Deyon, "A propos des rapports entre la
noblesse française et la monarchie absolue pendant la première moitié du XVIIe
siècle", *Revue Historique*, ccxxxi (1964), pp. 354-6.
[11] Cf. Goubert, *Louis XIV*, p. 67.
[12] See G. Pagès, "La vénalité des charges dans l'ancienne France" *Revue
Historique*, clxix (1932), pp. 492-3.
[13] See J. Meyer, *La Noblesse Bretonne au XVIIIe siècle*, 2 vols. (Paris, 1966),
i, pp. 46-7, ch. vi, *passim*, and ii, pp. 1245-6 for the conclusion that such

Despite Saint-Simon's jibes, all Louis's ministers enjoyed nobility.[14] His anti-aristocratic reputation in fact seems to rest mainly on his diminution of the political power wielded by a few *great* noblemen, a tiny handful of over-mighty subjects. Most of the aristocracy, for example, were left quite untouched by Louis's decision in 1661 not to call any prince, duke, peer or ecclesiastic to his policy-making councils. Such distant metropolitan manoeuvres were governmental changes, but hardly a new social policy. It was the same when Louis imposed restrictions on the powers and tenure of provincial governors, and indeed when he concentrated the magnates of the realm around his person at Versailles, away from their provincial power bases. Those affected were a relatively small group of notables. Moreover, when we examine the precise nature and the subsequent history of these innovations, we find either that they were not entirely novel, and were only partly reversed in the eighteenth century; or that, once made, they survived until the old order ended.

There was obviously a clear reaction in 1715 against the exclusion of princes, peers and clerics from policy-making. A system of *polysynodie* was introduced, an attempt to govern the kingdom through a series of executive councils staffed partly at least by great nobles;[15] but the most notorious fact about *polysynodie* is its short life, its failure to work. Within three years the experiment was abandoned. It is true that even after the collapse the categories excluded from policy-making by Louis XIV continued to play a part in the process. Princes like Orléans and Conti, peers like Choiseul, d'Aiguillon and Castries, clerics like Fleury, Bernis, Terray and Brienne are examples. To this extent there was something of a reaction, although it was century-long and certainly did not intensify as time went on. Yet it is arguable that a better description than reaction would be diversification of recruitment. Most of the personnel of the royal councils continued to be recruited from the upper echelons of the venal hierarchy, from the masters of requests and, ultimately, the sovereign courts. Louis XIV's innovation had been to confine recruitment to these groups, all noble,[16] but certainly not composed of men of "high consideration"[17] who might delude themselves that their

measures strengthened noble exclusivism rather than broke it down; see too R. B. Grassby, "Social Status and Commercial Enterprise under Louis XIV", *Econ. Hist. Rev.*, 2nd ser., xiii (1960-1), pp. 19, 25-6, 35.
[14] See below, p. 13.
[15] See M. Antoine, *Le Conseil du Roi sous le règne de Louis XV* (Paris Geneva, 1970), pp. 80-100.   [16] See below, pp. 13-14.
[17] *Mémoires de Louis XIV* (Paris, 1806 edn.), i, p. 7.

power was independent of the king's. Most of the personnel of the royal councils, in fact, was already drawn from their ranks before 1661,[18] and all Louis did was to exclude others and so in a sense professionalize his administration. This made it more exclusive too.[19] The eighteenth-century trend was to broaden recruitment once again, not restrict it.[20]

In other respects, the eighteenth century was remarkable for changing nothing. The concentration of the great at Versailles, for example, went from strength to strength, and the complex restrictions on access to the "honours of the court" which were elaborated in the eighteenth century were mainly a logistic device to stem the demand.[21] Similarly, provincial governorships, which Louis XIV kept as the preserve of the great nobility, remained in their hands until 1789. Admittedly Louis had restricted tenure of these offices to periods of three years, and this restriction apparently did not survive into the eighteenth century. But even under Louis himself appointments were normally renewed, the term being merely the guarantee of good conduct. He did deprive the governors of control of royal patronage, through which in the early seventeenth century they had been able to build up an extensive and semi-independent network of clientage, but this too was a permanent development. Indeed the eighteenth century saw a further decline in the governors' provincial power in the sense that from 1750 they were forbidden to reside in their provinces without royal permission.[22] The intendants too survived, concentrating in their own hands powers of justice, taxation and public works which the governors had often been able to usurp during years of internal disorder.[23] The powers of governors were above all military, and it is no coincidence that Louis XIV singled out those of frontier provinces as the most dangerous.[24] The policy of Louvois was to diminish these powers too by appointing subordinate commandants or lieutenants-general to exercise the

[18] R. Mousnier (ed.), *Le Conseil du Roi de Louis XII à la Révolution* (Paris, 1970), pp. 23-31.
[19] See below, pp. 18-19, for other links between exclusivism and profession-alization. [20] See below, p. 14.
[21] F. Bluche and P. Durye, *Les Honneurs de la Cour* (Paris, 1959); P. Du Puy de Clinchamps, *La Noblesse* (Paris, 1959), p. 62.
[22] On the governors, who deserve more attention, see P. Viollet, *Le Roi et ses Ministres pendant les trois dernières siècles de la Monarchie* (Paris, 1912), pp. 324-34; M. Marion, *Dictionnaire des Institutions de la France aux XVIIᵉ et XVIIIᵉ siècles* (Paris, 1923), pp. 259-61.
[23] G. Zeller, *Aspects de la Politique Française sous l'Ancien Régime* (Paris, 1964), ch. xii, *passim*; also J. H. Shennan, *Government and Society in France, 1461-1661* (London, 1969), pp. 60-2.
[24] *Mémoires*, i, pp. 15-16.

military authority theoretically at least still vested in the governors. These officers also continued into the eighteenth century, but since they were normally peers or great magnates of similar social standing to the governors themselves, the significance of their institution was limited.[25] On the other hand, we should beware of thinking that Louis reduced the governors to complete ciphers, and that ciphers they remained. In provinces with Estates especially, where local notables had to be managed and conciliated, the king relied heavily on their help.[26] From the mid-eighteenth century, when quarrels with provincial parlements became more bitter, the government resorted more and more to the help of the governors or commandants in order to coerce parlements undaunted by the authority of mere intendants, and this led to such famous disputes as those between the parlement of Toulouse and the duc de Fitz-James, or that of Rennes and the duc d'Aiguillon.[27] It was the governors and commandants who remodelled the provincial parlements on behalf of Maupeou in 1771, and they who received back the old ones in 1774-5.[28] But such a growth in the political rôle of these officers was hardly a sign of reaction; it was an institutional response to opposition among provincial parlements.

The parlements and the provincial Estates were also aristocratic institutions. In these spheres at least Louis XIV's policies affected more than the great nobility, although how far the latter would have regarded their position as linked in any way to those institutions is dubious. Louis kept a tight rein on the Estates, and the meetings of some were allowed to lapse. Yet most survived in all their aristocratic glory, and kept their powers, without increasing them, until the old order fell. In the case of the parlements, admittedly 1715 quite clearly saw a reaction against Louis's policies. In 1673 he had crowned a policy hostile to the pretentions of the sovereign

---

[25] Viollet, op. cit., pp. 361-5.

[26] Viollet, op. cit., p. 362, alludes to this neglected fact, but does not elaborate. For further substantiation, however, see A. Rebillon, Les Etats de Bretagne de 1661 à 1789: leur organisation, l'évolution de leurs pouvoirs, leur administration financière (Paris/Rennes, 1932), pp. 161, 183-5, 190; M. Bordes, "Les intendants de Louis XV", Revue Historique, cciii (1960), pp. 46-51; and R. C. Mettam, "The Role of the Higher Aristocracy in France under Louis XIV, with special reference to the 'Faction of the Duke of Burgundy' and the Provincial Governors" (Univ. of Cambridge Ph.D. thesis, 1966), pp. 200-384. Dr. Mettam shows that the active rôle of the governor in Brittany, often cited as an exception, had its counterparts in the Lyonnais, Boulonnais and Languedoc.

[27] For convenient summaries, see J. Egret, Louis XV et l'Opposition Parlementaire, 1715-1774 (Paris, 1970), pp. 149-56, 158-70.

[28] Ibid., p. 194.

courts ever since 1661 with the rule that henceforth remonstrances should follow the registration of laws and not precede it. In 1715 the government of the Regency reversed this rule and allowed remonstrances once more to precede registration.[29] The parlements built their whole constitutional position throughout the eighteenth century upon this reversal. By 1715 the aristocracy of their members was not in doubt.[30] Were they not, then, the vehicles of a broader aristocratic reaction? To prove rather than assume this we should have to demonstrate, first that they conducted a fairly conscious and successful campaign to increase their power in the state, and secondly that the policies they advocated were concerned with the promotion of aristocratic power. But neither of these propositions is self-evident.

The pattern of *parlementaire* resistance to royal authority over the eighteenth century is not one of crescendo. Up to about 1750 the provincial parlements remained relatively quiescent, and that of Paris was only sporadically active. They made no constitutional advances on what they had already achieved in 1715.[31] Nor were religion and finance, the two main issues which agitated the parlement of Paris in the troubled decades that followed, new ones. The religious question had been contentious even before Louis XIV died, and had been at the centre of the crises of the Regency and the early 1730s.[32] It had nothing whatever to do with the nobility and its aspirations. The finances had also been a constant subject of disagreement since 1715.[33] Naturally, in their protests against increasing taxation the magistrates sometimes alluded to the privileges of the nobility; but far more often they reiterated that the nation as a whole was overtaxed and would be ruined by further impositions.[34] Indeed the theme of *national* rights and *national* sovereignty is a far more striking feature of their remonstrances in the later eighteenth century than their occasional espousal of specifically noble interests.[35]

[29] *Ibid.*, p. 9.
[30] Ford, *Robe and Sword*, p. 59.
[31] Egret, *op. cit.*, pp. 45-9.
[32] J. D. Hardy, Jr., *Judicial Politics in the Old Regime : the Parlement of Paris during the Regency* (Baton Rouge, La., 1967), chaps. ii, iii, vii; J. H. Shennan, "The Political Role of the Parlement of Paris, 1715-23", *Historical Jl.*, viii (1965), pp. 183-5, 194-5, and "The Political Role of the *Parlement* of Paris under Cardinal Fleury", *Eng. Hist. Rev.*, lxxxi (1966), pp. 526-40; Egret, *Louis XV et l'Opposition*, pp. 17-33.
[33] Egret, *op. cit.*, pp. 34-43; Hardy, *op. cit.*, chaps. iv, vi, viii; Shennan, *op. cit.*, *Hist. Jl.*, pp. 186-94, and *Eng. Hist. Rev.*, pp. 522-6.
[34] Egret, *op. cit.*, pp. 107-9, 131-2. See too the remarks of Shennan, *op. cit.*, *Eng. Hist. Rev.*, p. 526.
[35] R. Bickart, *Les Parlements et la notion de Souveraineté Nationale au XVIIIe siècle* (Paris, 1933), *passim*; see too Mathiez, *La Révolution*, i, p. 8.

These remarks also apply to the provincial parlements, who began to make the pace in opposition after about 1750. Their main preoccupations were with taxes again, and with the powers of the government's local agents — intendants, governors, commandants. What was at stake was local autonomy; and it was not the localities and their parlements which sought change. If they were "reacting", it was not against a *status quo* going back to Louis XIV, but rather in defence of a *status quo* threatened by the ever-increasing encroachments of a revenue-hungry government. Allegations that the cry of public interest was a mask for noble ambitions will only take us so far; the parlements could not have achieved support as they did without a genuine and persistent defence of the interests of all, not just the nobility.[36] Support for the convocation of the Estates-General only spread when it became clear, from 1771, that the parlements were no longer defending the interests of all. This was not because they ceased to be willing to do so. It was because the work of Maupeou showed that in the last analysis they had not the power to do so. The last twenty years of the old régime, when we should expect to find the aristocratic reaction at its height, were in fact years of great weakness for the parlements, when their influence on the government fell back almost to pre-1750 levels.[37] The tax increases and extensions of the early 1780s passed with unprecedented ease. Even if we could call the zenith of their power, that is to say the 1750s and 1760s, part of a reaction (which is dubious), we should still have to admit that by the time of Louis XVI it had manifestly failed. The "noble revolt" of the summer of 1788 was not the confident knock-out blow aimed at a government tottering from previous aristocratic onslaughts. It was a desperate movement of non-co-operation with a government which had shown itself contemptuous of institutional checks on its power.

II

That the rule of Louis XIV provoked an "ideological" reaction in certain noble circles is well established. Around the prospect of the duc de Bourgogne coming to power congregated a group of great noblemen and supporters who saw France's salvation in an end to Colbertian mercantilism, the encouragement of agriculture and the

[36] Egret, *op. cit.*, pp. 230-1; see too Meyer, *Noblesse Bretonne*, ii, p. 1250, for the conclusion that the Breton nobility was on the defensive, and p. 1252 for noble defence of the general interest.
[37] W. Doyle, "The Parlements of France and the Breakdown of the Old Regime, 1771-1788", *French Historical Studies*, vi (1970), pp. 441-53.

suppression of the intendants. The assumption behind these ideas was that in implementing them great noblemen would resume the place in the state of which Louis was felt to have deprived them.[38] Fénelon, Boulainvilliers and Saint-Simon, the most notable leaders of the group, are often cited as the ideological prophets of the aristocratic reaction, which reached its most articulate expression in Montesquieu.[39]

It is undoubtedly true that all these writers were in favour of aristocratic power in the state; but it must be asked whether this general common feature was more important than the very considerable differences between them. Saint-Simon, for instance, was interested mainly in the claims of the peerage, a much more restricted group than the aristocracy as a whole.[40] Belesbat, Fénelon and Boulainvilliers, in favour of power for the aristocracy as a whole, nevertheless conceived of this body as essentially hereditary, and were hostile to ennoblement. This implied condemnation of the political and social pretentions of the magistracy, the whole category of nobles of the robe. Yet it was from this group that Montesquieu came, and it was the institutional power of the parlements that he saw as the best guarantee that the French monarchy would remain true to its nature and subject to the check of aristocratic intermediary bodies. Evidently there was no agreement among the ideologues of aristocracy as to what the aristocracy was, what powers it should have, or how they should be exercised. This suggests uncertainty and loss of direction rather than a new and self-conscious assurance.

It has, on the other hand, been argued that the events of the Regency proved the incompetence of the higher aristocracy, and that consequently they were led to abandon their own theorists and turn to support the parlements, with their well-established constitutional position.[41] Accordingly the full elaboration of Montesquieu's views in the *Esprit des Lois* of 1748 was a synthesis of all the various noble positions reflecting this "regrouping" over the previous half-century.[42] Yet it is also admitted that Boulainvilliers's theories "remained the symbol of the *thèse nobiliaire* prior to 1748",[43] and that

---

[38] L. Rothkrug, *Opposition to Louis XIV: the Political and Social Origins of the French Enlightenment* (Princeton, N.J., 1965), pp. 175-7, 242-86, 328-71; also Mettam, *op. cit.*, pp. 68-106.
[39] E.g. Soboul, *La France à la veille*, pp. 79-82.
[40] Ford, *Robe and Sword*, pp. 182-7; Mettam, *op. cit.*, pp. 120-2.
[41] Ford, *op. cit.*, ch. x.
[42] *Ibid.*, ch. xii, especially pp. 244-5.
[43] *Ibid.*, p. 227.

the similar feudal fantasies of La Curne de Sainte-Palaye could appear ten years after the *Esprit des Lois*.[44]   Above all it is assumed, but not proved, that the parlements united in the second half of the century, armed with Montesquieu, to press the claims of the whole nobility against the king.   Undoubtedly they often did cite Montesquieu in their remonstrances, and at no time more frequently than during the crisis of 1788.[45]   But he was never their consistent point of reference. They pillaged him as they did many other writers when they found it convenient, in a wide range of causes.   So did their opponents.[46] In any case all references to the authority of theorists were strictly secondary to arguments from the law.   Indeed it has been argued that the remonstrances of the parlements between 1660 and 1789 show a marked decline of interest in political theory, and an ever-growing emphasis on legal technicalities.[47]   There is no *prima facie* reason why legal arguments should always have the object of defending or refurbishing "privilege", however convenient it may be to assume this.   Nor need an increasing concern for legalistic constitutionalism always have been directed, consciously at least, towards concentrating power in aristocratic hands.

If, indeed, the aristocratic reaction is thought to have gathered pace over the eighteenth century, the conventional view of its ideological aspect has a further weakness.   Why are its spokesmen all writers of the seventeenth or the first half of the eighteenth century?   One would expect to find more, even if not greater, writers articulating aristocratic principles as time went on, if the reaction accelerated.   But even lesser works, like those of Mirabeau or the chevalier d'Arc, all appeared before 1760.   As Albert Soboul, who defines the "ideological reaction" most succinctly, is constrained to admit, after Montesquieu the aristocratic current "remained stationary" until the eve of the Revolution.[48]   The fact that it was still Montesquieu whose name was most invoked by discontented nobles in 1788 shows that the early masters had no heirs.

It might be said, of course, that the theory was for the struggle, and that the years of triumph after mid-century required none.   But it has already been suggested that in political terms the eighteenth century saw and required no struggle, and therefore no triumph. And this is even clearer if we turn to social developments.

[44] *Ibid.*, p. 245.
[45] E. Carcassonne, *Montesquieu et le problème de la Constitution Française au XVIIIe siècle* (Paris, 1927), ch. xi, *passim*.
[46] *Ibid.*, ch. vi, *passim*, and pp. 562-3.
[47] W. F. Church, "The Decline of French Jurists as Political Theorists, 1660-1789", *French Historical Studies*, iii (1967), pp. 1-40, *passim*.
[48] *La France à la veille*, p. 79.

III

The idea of a social reaction is one of the clearest and most persistent in the historiography of the old régime. Evidence by which it may be undermined accumulates daily, yet its significance is still largely ignored. So we may read, in a recent authoritative work by a group of very distinguished French historians, that:

> Kings no longer followed the prudent policy of Louis XIV. Under Louis XVI, all ministers, all councillors of state, all intendants (save one), all bishops and all abbots were nobles of old or very old "extraction"; new rules . . . effectually reserved for them the high ranks of the army; in the navy, they alone had access to the "grand corps". Against common or freshly ennobled talent, the doors were closing one by one.[49]

Here again, clearly, much of the argument depends on what we know of Louis XIV and those in office under him. As we have seen, Louis chose his advisers from the ranks of those already experienced in royal service but dependent for their continued worldly success on royal favour.[50] This alone ensured that they were noble, since most of the higher offices in the royal bureaucracy conferred nobility on their holders; but in any case, the families of Louis's secretaries of state had all enjoyed nobility for at least one generation, and that of most of them went back a good deal further. Such lineages were undistinguished compared to those of the dukes and peers whom Louis excluded from policy-making, but they still were noble ones; and what distinction they lacked in age, these families soon made up in alliances with the most ancient stock. The conclusion is clear:

> The personal reign of Louis XIV witnessed, in the high posts of the government, no commoners and no new men in the juridical sense of the word. This should be noted. We therefore conclude with a proposition exactly the contrary of that which is still held; Louis XIV governed without recourse to the collaboration of a single *bourgeois*.[51]

This then was Louis's "prudent policy". How far did matters change in the eighteenth century?

It is true that in the eighteenth century the king's ministers and secretaries of state included a number of princes, dukes and peers and clerics — men like Choiseul, d'Aiguillon, or Brienne. But it is

[49] F. Braudel and E. Labrousse (eds.), *Histoire économique et sociale de la France: des derniers temps de l'Age Seigneurial aux préludes de l'Age Industriel (1660-1789)* (Paris, 1970), p. 595.

[50] See above, pp. 6-7.

[51] F. Bluche, "L'origine sociale des secrétaires d'état de Louis XIV (1660-1715)", *XVIIe siècle*, nos. 42-3 (1959), pp. 15-16; see also Furet, "Le catéchisme", p. 274.

equally true that men of very humble extraction, such as Dubois or Sartine, could also attain these heights.[52] Most ministers and secretaries of state continued to be drawn under Louis XVI, as under Louis XIV, from the personnel of the privy council of state. The difference was that under Louis XVI more were recruited from outside its ranks. This meant that some great nobles attained office, but it also meant that other outsiders did so too. It is certainly difficult to believe that Louis XIV would ever have appointed a non-noble Swiss banker, like Necker, to manage his finances. Far then from closing, the doors to ministerial office seem to have been open to a wider and more diverse social range in the late eighteenth century than in the late seventeenth.

Of course, if most ministers and secretaries of state still came within reach of high office through being masters of requests, intendants or councillors of state, the true accessibility of the highest offices would reflect that of those subordinate ranks. But here the impression is confirmed. It was easier for newcomers to become councillors of state under Louis XV than under his predecessor, and there is no reason to believe that this state of affairs changed in the last years of the old order.[53] A study of the intendants yields similar conclusions.[54] Louis XIV's intendants were noble, like those of Louis XVI; having risen through the hierarchy of venal offices, they progressed in their careers through similar stages. It is the continuity of the pattern, rather than any change, which is striking. But in so far as it did change, there seems to have been a slight relative easing of access to intendancies for men of obscure origin under Louis XVI. In the last years of the old order the body of intendants, like that of the masters of requests from which it was recruited, comprised men of shorter lineage and more diverse background than ever before.

Admittedly this could not be said of the church hierarchy. There is no evidence of a diversification in its recruitment at the end of the old order; nobles practically monopolized the bench of bishops. But even under Louis XIV, between 1682 and 1700, at least 88 per

---

[52] F. Bluche, "L'origine sociale du personnel ministériel français au XVIIIᵉ siècle", *Bulletin de la Société d'Histoire Moderne*, 12th ser. (1957), pp. 9-13; and *Les Magistrats du Parlement de Paris au XVIIIᵉ siècle, 1715-1771* (Paris, 1960), p. 67; and Goodwin, "Social Origins", p. 397.

[53] Antoine, *Le Conseil du Roi*, pp. 255-60; see too his communication in Mousnier, *Le Conseil di Roi de Louis XII*, p. 44, and Furet, "Le catéchisme", p. 274.

[54] Gruder, *Royal Provincial Intendants*, ch. viii, *passim*.

cent of bishops were noblemen.[55] Any reaction there may have been, therefore, was hardly significant statistically.

But if the church stood still, other institutions were following the pattern of the royal councils and diversifying their recruitment. Provincial academics became broader in their interests and broader in their socio-professional recruitment as the century went on.[56] These were the very bodies singled out by Franklin Ford as noteworthy in the earlier part of the century for their aristocratic exclusivism, and their contribution to the evolution of an aristocratic ideology.[57] But, of course, Ford's book did not prove the existence of an aristocratic reaction; it took its existence for granted and set out to explain it.[58] This obviously affected both his researches and his findings. If the aristocratic reaction turns out to have been an illusion, we may find ourselves questioning more important points in his thesis — for instance, that "robe" and "sword" had united behind the parlements between 1715 and 1748 to form a solid aristocratic front down to 1789. Then we might remember that the spring of 1789 saw plenty of bickering between magistrates and other nobles,[59] and that magistrates ennobled by office were no more welcome at court under Louis XVI than under Louis XIV.[60] We might conclude that, despite the social fusion between "robe" and "sword" which seems conclusively proved, political and professional rivalry between different sections of the nobility fatally persisted until the old order

[55] N. Ravitch, *Sword and Mitre: Government and Episcopate in France and England in the Age of Aristocracy* (The Hague/Paris, 1966), pp. 69-71. It is true that Ravitch also concludes that there was a trend towards more exclusively "sword" recruitment, but such a category is dubious in itself, and he provides no means of checking his categorizations. Gruder, *op. cit.*, p. 222, n. 23, points out that the sources of Ravitch's data on types of nobility are not always reliable. On the other hand independent research cited by Furet, *loc. cit.*, has yielded similar conclusions to his.

[56] D. Roche, "Milieux académiques provinciaux et société des lumières. Trois académies provinciaux au XVIIIe siècle: Bordeaux, Dijon, Châlons sur Marne", in G. Bollème *et al.*, *Livre et Société dans la France du XVIIIe siècle* (Paris/The Hague, 1965), pp. 112-20.

[57] Ford, *Robe and Sword*, pp. 235-7.

[58] See his preface, pp. vii-ix.

[59] E.g. in Franche Comté — H. Carré, *La Fin des Parlements, 1788-90* (Paris, 1912), pp. 94-5; or Guyenne — M. Lhéritier, *La Révolution à Bordeaux dans l'Histoire de la Révolution Française: la Fin de l'Ancien Régime et la Préparation des Etats-Généraux (1787-1789)* (Paris, 1942), pp. 205-9, 222-5, 242-55.

[60] See Bluche and Durye, *Les Honneurs de la Cour*; and Goodwin, "Social origins", p. 396. R. Mousnier, *La Société Française de 1770 à 1789* (Paris, 1970), pp. 87, 107-110, is clearly sceptical of any claims that divisions within the nobility had disappeared.

fell.[61] Indeed, as more and more evidence emerges of social fusion even in the seventeenth century,[62] we might begin to wonder if these famous categories were ever more than professional ones, whose social significance was extremely limited. Clearly this would rob the Ford thesis of much of its point.

We should not, however, deceive ourselves that the notion of a a social reaction is based on no evidence at all. At the centre of it lies the all-too-solid evidence of the decisions of various parlements designed to exclude non-nobles and newcomers, and a series of military ordinances which restricted access to the officer corps. We cannot deny the existence of these; but we can investigate why they were passed, and whether they were enforced.

In the case of the parlements, the circumstances in which the excluding decisions of Rennes, Aix, Grenoble, Nancy and Toulouse were passed deserve further study. It may be that some of them emerged in the same way as that of Bordeaux in 1780, that is to say as bargaining counters in an internal quarrel, directed at a specific individual.[63] This would diminish their importance as assertions of general principle. In the case of Rennes some form of restrictive regulation had already been in force during the seventeenth century, so this was no new development.[64] Similarly, if the personnel of eighteenth-century parlements was noble, and included magistrates of very old lineage too, again the situation was often foreshadowed in the seventeenth century.[65] The proportion of magistrates of noble extraction in the parlement of Paris in 1771 was overwhelming, but this was equally the case in 1715.[66] Any changes were very minor and self-cancelling. The author of these conclusions believes that they demonstrate a noble reaction; but he provides no earlier evidence to substantiate the assertion. Even if he could, clearly it would not be a matter of the classic reaction of the last decades before the Revolution, but rather something of very long

[61] Furet, "Le catéchisme", p. 275, suggests that what had been called an aristocratic reaction was the manifestation in reality of just such conflicts. See also below, p. 19.
[62] See the remarks of P. Goubert in P. Goubert and J. Meyer, "Les problèmes de la noblesse au XVIIe siècle", paper read at the *XIII International Congress of Historical Sciences* (Moscow, 1970), p. 4; also Goubert, *Ancien Régime*, i, p. 165.
[63] W. Doyle, "Aux origines de l'Affaire Dupaty", *Revue Historique de Bordeaux et du département de la Gironde*, new ser., xvii (1968), pp. 5-16.
[64] Meyer, *Noblesse Bretonne*, ii, pp. 930-7.
[65] J. C. Paulhet, "Les parlementaires toulousains à la fin du XVIIe siècle", *Annales du Midi*, lxxvi (1964), pp. 6-8; also Goubert, "Les problèmes de la noblesse", p. 4.
[66] Bluche, *Les Magistrats*, pp. 76-7, 82-5.

standing indeed. Similar conclusions emerge from an analysis of the recruitment of the parlements as a whole between 1774 and 1789, which shows that, although the vast majority of those admitted to office in the parlements were noblemen, many had not the four quarterings or three degrees stipulated by the restrictive decisions even in places where such decisions existed (and they did not exist everywhere).[67] The majority of new recruits were in any case newcomers, with no *parlementaire* tradition behind them. Among these were the sons of both *parvenus* and old nobility. Again the impression is one of great diversity in recruitment,[68] and certainly no clear exclusivist trend.

The military evidence seems at first sight less ambiguous. In the navy, the *grand corps* of officers afloat was exclusively noble, and after 1775 entrance to officer cadet schools was confined to noblemen. In the army, the famous Ségur ordinance of 1781, "the classic example of the aristocratic reaction",[69] restricted entrance to the officer corps to those who enjoyed at least four degrees of nobility, following the restriction of military academies to noblemen in the 1770s. But these were not new principles of policy. The *grand corps* in the navy always had been noble by definition and Louis XIV had announced his desire to recruit naval cadets exclusively from the ranks of the nobility as long before as 1683.[70] The recruitment of army officers had been restricted as closely as in 1781, in 1718 and 1727.[71] Moreover there were important qualifications. The naval cadet schools, whose status and prestige fluctuated spectacularly over the century, never monopolized entrance to the officer class, and outside the *grand corps* the only requirements for recruits remained professional rather than social. The Ségur ordinance did not apply either to those already serving in the army (still in 1789 one quarter of all officers), or to the technical branches like the artillery, or to sons of *chevaliers de Saint-Louis*.[72] It was also to an extent, like the Bordeaux *arrêt* of 1780, the result of particular political circumstances rather than general policy, apparently being issued on the personal insistence of the comte

[67] J. Egret, "L'Aristocratie parlementaire française à la fin de l'Ancien Régime", *Revue Historique*, ccviii (1952), pp. 6-9; see too Furet, "Le catéchisme", p. 274.

[68] Egret, *op. cit.*, pp. 6, 11-12.

[69] M. Reinhard, "Élite et noblesse dans la seconde moitié du XVIIIe siècle", *Revue d'Histoire Moderne et Contemporaine*, iii (1956), p. 11.

[70] Marion, *Dictionnaire des Institutions*, p. 365.

[71] E. G. Léonard, *L'Armée et ses problèmes au XVIIIe siècle* (Paris, 1958), pp. 101 and 165; Mousnier, *La Société Française*, p. 126.

[72] Gruder, *Intendants*, pp. 223-4; Léonard, *L'Armée*, p. 286; Viollet, *Le Roi et ses Ministres*, p. 378.

d'Artois, brother of the king.[73]   All these circumstances make both the aims and results of the measures restricting the recruitment of officers less self-evident than would appear. What then was their intention? They were the culmination of two long-term trends. One was towards the professionalization of the armed forces. Ever since the 1750s the ideal of army reformers had been to diminish the influence of money, eliminate purchase by creating a professionally trained officer corps of noblemen. This had been the object of the edict creating a "military nobility" of 1750, and of the Saint-Germain reforms of the 1770s.[74]   Such a policy could only favour the petty nobility, too poor to pay the inflated price of commissions, but traditionally dependent on the army as a means of livelihood. Yet it did not necessarily exclude non-nobles either, if they chose to rise on their talents rather than their money. The military nobility of officers envisaged by the chevalier d'Arc and other mid-century writers was designed, like the higher judiciary, to ennoble recruits as well as to recruit nobles.[75]   Between 1750 and 1781 this was official policy too, and the 1781 ordinance explicitly claimed to be continuing it. In fact, by excluding those without a formidable noble lineage, it abandoned half the policy. Professionalization was sacrificed to another policy trend — making provision for the poor nobility.

Most of the apparent signs of reaction attributable to the government were part of this second trend. The restriction of access to the naval and military cadet schools was to keep out the rich and guarantee a career to the poor nobleman with no other resources. Similarly, if ecclesiastical benefices in the crown's gift were restricted to noblemen, the intention was explicit to help the poor nobility.[76] The problem was not new. Even in the seventeenth century the question of the poor nobility had preoccupied political writers. Then, as in the later period, they were torn between the conflicting solutions of urging the poor nobles into trade by suspending the law of *dérogeance*, or reinforcing their social separation by reserving certain positions for them alone.[77]   It is possible that over the

---

[73] Léonard, *op. cit.*, p. 286.

[74] *Ibid.*, p. 163-90, 244-50; Viollet, *op. cit.*, pp. 369-70; Reinhard, "Elite et noblesse", pp. 7-12; and A. Corvisier, *L'Armée Française de la fin du XVIIe siècle au ministère de Choiseul: le soldat*, 2 vols. (Paris, 1964), i, pp. 126-7.

[75] Léonard, *op. cit.*, pp. 181-90.

[76] Mme. Campan, *Mémoires sur la vie de Marie-Antoinette, Reine de France et de Navarre* (Paris, n.d.), p. 163. Also quoted in Ravitch, *Sword and Mitre*, p. 52.

[77] Grassby, "Social Status", *passim*, for the seventeenth century; Reinhard, "Elite et Noblesse", pp. 13-19, for the eighteenth. How far a feeling of

eighteenth century the problem became more acute. Certainly awareness of it was widespread, a fact reflected in the writings of the chevalier d'Arc, the abbé Coyer, or the marquis de Mirabeau. In a society where wealth opened every door, and yet where poor noblemen were largely debarred by their status from accumulating it, the pressure for some special provision became enormous.[78] Yet it was not so much against the competition of commoners that the poor nobility sought and were granted protection, as the glittering, well-connected courtiers of Versailles, and the new rich who so easily bought themselves ennoblement. It was against the nepotism of the former that the ecclesiastical appointments policy was mainly directed,[79] and against the wealth of the latter that the 1781 ordinance was framed.[80] If these measures were signs of a reaction, therefore, it was not so much noble against commoner, as one type of noble against another. They illustrate the deep chasms between rich and poor nobles, old and new nobles, metropolitan and provincial nobles, which remained a far more significant feature of old régime society than any possible fusion between the dubious categories of "robe" and "sword".

On the other hand, the very consciousness of these divisions fostered attitudes which from outside could only look reactionary. Petty provincial nobles reacted to the economic gap between themselves and the great at Versailles by attempting to play down other differences, falling back on doctrines of the unity and indivisibility of the nobility.[81] Rather than be treated as a separate and potentially inferior category, much less allow the court nobility a superior status, they resigned themselves to sharing the benefits of the Ségur ordinance with them, and ostentatiously applauded the decisions of those parlements which announced that they would no longer admit those whose only credentials were money. So that exclusivist or "reactionary" moves were finding a more receptive audience among some members of the nobility as the old régime ended, and from outside the Ségur ordinance and the restrictive rulings of the parlements must have looked like vehicles of

poverty in the poor nobility reflected their true position is, of course, a different matter. See J. Meyer, "Un problème mal posé: la noblesse pauvre. L'exemple breton, XVIIᵉ siècle", *Revue d'Histoire Moderne et Contemporaine*, xviii (1971), *passim*, but especially pp. 166, 188.

[78] See J. McManners, "France", in A. Goodwin (ed.) *The European Nobility in the Eighteenth Century* (London, 1953), pp. 36-8, and H. Carré, *La Noblesse de France et l'Opinion Publique au XVIIIᵉ siècle* (Paris, 1920), pp. 157 and 163.

[79] Campan, *loc. cit.*

[80] Furet, "Le catéchisme", p. 275.

[81] McManners, *loc. cit.*; E. Champion, *La France d'après les Cahiers de 1789* (Paris, 1867), pp. 89-90; Carré, *La Noblesse*, pp. 348-9.

aristocratic reaction.   In practice there was little movement towards greater exclusivism.   This was of little consolation to the aspiring bourgeois to whom even an unchanging degree of it might appear for various reasons increasingly intolerable.   But   that   is   another question.

IV

The idea that the last years of the old régime saw a "feudal" or "seigneurial" reaction in the countryside seems to go back to the last years of the nineteenth century.[82]   As then outlined, it had two main features.   On the one hand, lords or their agents fraudulently or unilaterally increased the burden of seigneurial rights and dues by new assessments.[83]   On the other, old rights of undoubted legality which had fallen into disuse were revived and exercised, as terriers were remade by a zealous breed of agents (*feudistes*).[84]   These developments contributed to the aggravation of the burden borne by peasants in 1789 and thus played a crucial rôle in the peasant risings of that summer.

As early as 1902 the suggestion that dues were arbitrarily increased came under attack,[85] and the greatest agrarian historian of the next generation remained unconvinced.[86]   By 1946, even the father of the idea felt constrained to admit that "It is difficult to prove a direct and written increase",[87] and most modern authorities carefully avoid committing themselves on this aspect,[88] confining themselves to the better-established fact that many terriers were remade and old rights revived under Louis XVI, and quite legitimately too.   This at least seems irrefutable, and has passed into most textbooks.   Revival of

---

[82] A. Chérest, *La Chute de l'Ancien Régime,* 3 vols. (Paris, 1884), i, pp. 48-56; Champion, *La France d'après les Cahiers,* pp. 150-1; P. Sagnac, *Quomodo jura dominii aucta fuerint regnante Ludovico sexto decimo* (Le Puy, 1898).

[83] Champion, *op. cit.,* pp. 149-50.   I cannot claim to have read, or even to be able to read, Sagnac's thesis, but it is fairly fully summarized in Mousnier, *La Société,* pp. 166-75.

[84] Champion, *op. cit.,* pp. 152-3.

[85] M. Marion, *Etat des classes rurales au XVIIIe siècle dans le généralité de Bordeaux,* (Paris, 1902), pp. 74-6.

[86] G. Lefebvre, *Les Paysans du Nord pendant la Révolution Française,* new edn. (Bari, 1959), pp. 158-60.

[87] P. Sagnac, *La Formation de la Société Française Moderne,* 2 vols. (Paris, 1946), ii, p. 221.

[88] E.g. Soboul, *La France à la veille,* p. 85, and, at greater length, "De la pratique des terriers à la veille de la Révolution", *Annales, E.S.C.,* xix (1964), p. 1049; but A. Davies, "The Origins of the French Peasant Revolution of 1789", *History,* new ser., xlix (1964), p. 36, is reluctant to abandon the idea entirely.

obsolete or half-forgotten dues when terriers were remade still meant that there was a reaction in which the peasants' burden increased. Yet even this did not find universal acceptance when it was first suggested. In 1914 Alphonse Aulard, while admitting that he did not have the volume of evidence to demolish it completely, suggested that the *cahiers*, the most persuasive source for the idea, were not always reliable as precise evidence, being often vague and general in their allegations.[89] He also pointed out the dangerous complexities in the use of other evidence, such as the comparison of terriers,[90] and the selection of untypical cases of profiteering and abuse among *feudistes*.[91] His conclusion was that "there is no certainty about the degree of worsening of feudalism under Louis XVI, if indeed this feudalism did worsen".[92] The only certainty was that people complained more about the burden, and that, for reasons like foreign examples of alleviation and the spread of enlightenment, they found it less tolerable.[93]

Curiously enough nobody followed this lead. General works ignored the doubts,[94] while particular studies seemed to confirm that revision of terriers, revival of old dues, and therefore a seigneurial reaction, did occur.[95] Most leading historians therefore continue to take them for granted. Even Alfred Cobban, who forced us to look afresh at so much in this period, accepted the fact of a reaction, although he did suggest that the increase in the peasants' burden came from a "growing commercialisation" in the management of rights, rather than a return to archaic demands and harsher ways of management.[96] After all, evidence has continued to accumulate that pre-revolutionary landlords *were* remaking terriers and reviving dues,[97] which seems to confirm the repeated complaints of the rural *cahiers*.

---

[89] A. Aulard, *La Révolution Française et le Régime Féodal* (Paris, 1919), pp. 58-9, 66-9. The book was in fact written in 1914. For a translation of Aulard's earlier views on the subject, see R. W. Greenlaw (ed.), *Economic Origins of the French Revolution: Poverty or Prosperity?* (Boston, 1958). Only recently have new doubts arisen as to the exact value and meaning of the *cahiers* as evidence: see Furet, "Le catéchisme", pp. 266-8.

[90] Aulard, *op. cit.*, pp. 57-8.

[91] *Ibid.*, pp. 60-1.

[92] *Ibid.*, p. 69.

[93] *Ibid.*, pp. 69, 75.

[94] Mathiez, *La Révolution*, i, pp. 16-17.

[95] Lefebvre, *Paysans du Nord*, pp. 157-71.

[96] Cobban, *Social Interpretation*, p. 52.

[97] See R. Forster, *The Nobility of Toulouse in the Eighteenth Century: a Social and Economic Study* (Baltimore, 1960), pp. 49-53, for a much-cited example; and Davies, "The Origins", pp. 35-7, for a general statement of the case.

Unfortunately much of this evidence remains inconclusive on logical grounds alone. The remaking of terriers and complaints about it only prove that a reaction was taking place if they were not being remade, or were being remade much less extensively, in previous years. The discovery of new terriers in the 1780s means far less if they can also be found in the 1750s, for example, or even earlier. It is the same methodological problem which lies at the heart of other aspects of the so-called reaction. Long histories of individual fiefs are needed, and in large numbers, if we are ever to resolve this aspect of the problem satisfactorily.[98] Meanwhile, our materials are as statistically inadequate as Aulard's were, and certainly not enough to justify our dismissing him out of hand. Quite the reverse, in fact: there is evidence to suggest that a thorough inquiry might do much to vindicate his doubts.

First of all historians have uncovered "feudal" or "seigneurial" reactions in other, earlier, periods. From the Hundred Years' War onwards seigneurial administration became better organized and more regularly documented throughout France;[99] the reconstruction of domains in the Bordelais after that war demonstrates many of the classic elements of "reaction" — renewal of half-forgotten obligations, foreclosures on accumulated debts, prior purchase by lords (retrait féodal), and reconstruction of terriers.[100] More significantly, a similar process of reconstruction occurred on lands around Dijon after the Thirty Years' War in the seventeenth century; in this area ravaged by war and plagued by lost records, the reaction seems to have been far more severe than anything the eighteenth century might have witnessed.[101] But terriers were being reconstructed in the seventeenth century even where war did not rage, as the case of the Beauvaisis shows.[102] Recently it has been suggested that this was going on, and that feudistes were at work, all over France in that period.[103] There was, then, nothing unique about what happened under Louis XVI. It had happened before.

[98] See the appeal in Mousnier, La Société, pp. 191-2.
[99] M. Bloch, Les Caractères Originaux de l'Histoire Rurale Française, 2 vols. (Paris, 1964), i, p. 135.
[100] R. Boutruche, La Crise d'une Société: Seigneurs et Paysans du Bordelais pendant la Guerre de Cent Ans (Paris, 1963), pp. 333-9. On p. 338 he actually calls it "an attempt at seigneurial reaction".
[101] G. Roupnel, La Ville et la Campagne au XVIIe siècle: étude sur les populations du Pays Dijonnais (Paris, 1955), pp. 250-67.
[102] P. Goubert, Beauvais et le Beauvaisis de 1600 à 1730: contribution à l'histoire sociale de la France du XVIIe siècle (Paris, 1960), pp. 530-2. On p. 543 he speaks of a "sort of first 'feudal' reaction".
[103] In Braudel and Labrousse, Histoire Economique et Sociale, pp. 591-2. See too Goubert, Ancien Régime, i, p. 170.

This suggests a further reflection; perhaps it was always happening, all the time. In any system where lordship and ownership are not congruent, any records of debts owed and properties on which they are owed are bound to become outdated very quickly as land changes hands; and as soon as they do, exact dues may cease to be levied. On the other hand, if dues went unexacted for thirty years, then rights lapsed. This meant that terriers had to be revised every twenty-nine years at the least, which explains why arrears which peasants complained had built up, were seldom more than twenty-nine years behind.[104] Every generation of lords had to remake its terriers, or lose its rights for ever. This would mean that the main characteristics of what has been called a reaction were in fact permanent features of that structure of property which for convenience we call "feudal" or "seigneurial". It would mean that the reaction which supposedly began around 1770,[105] was in fact only the last phase of a perpetual process, complained about by those peasants who happened at the time to be undergoing it.[106] It would certainly mean that we could no longer accept massive accumulations of evidence for a reaction under Louis XVI, such as those for the Nord,[107] unless it could also be demonstrated that such evidence could not be found in the same area for the earlier decades of the century. In the present state of knowledge, this cannot be taken for granted, as a brief survey reveals.

The seigneurial burden was probably generally lighter in southern than in northern France,[108] but even there terriers were remade and old rights exacted. But when? Foreclosures and prior purchases cited as examples of seigneurial reaction in the Bordelais are drawn from the whole century.[109] The two examples of collections of accumulated arrears in a study of the nobility of Toulouse come from

---

[104] Soboul, "De la pratique des terriers", pp. 1062-3; Meyer, *Noblesse Bretonne*, ii, pp. 788-9. In some areas the limit of legal memory was twenty years. It is noteworthy that the two seigneurial offensives of the Saulx-Tavanes family, in 1765 and 1785, coincided with the estates changing hands: R. Forster, *The House of Saulx-Tavanes: Versailles and Burgundy, 1700-1830* (Baltimore and London, 1971), p. 92. It is only fair to add that the sharpening of seigneurial demands in this Burgundian duchy after 1750 seems irrefutable evidence of a reaction there. It remains astonishing, however, that there had been no general revision of terriers since 1610 (p. 95).
[105] Sagnac, *La Formation*, ii, pp. 129-30.
[106] Mousnier, *La Société*, pp. 191-2, employs a similar argument, suggesting that terrier renovation occurred whenever a fief was sold.
[107] Lefebvre, *op. cit.*, pp. 158-9.
[108] Goubert, *Ancien Régime*, i, pp. 83-123; Furet, "Le catéchisme", pp. 264-5.
[109] R. Forster, "The Noble Wine Producers of the Bordelais in the Eighteenth Century", *Econ. Hist. Rev.*, 2nd ser., xiv (1961-2), pp. 29-30.

1750 and 1724.[110]   In Auvergne, the burden, though light, increased over the century, but only as a proportion of net produce.[111]   In lower Provence, there was no reaction at all either in the long or short term, either by the extension of seigneurial domains or in the increase of burdens on the peasants.[112]   It was the same in the Albigeois.[113]   Even further north there were areas where the burden was slight.   In what was to become the department of the Sarthe, seigneurial rights were very unremunerative, disturbed the peasants little, and did not obviously increase in weight with the remaking of the terriers.   Their historian concludes that terriers were only remade at all as part of the waste-clearing mania of the 1760s, and because they were bound to get out-of-date as owners changed.[114]   Even in parts of northern France, like the Nord, terriers were being remade at least as early as 1759.[115]   Admittedly in certain areas of a traditionally heavy seigneurial burden, like Burgundy, some aggravation may have taken place in the old régime's last years.[116] In the Duchy of Saulx-Tavanes, the courtier landlord was determined to squeeze the last penny from his rights, and used the occasion of his elevation to a dukedom in 1786 to double his demands for the year under a custom not invoked since the thirteenth century.[117]   A general study of the whole of northern Burgundy also emphasizes a more intensive approach to exercising seigneurial rights later in the century.[118]   Yet the same study also reveals renovation of terriers and scrupulous attention to seigneurial rights throughout the first half of the century.[119]   Its author concludes that the reaction

---

[110] Forster, *Nobility of Toulouse*, p. 51.
[111] A. Poitrineau, *La Vie Rurale en Basse Auvergne au XVIIIe siècle 1726-1789*, 2 vols. (Paris, 1965), i, pp. 342 ff.
[112] R. Baehrel, *Une Croissance: la Basse-Provence rurale (fin XVe siècle — 1789)* (Paris, 1961), pp. 451-2.
[113] P. Rascol, *Les Paysans de l'Albigeois à la fin de l'Ancien Régime* (Aurillac, 1961), pp. 102-13.
[114] P. Bois, *Paysans de l'Ouest: des structures économiques et sociales aux options politiques depuis l'époque révolutionnaire dans la Sarthe* (Le Mans, 1960), pp. 391-4.   [115] Lefebvre, *Paysans du Nord*, p. 149.
[116] R. Robin, *La Société Française en 1789: Semur en Auxois* (Paris, 1970), p. 153, calls this a certainty, on the grounds that lords were employing the right to a segment of divided commons *(triage)* more frequently. The examples she gives for her own community, however (pp. 154-7), do not relate to this practice, nor does she prove there was anything about them peculiar to the pre-revolutionary decades.
[117] Forster, *House of Saulx-Tavanes*, pp. 100-1; for the general intensification of pressure on this estate see pp. 92-108.
[118] P. de Saint-Jacob, *Les Paysans de la Bourgogne du Nord au dernier siècle de l'Ancien Régime* (Paris, 1960), p. 425.
[119] *Ibid.*, pp. 223-5, 243-4. Roupnel, *La Ville et la Campagne*, pp. 250-67, shows it going on earlier still.

was century long, and that what happened later in the century was merely a "new chapter" in proceedings by no means new in themselves.[120] In Brittany, noble concern for exactitude in the levy of dues went back to the late seventeenth century or even before. It resulted, moreover, not so much from the greed of landlords as the policies of a royal administration determined to deprive them of all rights they could not document,[121] and from constant attempts by a resourceful peasantry to whittle away their lords' rights whenever their vigilance relaxed. Such tendencies forced lords to make their claims precise, either in periodic new terriers or at each change of ownership. As the historian of the Breton nobility puts it:

> The expression "seigneurial reaction" is inadequate because it has been applied to too short a period (the end of the eighteenth century), when its judicial symptoms were appearing from the end of the sixteenth. It is also incomplete in that it leaves aside not only the permanence of seigneurial pressure, but also that of erosion by the peasants (*grignotage paysan*).[122]

The overall impression left by recent studies, therefore, is that the maintenance of seigneurial rights was a constant process, of which the remaking of terriers under Louis XVI, where it occurred, was merely the last manifestation. Only very occasionally were new dues levied or old ones increased. It was mostly a question of not allowing existing ones to lapse.

This is not to say that the seigneurial order saw no new developments as the eighteenth century progressed. The rise in prices must have diminished the weight of dues in cash, a positive alleviation of the burden.[123] On the other hand it must have increased the weight of dues in kind. Improved surveying techniques must have made terriers more precise as time went on.[124] A new table of duties payable on terrier work, of 1786, certainly increased the cost of revising these documents, costs which the tenant rather than the lord usually bore.[125] It seems too that more lords were farming out their assets to professional agents or farmers, who were perhaps harsher managers than the lords themselves.[126] In these ways, the burden of the seigneurial structure may have been increasing. For these reasons, the peasants complained when the *cahiers* presented them with the opportunity.

---

[120] Saint-Jacob, *op. cit.*, pp. 249, 425, 434.
[121] Meyer, *Noblesse Bretonne*, ii, pp. 784-5.
[122] *Ibid.*, p. 788.
[123] E.g. in Provence, a point made by Baehrel, *op. cit.*, pp. 450-1.
[124] Davies, "The Origins" (cited n. 88), pp. 36-7; Soboul, "De la pratique", pp. 1058-63; Meyer, *op. cit.*, ii, pp. 790-1.
[125] Aulard, *Féodalité*, pp. 51-3; Davies, *op. cit.*, p. 36.
[126] See Cobban, *Social Interpretation*, pp. 48-50; Forster, *House of Saulx-Tavanes*, pp. 94-104.

But little of this resulted from any "reaction" among lords. The rise in prices and the improvement of surveying techniques were beyond their control. So was royal fiscal policy. The employment of farmers suggests disinterest in the means of assuring returns, rather than renewed attention.[127]   And the remaking of the terriers, collection of arrears, and all the other multifarious exactions of the system, were processes as old as the system itself, which had no occasion to be revived, since they had never died out.

V

Those historians who have tried to synthesize all the elements analysed here into one immense reaction have often been shown to be vulnerable.   Critics have seized upon their convenient confusion of terms, like "noble" or "aristocratic" or "feudal" or "seigneurial", none of which are entirely synonymous and some of which are very different indeed.[128]   The foregoing survey should add to these doubts.   The "feudal" or "seigneurial" reaction was an idea developed quite independently of the others, and whatever tenuous connection it could be said to have with political or social reactions, in that it was conducted by aristocrats,[129] now seems weaker than ever. Similarly, if there was an ideological reaction, or a political one, they did not coincide chronologically with what has been supposed to be the social reaction of the later eighteenth century.   Even accepting that these various different phenomena did occur, the single broad "aristocratic reaction" has been synthesized only at the cost of glossing over many such obstinate difficulties.

Meanwhile it seems increasingly doubtful whether even the particular reactions can be substantiated.   In political terms, the only irrefutable reaction was confined to the years of the Regency, and that was short-lived. Nothing after it appears unambiguous enough to deserve the name reaction, at least until the sudden emergence of the social question in 1787-8, which is rather a different problem. In ideological terms, there was no unanimity among theorists on anything more precise or less superficial than increased power for aristocrats, a theme which seems to peter out, or at least petrify,

---

[127] On these grounds Cobban, *loc. cit.*, goes so far as to call the "feudal reaction" a misnomer.

[128] E.g. M. Reinhard, "Sur l'Histoire de la Révolution Française", *Annales, E.S.C.*, xiv (1959), pp. 568-9; Cobban, *Social Interpretation*, ch. iv, *passim*; Furet, "Le catéchisme", p. 264.

[129] Which incidentally ignores the fact that as often as not the landlords or farmers concerned were bourgeois.

between about 1750 and 1787. In social terms, most institutions in France seem to have become less, not more exclusive in their recruitment as the century went on. And although a hostile awareness of this trend seems to have been spreading among certain noblemen, it had made little impact on the trend by the time of the Revolution. In the countryside, the burden of the seigneurial property structure may have grown more heavy, but in most areas this had little to do with any reaction. Over-exclusive study of the years immediately preceding the Revolution seems to have produced a historian's illusion. But the ship has now sunk. Not without trace; a few masts obstinately protrude above the surface to mark where the wreck lies. But wreck it remains. Can anything be salvaged?

Little remains for the supposed reaction under Louis XVI, at least prior to the collapse of the government's reform plans in the summer of 1788. There were those who felt that the barriers of privilege should be strengthened, if only to help the petty nobility. There were moves, like the Ségur ordinance, in that direction. But they had little to do with the collapse of the established political order which produced the real reaction, in the form of moves to capture control of the political machinery of the future for the provincial nobility. Perhaps, with no revolution, the moves towards exclusivism would have snowballed: the new army regulations of 1788, for example, would have had the effect of closing many of the loopholes which the Ségur ordinance had left open.[130] But, however much they inflamed a public opinion whose hostility was perhaps growing,[131] the practical impact of exclusivist sentiment remained small, and wealth, rather than privilege, remained the key to social success before 1789.[132] Such "reactionary" tendencies as there were, were precisely directed at altering this state of affairs. But no reaction was necessary to ripen conditions for a revolution; all that was needed was a growing consciousness among those whom the old régime had always excluded from honour, of the injustice of their exclusion.

Some historians, seeing the limitations of the idea of a reaction under Louis XVI alone, have preferred to speak of a longer process, of a century or more. This certainly lessens the chronological difficulties in synthesizing such a movement, and outflanks many of

[130] See J. Egret, *La Pré-Révolution Française (1787-1788)* (Paris, 1962), pp. 87-94; and Mousnier, *La Société*, pp. 128-9.
[131] Carré, *Noblesse de France*, p. 313.
[132] See J. McManners, "France" in Goodwin (ed.), *European Nobility,* for the most elegant expression of this view.

the arguments which demonstrate that things were much the same under Louis XVI as under Louis XIV. Noble pressure for the revival in the early and mid-seventeenth century of the long-dormant law against *dérogeance* might suggest that such a long-term reaction may have been beginning then.[133] This may be so; but it is doubtful whether, thus extended, the concept has much meaning, especially when considered as a factor in the origins of the Revolution. By the later eighteenth century it would be important as a structural characteristic of the old order, but hardly by then a development peculiarly significant in precipitating the revolution which overthrew that order. Nor would anything, except some element of dramatic contrast, be lost by such a disappearance. There is still more than enough in the circumstances of Louis XVI's reign to explain the outbreak of revolution.

Besides, behind the idea of a long, secular reaction would still lie the assumption of a different order in previous centuries, a less artistocratic France in the fifteenth, sixteenth, or early seventeenth centuries. Such assumptions may prove justified, but until their truth is demonstrated we should beware of them. A critical examination of the supposed "reaction" on the eve of the Revolution justifies such reservations. Historical *clichés* invite confirmation by research as much as they stimulate criticism, and most scholars have set out to explain and illustrate the aristocratic reaction. Yet by looking beyond the period characterized by the supposed reaction we find plenty of justification for questioning it. Perhaps future research will still show that institutions did become more aristocratic, or that more terriers were remade, in the later eighteenth century. But that research is essential if we are to establish beyond doubt that such things did take place. In the meantime much of the evidence points in quite the opposite direction.

NOTE, 1976

Since the present article was first published, the question of a social reaction has been examined at greater length than I found possible by D. D. Bien, "La réaction aristocratique avant 1789: l'exemple de l'armée", *Annales, E.S.C.*, xxix (1974), pp. 23-48 and 505-34. After a very exhaustive survey of both old and new evidence, Professor Bien reaches conclusions broadly similar to mine.

[133] Grassby, "Social Status", p. 19.

2. The Revolution and the Rural Community in Eighteenth-Century Brittany

T. J. A. LE GOFF AND D. M. G. SUTHERLAND

ONE OF THE MOST POWERFULLY DEVELOPED THEMES IN TOCQUEVILLE'S study of the old régime in France was the extent to which the French kings had undermined the autonomy of local institutions and government, subordinating the lives of Frenchmen to daily surveillance by a powerful central authority.[1] Since Tocqueville's day, historians have pointed out how uneven the centralizing action of the Bourbon monarchy had in fact been. If the king's servants in Versailles and his agents in the provinces did have a great deal of authority over some regions, municipalities and village councils, most ordinary people could still live almost entirely outside the influence of the state. The Revolution came as an unprecedented and often unwelcome intrustion into the lives of many such people. After 1790, the demands the central government made on citizens for attention, activity and loyalty went far beyond the claims of the ramshackle administration of the old régime.

The impact of the revolution in government on the largely rural local communities of France is a problem for historians of popular culture, since the reception these changes received in different regions varied considerably. Brittany is an obvious choice for a study of this impact, for it was one of the regions of France where popular counter-revolution gained wide support in the countryside. By looking at the relations between the royal and provincial governments and the local communities over which they ruled, and the changes in these relationships which the Revolution brought with it, one may begin to understand some of the reasons why this rejection of the new régime took place. Such a local study may also suggest a new approach to the reactions to the revolutionary settlement of other rural communities in the rest of France.

One prime source for the study of these relationships is the judicial collections of the old régime and revolutionary courts. Judicial

---

[1] A. de Tocqueville, *L'ancien régime et la Révolution* (first published in 1856), in *Oeuvres complètes*, ed. J.-P. Mayer, 2 vols. (Paris, 1952), ii, pp. 107-42, 284-6.

records can be used — and have been, to great effect — for the study of criminality in pre-industrial societies,[2] but they are no less important as sources for the history of popular mentalities. The judicial records of the old régime in France have the great advantage in this that they give an account of all phases of the investigation of a crime, since every aspect of the inquiry and trial was considered a part of the judicial process. In an English investigation and trial, rumour, hearsay and much superfluous detail about the background of a crime are elicited and used by investigators but are inadmissible or irrelevant in court; in France, the judges themselves ran the investigation, and depositions, examinations and confrontations of witnesses, and lengthy interrogations of suspects formed an integral part of the judicial dossier. This wealth of direct testimony by ordinary people can be used as a unique kind of listening device to reveal the day-to-day tensions within rural society and the way in which rural people regarded, used or were the victims of the state. Such records establish a remarkable continuity between rural reactions to outside authority in the old régime and during the Revolution. The criminal records of the *parlement*, the *présidiaux* and seigneurial courts, and of the revolutionary courts which replaced them help us understand how much the attitudes and assumptions of the rural community expressed in the *chouannerie* — the royalist guerilla wars in Brittany from 1793 to 1815 — had vivid precedents in earlier experience. In this study, we have used records from two regions in Brittany: the largely Breton-speaking area which became the District of Vannes in 1790, and the French-speaking areas around Rennes, Vitré and Fougères.

Government presupposes the existence of some form of repressive authority. Frenchmen in the eighteenth century thought their society was very well policed indeed; on learning of the Gordon Riots, L.-S. Mercier remarked that such anarchy could never take place in Paris for this reason. For us, the surprising thing about France in the old régime is how ineffectual and erratic the instruments of legal repression were. Apart from towns, where a few *sergents* and *huissiers* of the courts might be expected to keep order, France was virtually unpoliced. In Brittany, as in the rest of France, the *maréchaussée* — the mounted police which was the predecessor of the present-day *gendarmerie* — was the sole permanent force of order; during most of the eighteenth century it numbered about two hundred men for a

---

[2] See the studies and comprehensive bibliography in A. Abbiateci, F. Billaçois et al., *Crimes et criminalité sous l'ancien régime, 17e-18e siècles* (Paris, 1971).

population of some two million.[3]   The result was that organized force alone could not maintain order.   Weak, scattered about the province and, for much of the century, under-financed, governmental institutions needed allies to execute the law.   If one of the chief duties of the state may be fairly considered to be the maintenance of law and order, it is safe to say that the government of the old régime was sadly inefficient.   The repression of crime in the countryside lay in the hands of individual and community initiative.   Virtually all the criminal cases which came before the tribunals, great and small, got there because individuals had complained to the courts, seigneurial and royal, of wrongs done to them.

If the repression of crime by constituted authority took place only when such personal appeals were made, it is of some significance to know how the rural population regarded that authority.   In old régime Brittany, the rural communities had always accepted outside authority with reluctance.   The normal taxes of the Bourbon monarchy were resisted up to the end of the old régime with considerable success.   Everyone knows of the revolt of the *papier timbré* in 1675 which had, at least as its pretext, the introduction, real and supposed, of new royal taxes to the province.   Only with the greatest difficulty, and through the intervention of royal troops, and, by no means less significant, the energetic preaching of the famous missionary Fr. Maunoir and other Jesuits was it put down.[4]   This, however, was but one example of resistance to royal fiscalism.   In 1719-20, tax revolts against the *capitation* broke out sporadically, and the menace of another anti-fiscal uprising, abetted by the nobles of the province, haunted the royal administration through the 1720s and '30s.   The *vingtième* was only established in Britanny in the 1750s after considerable compromise with local nobles and peasants, and the Breton Estates managed, down to the end of the old régime, to keep out the hated *gabelle* and *tailles*.[5]

One of the fruits of such compromises was the establishment of the *Commission intermédiaire* of the Breton Estates.   This institution had

---

[3] E. Bertin-Meurot, "La Maréchaussée en Bretagne au xviiie siècle" (Université de Rennes, Thèse de doctorat en droit, 1969), pp. 119, 163.

[4] Summary accounts can be found in, among others, R. Mousnier, *Fureurs paysannes* (Paris, 1967), pp. 123-56; J. Delumeau (ed.), *Histoire de Bretagne* (Toulouse, 1969), pp. 291-2; and L. Bernard, "French society and popular uprisings under Louis XIV", *French Historical Studies*, iii (1964), pp. 468-75.

[5] H. Fréville, *L'Intendance de Bretagne (1689-1790)*, 3 vols. (Rennes, 1953), i, pp. 256-60, 441-62; A. Rebillon, *Les Etats de Bretagne de 1661 à 1789 . . .* (Paris-Rennes, 1932), pp. 313-21; J. Meyer, *La noblesse bretonne au xviiie siècle*, 2 vols. (Paris, 1966), ii, p. 1,067.

become permanent by mid-century and by the end of the old régime had managed to wrest the administration of most taxes from the hands of the crown.   The commission is chiefly known to historians as one of the bulwarks which enabled the Breton nobility to resist the encroaching absolutism of Versailles.   Equally important, however, was that it relied for the success of its operations on the local contacts of the commissioners in each diocese, who themselves worked out the division of taxes with the petty peasant notables of each parish.   The intrusion of the royal *commis* into the countryside was thus reduced to a minimum.   Moreover the Estates and the commissioners kept down the taxes.   At the end of the old régime, Necker estimated that the average tax levy *per capita* and per unit of land was about one third less in Brittany than in the rest of France. [6]

The power of the royal government depended on compromises like this; so did that of other forms of external authority.   The church's "invasion" of rural society, for instance, if it went back to Gallo-Roman times, had to be renewed constantly, as it had been by the vigorous programme of parish missions, retreats and popular devotions in the seventeenth and eighteenth centuries; but here too, the church only penetrated the rural areas by transforming itself in the image of the rural community: by Christianizing the pagan gods, menhirs, and holy wells in Merovinigian times, by adopting the doctrines of seventeenth-century French mysticism to simple visual presentation, and by undergoing a massive invasion of the rural clergy by priests of peasant stock in the eighteenth and nineteenth centuries. [7]

Seigneurial authority was in some ways another of the forms of external power with which the rural community had to deal.   The attitude of the common people to seigneurial authority was often ambivalent.   Estate agents were the victims of universal petty fraud when they tried to revise *terriers*, even when the sums of money they tried to collect were derisory.   On the other hand, the peasants often relied on the seigneurial courts to render justice, and they expected their seigneurs to provide entertainments, charity and endowments. Seigneurial authority was also employed on some occasions as an

[6] A. Rebillon, *Histoire de Bretagne* (Paris, 1957), p. 145.   A proper study of the operation of the *Commission intermédiaire* is still to be written; the conclusions here are based on research in the Archives départementales du Morbihan (hereafter cited as A. D. Morbihan, C — Commission intermédiaire (unclassified series), and on Rebillon, *Les Etats de Bretagne*, pp. 251-3, 290-312 and *passim*.

[7] Meyer, *La noblesse bretonne*, ii, pp. 1,151-3; T. Le Goff, "A social and economic study of the town of Vannes and its region during the eighteenth century" (University of London Ph.D. thesis, 1970), pp. 254-62; and C. Langlois, *Le diocèse de Vannes au XIXe siècle 1800-1830* (Rennes, 1974), pp. 298-320, 530-89.

instrument of royal control but whether the seigneur acted on his own behalf or that of the king, seigneurs had to conform to certain expectations in order to carry some weight in the rural community.[8]

If royal and ecclesiastical authority gained some foothold in rural Brittany, there were other forms of external authority which were resisted tenaciously. One such authority was the *fermes du tabac* and the *fermes des devoirs*, the government monopolies of tobacco and alcohol which were leased out to entrepreneurs. In the region of Vannes, for example, the landing of contraband tobacco from Jersey in the numerous small coves off the coast appears to have been a regular occurrence. In 1775, two employees of the *ferme* described how, on a moonlit December night, a band of some three hundred men, mostly peasants and the rest smugglers belonging to an organization of long standing known as the Bande Angevine, all with blackened faces, armed with cudgels and pistols, and equipped with sixty to seventy horses, assembled on the coast near St.-Gildas-de-Rhuys to cover the landing of contraband from a sixteen-ton coasting vessel. To prepare for the landing, after terrorizing the monks and women of the *bourg* of St.-Gildas for a couple of hours, they rounded up all the customs officers in the area, tried to elicit from them the whereabouts of their captain-general in order to "have the pleasure of seeing him and garroting him", and debated whether they ought to drown or beat to death their captives (they were finally let go with a warning not to interfere with these operations in the future).[9] Attempts by the agents of the tax farmers to repress such activities could lead to revolts by whole parishes, as occurred in 1761 at Ambon, where the excisemen attempted to arrest a soldier for selling contraband tobacco to the inhabitants.[10]

Even more frequent, apparently, were infractions against the *ferme des devoirs*. Fifty-eight prosecutions for fraud concerning the sale of wine, cider and other drinks in the rural area around Vannes were brought to court between 1760 and 1764. This amounted to almost as many as the total number of criminal cases in the same period. About one in eight of these culminated in some form of

---

[8] Le Goff, "Vannes", pp. 225-32; Meyer, *La noblesse bretonne*, ii, pp. 777-801, 1,111-12.

[9] Archives départementales d'Ille-et-Vilaine (cited hereafter as A.D. I.-V.), 1 B h 14: Requête de Laurent David, adjudicataire des fermes royales ..., 2 Aug. 1776; cf. A. D. Morbihan, L 135, 29 Nov. 1792.

[10] A. D. Morbihan, B 1267: Présidial de Vannes, procédures, 1760; *ibid.*, 14 B 10: Traites de Vannes, 1761. Cf. H. Sée, "Quelques aperçus sur la contrebande en Bretagne au xviiie siècle", in J. Hayem (ed.), *Mémoires et documents pour servir à l'histoire du commerce et de l'industrie en France*, 9e série (Paris, 1925), pp. 227-35.

violence against the excisemen. The scenario of such raids had something of the formality of classical farce: the *commis des devoirs* who, having been "informed" that a peasant was selling his own wine or cider, or Nantes wine fraudulently, would venture out to the hamlet or *bourg*, observe the drinkers through the window, and suddenly push open the door. A woman (for some reason it is always the woman who serves) cries out "The excisemen! We're done for." The drinkers protest that they are merely "friends" of the householders, but in vain, for the wary excisemen observe that the wine is "genuine full-quality commercial wine of the latest vintage", and that it comes from the family barrel, which has been emptied at a dangerously fast rate. Often the enraged drinkers, with the assistance of neighbours, would compel them to leave by starting fist fights, and then would pursue them with insults, stones and even gunfire.[11] There were certain areas such as this where royal authority made little impression on rural people.

Outside authority was, then, kept at a healthy distance in the rural communities of Brittany, and appealed to only in certain circumstances. The *maréchaussée* were not popular, and their interventions, even when carried out with the best of intentions, were unwelcome. Thus in 1790, on a market-day in Fougeray in July 1790, the *maréchaussée* tried to stop a fight; one of the brawlers seeing his chance, enlisted the support of a crowd of some three hundred, led by the clerk of the village. The police beat a hasty retreat.[12]

To call in the *maréchaussée* or the *huissiers* against outsiders of course offended no one and was safe, if the outsiders were not dangerous. Thus, one October evening in 1764, a prosperous *métayer* of Séné, Gervais le Guerer, returned home to find that he had been robbed of a loaf of bread and two shirts. Le Guerer gathered up a group of harvest workers from the taverns of the parish, and together they tracked down and delivered to the *maréchaussée* a hapless young pair of wandering beggars, one an ex-sailor, the other a cowherd. In 1788, wary peasants in Montautour denounced Louis Orière, an itinerant and shiftless roofer, to the *maréchaussée* for the theft of two bed-sheets and some farm tools.[13] One could call upon

---

[11] A. D. Morbihan, B 1137-41, 1172-9, 1267, 1273: Présidial de Vannes, Minutes, 1730-2, 1760-4; *ibid.*, B (unclassified): Sénéchaussée de Rhuys, Minutes 1732-2, 1760-4; A.D. I.-V., 2B 674-6, 684-7, 693-4: Présidial de Rennes, ferme des devoirs 1750-71, 1788-90, where the incidence of fraud seems comparable.

[12] A.D. I.-V., 8B 60, 10 July 1790.

[13] A. D. Morbihan, B 1373: Présidial de Vannes, Minutes, 1764; A.D. I.-V., 1 B^n 2910: Tournelle.

the courts and their servants against a marginal member of the rural community, whom none liked. In 1763, two *laboureurs* of Plescop denounced, apparently with no hesitation, one Joachim Jouan, an itinerant cattle-merchant and butcher living for the time in the parish, for stealing their cows. On another occasion, a drunken Guillaume Fourcault of Betton was seized by some local people and delivered to the *maréchaussée* for the apparently trivial offence of cutting the tails off his employer's horses while they were grazing.[14] If a victim knew that there was a danger of reprisal by his aggressor, he thought twice before going to the courts. In 1753, the *procureur du roi* of the *présidial* of Vannes complained that he had only just learned by public rumour of the activities of a gang of thieves operating in the countryside around Vannes during the previous ten years. The *maréchaussée*, he claimed, knew more than he of their activities, and did nothing, and the band carried on with impunity by threatening to burn the houses of their victims if they talked. An ecclesiastical *monitoire* of 1764 demanded information, under the customary pain of excommunication, from anyone with knowledge of the brigands responsible for no less than four murders, thirteen violent robberies and one assault which had occurred over the previous twenty-three years around the tavern of Belair in the parish of Bourg-des-Comptes on the high road between Rennes and Poligné. No one came forward.[15]

To denounce one's enemies, then — and some did — one had either to be in a strong position oneself, or to fear no reprisals from a weak adversary. But even where there was no apparent risk, countryfolk showed considerable reluctance to go to the trouble of denouncing their neighbours; it was somehow not fitting. "So your husband has gone to Vannes to make trouble for us", cried the tavern-keeper Marie Conan of Plaudren in 1763 before kicking and biting her neighbour Michelle Thomas. In 1764, Guillaume Payen, his brother Julien Payen and Julien's son, *laboureurs* in Elven, were accused by their brother-in-law, Julline Richard, of attempted murder. They admitted that they had tried to beat Richard, but only after he had stolen 480 *livres* from Guillaume Payen's house the night Guillaume's brother, a priest, had died. Moreover, Richard had refused to pay money he owed to his other relatives, and was even accused of having tossed arsenic into Payen's bed; "Guillaume Payen

[14] A. D. Morbihan, B (unclassified): Regaires de Vannes, Minutes, 1763; A.D. I.-V., 2B 947: Présidial de Rennes.
[15] A.D. I.-V., 1Bⁿ 2069: Tournelle, 1753-4; *ibid.*, 2B 958: Présidial de Rennes.

believed he was going to die, so extraordinarily did his head swell up". All this, needless to say, would never have been brought to court but for Richard's complaint.[16] Cases like this suggest that the courts were used as a kind of final resort, a terminal stage in long-standing private feuds. In fact, the reason why judgements in so many cases of this sort pleaded in the lower courts are difficult to find is that many were settled privately, for a sum of money, before a notary, after the appropriate menace of prosecution had been made.[17] As in this case, the actual criminal case represents a kind of ultimate step in a feud or a quarrel. (But how many similar disputes must there have been which never reached this stage . . . !) One applied to authority, then, when offenders were outsiders, or were disliked, or were too weak to retaliate, or when the offender had gone too far.

The wide latitude that was permitted local transgressors can be illustrated by an examination of two cases of arson. The first, which occurred in Romillé in July 1771, also shows how quickly and in this case unjustifiably the community picked on outsiders who were perceived as a threat to lives and property. An accidental fire in the *bourg* of Romillé was rumoured to have been set so that two men previously arrested on suspicion of spying for brigands and known already as tobacco smugglers and alms-box robbers could escape from the seigneurial gaol. Rumour quickly incriminated two possible accomplices in the alleged arson, Marie Chiennefront and her brother François. Their quarrelsome and dishonest behaviour in the past convinced everyone that the two were quite capable of helping criminals and committing arson. Everyone knew François had already feigned blindness to improve his chances of gaining alms while begging, and everyone had heard a tale that he had stolen church ornaments in nearby Bédée. Marie was known to be a petty thief. However, she had never been denounced to the courts despite the sore provocation that the repeated truculent denials and threats of arson she made to her accusers must have been; up to then, people had been satisfied with forcing her to restore her plunder. The thick dossier detailing the case is particularly interesting because at no time was evidence ever produced to link the Chiennefronts to the brigands. Nor had the Chiennefronts' violations of the law over the

---

[16] Both cases in A. D. Morbihan, B (unclassified): Largouet-sous-Vannes, Minutes, 1764.

[17] Numerous examples in A. D. Morbihan, E^n: Fonds des notaires; e.g. E^n 693 (Perrigaud), 9 Oct. 1723, 22 Nov. 1723. Cf. J.-C. Gégot, "Etude par sondage de la criminalité dans le bailliage de Falaise (xviie-xviiie siècle). Criminalité diffuse ou société criminelle?", *Annales de Normandie*, xvi (1966), p. 119.

years ever been investigated.[18] As locals, they enjoyed a tolerance which was quite obviously not extended to the prisoners who, as outsiders, were capable of anything and therefore to be feared. Only when someone went beyond a certain threshold of tolerated behaviour were they turned over to outside justice, as the second case of arson illustrates. A fifty-year-old widow named Marie Besnard, in love with a young notary half her age named Pierre Evallet, tried to force him to marry her. She falsely claimed that he had made her pregnant, she slandered his mother, and told everyone that when Evallet refused her entreaties, the devil "wearing great horns" had seduced him and the parish priest had had to re-baptize him. All to no avail. When Evallet became engaged to someone else, Marie cut the ears and tail off his horse and nailed them to his fiancée's door. She also tried, unsuccessfully, to interrupt the marriage ceremony by hiding under the altar and making rude noises. None of this won Evallet's affections. But what is remarkable in this year-long campaign of harassment is the restraint Evallet and his family showed. He did nothing to stop the woman, even when she mutilated his horse. It was only when Marie, in an act of frustration and revenge, set fire to Evallet's house that the law was called in.[19] It is doubtful that the same sort of understanding tolerance would have been extended to an outsider.

It would seem, then, that much of rural crime went unpunished by legal authorities. Indeed, the rural community resisted uninvited intervention when it was felt to conflict with the moral order of the community, or of a majority of the community. An important place in this moral order was occupied by beggars who, if covertly feared and disliked at times, still retained in the Breton countryside much of the sacred character of the medieval poor. In 1786, three cavaliers of the *maréchaussée*, after taking in tow a man and two women who were begging near Pont-Scorff, stopped to watch a *pardon* at a nearby chapel and were promptly set upon by an enraged crowd, who liberated the prisoners. In 1770, the *maréchaussée* tried to arrest beggars at the fair of Le Nedo, in Plaudren, and provoked a full-scale riot.[20] This sort of resistance does not mean of course that crime went totally unpunished, or that the poor lived an idyllic life in a village community that took care of their every need.

---

[18] A.D. I.-V., 1B^n 2544: Tournelle, 1771-4.
[19] A.D. I.-V., 1B^n 2457: Tournelle, 1771.
[20] E. Guéguen, "La mendicité au pays de Vannes dès la deuxième moitié du xviiie siècle", *Bulletin de la société polymathique du Morbihan*, 1970, pp. 111-12.

Demonstrated cases of punishments exercised by the community are of their nature bound to occur only rarely in legal, or any other documents, but here and there one finds enough evidence to know that they existed. We have seen how Marie Chiennefront's petty thefts had been frustrated by forced restitution. Similarly, Joseph Lemabe, aged twenty-two, a former tobacco smuggler who made himself a nuisance to the *bourg* of Elven by several thefts in 1791, had half his hair cut off by the inhabitants.[21] As for the poor, while they enjoyed a certain licence and a certain consideration because of the church's teaching, they were considered by many as an annoyance, and if they had a place at the wedding feast, it was at the end of the table. In 1732, Jacques Le Mauf, a professional beggar, was dragged out of a wedding banquet at Trefflean and locked up because he took wine, bread and meat from the table out of turn.[22] All these were people who had broken unwritten rules, and paid a price exacted by common consent.

Given the slowness and inefficiency of justice in the lower courts, community self-regulation was considerable and a necessity. It was also possible, however, for the victim to take direct action against wrongdoers alone, or with the aid of his family, friends or allies. Often, for example, when tenants were evicted from their tenures held under precarious tenure — *métayage, fermage* or *domaine congéable*[23] — they retaliated against the new tenants with blows, threats, gunshots and arson. In 1761, Joseph Le Luhern, a *laboureur* of Séné, was pursued by the dogs of a certain Jullien Le Bras, and set on by Jullien, his son and his farm-hand who threw him into a mill-pond and beat him with their cudgels because he had tried to take over the lease of Le Bras' holding. "He'll remember Le Bras of Perenno for a while", growled the old man as he moved off; no doubt he did.[24]

A fascinating case of an eight-year feud between two families of Grand-Champ shows vividly how long this kind of quiet warfare could go on. Around 1777 a *laboureur*, Gervais Corsmat, the head of a family which included five sons, took over the lease of a tenure under *domaine congéable* from the Le Pallud family against the latter's will. On the day the land was surveyed for the transfer, Janne Le Pallud

[21] A. D. Morbihan, L^z 287^1: Tribunal criminel du district, 1791.

[22] A. D. Morbihan, B (unclassified): Largouet-sous-Vannes, Minutes.

[23] A system of tenure somewhat less precarious than a leasehold, but less permanent than a *censive*. It gave the tenant proprietorship of buildings and most crops, but not of the ground itself, which was leased from a landlord.

[24] A. D. Morbihan, B (unclassified): Regaires, Minutes, 1762; for further examples, see Le Goff, "Vannes", pp. 211-13.

tried to hit the patriarch of the Corsmats with her sabot, and this seems to have been the first in a long series of battles between the families. Since that time, according to the Corsmats, the Palluds ambushed them after every fair. As the nine-year lease on the tenure began to run out, the Palluds outbid the Corsmats for the new lease, setting off a campaign of terror by the Corsmats, who publicly threatened vague but certain violence against their rivals, upset the Pallud's cart when it was loaded, began cutting down apple trees on their tenement before they had to move out, and paid a visit to a relative of the Palluds' who was lending them the money to finance their new bid on the lease; a visit at which, according to Corsmat, they did no more than talk about the weather — but that was not their rivals' story! The feud culminated in a slanging match and pitched battle between the two families in 1785.[25]   In the same sort of way, little wars between neighbouring parishes or sections of large parishes could occur, such as the one between the village of Penerf and that of La Tour du Parc on the peninsula of Rhuys, over the right to collect seaweed to use as fertilizer.[26]

But direct, indeed violent, action was resorted to for much less. A woman who, for example, put flax to ret in a pond her neighbours used for drinking-water for their cattle narrowly escaped serious injury, along with her family, from her enraged neighbours.[27] In 1789, in Betton, Julien Vincent badly beat a fellow farm-worker for no other reason than because the latter had been sleeping in his bed.[28] In 1762, a pregnant woman from Elven was beaten and kicked, her child was stillborn as a result, and she was attacked again five days later because she reproached a neighbour with letting his cows wander in her field.[29] A *laboureur*, Yves Le Nevé of Trefflean, was killed by a stone from another neighbour for complaining of the same offence.[30] In 1761, Pierre Cottier of Bruz, a farm servant, shot Pierre Maunnier, another domestic, in the leg in a dispute over the right of the former to lead his employer's horses over the property of Cottier's employer.[31]

The countryside was a turbulent world which had its own ways, usually effective, of righting wrongs and redressing injuries, indeed

---

[25] A.D. I.-V., 1B^n 3615: Tournelle, 1785-6.
[26] A. D. Morbihan, B (unclassified): Sénéchaussée de Rhuys, Minutes, 1771, 1773; *ibid.*, L 1463: Population, District de Vannes, 1790.
[27] A. D. Morbihan, B (unclassified): Regaires, Minutes, 1763.
[28] A.D. I.-V., 2B 948: Présidial de Rennes.
[29] A. D. Morbihan, B (unclassified): Largouet-sous-Vannes, Minutes, 1762.
[30] A. D. Morbihan, B (unclassified): Largouet-sous-Vannes, Minutes, 1761.
[31] A.D. I.-V., 2B 856: Présidial de Rennes.

even for containing quarrels and letting off steam. Thus, the primitive form of football played in Brittany in the seventeenth and eighteenth centuries, *soule* (at which, according to family tradition, the father of the *chouan* hero Georges Cadoudal excelled), was little more than a ritualized battle between parishes.[32] Such behaviour was part of a coherent set of understandings and part of normal life. Except when matters got out of hand, when people were killed or seriously injured, or decided to put an end to harassment, it rarely came to the notice of townsfolk or government officials who, for their part, had few contacts with the countryside.

It is hard to escape the conclusion that under the old régime as it had existed in Brittany, perhaps in most of rural France, as long as the violence, rowdyism, feuding, petty thieving and the like which were contained, tolerated or repressed within the rural communities, did not interfere with the collection of taxes and general order, the state preferred not to interfere. And this was a situation which generally suited the country people, who dealt with discontent and violations of their social order in their own way. To be sure, the state was a necessary part of the moral order, to be appealed to against outsiders and the weak, and as a last resort, but it was a lesser part. The state, too, was able to exploit the prestige of the local parish priests, who possessed a double advantage: not only did they fulfil a sacred office, but they were often the only persons with real social ascendancy in the parish. Without the co-operation of the clergy, the monarchy would have had no idea of the movement of the population, the annual state of the harvest, the problem of poverty and all the other information required by an increasingly complex state. Yet as we have seen, even the influence of the clergy could not prevent rural people from rejecting certain aspects of monarchical authority. The relations of the *maréchaussée* with the peasant communities were extremely delicate; those of the agents of the tax-farms and tobacco monopoly even more so. In the old régime, as long as government was distant, it was generally respected.

No doubt the same pattern of internal regulation which characterized the rural community in the old régime continued into the Revolution.[33] However, a fundamental difference became apparent soon after 1789: the state and outside authority no longer filled the same

---

[32] A.-F. Rio, *La petite chouannerie ou histoire d'un collège breton sous l'Empire* (London, 1842), pp. 47-50; and Y. Brekilien, *La vie quotidienne des paysans en Bretagne au xixe siècle* (Paris, 1966), pp. 208-9.

[33] Much has been made in recent studies of crime in old régime France of a supposed evolution away from crimes against persons towards a more "professional" criminality in the years immediately preceding the Revolution. The evidence for this in Normandy and the Nord, where most of the studies on

rôle of a distant arbiter.   After 1789 most of the country people had lost all confidence in outside authority.   To appeal to it became a political act which marked one off from the rest of the community. Within a few months of the beginning of the Revolution, the impact of government on a rural community changed drastically.   For the first time, the Revolution brought the government into close and regular contact with the rural community and thereby it lost its respect. The administrative revolution of 1790-1 changed the nature of a hitherto vague and undemanding "outside" authority.   The changes upset the delicate balance between administration and country by demanding that country people participate in government in ways previously unknown.   In the process, the revolutionaries destroyed the moral force of the clergy by transforming them into paid civil servants who were expected to be apologists for the new régime. And, when the countryside showed its reluctance, the revolutionaries had no principle of authority to which they could appeal other than force, which they were increasingly obliged to use after 1790 to maintain the Revolution in the countryside.   There was no uniform response to these changes.   Some parishes accepted them with varying degrees of enthusiasm.   Some balked or delayed, some refused outright.   The reasons why each parish, each hamlet and each family were disposed to make their decision for or against the Revolution had much to do with the economic structure of each parish and region.   On this level, various explanations of the counter-revolutionary behaviour of most of western France are possible, and it is not our intention to rehearse here the conclusions of Paul Bois,

rural and semi-rural criminality have been done, is rather ambiguous, but if there is any truth to the thesis, Brittany may well have been characterized by a rather different, "static" pattern of crime in which no such evolution took place.   On Normandy, see B. Boutelet, "Etude par sondage de la criminalité dans le bailliage du Pont-de-l'Arche (xviie-xviiie siècles).   De la violence au vol: en marche vers l'escroquerie", *Annales de Normandie*, xii (1962), pp. 235-52; P. Crépillon, "Un 'gibier de prévôts'.   Mendiants et vagabonds au xviiie siècle entre la Vie et la Dives 1720-1789", *Annales de Normandie*, xvii (1967), pp. 223-52; V. Boucheron, "La montée du flot des errants de 1760 à 1789", *Annales de Normandie*, xxii (1971), pp. 55-86; Gégot, "Etude par sondage"; some of these conclusions seem rather forced.   On the Nord, see P. Deyon, "Délinquance et répression dans le Nord de la France au xviiie siècle", *Bulletin de la Société d'Histoire moderne*, 14th ser., no. 20 (1972), pp. 10-15.   In the area around Vannes, we have found that crimes against property accounted for less than one third of rural crime in 1730-2, but only 11% of rural crime in 1760-4; and in the jurisdiction of the présidial of Rennes, Mlle. Muracciole has found no significant evolution towards rural "professional" crime in her study "La criminalité de 1758 à 1790, d'après le fonds du présidial de Rennes, étude par sondage" (Université de Rennes, mémoire de maîtrise, 1969).   The virtual breakdown of government in the countryside in Brittany after 1791 and the multiplication of special tribunals and political crimes make statistics of crime after that date meaningless.

Marcel Faucheux or Charles Tilly.[34] In their work it is possible to discern a common theme, which is perhaps not worked as fully as it might be: that in general the mass of the poor who inhabited the French countryside profited little if at all from the Revolution, and that in counter-revolutionary areas it was such people who gave desperation, and sometimes the force of numbers, to discontent and risings. It might be possible to take this further and say that acceptance of the changes the Revolution brought depended in large part on the attitude of the more prosperous set of peasants — and their numbers — in any given region. What we are concerned with here is, however, less the conditions which may have predisposed certain regions to revolution than with the nature of the changes in the balance of power within the rural community and between the community and the outside world which made the Revolution insufferable to large numbers of people.

The Revolution shifted the initiative from the community to government and at the same time gave government a power to coerce which its counterpart in the old régime had never possessed. The effect on the moral unity of the countryside was traumatic. The petty notables of the rural community who had accepted the Revolution became increasingly isolated. To their fellow parishioners, they were now the instruments of the new political régime. But if they were the willing tools of outside authority, they also profited from their new power, using it to gain their own way in local disputes, even to the extent of calling in the National Guard and the army. Against them, the sense of communal solidarity felt by the remainder of the parish community was heightened. The seizure of power by such petty notables appears to have taken place throughout most of France. *Chouannerie*, in Brittany, originated as a protracted civil war in those parishes where this new ascendancy did not evoke a sense of legitimacy nor call out sufficient support.

Others have described the actual institutional changes which the Constituent Assembly instituted in the provinces.[35] What is necessary here is to outline the impact of these changes on Breton society, for it was through the reforms and the way they were applied

[34] P. Bois, *Paysans de l'Ouest* (Le Mans, 1960); M. Faucheux, *L'insurrection vendéenne de 1793* (Paris, 1964); C. Tilly, *The Vendée* (London, 1964). The conclusions are summarized and evaluated in H. Mitchell, "The Vendée and counterrevolution: a review essay", *French Historical Studies*, v (1967-9), pp. 405-29.

[35] J. Godechot, *Les institutions de la France sous la Révolution et l'Empire* (Paris, 1951). At the local level: J. Bricaud, *L'administration du Département d'Ille-et-Vilaine au début de la Révolution (1790-1791)* (Rennes, 1965); D. Jouany, *La formation du Département du Morbihan* (Paris-Vannes, 1920).

that the Revolution gradually lost its moral force in rural Brittany. In the first place, the Constituent Assembly procrastinated over the two issues — the seigneurial system and tax reform — which had held so important a place in the rural *cahiers* in 1789. In Upper Brittany the *cahiers* had demanded that the seigneurial régime be abolished outright or that the nobles be forced to play a more positive rôle in the countryside.[36] The Constituent Assembly did neither of these, and by demanding compensation for the old payments merely perpetuated the most contentious aspects of the seigneurial system. In the end the peasants generally refused to pay either dues or the compensation payments.[37] On the issue of tax reform, the peasants had hoped that the abolition of privilege would lighten their own burden. On the whole, this did not happen. By some complicated arithmetic, it is possible to show that the over-all level of direct taxation did not change significantly after 1790.[38] Moreover, by allowing proprietors to add the equivalent of the former tithes to leases, the Constituent Assembly made it just as difficult for tenant farmers to pay as in the old régime. In Lower Brittany, to obtain the support of the peasants in 1788-9, some of the urban revolutionaries had told them that the *domaine congéable*, the predominant form of tenure, was "feudal" and ought to be abolished. The local landlords — and the Constituent Assembly, whom the landlords lobbied energetically — disagreed, and it was not until August 1792 that the system was significantly altered.[39] Measured against the unprecedented demands

[36] H. Sée and A. Lesort, *Cahiers de doléances de la Sénéchaussée de Rennes pour les Etats-Généraux de 1789*, 4 vols. (Paris, 1909-12). The former is the more usual demand, but examples of the latter can be found, e.g. *ibid.*, i, pp. 161 (Balazé), 196 (Ste.-Colombe), 225 (Billé), 403 (Drouges), 565 (Amanlis), 258 (Cornillé), 455 (Rétiers).

[37] One can follow this process in the account books of the marquis de Piré in A.D. I.-V., 2E^r 340, where no compensation was ever paid, and the peasants gradually stopped paying all feudal dues.

[38] It is difficult to compare the old and new tax structures because most taxes in the old régime were indirect, falling on articles of consumption and therefore to a large extent on the towns. The Constituent Assembly's shift to direct taxation must have adversely affected the countryside more than the towns. The direct *per capita* taxation in the Ille-et-Vilaine doubled from 2 livres 10 sols to 5 livres. This calculation is based on: the tables in the *Almanach du District de Fougères* (Fougères, 1791); the *états de répartition* in A.D. I.-V., C 3981, 4595, 4599 and 4627-8; the population lists in A.D. I.-V., L 503; and the tables in Bricaud, *L'administration . . . d'Ille-et-Vilaine*, pp. 545-8. On the other hand, the adjustment of seigneurial dues, the abolition of the tithe and continuing high grain prices made it easier for some — but not all — peasants to support the higher taxes.

[39] Le Goff, "Vannes", pp. 320-39, and "Les doléances des paysans du Vannetais à la veille de la Révolution", *Bulletin de la Société polymathique du Morbihan*, 1969, pp. 31-50; L. Dubreuil, *Les vicissitudes du domaine congéable en Bretagne à l'époque de la Révolution*, 2 vols. (Rennes, 1915).

it imposed, the Revolution offered few compensating benefits to most peasants.

The effect of the Constituent Assembly's reforms on local institutions was to increase immensely the ability of government to influence the countryside. In the old régime, rural local government had been in the hands of a self-appointing oligarchy which dealt with fairly minor measures such as secondary roads, church repairs and so on. Only rarely did the Intendant and the Parlement intervene in local affairs.[40] The revolutionary rural communes were radically different in that they were designed to by-pass the administrative authority of the parish clergy and to be the direct executors of the will of the Districts and Departments.

Besides being more closely linked to the executive than ever before, local institutions were also expected to do more. For instance, in the first year of the new régime, local municipal officers were expected to draw up a rough land-survey, a census, a list of all ecclesiastical holdings and their values, lists of active citizens, lists of the poor and mendicants, and to re-apportion taxation along new lines. In co-operation with judicial authorities, they also apprehended criminals, reported on opinion and disturbances, assured the smooth functioning of the grain trade, assisted at fêtes and federations and supervised the formation of the rural National Guard and various electoral meetings.[41] Citizenship became a turbulent and time-consuming business for most revolutionary Patriots in the countryside.

While government now demanded the active co-operation of the rural community as a whole, actual power devolved into the hands of a relatively small and select group of men. This was the combined effect of the electoral laws and the system of indirect elections. The distinction between active and passive citizens actually achieved in Brittany what it was intended by the Constituent Assembly to achieve everywhere in France: it disenfranchised a substantial minority of tax-paying citizens — some 25 to 35 per cent of the adult males in the Department of the Ille-et-Vilaine and 40 to 50 per cent in the District of Vannes.[42] Coincident with this, the system of indirect elections

[40] Potier de la Germondaye, *Introduction au gouvernment des paroisses, suivant la jurisprudence du Parlement de Bretagne* (St.-Malo-Rennes, 1777), *passim.*

[41] Bricaud, *L'administration . . . d'Ille-et-Vilaine*, pp. 52-4, 291-2, 339-42.

[42] Calculated (1) for the Ille-et-Vilaine by comparing the numbers of active citizens in 1790-1 in Bricaud, *L'administration . . . d'Ille-et-Vilaine*, pp. 538-42, with the number of voters in 1793 in A.D. I.-V., L 337-9, 346; (2) for the District of Vannes by comparing the same data in L 234: État général du département du Morbihan . . . 1790, with Archives Nationales (cited hereafter as A.N.), F²⁰ 361 pc. 54: Population, Dénombrement, 1793. In both areas, around half the active citizens were not permitted to be eligible as electors.

gave day-to-day authority at the District and Departmental level to an élite of bourgeois and the wealthier sort of peasant. There are some indications that this happened at the municipal level as well.[43] By and large then, political power became the preserve of men who were economically and socially unrepresentative of their constituents and who, in every sphere but the political, had no preponderant influence over their fellow citizens.[44]

Outside authority now became much more immediate in the countryside and its local agents quickly became the tools of a new authority which was willing to impose its values on the rural community. Typical of these were men like the sieur Joulan, a municipal councillor in Gahard, who in a dispute with the parish priest over his rights to sit on the council, claimed "that he had a better title to be there than him, since he had more property in the parish".[45] The meaning of the Revolution also became apparent to the parishioners of St.-Didier in August 1790 when the mayor and National Guard captain could stand up in church on successive Sundays and loudly demand that prayers no longer be said for the former seigneurs.[46] One could cite dozens of examples of the new élite challenging the position and influence of the rectors, but it should be noted that the political power handed over to the more socially prominent members of the rural community was used in other spheres as well.

The coalition of urban politicians and rural petty notables who assumed power in 1789 took advantage of the situation to eliminate real or imagined threats to their authority and to remove affronts to bourgeois morality. In the parish of Ploeren, the local *laboureurs*, encouraged by the constitutional priest Le Quinio, arrested a band of beggars established in the area. As the beggars were led off to Vannes by the *gendarmerie*, they were heard to say "that ever since the country folk had begun arresting vagabonds, they had no luck with their harvests; that the houses of the rich and solid peasants would have to be burned".[47] At the fair of Mangolerian in Plaudren, in

---

[43] A.D. I.-V., L 337; A. D. Morbihan, L 234-6, 1420. In the Ille-et-Vilaine, the status and wealth of the municipal officers have been derived by comparing the names of municipal officers writing to the Districts, e.g. in A.D. I.-V., L 441, 31 Oct. 1790 (St.-Didier), and *ibid.*, L 1426, 13 June 1791 (Balazé), with the *capitation* the officers paid in 1788, found in A.D. I.-V., C 4264.

[44] On the absence of a "rural bourgeoisie", see Le Goff, "Vannes", pp. 221-4, and the 1974 thesis of D. Sutherland in the University of London on "The Social Origins of Chouannerie in Upper Brittany".

[45] A.D. I.-V., 2B 945: deposition of Sr. Petitjean, rector of Gahard, Mar. 1789.

[46] A.D. I.-V., L 441: Procès-verbal of the mayor and notables of St.-Didier, 31 Oct. 1790, "Réponse du recteur de St.-Didier . . . ", 16 Nov. 1790; petition of the National Guards of St.-Didier [n.d.].

[47] A. D. Morbihan, L^z 273^2: Tribunal criminel du district, 1791.

July 1790, the priests, municipal officers and some *laboureurs* helped the *maréchaussée* to arrest an itinerant professional gambler and army deserter; as the police led him to the edge of the fairground, they were set upon by about two hundred men and boys, armed with stones.[48] In 1789-90, the *maréchaussée* arrested in and around Rennes and Vannes an unprecedented number of women of ill repute, denounced by the new municipal council because their presence threatened the health of the soldiers, and by some peasants because their activities, sometimes carried out in the fields outside the towns, were ruining the crops.[49]   Such repressive action was not new, of course, as we have seen from some of the earlier examples, but it seems to have increased in scope under the Revolution — partly perhaps because so many rootless people seemed set adrift by the economic crises of these years. And before the Revolution, for local petty notables to use the repressive force of the state against the poor so openly would have been rather dangerous.

The new holders of power were also able to use it to repress opinions which they had previously encouraged.   In the electoral campaign of 1789, the urban politicians had invited the peasants to attack the seigneurial system as a means of undercutting the nobility.[50]   A year later, when a series of minor anti-seigneurial riots broke out between Rennes and Ploermel, the politicians sent out the urban National Guard to repress them.[51]   National politics and a newly-found respect for all forms of property no longer required or allowed a vigorous attack on the nobility.   In general, then, the repressive machinery of government was used in entirely new directions to attack the local clergy and to impose the values of the revolutionary élite on the countryside.   It was also used more vigorously and more frequently in an attempt to support the new authority.

Nor was this repressive machinery the same as the old one in the

[48] A. D. Morbihan, B 1340: Présidial de Vannes, Minutes, 1790.

[49] A. D. Morbihan, B 1340: Présidial de Vannes, Minutes, 1789-90; *ibid.*, L 1699: Registre d'écrou, 1787-93; A.D. I.-V., 8B 60, 8B 76-7: Maréchaussée de Bretagne, Procédures prévotales, 1786-90.

[50] Le Goff, "Les doléances des paysans du vannetais", pp. 35-7; and R. Dupuy, "Contre-révolution et radicalisation. Les conséquences de la journée des 'Bricolles' à Rennes, 26 et 27 janvier 1789", *Annales de Bretagne*, lxxix (1972), p. 441.   It is also worth noting that the urban politicians were concerned with the question of seigneurial rights only after the noble-inspired *coup* in Rennes in Jan. 1789 convinced them that the nobility would stop at nothing to protect their privileges.

[51] H. Sée, "Les troubles agraires en Haute-Bretagne, 1790-91", *Bulletin d'Histoire économique de la Révolution*, 1920-1, pp. 231-370; R. Dupuy, *La Garde nationale et les débuts de la Révolution en Ille-et-Vilaine (1789-mars 1793)* (Paris, 1972), pp. 108-20, 182-97.

mind of the country folk; the authority of the old régime had been an intermittently exercised force, backed up by centuries of custom, the sanction of Divine Right, and the concurrence of the clergy. In 1675, the King had had not only troops, but also Fr. Maunoir's missionaries to restore order in Brittany; after 1789, the revolutionaries had only the moral force of the Nation behind them, a concept void of significance for most country people: "We have no more king, we have no more priests, we want to grapple with the Nation! We want to know by what authority they think they can recruit us .... We no longer recognize any ...", the peasants who invaded Vannes in 1793 were reported as saying[52] — a protest which neatly sums up the total collapse of the moral authority of the new order.

Even within their own terms, the revolutionary politicians used their power arbitrarily if not illegally and tolerated violence from their own supporters. The countryside had already had a taste of this as early as the summer of 1789. As royal authority disintegrated in Brittany and the Intendancy withered away, effective control passed to the municipalities and the National Guards. Throughout the summer, they requisitioned grain and arrested suspects on their own authority.[53] Even constituted authority could be arbitrary. Later, in January 1791, the Department of the Ille-et-Vilaine tried to force the parish priests into taking the oath to the Civil Constitution of the Clergy by threatening — quite illegally — to withhold the pensions of refractories. The Department and the Districts also interned and exiled refractory priests. In 1792 they tried to impose their own oath to the Civil Constitution on the refractory priests and to arrest those who refused it. Royal vetoes of this and similar local legislation were ignored. Later in the summer of 1792, the Department, before it had received authorization from the Legislative Assembly, decreed the deportation of all but a handful of refractory priests on its territory. All of this was justified in their eyes because "the evident danger to general security forced us to disregard the constitutional guarantee of individual liberty".[54] The terrorist mentality had already appeared.

Despite the energetic character of these measures, few of them

---

[52] A. D. Morbihan, L 149: Procès-verbal des autorités constitués en permanence à Vannes, 14 mars-2 avril 1793.

[53] Dupuy, *La Garde nationale*, pp. 93-108; Le Goff, "Vannes", pp. 320-1.

[54] Cited in Bricaud, *L'administration ... d'Ille-et-Vilaine*, p. 386, note 82. Copies of the *arrêtés* and some of the correspondence can be found in A.N., F[19] 430, most of which has been reprinted in A. Lemasson, *Les actes des prêtres insermentés en 1794* (Rennes, 1927), pp. 2-12.

worked. The country people protected the priests to such an extent that relatively few were arrested and only a minority of the refractories were deported.[55] By the summer of 1792, the countryside had effectively broken its tenuous links with the urban governments. In full consciousness of the futility of legal measures, the National Guard in the eastern Ille-et-Vilaine began a continuous campaign of harassment against "aristocratic" parishes — a campaign which the authorities were powerless to stop. It usually took the form of closing down churches, chasing out refractory priests and lending support to local Patriots. One of the best examples occurred in the spring of 1792 when two thousand National Guards descended on the hapless parish of Acigné. The priests having long since fled, the Guardsmen settled down to an afternoon of pillaging local wine cellars. By the time armed forces arrived from the Department, the men were threatening to set fire to the *bourg* if anyone tried to arrest them. In the end, the authorities had to let the Guardsmen stagger home. This and dozens of other incidents like it had a shattering effect on the countryside.[56] Municipalities expressed their loss of confidence in the revolutionary authorities. The co-operation the Revolution needed to function in the countryside vanished.[57] Loss of confidence also led to thoughts of revenge. All the parishes but two which had been victims of National Guard attacks in 1792 were classed as *chouan* in 1795 in the Ille-et-Vilaine.[58] The struggles of 1792 merely continued through the Directory under different names: *chouans* on one side, *gardes territoriales* on the other — a struggle so fierce that it was bitterly remembered as late as the 1840s.[59]

[55] Cf. the lists of priests taking the departmental oath and those interned in April 1792 in A.D. I.-V., L 1005, 1007. By 9 Sept. 1792, only 58 priests had been deported to Jersey, according to Lemasson, *Les actes des prêtres*, pp. 259-61. Although there were more deported later — cf. Public Record Office, H.O. 98/2 — the number of those deported, imprisoned or executed in the Year II does not approach that of the 648 refractories of 1791.

[56] A.N., F⁷ 3679¹, report of Julien Guyot, commissaire du directoire du district de Rennes, 16 April 1792. See also *ibid.*, 13 Nov. 1792, and A.D. I.-V., L 441, 996, 1246 and 1412. On other attacks, see Dupuy, *La Garde nationale*, pp. 197-203, 271-3; C.-L. Chassin, *La Vendée patriote*, 3 vols. (Paris, 1893-5), ii, pp. 164-70; F.-A. Aulard, *Recueil des actes du Comité de Salut public*, 27 vols. (Paris, 1889-97), ii, pp. 567 ff.; A.-R. Du Chatellier, *Histoire de la Révolution dans les départements de l'ancienne Bretagne*, 6 vols. (Paris-Nantes, 1835-6), ii, pp. 323-4; R. Cobb, *Les armées révolutionnaires*, 2 vols. (Paris-La Haye, 1963), ii, pp. 555-6, 582-7.

[57] E.g.: A.N., F⁷ 3679¹: extract of deliberations of municipal council of La Chapelle Erbrée, 3 Aug. 1792; and Le Goff, "Vannes", p. 328.

[58] A.D. I.-V., L 379: Tableaux de l'état politique et militaire des communes, Year III.

[59] P. de Pontbriand (ed.), *Mémoires du colonel de Pontbriand sur les guerres de la chouannerie* (Paris, 1897), p. 205.

The intrusion of government into the countryside, its arbitrariness and authoritarianism, its willingness to use its power against the priests who had previously done so much to aid Bourbon absolutism and the monopolization of that power by a rather small group of local politicians gradually left only physical force to regulate rural-urban relations. Any rural politician who continued to co-operate with authority cut himself off from the rural community and allied himself with an alien system. The moral unity of the community, which had operated in the old régime against the weak, the marginal members, the outsiders, or those who violated accepted standards, was turned upon those who sympathized with the Revolution, who had tried to lead the rural world into the new national politics, or, less creditably, to use the great slogans of national politics, to further their local ends. But since the revolutionaries could not be turned over to an authority which was, after all, their ally, they were ostracized instead. The rector of La Chapelle-Janson was jeered because he took the oath to the Civil Constitution of the Clergy: "The people treated me as an intruder (*intrus*)", he reported indignantly, "though I have occupied my functions for forty years".[60] A seamstress, Marie Halen of Luitré, admitted that since the beginning of the Revolution "she had sown discord in treating as intruders the priests who took the oath and those who followed them"; she even claimed to be able to sense "a horrid stench in the house [of a neighbour] of the intruders who had been to mass".[61] Municipal officers, like Bertrand Gravier, *agent national* of Argentré, who tried to maintain their authority were given the same treatment. "Where's Gravier, your husband, that bugger of an intruder?" a band of *chouans* demanded of his wife; "Where's the intruder, that buggering madman?"[62] All such men became outsiders, the agents of a godless state, fair game for any *chouan* band to pillage and rob. For the *chouans*, any outrage against them was allowable because they had violated the community's supposedly unanimous attitude to the Revolution and forfeited their right to be considered its members.

The *chouan* parishes were too weak militarily to keep authority as distant as it had been before 1789. This did not stop them, however, from rejecting the symbols and vocabulary of the Republic. A rural republican became a "citoyen", a man to be despised almost as a different being. "How can you think I resemble you?" said a *chouan* to Jeanne Bouin of Bréal, "I am a good *émigré*, a good

[60] A.D. I.-V., L 438: Guérin to Gavard, 14 Oct. 1791.
[61] A.D. I.-V., L 1486: interrogation of Marie Halen, 2 Floréal Year II, comité de surveillance de Rennes.
[62] A.D. I.-V., 1F 1665: declaration of Perrine Belloir, 10 Brumaire Year III.

Christian and a good royalist".[63] Indeed, words like "citoyen", "bleu", "nation", "lois", and so on, words charged with sacred meaning to a *sans-culotte*, became words of contempt and derision in *chouan* country. As late as 1833, a popular song had it that Bretons would rather die than fight for "la patrie".[64] Mathurin Mangodin of Fleurigné expressed this sense of rejection succinctly when he harangued his neighbours during a *chouan* occupation of the parish: "You know we are no longer under the laws of the nation or of tyranny . . .".[65] The law of such a demanding outside authority was considered a kind of despotism.

At the same time as outside authority and its local supporters were rejected, the rural community affirmed as never before its right to moral existence. In retrospect at least, the unified community of the old régime was idealized, as the country people became aware of a profound sense of loss. Joseph Thomas, a *laboureur* of Landéan, freely admitted that he "regrets the old régime, because every one was happy then and we all were as one, whereas today we are two".[66] Someone else observed that "the more that happens, the worse the people's lot gets".[67] This association of communal unity and happiness was easily linked to the visible symbols of the old régime, most notably to the king and clergy. The same Joseph Thomas said that "he would prefer a king, since everyone would be contented and happy . . . I want him back, and also Monsieur Baro [Barreau] de Girac, the previous non-juring bishop of Rennes".[68] The same association of ideas was present in the mind of Louise Geogaut, a domestic servant from Yrodouer, when she said that the *chouans* "were meeting in order to bring back the king and the good priests just as they had been before".[69] To some extent at least, the *chouans'* royalism and catholicism derived from their nostalgia for an

---

[63] A.D. I.-V., L (supplément), liasse 3, 1er cahier: interrogation of Jeanne Bouin, 5 Pluviôse Year II.
[64] On the use of vocabulary, see A.D. I.-V., 1F 1665: anonymous note of 17 Feb. 1794, declaration of Pierre Douard, 3 Floréal Year II, and "Chanson trouvée sur un chouan, le 2 avril 1833"; A.D. I.-V., L (supplément), liasse 30, 3e cahier, fo. 15v: interrogation of Perrine Boquais [n.d.]; *ibid.*, liasse 29: declaration of Jean Chalmel, 2 Nivôse Year II.
[65] A.D. I.-V., L (supplément), liasse 29, dossier 234: deposition of Julien Poirier, 27 Ventôse Year II.
[66] A.D. I.-V., L (supplément), liasse 31, dossier 283: interrogation of Joseph Thomas, 2 Floréal Year II.
[67] A.D. I.-V., L (supplément), liasse 31, dossier 285: interrogation of Jeanne Bechet, 6 Ventôse Year II.
[68] A.D. I.-V., L (supplément) liasse 31, dossier 283, 2 Floréal Year II.
[69] A.D. I.-V., L 1485: interrogation of Louise Geogaut femme Bardon, 12 Nivôse Year II.

ideal community located in the immediate past when, it seemed, everyone knew his proper place in society.

This conception of a proper moral order may perhaps explain some of the more curious actions of the *chouans*. They did not always kill or rob their victims, who, incidentally, were rarely tortured or maimed, unlike the victims of the White Terror in the Midi whose grim fates Richard Cobb has recently recalled.[70] Instead, they often engaged in a practice which may have its roots in rural custom and which the insensitive urban administrators interpreted as simple pillage: the *chouans* forced rural republicans to give whole bands food and drink, berating them all the while for their actions and threatening reprisals if they did not mend their ways.[71] This reminder of communal responsibilities could show itself also in the form of a public humiliation. A dramatic example took place in the parish of Fleurigné when a band of *chouans* prodded Jean Chalmel into climbing the church belfry, and, as he clung perilously to the steeple, forced him to wave a white flag and shout "Vive Louis XVII".[72] In another public ceremony, reminiscent of the charivaris of perhaps happier days, some *chouans* forced one Julienne Langlais to her knees while the leader of the group held an image of the Sacred Heart before her and said "Look upon the heart of Jesus; you must be reconciled to Him".[73] Reconciliation with the community through political and religious symbols which recalled an idealized past, and through humiliation, penance and repentance was evidently possible for some local people. Just as some actions were tolerated before 1789, so others were forgiven afterwards, provided that the transgressors had not gone too far.

Doubtless the *chouans* and their supporters had greatly idealized the way of life in the rural community before the Revolution. In many ways, relations of rural people with the outside world had been difficult, just as they were with neighbours. The rural community perpetuated injustices and made life difficult for the weak, even though it partly assumed responsibility for them. Its notions of justice, its settling of accounts had reflected the roughness of everyday life and manners. Nevertheless, the *chouans* were right in believing

[70] R. C. Cobb, *The Police and the People. French Popular Protest, 1789-1820* (Oxford, 1970), pp. 133, 146, 337-9; and *Reactions to the French Revolution* (London, 1972), pp. 22, 230, 245.

[71] A. D. Morbihan, L 333-7: Secours pour pertes, 1790-Year VIII; A.D. I.-V., L 480-1: Etats des pertes.

[72] A.D. I.-V., L (supplément), liasse 29: declaration of Jean Chalmel, 2 Nivôse Year II.

[73] *Ibid.*: declaration of Julienne Langlais [n.d.].

that the Revolution had introduced great changes in the internal order of their miniature societies.   The old régime had governed largely by not governing; it allowed the rural communities to settle the bulk of their own affairs.   For perfectly understandable reasons, the Revolutionary authorities in Paris and in the Departments and Districts of the new régime had to change this.   But the disruption these changes caused in the balance of power within the rural community was traumatic.   Invaded and put upon by the urban revolutionaries and their friends inside the parishes, the rural communities of Brittany became more conscious of their distinctness, vague and shifting as it was, defining it in political terms, terms which in themselves took on different meanings from those which Parisian assemblies assigned to them at the time and which political historians have given them since.   Individuals within the rural world were considered, as before, as "insiders" or "outsiders", but now they were branded as "revolutionaries", "aristocrats" and "intruders" as well. The consciousness of the rural community was reaffirmed as violent political opposition to a régime harsher and more demanding, and yet more arbitrary and lacking in moral force, than the monarchy of the old régime had ever been.

3. The High Enlightenment and the Low-Life of Literature in Pre-Revolutionary France

ROBERT DARNTON

> Where does so much mad agitation come from? From a crowd of minor clerks and lawyers, from unknown writers, starving scribblers, who go about rabble-rousing in clubs and cafés. These are the hotbeds that have forged the weapons with which the masses are armed today.
>
> *P. J. B. Gerbier, June 1789.*
>
> The nation's rewards must be meted out to those who are worthy of them; and after having repulsed despotism's vile courtiers, we must look for merit dwelling in basements and in seventh-storey garrets.... True genius is almost always *sans-culotte*.
>
> *Henri Grégoire, August 1793*

THIS ESSAY IS INTENDED TO EXAMINE THE LATE ENLIGHTENMENT AS historians have recently studied the Revolution — from below. The summit view of eighteenth-century intellectual history has been described so often and so well that it might be useful to strike out in a new direction, to try to get to the bottom of the Enlightenment, and perhaps even to penetrate into its underworld.

Digging downward in intellectual history calls for new methods and new materials, for grubbing in archives instead of contemplating philosophical treatises. As an example of the dirt that such digging can turn up, consider the following titles taken from a manuscript catalogue that circulated secretly in France around 1780 and that were offered for sale under the heading "philosophical books":[1] *Venus in the Cloister or the Nun in a Nightgown, The Woman of Pleasure, The Pastime of Antoinette* (a reference to the Queen), *Authentic Memoirs of Mme. la Comtesse Du Barry, Monastic News or the Diverting Adventures of Brother Maurice, Medley by a Citizen of Geneva and Republican Advice dedicated to the Americans, Works of La Mettrie, System of Nature.* Here is a definition of the "philosophical" by a publisher who made it his business to know what eighteenth-century Frenchmen wanted to read. If one measures it against the view of the philosophic movement that has been passed on piously from textbook to textbook, one cannot avoid feeling uncomfortable: most of those titles are completely unfamiliar, and they suggest that a lot of trash somehow got mixed up in the eight-

[1] Papers of the Société Typographique de Neuchâtel, Bibliothèque de la Ville de Neuchâtel, Switzerland, MS. 1108.

eenth-century idea of "philosophy". Perhaps the Enlightenment was a more down-to-earth affair than the rarified climate of opinion described by textbook writers, and we should question the overly highbrow, overly metaphysical view of intellectual life in the eighteenth century. One way to bring the Enlightenment down to earth is to see it from the viewpoint of eighteenth-century authors. After all, they were men of flesh and blood, who wanted to fill their bellies, house their families, and make their way in the world. Of course the study of authors does not solve all the problems connected with the study of ideas, but it does suggest the nature of their social context, and it can draw enough from conventional literary history for one to hazard a few hypotheses[2].

A favourite hypothesis in histories of literature is the rise in the writer's status throughout the eighteenth century. By the time of the High Enlightenment, during the last twenty-five years of the Old Régime, the prestige of French authors had risen to such an extent that a visiting Englishman described them exactly as Voltaire had described English men of letters during the early Enlightenment: "Authors have a kind of nobility".[3] Voltaire's own career testifies to the transformation of values among the upper orders of French society. The same milieux who had applauded the drubbing administered to him by Rohan's toughs in 1726 cheered him like a god during his triumphal tour of Paris in 1778. Voltaire himself used his apotheosis to advance the cause of his "class" — the "men of letters" united by common values, interests, and enemies into a new career group or "estate". The last twenty years of his correspondence read like a continuous campaign to proselytize for his "church", as he called it, and to protect the "brothers" and the "faithful" composing it. How many youths in the late eighteenth century must have dreamt of joining the initiate, of lecturing monarchs, rescuing outraged innocence, and ruling the republic of letters from the Académie française or a château like Ferney. To become a Voltaire or d'Alembert, that was the sort of glory to tempt young men on the make. But how did one "make it" as a *philosophe?*

Consider the career of Jean-Baptiste-Antoine Suard, a leading

---

[2] Among these histories, the following were found to be most useful: Maurice Pellisson, *Les hommes de lettres au XVIIIe siècle* (Paris, 1911); Jules Bertaut, *La vie littéraire au XVIIIe siècle* (Paris, 1954); and John Lough, *An Introduction to Eighteenth Century France* (London, 1964), chaps. vii and viii.

[3] Quoted in Marcel Reinhard, "Élite et noblesse dans la seconde moitié du XVIIIe siècle", *Revue d'histoire moderne et contemporaine,* iii (Jan.-March 1956), p. 21. For Voltaire's view, see the famous 23rd letter of his *Lettres philosophiques* (London, 1734).

candidate for a representative *philosophe* of the High Enlightenment. Others — Marmontel, Morellet, La Harpe, Thomas, Arnaud, Delille, Chamfort, Roucher, Garat, Target, Maury, Dorat, Cubières, Rulhière Cailhava — might do just as well. The advantage of Suard's case is that it was written up by his wife. A *philosophe's* rise to the top is indeed revealing when seen from his wife's viewpoint, and especially when, as in the case of Mme. Suard, the wife had an eye for domestic detail and the importance of balancing the family accounts.[4]

Suard left the provinces at the age of twenty and arrived in Paris just in time to participate in the excitement over the *Encyclopédie* in the 1750s. He had three assets: good looks, good manners, and a Parisian uncle, as well as letters of introduction to friends of friends. His contacts kept him going for a few months while he learned enough English to support himself as a translator. Then he met and captivated the abbé Raynal, who functioned as a sort of recruiting agent for the socio-cultural élite known as *le monde.*[5] Raynal got Suard jobs tutoring the well born, encouraged him to write little essays on the heroes of the day — Voltaire, Montesquieu, Buffon — and guided him through the salons. Suard competed for the essay prizes offered by provincial academies. He published literary snippets in the *Mercure*; and having passed at Mme. Geoffrin's, he began to make frequent appearances in *le monde* — a phrase that recurs with the regularity of a leitmotive in all descriptions of Suard.[6] With doors opening for him in the salons of d'Holbach, Mme. d'Houdetot, Mlle. de Lespinasse, Mme. Necker and Mme. Saurin, Suard walked into a job at the *Gazette de France*: lodging, heating, lighting, and 2,500 livres for a half day's work of putting polish on the materials provided every week by the ministry of foreign affairs. At this point Suard took his first unorthodox step: he got married.

[4] The following is based on Mme. Suard's *Essais de mémoires sur M. Suard* (Paris, 1820), supplemented by the almost equally interesting reminiscences of D.-J. Garat, *Mémoires historiques sur la vie de M. Suard, sur ses écrits, et sur le XVIIIe siècle*, 2 vols. (Paris, 1820). Although Suard is a forgotten figure today, he was one of the most prominent writers of the High Enlightenment. He never produced a major work, but he made a reputation by journal articles, academic discourses, and translations, whose studied tastefulness may be appreciated from his *Mélanges de littérature*, 5 vols. (Paris, 1803-1805).

[5] Garat described Raynal as follows (*Mémoires historiques, op. cit.*, i, p. 107): "In the capital of France and of philosophy, he acted as a grand master of ceremonies, who introduced beginners with talent to talented celebrities and men of letters to manufacturers, merchants, farmers, generals, and ministers".

[6] Garat described Suard as the epitome of the *savoir-faire* and respect for social rank that made a man of *le monde* (see especially *ibid.*, i, pp. 133-6), and he defined *le monde* as a milieu of "men powerful by virtue of position, wealth, literary talent and birth . . . those three or four conditions that are the real sources of power in society", *ibid.*, i, p. 263.

Philosophes did not generally marry. The great figures of the early Enlightenment — Fontenelle, Duclos, Voltaire, d'Alembert — remained bachelors; or, if they fell into matrimony, as in the case of Diderot and Rousseau, it was with someone of their own station — shop girls and servants.[7] But the elevated status of the *philosophe* in Suard's time made marriage conceivable. Suard picked a girl of good bourgeois stock like himself; overcame the objections of her brother, the publisher Panckoucke, and of Mme. Geoffrin, who held old-fashioned ideas about the incompatibility of professional writing and family life; and set up house in the apartment that went with his job on the *Gazette de France*. Mme. Suard trimmed her wardrobe to fit their tight budget. Friends like the prince de Beauvau and the marquis de Chastellux sent them game from the hunts every week. And princely patrons like Mme. de Marchais sent carriages to carry the couple off to dinners, where the bride marvelled at "the rank and the merit of the guests".[8] This was something new: Madame Philosophe had not accompanied her husband on his forays into *le monde* before. Mme. Suard followed her husband everywhere and even began to form a salon of her own, at first a modest supper for literary friends. The friends and patrons responded so enthusiastically that something of a cult grew up around the "petit ménage" as it was known from a poem celebrating it by Saurin. Formerly a fringe character picked up for amusement by the salons and readily turned out into the street for drubbings, begging, and *embastillement*, the *philosophe* was becoming respectable, domesticated, and assimilated into that most conservative of institutions, the family.

Having made it into *le monde*, Suard began to make money. By taking over the entire administration of the *Gazette de France*, he and his collaborator the abbé Arnaud, boosted their income from 2,500 to 10,000 livres apiece. They succeeded by appealing over the head of a bureaucrat in the ministry of foreign affairs, who was "astonished that men of letters shouldn't consider themselves rich enough with 2,500 l. of revenue",[9] to the foreign minister, the duc de Choiseul, whose sister, the duchesse de Grammont, was an intimate of the princesse de Beauvau, who was a friend of the Suards and of Mme. de Tessé, who was the protector of Arnaud. Such obliging *noblesse* was vulnerable to the vagaries of court politics, however;

---

[7] Of course well-born and wealthy *philosophes* like Montesquieu, d'Holbach and Helvétius did not fit into this pattern. Humbler writers were expected to take mistresses or to marry when their fortune was made. Maupertuis, Marmontel, Piron, and Sedaine were famous and past fifty when they married.   [8] Mme. Suard, *Essais de mémoires, op. cit.,* p. 59.

[9] *Ibid.,* p. 94.

and when d'Aiguillon replaced Choiseul, the Suards were turned out of their *Gazette* apartment. Once again *le monde* rallied to the defence of its *petit ménage*. Suard received a compensatory pension of 2,500 livres from d'Aiguillon, who was persuaded by Mme. de Maurepas, who was moved by the duc de Nivernais, who was touched by the sight of Mme. Suard weeping in the Académie française and by the prodding of d'Alembert and La Harpe. Then a gift of 800 livres in *rentes perpétuelles* arrived from the Neckers. The Suards rented a house in the rue Louis-le-Grand. Suard managed to get the lucrative post of literary correspondent to the Margrave of Bayreuth. His friends arranged a pension for him of 1,200 l. on the income from the *Almanach Royal*. He sold his collection of English books to the duc de Coigny for 12,000 l. and bought a country house. He became a royal censor. Election to the Académie française came next, bringing an income of up to 900 l. in *jetons* (doubled in 1786) and far more in indirect benefits, such as a position as censor of all plays and spectacles, worth 2,400 livres and later 3,700 livres a year. When the *Journal de Paris* was suspended for printing an irreverent verse about a foreign princess, the keeper of the seals called in Suard, who agreed to purge all future copy and to share the profits: another 1,200 livres. "He took a cabriolet, which transported him after he fulfilled the duties of his posts, to the lovely house he had given to me",[10] Mme. Suard reminisced. They had reached the top, enjoying an income of ten, perhaps over twenty thousand livres a year and all the delights of the Old Régime in its last days. The Suards had arrived.

The most striking aspect of the Suard success story is its dependence on "protection" — not the old court variety of patronage, but a new kind, which involved knowing the right people, pulling the right strings, and "cultivating", as it was known in the eighteenth century. Older, established writers, wealthy bourgeois, and nobles all participated in this process of co-opting young men with the right style — the perfect pitch of *bon ton* — into the salons, academies, privileged journals, and honorific posts. The missing element was the market: Suard lived on sinecures and pensions, not on sales of books. In fact, he wrote little and had little to say — nothing, it need hardly be added, that would offend the régime. He toed the party line of the *philosophes* and collected his reward.

But how many rewards of that kind were there, and how typical was Suard's *cas typique*? Part of the answer to those questions lies

<hr/>

[10] *Ibid.*, p. 137.

in a box in the Archives Nationales containing a list of 147 "Men of Letters Who Request Pensions" and ten dossiers crammed with material on writers and their sources of support.[11] The list reads like a "Who's Who" of the literary world drawn up by officials in the *Contrôle général* to guide Calonne, who had decided in 1785 to increase and systematize the award of literary pensions, "gratifications", and "traitements". Calonne was also guided by a committee composed of Lenoir, the former lieutenant general of police, Vidaud de Latour, the director of the book trade, and two courtier-academicians, the maréchal de Beauvau and the duc de Nivernais. Hardly a revolutionary group. The pension list, with the recommendations of Calonne's officials and his own notes scrawled in the margins, gives a corresponding impression. It shows a strong bias in favour of established writers, especially academicians. Here Morellet appears with his 6,000 livres a year from the Caisse de commerce; Marmontel with 3,000 livres as "historiographe de France" and 2,000 livres as perpetual secretary of the Académie française; La Harpe complains of receiving a mere 600 livres from the *Mercure*, the maréchal de Beauvau pushes to get him pensioned for 1,500, and the pension is granted, despite a subordinate official's observation that La Harpe also collects 3,000 livres for lecturing in the Lycée. And so the list goes, one figure of the High Enlightenment succeeding another: Chamfort (granted 2,000 livres in addition to 1,200 on the *maison du roi*), Saint-Lambert (requested 1,053 livres, decision delayed), Bernardin de Saint-Pierre (1,000 livres), Cailhava (1,000 livres) Keralio, Garat, Piis, Cubières, des Essarts, Aubert, and Lemierre.

Blin de Sainmore, a solid citizen in the republic of letter's lesser ranks, exemplified the qualities required for getting a pension. He

[11] Archives Nationales, F17a1212. Some unsigned, undated "Observations préliminaires" in the first dossier explained that the list was drawn up in order to implement an edict of 3 September 1785 which announced the government's intention of aiding men of letters more systematically than had been done before. The author of the "Observations" (probably Gojard, *premier commis* to the controller-general) evidently thought the proposed subsidies excessive: "Aside from the sums paid by the Royal Treasury to men of letters, and which amount to 256,300 livres, there are also pensions attached to journals and to the *Almanach royal*; and it is possible that they have been given to several authors who are applying today without having declared [that other income], as they should have done according to the terms of the first article of the edict". An incomplete (21 names missing) version of the master list in the Archives Nationales was sold at an auction and later published by Maurice Tourneux in *Revue d'histoire littéraire de la France*, viii (1901), pp. 281-311. Lacking the supplementary information, which he vainly sought in the series O of the Archives, Tourneux was unable to explain the circumstances of the pension scheme and wrongly linked it with the baron de Breteuil. Much of the material in F17a1212 also covers the period 1786-8.

was a royal censor, "historiographe de l'Ordre du Saint-Esprit", and protégé of the princesse de Rochefort. "I will further add, Monseigneur, that I am the head of a family, that I was born without fortune, and that I have nothing for the support and education of my family except the post of historiographer of the king's orders, whose income is barely sufficient for me alone to live in a decent style".[12] Thus the pensions went for charity as well as good works. Saurin's widow applied because his death had left her destitute, since he had lived entirely from "the beneficence of the government".[13] And Mme. Saurin specified:

Pension of the Académie française	2,000
Pension on the General Farms	3,000
As the son of a converted [Protestant] minister	800
As a censor	400
On an office of *trésorier du pavé de Paris*	2,400
Total	8,600

This "beneficence" generally went to serious, deserving writers but not to anyone unconnected with *le monde*. Academicians were first on the government's list — to such an extent that one ministerial aide jotted in a margin, "There is some danger that the title of academician might become a synonym for pensioner of the king".[14] Ducis demanded 1,000 livres a year for life on the grounds that "most of our confrères, either of the Académie française or of the Académie des Inscriptions, have obtained pensions that have the character of a permanent grace".[15] This favouritism offended Caraccioli, who wrote testily, "I am pretentious enough to believe that you will have heard of my works, all of which have religion and sound morality as their object. I have been writing in this genre for thirty-five years; and despite the frivolity of the century, [my works] have spread everywhere and have been translated into various languages. Nevertheless, under ministers who preceded you and who made me the most beautiful promises, I never obtained anything, although living in a modest state that might well be called indigence. And I have seen gratifications as well as pensions pour down . . .".[16]

As Caraccioli's comments suggest, "sound" opinions were con-

---

[12] Blin de Sainmore to the Contrôleur général, 22 June 1788, Archives Nationales F17a 1212, dossier 10.   [13] *Ibid.*, dossier 6.

[14] *Ibid.*, dossier 3.

[15] Ducis to Loménie de Brienne, 27 November 1787, *ibid.*, dossier 6. See also the similar letter of A. M. Lemierre of 8 March 1788, *ibid.*, dossier 10.

[16] Caraccioli to the Directeur général des finances, 13 August 1788, *ibid.*, dossier 6. See also Caraccioli's letter of 8 April 1785, *ibid.*, dossier 10: "I am the only author of my advanced age who has never had either a pension or a grant".

sidered as a necessary qualification for a pension. In some cases the government subsidized writers who had produced propaganda for it. It looked favourably on the abbé Soulavie, because "he has submitted some manuscripts on financial matters to M. le contrôleur général".[17] Conversely, the government avoided making payments to anyone whose loyalties were in doubt. It turned down J.-C.-N. Dumont de Sainte-Croix, a minor author on jurisprudence, because, according to the marginal note next to his name, "All the new systems of this genre would merit some encouragement, if they were made only to be known by the government and not by the public, which is incited to rebel against the established laws instead of becoming enlightened as to the means of making them better". Then, in another hand: "Nothing".[18] Rivarol also received nothing, but only because he already had a secret pension of 4,000 livres: "He is very clever, and an encouragement, which could be paid to him each year, if he remains faithful to sound principles, would be a way of preventing him from following his inclination toward those which are dangerous".[19]

So several considerations determined the state's patronage. As in the case of modern institutions like the French "Centre National de la Recherche Scientifique", the monarchy supported serious *savants*, perhaps even with the intention of recruiting a fresh intellectual élite.[20] It also dispensed charity. And it used its funds to encourage writing that would make the régime look good. In each instance, however, it restricted its subsidies to men with some standing in the world of letters. A few fringe characters like Delisle de Salles, Mercier, and Carra presumed to apply for the pensions; but they received nothing. Lenoir later revealed that he and his colleagues had turned down Carra, Gorsas, and Fabre d'Eglantine because "the academicians described them as the excrement of literature".[21] While the literary rabble held out its hands to the government, the government gave its handouts to writers situated safely within *le monde*.

It dispensed them on a large scale. A note by a subordinate official put the total payments at 256,300 livres, to which 83,153 livres were added in 1786. But that sum represented only the direct dole from the royal treasuries. Far more money flowed into the

---

[17] *Ibid.*, note in dossier 3.   [18] *Ibid.*, dossier 1.
[19] *Ibid.*, dossier 1.
[20] The documents in the Archives Nationales would therefore tend to support the argument advanced by Marcel Reinhard in "Elite et noblesse", *op. cit.*, n. 3.
[21] Lenoir papers, Bibliothèque municipale d'Orléans, MS. 1422.

purses of "sound" writers from the appointments at the government's disposal. Journals, for example, provided an important source of income for the privileged few in the literal sense of the word. Royal privileges reserved certain subjects for the quasi-official periodicals like the *Mercure, Gazette de France,* and *Journal des savants,* which exploited their monopolies without worrying about competitors (the government permitted some discreet foreign journals to circulate, provided they passed the censorship and paid compensation to a privileged journal) and which turned over part of the take to writers named by the government. In 1762 the *Mercure* paid out 30,400 livres to twenty subluminaries of the High Enlightenment.[22] Then there were many sinecures. Not only did the king require an official historiographer, but he subsidized "historiographes de la marine", "des bâtiments royaux", "des menus-plaisirs", and "de l'Ordre du Saint-Esprit". The branches of the royal family were loaded with readers, secretaries, and librarians — more or less honorific posts that one had to work *for* but not *at,* that one acquired by waiting in antechambers, improvising eulogies, cultivating acquaintances in salons, and knowing the right people. Of course it always helped to be a member of the Académie française.[23]

The dozens of volumes about the history and *petite histoire* of the academy in the eighteenth century,[24] whether written in love or in hatred, reveal a dominant theme: the Enlightenment's successful campaign to win over the French élite. After the "chasse aux Pompignans" of 1760, the election of Marmontel in 1763, and d'Alembert's elevation to the perpetual secretaryship in 1772, the academy fell to the *philosophes*. It became a sort of clubhouse for them, an ideal forum for launching attacks against *l'infâme,* proclaiming the advent of reason, and co-opting new *philosophes* as fast as the old guard academicians would die off. This last function, virtually a monopoly of the philosophic salons, assured that only party men would make it to the top. And so Voltaire's church was besieged by converts. The spectacle of a new generation taking up the torch warmed the old man's heart. When he congratulated Suard on his election, Voltaire exulted, "Voilà, God be thanked, a new career assured .... At last I see the real fruits of philosophy, and I begin to believe that I shall die content".[25] Thus Suard and his circle,

[22] Pellisson, *Les hommes de lettres, op. cit.,* p. 59.
[23] See the appointments listed after the names of the academicians in the annual issues of the *Almanach royal.*
[24] The most revealing of these is Lucien Brunel, *Les philosophes et l'Académie française au dix-huitième siècle* (Paris, 1884).
[25] Printed in Garat, *Mémoires historiques, op. cit.,* p. 342.

62   ROBERT DARNTON

the high priests of the High Enlightenment, took over the summit
of the literary world, while the mid-century *philosophes* declined and
died.   The new men included both writers like Thomas, Marmontel,
Gaillard, La Harpe, Delille, Arnaud, Lemierre, Chamfort, and Rulhière, and philosophically-minded *grands*, powerful courtiers and
clergymen, like the marquis de Chastellux, the maréchal de Duras,
Boisgelin, archbishop of Aix, and Loménie de Brienne, archbishop
of Sens.

The fusion of *gens de lettres* and *grands* had been a favourite theme
of philosophic writing since the mid-century.   Duclos had proclaimed it triumphantly in his *Considérations sur les moeurs de ce
siècle* (1750).   Writing had become a new "profession", which
conferred a distinguished "estate" upon men of great talent but modest
birth, he explained.   Such writers became integrated into a society
of courtiers and wealthy patrons, and everyone benefited from the
process: the "gens du monde" gained amusement and instruction,
and the "gens de lettres" acquired polish and standing.   It went
without saying that promotion into high society produced some
commitment to the social hierarchy.   Duclos had a keen eye for all
the subtleties of status and rank; and although he took pride in the
man of letter's ability to rise by sheer talent, he showed equal respect
for what made a man of *le monde*: "One is an *homme du monde* by
birth and by position".[26]   Voltaire, the arch-apologist for *le mondain*,
shared the same attitudes.   His article entitled "Gens de lettres" in
the *Encyclopédie* emphasized that in the eighteenth century "the spirit
of the age made them [men of letters] for the most part as suitable
for *le monde* as for the study.   They were kept out of society until
the time of Balzac and Voiture.   Since then they have become a
necessary part of it".   And his article "Goût" in the *Dictionnaire
philosophique* revealed the élitist bias in his conception of culture:
"Taste is like philosophy.   It belongs to a very small number of
privileged souls . . . .   It is unknown in bourgeois families, where
one is constantly occupied with the care of one's fortune".   Voltaire
— who incessantly cultivated courtiers, tried to become one himself,
and at least managed to buy his way into the nobility — thought that
the Enlightenment should begin with the *grands*: once it had captured
society's commanding heights, it could concern itself with the masses
— but it should take care to prevent them from learning to read.
D'Alembert believed in essentially the same strategy, but he did

[26] Charles Pinot-Duclos, *Considérations sur les moeurs de ce siècle*, ed.
F. C. Green (Cambridge, Eng., 1939, 1st. edn. 1750), p. 140 and, in general,
chaps. xi and xii.

not share his "master's" taste for the court.[27] His *Essai sur les gens de lettres et les grands* (1752), published two years before his election to the Académie française, amounted to a declaration of independence for writers and writing as a proud new profession (not in the present sociological sense of the term, but as it was used by Duclos). Yet despite some strong language advocating a "democratic" republic of letters in contrast to the humiliating practices of patronage, d'Alembert stressed that society was and ought to be hierarchical and that the *grands* belonged on top.[28] By the time he wrote his *Histoire des membres de l'Académie française* (1787), when he ruled the academy as Duclos's successor in the perpetual secretaryship, d'Alembert reformulated Duclos's theme in a conservative vein. He castigated the "horde of literary rebels (*frondeurs littéraires*)" for venting their frustrated ambitions in attacks on the academy. He defended the academy's mixture of "grands seigneurs" and writers. And he emphasized the rôle of courtiers, as experts in the realm of taste and language, in a very élitist Enlightenment — a process of gradual, downward diffusion of knowledge, in which the principle of social equality could play no part. "Is a great effort of philosophy necessary to understand that in society, and especially in a large state, it is indispensable to have rank defined by clear distinctions, that if virtue and talent alone have a claim to our true homage, the superiority of birth and position commands our deference and our respect . . . ? And how could men of letters envy or misconstrue the so legitimate prerogatives of other estates?"[29] As spokesmen for the writer's new "estate" (but not for the brand of *philosophe* represented by Diderot and d'Holbach), Duclos, Voltaire, and d'Alembert urged their "brethren" to profit from the mobility available to them in order to join the élite. Rather than challenge the social order, they offered a prop to it.

But what was the meaning of this process? Was the establishment becoming enlightened or the Enlightenment established? Probably both, although it might be best to avoid the overworked term "estab-

[27] On the strategical agreement and tactical differences between Voltaire and d'Alembert and their disagreements with the d'Holbach group (which apparently left Diderot somewhere in the middle), see John N. Pappas, *Voltaire and d'Alembert* (Indiana University Humanities Series, number 50, Bloomington, 1962).

[28] D'Alembert, *Essai sur la société des gens de lettres et des grands, sur la réputation, sur les Mécènes, et sur les récompenses littéraires* in *Mélanges de littérature, d'histoire et de philosophie* (Amsterdam, 1773, 1st. edn. 1752); see especially pp. 403 and 367.

[29] D'Alembert, *Histoire des membres de l'Académie française morts depuis 1700 jusqu'en 1771* (Paris, 1787), i, pp. xxiv and xxxii.

lishment"[30] and to fall back on the eighteenth-century expression already cited, *le monde*. After fighting for their principles in the mid-century and consolidating their victories during the last years of Louis XV's reign, the great *philosophes* faced the problem that has plagued every victorious ideology: they needed to find acolytes worthy of the cause among the next generation. Admittedly, "generation" is a vague concept.[31] Perhaps there are no real generations but only demographic "classes". Still, the great *philosophes* form a fairly neat demographic unit: Montesquieu 1689-1755, Voltaire 1694-1778; and then Buffon 1707-1788, Mably 1709-1785, Rousseau 1712-1778, Diderot 1713-1784, Condillac 1715-1780, and d'Alembert 1717-1783. Contemporaries were naturally struck by the deaths, not the births, of great men. Voltaire, Rousseau, Diderot, Condillac, d'Alembert, and Mably all died between 1778 and 1785; and their deaths left important places to be filled by younger men, who were born, for the most part, in the 1720s and 1730s.

As age overcame them, the great *philosophes* made the rounds of the salons, searching for successors. They tried to find another d'Alembert — and came up with Marmontel, the champion of *Gluckisme*. They tried to persuade themselves that Thomas could thunder like Diderot and La Harpe bite like Voltaire. But it was no use. With the death of the old Bolsheviks, the Enlightenment passed into the hands of nonentities like Suard: it lost its fire and became a mere tranquil diffusion of light, a comfortable ascent toward progress. The transition from the heroic to the High Enlightenment

[30] See Henry Fairlie, "Evolution of a Term", *The New Yorker*, 19 October 1968, pp. 173-206.

[31] Although birth and death dates overlap too much to fall into clear categories, "generations" might be differentiated by the experience of events. Whether we are thirty or fifteen, a chasm of experienced time separates those of us who did not live through World War II from those who participated in it or who read about it in the newspapers while it took place. Perhaps a similar line of experience divided the men who wrote and read the great works of the Enlightenment when they appeared in the mid-century from those who read them after they had already begun to congeal into "classics". Suard (1734-1817) recalled, "I entered *le monde* at the time of that explosion of the philosophical spirit which has marked the second half of the eighteenth century. I read *L'Esprit des lois* at the age of nineteen [i.e. in 1753, five years after its publication]. I was in the provinces, and that reading delighted me. *L'Histoire naturelle* [of Buffon] and the works of Condillac appeared soon afterwards, the *Encyclopédie* in 1752, as did the *Découverte de l'irritabilité* by Haller" (quoted in Garat, *Mémoires historiques*, *op. cit.*, ii, p. 445). For a survey of the literature on the problem of generations and periodization, see Clifton Cherpack, "The Literary Periodization of Eighteenth-century France", *Publications of the Modern Language Association of America*, lxxxiv (March 1969), pp. 321-8.

domesticated the movement, integrating it with *le monde* and bathing it in the *douceur de vivre* of the Old Régime's dying years. As Mme. Suard remarked after reporting the receipt of their last pension, "I have no more events to recount, other than the continuation of a soft and varied life, until that horrible and disastrous epoch [the Revolution]".[32] Her husband, turned censor, refused to approve Beaumarchais's not so very revolutionary play, *Le mariage de Figaro*. And Beaumarchais put most of his energy in investing — and ultimately in building the biggest townhouse in Paris — "a house that is talked about" — the *arriviste's* dream.[33]

The establishment of the Enlightenment did not blunt its radical edge, however, because just as a generation gap separated the high *philosophes* from their predecessors, a generation split cut them off from the low life of literature, from their contemporaries who failed to make it to the top and fell back into Grub Street.

Perhaps the literary world has always divided into a hierarchy whose extremes might be labelled a *monde* of mandarins on the one hand and Grub Street on the other. Such milieux existed in the seventeenth century and exist today. But the social and economic conditions of the High Enlightenment opened up an unusual gulf between the two groups during the last twenty-five years of the Old Régime, and this split, if examined in all its depth, ought to reveal something about one of the standard questions posed by the pre-revolutionary era: what was the relation between the Enlightenment and the Revolution?

At first glance, it seems that the writer's lot should have improved substantially by the reign of Louis XVI. The relevant data, flimsy as they are, all point in the same direction: a considerable expansion in

---

[32] Mme. Suard, *Essais de mémoires, op. cit.,* p. 155.

[33] Quoted in Louis de Loménie, *Beaumarchais et son temps* (Paris, 1856), ii, p. 424. Suard did not object to *Le mariage de Figaro* because he found it radical but because he considered its treatment of sex unsuitable for the stage (Mme. Suard, *Essais de mémoires, op. cit.,* p. 133). One could cite a dozen contemporary references indicating the same attitude. Even Lenoir, more involved in the business of sniffing out sedition than anyone in France, reported on Beaumarchais: "Almost all the plays of that author were prevented from opening on the grounds of being offensive to morality, but he succeeded by his intrigues in forcing his way through the censorship. More than once I received an order to let pass plays of his that had been held up for a long time without receiving the necessary approbation and permission": Bibliothèque municipale d'Orléans, MS. 1423. The "revolutionary" message of *Le mariage de Figaro*, if it exists, went unnoticed in pre-revolutionary France. Is not the play's refrain a formula for political quietism: "Everything finishes with a song"? Beaumarchais was a wealthy, ennobled man-on-the-make like Voltaire, and he devoted much of his fortune to re-editing Voltaire's works.

demand for the printed word.[34]   Literacy probably doubled in the course of the century, and the general upward swing of the economy, combined with improvements in the educational system, very likely produced a larger, wealthier, and more leisured reading public. Certainly book production soared, whether measured by demands for privileges and *permissions tacites* or indirectly by the number of censors, booksellers, and printers.   But there is little evidence that writers benefited from any publishing boom.   On the contrary, everything indicates that while the mandarins fattened themselves on pensions, most authors sank into a sort of literary proletariat.

Admittedly, information about the growth of Grub Street comes from anecdotal sources, not statistics.   Mallet du Pan claimed that three hundred writers, including a heavy dose of hacks, applied for Calonne's pensions, and he concluded, "Paris is full of young men who take a little facility to be talent, of clerks, accountants, lawyers, soldiers, who make themselves into authors, die of hunger, even beg, and turn out pamphlets".[35]   Crébillon fils, who reportedly gave out *permissions de police* for 40,000-50,000 verses of pamphlet poetry every year, was besieged by a "multitude of versifiers and would-be authors" who flooded into Paris from the provinces.[36]   Mercier found these "famished scribblers", "these poor hacks" (*écrivailleurs affamés, ces pauvres barbouilleréus*) everywhere,[37] and Voltaire constantly hammered at the theme of the "ragged rabble" (*peuple crotté*) crowding the bottom of the literary world.   He placed "the miserable

---

[34] For information on literacy, education, and book production in eighteenth-century France, see Michel Fleury and Pierre Valmary, "Les progrès de l'instruction élémentaire de Louis XIV à Napoléon III", *Population*, xii (Jan.-March 1957), pp. 71-92; Pierre Gontard, *L'enseignement primaire en France de la Révolution à la loi Guizot (1789-1833)*, (Lyons, 1959); Robert Estivals, *La statistique bibliographique de la France sous la monarchie au XVIIIe siècle* (Paris and The Hague, 1965); and François Furet, "La 'librairie' du royaume de France au dix-huitième siècle", *Livre et société dans la France du XVIIIe siècle* (Paris and The Hague, 1965), pp. 3-32.   The *Almanach de la librairie* for 1781 lists 1,057 booksellers and printers, of whom about one fifth did business in Paris.   No editions of the *Almanach* go back before 1778, so comparisons cannot be made with the early eighteenth century.   But the *Almanach royal* for 1750 lists 79 royal censors, and the *Almanach royal* for 1789 lists 181, an increase that represents a greater output of books, not greater severity in controlling them. It will probably never be possible to make estimates of the number of authors in the eighteenth century, not only because of a lack of statistics but because of the problem of defining what an author was.   Robert Escarpit made a brave but unsuccessful attempt in *La sociologie de la littérature* (Paris, 1958).

[35] *Mémoires et correspondance de Mallet du Pan pour servir à l'histoire de la Révolution française, recueillis et mis en ordre par A. Sayous* (Paris, 1851), i, p. 130.   Lenoir estimated the number of applicants for pensions at "4,000" (probably a slip for 400): Bibliothèque municipale d'Orléans, MS. 1422.

[36] L.-S. Mercier, *Tableau de Paris*, 12 vols. (1789), x, pp. 26-7.

[37] *Ibid.*, p. 29.

species that writes for a living" — the "dregs of humanity", "the riff-raff of literature" (*lie du genre humain, canaille de la littérature*) — at a social level below prostitutes.[38] Writing in the same spirit, Rivarol and Champcenetz published a mock census of the undiscovered Voltaires and d'Alemberts crammed into the garrets and gutters of Paris. They produced articles on well over five hundred of these poor hacks, who scribbled for a while in obscurity, and then vanished like their dreams of glory — except for a few: Carra, Gorsas, Mercier, Restif de la Bretonne, Manuel, Desmoulins, Collot d'Herbois, and Fabre d'Eglantine. The names of those future revolutionaries look strange in Rivarol's roll-call of "the five or six hundred poets" lost in the legions of "la basse littérature" — but Rivarol put them rightly in their place.[39]

That place was Grub Street, and its population, combustible at any time, was exploding during the last twenty-five years of the Old Régime. Of course this interpretation may be only a demographic fantasy based on subjective, literary sources, but the sources seem suggestive enough to warrant giving the fantasy rein. They continually stress the theme of the provincial lad who reads some Voltaire, burns with the ambition to become a *philosophe*, and leaves home only to smoulder helplessly and expire down and out in Paris.[40] Even Duclos worried about this corollary to his formula for success.[41] And Voltaire, obsessed by the overpopulation of young writers in Paris ("Egypt of old had fewer locusts"), claimed that he attacked Grub Street in order to warn youth away from it.[42] "The number of those who are lost as a result of this passion [for the "career of letters"] is prodigious. They render themselves incapable of any

[38] See *Le pauvre diable* and the articles in the *Dictionnaire philosophique* from which the quotations are taken: "Auteurs", "Charlatan", "Gueux", "Philosophe", and "Quisquis".

[39] *Le petit almanach de nos grands hommes* (1788), quotation from p. 5. In the preface Rivarol explained that he would exclude all established writers from his survey: "I will gladly descend from these imposing colossi to the tiniest insects . . . to that inumerable mass of families, tribes, nations, republics, and empires hidden under a leaf of grass" (p. vi).

[40] For a particularly striking example of this theme, see the first chapters of J.-P. Brissot's *Mémoires*, ed. Claude Perroud (Paris, 1910). Mercier often remarked on the influx of provincial writers and even wrote a sort of parable about it: *Tableau de Paris, op. cit.*, x, pp. 129–30. He claimed that some of them roamed the capital in bands, so that the native Parisian writer ". . . has to combat Norman writers, who form a corps, and especially The Gascons, who go around citing Montesquieu, to whom they consider themselves as successors" (xi, p. 103).

[41] *Considérations sur les moeurs, op. cit.*, p. 141.

[42] Voltaire, *Le pauvre diable* in *Oeuvres complètes de Voltaire* (1785, no place of publication), xiv, quotation from p. 162. Of course Voltaire used this theme to satirize his enemies, but it can be taken as social comment.

useful work . . . . They live off rhymes and hopes and die in destitution".[43] Voltaire's attacks wounded Mercier, who rose to the
defence of the "poor devils" in opposition to the pampered, pensioned
darlings of the academies and salons. Mercier protested that the
"poor" of the "low literature" (*basse littérature*) in the Faubourg
Saint-Germain had more talent and integrity than "the rich" in the
"high literature" (*haute littérature*) of the Faubourg Saint-Honoré.
But even he concluded pessimistically, "Ah! keep away from this
career you who do not want to know poverty and humiliation".[44]
Linguet, another anti-Voltairean, devoted a whole book to the same
theme. A constant target of would-be authors in search of a protector, he had reason to lament that "secondary schools have become
a seed-bed of child authors, who hurriedly scribble tragedies, novels,
histories, and works of all sorts" and then "spend the rest of their
lives in destitution and despair".[45]

The provincials flocked to Paris in search of glory, money, and the
improved "estate" promised to any writer with sufficient talent.
They did not necessarily share the motivations of the early *philosophes*,
who were often nobles and clergymen enjoying enough leisure to
write when the spirit moved them and who wrote before the time
when "literature became a *métier*", as Meister distastefully observed[46].
J. J. Garnier, a writer with a highly developed sense of profession-
alism, noted that by 1764 many men of letters were moved by "the
hope of gaining reputation, influence, wealth etc. The avenues of
advancement having been closed to them because of their humble
birth and modest fortunes, they observed that the career of letters,
open to everyone, offered another outlet for their ambition".[47]
Mercier agreed that the immigrant from the provinces could hope

---

[43] *Ibid.*, p. 164.
[44] *Tableau de Paris, op. cit.*, xi, p. 187. See especially the chapters entitled
"Auteurs", "Des demi-auteurs, quarts d'auteurs, enfin métis, quarterons",
"Misère des auteurs", "La littérature du Faubourg Saint-Germain et celle du
Faubourg Saint-Honoré", "Les grands comédiens contre les petits" and "Le
musée de Paris".
[45] S.-N.-H. Linguet, *L'aveu sincère, ou lettre à une mère sur les dangers que
court la jeunesse en se livrant à un goût trop vif pour la littérature* (London, 1763),
pp. v and vii. Linguet explained, p. iv, "I address myself to those ingenuous
and inexperienced souls who could be deceived by the glory that they see
surrounding the great writers".
[46] *Correspondance littéraire, philosophique et critique par Grimm, Diderot,
Raynal, Meister, etc.*, ed. Maurice Tourneux (Paris, 1880), xii, p. 402: "Since
literature has become a job (*métier*), and, what's more, a job whose practice has
been made easy and common, owing to the numerous models to emulate and the
simplicity of its techniques . . .".
[47] J.-J. Garnier, *L'homme de lettres* (Paris, 1764), pp. 134-5.

to shake off his humble origins and climb to the top in Paris.[48]   But the top of Paris, the *tout Paris*, had little room for ambitious young men on the make — perhaps because, as sociologists claim, rising status groups tend to become exclusive, perhaps because of a literary version of the Malthusian crush, or because France suffered from a common ailment of developing countries: a surplus population of over-educated and under-employed *littérateurs* and lawyers.   In any case, it seems that the attractiveness of the new career celebrated by Duclos and the new church proclaimed by Voltaire resulted in a record crop of potential *philosophes* — far more than could be absorbed in the archaic system of protections.   Of course the lack of statistics and the confusion of social categories in pre-revolutionary France (how does one define a "man of letters"? someone with a literary reputation, someone who has published a book, or someone who lives by his pen?) makes these hypotheses unverifiable.   But there is no need for a complete census of eighteenth-century writers in order to make sense of the tension betweeen the men of Grub Street and the men of *le monde* on the eve of the Revolution.   The facts of literary life at that time speak for themselves.

The most salient fact is that the market place could not support many more writers than in the days when Prévost and Le Sage proved that it was possible — barely possible — to live from the pen instead of pensions.   Although publishers offered somewhat better terms than earlier in the century, authors were caught between the masters of the publishing-bookselling guilds, who paid little for manuscripts, and pirate publishers, who paid nothing at all.[49]   None of the great mid-century *philosophes* relied much on sales except for Diderot, who never fully extricated himself from Grub Street. Mercier claimed that in his day only thirty hard-core "professionals"

[48] Mercier, *Tableau de Paris, op. cit.*, xi, pp. 104-5: "The man of letters from the provinces finds in Paris an equality that does not exist at all among the men of his small town: here his origins are forgotten; if he is the son of a tavern keeper, he can call himself a count; no one will dispute his claim".   Mercier probably had Rivarol in mind when he wrote those lines.

[49] On the financial relations between authors and publishers, see Pellisson, *Les hommes de lettres, op. cit.*, chap. iii; Lough, *An Introduction to Eighteenth Century France, op. cit.*, chap. vii; and G. d'Avenel, *Les revenues d'un intellectuel de 1200 à 1913* (Paris, 1922), although d'Avenel's study is flawed by an attempt to translate all financial transactions into francs of 1913.   For vivid contemporary accounts of the dealings between authors and publishers, see P. J. Blondel, *Mémoires sur les vexations qu'exercent les libraires et imprimeurs de Paris*, ed. Lucien Faucou (Paris, 1879), which hits the publishers very hard, and Diderot's *Lettre sur le commerce de la librairie* in his *Oeuvres complètes*, eds. J. Assézat and M. Tourneux (Paris, 1876), xviii, which also deals some damaging blows, although Diderot was evidently writing as their paid propagandist.

supported themselves by writing.[50] The open, "democratic"
market that could feed large numbers of enterprising authors did
not appear in France until well into the nineteenth century. Before
the day of the steam press and the mass reading public, writers lived
by scavenging along the road to riches that worked so well for Suard
— or they dropped by the wayside, in the gutter.

Once he had fallen into Grub Street, the provincial youth who had
dreamt of storming Parnassus never extricated himself. As Mercier
put it "He falls and weeps at the foot of an invincible barrier . . . .
Forced to renounce the glory for which he so long has sighed, he
stops and shudders before the door that closes the career to him".[51]
The nephews and grand-nephews of Rameau really faced a double
barrier, both social and economic; for after Grub Street had left its
mark on them, they could not penetrate into polite society where the
plums were passed around. So they cursed the closed world of
culture. They survived by doing the dirty work of society — spying
for the police and peddling pornography; and they filled their
writings with imprecations against the *monde* that humiliated and
corrupted them. The pre-revolutionary works of men like Marat,
Brissot, and Carra do not express some vague, "anti-Establishment"
feeling; they seethe with hatred of the literary "aristocrats" who had
taken over the egalitarian "republic of letters" and made it into a
"despotism".[52] It was in the depths of the intellectual underworld
that these men became revolutionaries and that the Jacobinical
determination to wipe out "the aristocracy of the mind" was born.

To explain why Grub Street had no exit and why its prisoners felt
such hatred for the *grands* at the top it is necessary to say a word about
the cultural modes of production during the late eighteenth century;
and that word is the term one meets everywhere in the Old Régime
— privilege.[53] Books themselves bore privileges granted by the

---

[50] L.-S. Mercier, *De la littérature et des littérateurs* (Yverdon, 1778), pp. 38-9.
[51] *Tableau de Paris, op. cit.,* viii, p. 59.
[52] For documentation of this trend in the sub-culture of scientists and pseudo-scientists in pre-revolutionary Paris, see Robert Darnton, *Mesmerism and the End of the Englightenment in France* (Cambridge, Mass., 1968), chap. iii.
[53] A trade war in the late seventeenth century had left the publishing industry in the grip of the Parisian *Chambre royale et syndicale de la librairie et imprimerie,* and the Parisian guild tightened its hold throughout the eighteenth century, despite the government's attempts to impose some reforms in 1777. The archaic, "Colbertist" conditions of the book trade may be appreciated from the texts of the edicts regulating it: see *Recueil général des anciennes lois françaises,* eds. F. A. Isambert, Decrusy, and A. H. Taillandier (Paris, 1822-33), xvi, pp. 217-51 and xxv, pp. 108-28. The transition from seventeenth- to eighteenth-century conditions is explored in the recent thesis by Henri-Jean Martin, *Livre,*

"grace" of the king. Privileged guilds, whose organization showed the hand of Colbert himself, monopolized the production and distribution of the printed word. Privileged journals exploited royally-granted monopolies. The privileged Comédie française, Académie royale de musique, and Académie royale de peinture et de sculpture, legally monopolized the stage, opera, and the plastic arts. The Académie française restricted literary immortality to forty privileged individuals, while privileged bodies like the Académie des Sciences and the Société Royale de Médecine dominated the world of science. And above all these "corps" rose the supremely privileged cultural élite who kept *le monde* all to themselves.

It may have been appropriate for a corporate society to organize its culture corporately, but such archaic organization constrained the expansive forces that might have opened up the cultural industries and supported more of the overpopulated underworld of letters. As it was, the bookdealers' guilds acted far more effectively than the police in suppressing unprivileged books, and underprivileged youths like Brissot were forced into destitution, not so much because their early works were radical as because the monopolies prevented them from reaching the market.[54] Writers therefore fed their families either from the pensions and sinecures reserved for the members of *le monde* or from the scraps tossed into Grub Street.

The corporate organization of culture was not simply an economic matter, because it contradicted the basic premises under which the young writers had flocked to Paris in the 1770s and 1780s. They had come with the conviction that the republic of letters really existed as it had been described in the works of the great *philosophes* — as the literary counterpart to the "atomic" individualism of Physiocratic theory, a society of independent but fraternal individuals, in which the best men won but all derived dignity, as well as a living, from service to the common cause. Experience taught them that the real world of letters functioned like everything else in the Old Régime: individuals got ahead as best they could in a labyrinth of baroque institutions. To have an article published in the *Mercure*, to get a play accepted by the Comédie française, to steer a book through the Direction de la librairie, to win membership in an

pouvoirs et société à Paris au XVIIe siècle (1598-1701), 2 vols. (Geneva, 1969). On the even more monopolistic conditions in the theatre, see Jules Bonnassies, *Les auteurs dramatiques et la Comédie française aux XVIIe et XVIIIe siècles* (Paris, 1874).

[54] Robert Darnton, "The Grub Street Style of Revolution: J.-P. Brissot, Police Spy", *Jl. of Modern History,* xl (Sept. 1968), pp. 301-27.

academy, entry in a salon, or a sinecure in the bureaucracy required resorting to the old devices of privilege and protection, not merely the demonstration of talent.

Talent certainly carried some to the top.   Maury was the son of a poor cobbler in a village of the Venaissain, Marmontel of a poor tailor in the Limousin, Morellet of a small-time paper merchant of Lyons, Rivarol (who called himself a count) of an inn-keeper in Languedoc; La Harpe and Thomas were orphans.   All rose through skill and scholarships, and they were not the only examples of rapid upward mobility.   But as de Tocqueville observed, it was the erratic opening up of mobility, not the absence of it, that produced social tensions.   Nowhere was this general phenomenon more important than in the world of letters, because the attractiveness of writing as a new kind of career produced more writers than could be integrated into *le monde* or supported outside of it.   To the outsiders, the whole process looked rotten, and they were not inclined to blame their failures on their own inability: on the contrary, they tended to see themselves as successors to Voltaire.   They had knocked on the door of Voltaire's church, and the door remained closed.   Not only did their status fail to rise as fast as their expectations; it plummeted, dragging them down to a world of opposites and contradictions, a *monde* turned upside down, where "estate" could not be defined at all, and dignity dissolved in destitution.   Seen from the perspective of Grub Street, the republic of letters was a lie.

If the institutional realities of the established literary world contradicted its principles, at least from the viewpoint of those who failed to reach the top, what were the realities of life for those at the bottom? Grub Street had no principles, and it had no institutions of a formal kind.   It was a world of free-floating individuals — not Lockean gentlemen abiding by the rules of some implicit game, but Hobbesian brutes struggling to survive.   It was as far removed from *le monde* as was the café from the salon.[55]

Despite the democratic play of wit, the salon remained a rather formal institution.   It did not allow any putting of elbows on the table or any admission to those without introductions.   During the last decades of the Old Régime, the salon became increasingly a

[55] Because Grub Street remains unexplored territory (I hope at least to map it in a later work), there are no secondary works on it.   For an example of how it wrapped its tentacles around one future revolutionary, see Robert Darnton, "The Grub Street Style of Revolution: J.-P. Brissot, Police Spy", *op. cit.* See also the fascinating biography by Paul Robiquet, *Thévenau de Morande: étude sur le XVIIIe siècle* (Paris, 1882).   Morande acted as the dean of the *libellistes* and lived with a collection of underworld characters that makes some of the extravagant comments in *Le neveu de Rameau* seem mild indeed.

preserve for the high *philosophes*, who generally abandoned the cafés to the lower species of *littérateur*. The café functioned as the antithesis of the salon. It was open to everyone, just one step from the street, although there were degrees in its closeness to street life. While the great names gathered in the Procope or La Régence, lesser figures congregated in the notorious Caveau of the Palais-Royal, and the humblest hacks frequented the cafés of the boulevards, blending into an underworld of "swindlers, recruiting agents, spies, and pickpockets; here one finds only pimps, buggers, and *bardaches*".[56]

Grub Street may have lacked the corporate structure of the established culture, but it was not sheer anarchy. It had institutions of a sort. For example, the *musées* and *lycées* that sprang up in such numbers during the 1780s responded to the needs of obscure writers for a place to exhibit their wares, to declaim their works, and to make contacts. These clubhouses formalized the functions of the cafés. The *musées* of Court de Gébelin and P.C. de La Blancherie seem even to have served as counter-academies and anti-salons for the multitude of *philosophes* who could not get a hearing elsewhere. La Blancherie published a journal, *Les nouvelles de la République des lettres et des arts*, which vented some of the frustrations of the *musée* members both by sniping at academicians and by reviewing works that were beneath the notice of the *Journal de Paris* and the *Mercure*[57]. But the most effective sniper and the most influential outsider of pre-revolutionary France was Simon Henri-Linguet. While respecting the crown and the church, Linguet blasted at France's most prestigious institutions, especially the Parisian bar and the Académie française. His polemical genius made his pamphlets, judicial *mémoires*, and journals best-sellers; and his tirades against "aristocratic" and "despotic" corporateness reverberated up and down Grub Street, setting the tone for some of the anti-élitist propaganda of the Revolution.[58]

[56] Charles Thévenau de Morande, *La gazette noire par un homme qui n'est pas blanc* (1784, "imprimé à cent lieues de la Bastille . . ."), p. 212. The literature on salons and cafés is brought together in the works of Pellisson and Bertaut, cited above. See also the revealing remarks by Karl Mannheim in *Essays on the Sociology of Culture,* ed. Ernest Manheim (London, 1956), pp. 91-170.

[57] The only copy of *Les nouvelles de la République des lettres et des arts,* 7 vols. (Paris, 1777-87) that I have been able to locate is incomplete: Bibliothèque Nationale, Réserve Z 1149-1154. See also La Blancherie's *Correspondance générale sur les sciences et les arts* (Paris, 1779), Rz. 3037 and 3392. There is a great deal of information on the *musées* and *lycées* of the 1780s scattered through the *nouvelles à la main* published as *Mémoires secrets pour servir à l'histoire de la République des lettres en France* and commonly known as the *Mémoires secrets* of Bachaumont.

[58] See especially Linguet's widely read *Annales politiques, civiles et littéraires du dix-huitième siècle,* which attacked the cultural élite with declamations like

Grub Street therefore had a few organs and organizations to express itself. Perhaps it even had an inchoate stratification system of its own, for the underground contained several levels. Having cultivated an established *philosophe* or got some verses published in the *Almanach des muses,* some writers lived just below *le monde.* Mirabeau maintained a mandarin style of life even when in prison and in debt. He kept a stable of pamphleteers (who referred to him simply as "le comte") to produce the works published under his name.[59] Lesser figures put together the encyclopedias, diction- aries, digests, and anthologies that circulated in such profusion in the last half of the eighteenth century. Even cruder hack work could be relatively respectable — writing for ministers, pamphlet- eering for the *baissiers* fighting the *haussiers* on the Bourse, and producing *nouvelles à la main*; or it could be demeaning — manufac- turing smut, peddling prohibited works, and spying for the police. Many writers lived on the fringes of the law, calling themselves lawyers or law clerks and taking on the odd jobs available in the *basoche* of the Palais de Justice. Some, at the bottom of the literary underworld, sank into criminality. Charles Thévenau de Morande, one of Grub Street's most violent and virulent pamphleteers, lived in a demi-monde of prostitutes, pimps, blackmailers, pickpockets, swindlers, and murderers. He tried his hand at more than one of these professions and gathered material for his pamphlets by skim- ming the scum around him. As a result, his works smeared every- thing, good and bad alike, with a spirit of such total depravity and alienation that Voltaire cried out in horror, "There has just appeared one of those satanic works [Morande's *Gazetier cuirassé*] where every- one from the monarch to the last citizen is insulted with furore; where the most atrocious and most absurd calumny spreads a horrible poison on everything one respects and loves".[60]

Grub Street stifled respect and love. Its grim struggle for survival brought out baser sentiments, as is suggested by the following excerpts from reports submitted to the Parisian police by its legions

the following (vi, p. 386): "There was nothing in France that was not sub- ordinate to it. The ministry, the judiciary, science, literary bodies, everything had been invaded by it: [the "faction" of the established *philosophes*] controlled everything, even reputations. It alone opened the gateway to glory and wealth. It filled every position with philosophizing *parvenus.* The academies as well as the courts were in its grip; the press, the censors, the journals were at its command".

[59] See Jean Bouchary, *Les manieurs d'argent à Paris à la fin du XVIIIe siècle* (Paris, 1939-43), i; and Jean Bénétruy, *L'atelier de Mirabeau: quatre proscrits genevois dans la tourmente révolutionnaire* (Geneva, 1962).

[60] *Dictionnaire philosophique,* article entitled "Quisquis".

of spies and secret agents, many of them underworld writers themselves with their own dossiers in the archives of the police.[61]

GORSAS: proper for all kinds of vile jobs. Run out of Versailles and put in Bicêtre [a jail for especially disreputable criminals] by personal order of the king for having corrupted children whom he had taken in as lodgers, he has withdrawn on to a fifth floor of the rue Tictone. Gorsas produces *libelles*. He has an arrangement with an apprentice printer of the Imprimerie polytype, who has been fired from other printing shops. He [Gorsas] is suspected of having printed obscene works there. He peddles prohibited books.

AUDOUIN: calls himself a lawyer, writes *nouvelles à la main*, peddler of forbidden books; he is connected with Prudhomme, Manuel, and other disreputable authors and book-peddlers. He does all kinds of work; he will be a spy when one wants.

DUPORT DU TERTRE: solicits a position in the offices of the police; is a lawyer who is not often employed in the Palais, although he is not without merit. He failed to get a position in the Domaines. He lives in a modest, fourth-storey apartment; he hardly gives off an air of wealth (*il ne respire pas l'opulence*). He is generally well spoken of; he has a good reputation in his neighbourhood.

DELACROIX: lawyer, writer, expelled from the bar. He produces [judicial] *mémoires* for shady cases; and when he has no *mémoires* to write, he writes scurrilous works.

MERCIER: lawyer, a fierce, bizarre man; he neither pleads in court nor consults. He hasn't been admitted to the bar, but he takes the title of lawyer. He has written the *Tableau de Paris*, in four volumes, and other works. Fearing the Bastille, he left the country, then returned and wants to become attached to the police.

MARAT: bold charlatan. M. Vicq d'Azir asks, in the name of the Société Royale de Médecine, that he be run out of Paris. He is from Neuchâtel in Switzerland. Many sick persons have died in his hands, but he has a doctor's degree, which was bought for him.

CHENIER: insolent and violent poet. He lives with Beauménil of the Opéra, who, in the decline of her charms, fell in love with him. He mistreats her and beats her — so much that her neighbours report that he would have killed her had they not come to her rescue. She accuses him of having taken her jewels; she describes him as a man capable of any crime and doesn't hide her regrets at having let herself be bewitched by him.

[61] "Extraits de divers rapports secrets faits à la police de Paris dans les années 1781 et suivantes, jusques et compris 1785, concernant des personnes de tout état et condition [ayant] donné dans la Révolution", Lenoir papers, Bibliothèque municipale d'Orléans, MS. 1423. As their gossipy tone indicates, these reports should not be taken as factually accurate, but they do suggest the general character of life at the bottom of the literary world. In a note at the end of the reports, Lenoir explained that he cut out sections that would incriminate respectable persons but that the remaining excerpts were untouched and could be verified by comparison with other police records (which have been destroyed since he wrote). In general, Lenoir's papers seem reliable. In the case of Manuel, for example, they contain several remarks about Manuel's life in the literary underworld which are corroborated by his dossier in the Archives Nationales, W 295, and by an anonymous *Vie secrète de Pierre Manuel* (n.p., 1793).

> FRÉRON: who has neither the wit nor the pen of his father, is generally despised. It is not he who writes the *Année littéraire*, although he has its privilege. He hires young unemployed lawyers. He's an insolent coward, who has received his share of beatings — and doesn't boast about it — most recently from the hand of the actor Desessarts, whom he had called a "ventriloquist" in one of his issues. He is connected with Mouvel, who was expelled from the Comédie for pederasty.

> PANIS: young lawyer of the Palais, protected by M. le Président d'Ormesson because of Panis's parents, who are his [d'Ormesson's] *fermiers*; is employed by Fréron on the *Année littéraire*. Panis has as a mistress a woman branded by the hand of the executioner.

Life in Grub Street was hard, and it took a psychological toll, because "the excrement of literature" had to face not merely failure but degradation, and they had to face it alone. Failure breeds loneliness, and the conditions of Grub Street were peculiarly suited to isolate its inhabitants. Ironically, the basic unit of life in *la basse littérature* was the garret (stratification went more by storey than by neighbourhood in eighteenth-century Paris). In their fourth and fifth-floor *mansardes*, before Balzac had romanticized their lot, the undiscovered *philosophes* learned that they were what Voltaire had called them: the "canaille de la littérature". But how could they come to terms with such knowledge?

Fabre d'Eglantine is a case in point. A drifter and a *déclassé* who saw himself as the successor of Molière, he went down in the police dossiers as a "poor poet, who drags about in shame and destitution; he is despised everywhere; among men of letters he is considered an execrable subject (poète médiocre qui traîne sa honte et sa misère; il est partout honni; il passe parmi les gens de lettres pour un exécrable sujet)".[62] Sometime before the Revolution, Fabre wrote a play that reads like an escapist fantasy of an author trapped in Grub Street. The hero, an unappreciated Twenty-eight-year-old genius from the provinces, writes his heart out in a Parisian garret, mocked and exploited by the evil élite that dominates French literature: mercenary publishers, crass journal editors, and the perfidious *beaux-esprits* who monopolize the salons. He is about to succumb to disease and poverty when, by a stroke of good fortune, a virtuous bourgeois tycoon discovers him, appreciates his talent and superior morality, and carries him off to the provinces, where he writes masterpieces happily ever after. The play breathes hatred of the cultural élite and a fierce egalitarianism, which confirms La Harpe's description of the pre-revolutionary Fabre as an embittered failure, "envenomed with hatred, like all the persons of his sort, against everyone who

[62] Bibl. Mun. d'Orléans, MS.1423.

called himself an *homme du monde*, against everything that had a rank in society — a rank that he did not have and should not have had".[63]

Others probably sought refuge in similar fantasies. Marat dreamed of being whisked away to preside over an academy of sciences in Madrid.[64] Both he and Carra found solace in imagining that they had outstripped Newton, despite society's failure to appreciate them. But no amount of fantasy could erase the contradictions between life at the top and the bottom of the world of letters and between what those at the bottom were and what they wanted to be. The established writers enjoyed an "estate"; they derived honour and wealth from the established cultural institutions. But the literary proletariat had no social location. Its ragged pamphleteers could not call themselves "men of letters"; they were just *canaille*, condemned to gutters and garrets, working in isolation, poverty, and degradation, and therefore easy prey to the psychology of failure — a vicious combination of hatred of the system and hatred of the self.

The Grub Street mentality made itself heard with exceptional vehemence during the last years of the Old Régime. It spoke through the *libelle*, the hack writers' staff of life, their meat, their favourite genre, and a genre that deserves to be rescued from the neglect of historians, because it communicates the Grub Street view of the world, a spectacle of knaves and fools buying and selling one another and forever falling victim to *les grands*, The *grand monde* was the real target of the *libelles*. They slandered the court, the church, the aristocracy, the academies, the salons, everything elevated and respectable including the monarchy itself with a scurrility that is difficult to imagine today, although it has had a long career in underground literature. For pamphleteers had lived by libel since the time of Aretino. They had exploited all the great crises in French history — in the propaganda produced by the Catholic League during the religious wars, for example, and in the *Mazarinades* of the Fronde. But the ultimate crisis of the Old Régime gave them an unusual opportunity, and they rose to the occasion with what seems to have been their greatest barrage of anti-social smut.[65]

[63] J. F. de La Harpe, *Lycée ou cours de littérature ancienne et moderne* (Paris, Year VII to Year XIII), xi, part 2, p. 488. Fabre's play, *Les Gens de lettres*, was published posthumously in *Mélanges littéraires par une société de gens de lettres* (Paris, 1827).

[64] See Marat's letters to Roume de Saint Laurent in *Correspondance de Marat, recueillie et annotée par Charles Vellay* (Paris, 1908).

[65] This interpretation, which maintains that the *libelles* increased in number and importance during the régime's last years, is based only on impressions from extensive reading in the pamphlet collections of the Bibliothèque Nationale

Although a survey of *libelles* published between 1770 and 1789 cannot be undertaken here,[66] it should be possible to capture some of their flavour by explicating one of their texts. Perhaps the most typical *libelle* — a pamphlet so sensational and so widely read that it became virtually a prototype of the genre — was the work that especially horrified Voltaire: *Le Gazetier cuirassé* by Charles Thévenau de Morande. Morande mixed specific calumny and general declamation in brief, punchy paragraphs, which anticipated the style of gossip columnists in the modern yellow press. He promised to reveal "behind-the-scenes secrets" (*secrets des coulisses*)[67] in the tradition of the *chronique scandaleuse*. But he provided more than scandal:

> The devout wife of a certain Maréchal de France (who suffers from an imaginary lung disease), finding a husband of that species too delicate, considers it her religious duty to spare him and so condemns herself to the crude caresses of her butler, who would still be a lackey if he hadn't proven himself so robust.[68]

This sexual sensationalism conveyed a social message: the aristocracy had degenerated to the point of being unable to reproduce itself;[69] the great nobles were either impotent or deviant;[70] their wives were forced to seek satisfaction from their servants, representatives of the more virile lower classes; and everywhere among *les grands* incest and venereal disease had extinguished the last sparks of humanity.[71] Vivid detail communicated the message more effectively than abstractions; for although the reader might at first merely be shocked by a particular incident . . .

> The Count of Noail . . . , having taken some scandalous liberties with one of his lackeys, this country bumpkin knocked over Monseigneur with a slap that kept his lordship in bed for eight days . . . . The lackey . . . is a Picard of the first order who had not yet been instructed how to serve a Spanish

and the British Museum, but it is supported by the similar impressions of Louis XVI's lieutenant general of police: see Lenoir's essay, "De l'administration de l'ancienne police concernant les libelles, les mauvaises satires et chansons, leurs auteurs coupables, délinquants, complices ou adhérents", Bibliothèque municipale d'Orléans, MS. 1422.

[66] For a more detailed discussion of *libelle* literature, see Robert Darnton, "Reading, Writing, and Publishing in Eighteenth-Century France: A Case Study in the Sociology of Literature", *Daedalus* (Dec. 1970).

[67] Charles Thévenau de Morande (anonymously), *Le Gazetier cuirassé: ou Anecdotes scandaleuses de la cour de France* (1771, "Imprimé à cent lieues de la Bastille, à l'enseigne de la liberté"), p. 128.

[68] *Ibid.*, pp. 167-8.

[69] *Ibid.*, pp. 169-70.

[70] As examples of Morande's characteristic emphasis on impotence and sodomy, see *ibid.*, pp. 51-2 and 61.

[71] *Ibid.*, pp. 79-80.

grandee, Knight of the Royal Orders, Lieutenant General, Governor of Vers . . . , Prince of P . . . , Lord of Arpa . . . , Grand Cross of Malta, Knight of the Golden Fleece, and secular member of the Society of Jesus, etc., etc., etc., etc.[72]

. . . he would know what to conclude after he had recovered from the shock. Morande led the reader toward general conclusions by piling up anecdotes and slanting them in the same direction — against *le monde*. He showed that the summit of society had decayed beyond the point of recovery, both morally and physically:

> The public is warned that an epidemic disease is raging among the girls of the Opera, that it has begun to reach the ladies of the court, and that it has even been communicated to their lackeys. This disease elongates the face, destroys the complexion, reduces the weight, and causes horrible ravages where it becomes situated. There are ladies without teeth, others without eye-brows, and some completely paralysed.[73]

Morande's chronical of cuckoldry, buggery, incest and impotence in high places therefore read as an indictment of the social order. And Morande did not merely leave the reader with a general impression of corruption. He associated the aristocracy's decadence with its inability to fulfil its functions in the army, the church, and the state.

> Of approximately two hundred colonels in the infantry, cavalry, and dragoons in France, one hundred and eighty know how to dance and to sing little songs; about the same number wear lace and red heels; at least half can read and sign their names; and in addition not four of them know the first elements of their craft.[74]

> As the king's confessor was disgraced for having been discovered flirting with some pages, there is now open competition for that position, which will go to the prelate who will be easiest on the king's conscience. The Archbishop of R . . . has been proposed but rejected, because of the scandalous relations he has maintained for such a long time with one of his grand vicars. The cardinals of Gèv . . . and of Luy . . . were designated to serve by alternate semesters; but since the first doesn't know how to read and the second hasn't recovered from being slapped [a reference to a scandal involving homosexuality], one can't be sure of His Majesty's decision.[75]

Morande constantly stressed the connection between sexual and political corruption by news "flashes" like the following:[76] "Having a pretty wife of whom he was very jealous, the unfortunate Baron of Vaxen was sent to prison by a *lettre de cachet* in order to learn the customs of *le monde*, while the duke [La Vrillière, one of Louis XV's favourite ministers] sleeps with his wife". The monarchy had degenerated into despotism, this message stood out on every page: the

---

[72] *Ibid.*, pp. 182-3.
[73] *Ibid.*, pp. 131-2.
[74] *Ibid.*, pp. 80-1.
[75] *Ibid.*, p. 53.
[76] *Ibid.*, pp. 36-7.

ministers have hired an extra team of secretaries just to sign *lettres de cachet*; the Bastille and Vincennes are so overcrowded that tents have been set up inside their walls to house the guards; a new élite police corps, modelled on Louis XIV's dragonades, has been created to terrorize the provinces; the government is experimenting with a new machine that can hang ten men at a time; and the public executioner has resigned, not because he is worried about automation, but because the new Maupeou ministry offends his sense of justice. In case any reader could possibly miss the point, Morande stated it explicitly:[77] "According to Chancellor Maupeou, a monarchical state is a state where the prince has the right of life and death over all his subjects, where he is proprietor of all the wealth in the kingdom, where honour and equity are founded on arbitrary principles, which must always conform with the interests of the sovereign."

What was the king's place in this political system? "The chancellor and the Duke d'Aiguillon have come to dominate the king so much that they leave him only the liberty of sleeping with his mistress, petting his dogs, and signing marriage contracts".[78] Deriding the idea of a divine origin to royal sovereignty,[79] Morande reduced the king to the level of the ignorant, crapulous court. He made Louis XV look ridiculous, a trivial figure, even in his despotism:[80] "A notice has been published in the hopes of finding the sceptre of one of the greatest kings of Europe. After a very long search, it was found in the *toilette* of a pretty woman called a countess, who uses it for playing with her cat". The real rulers of France and the villains of the book were the Countess DuBarry and the ministerial triumvirate of Maupeou, Terray, and d'Aiguillon. Seizing on Mme. DuBarry as a symbol of the régime, Morande dwelt on every detail about her that he could fabricate or extract from *café* gossip: her supposedly illegitimate birth to a servant girl who had been seduced by a monk, her career as a common whore, her use of the king's power to help her former colleagues by forbidding the police to set foot in brothels, her lesbianic relations with her maid, and so on. Similarly, Morande

---

[77] *Ibid.*, p. 80. This remark introduced the following reference (p. 80) to Maupeou's fellow minister, the Duke d'Aiguillon: "The peerage used to be in France a rank where the slightest stain was inadmissable; but today a peer [i.e. d'Aiguillon] can empoison, ruin a province and intimidate witnesses, provided he possesses the art of the courtier and can lie well".

[78] *Ibid.*, p. 31.

[79] *Ibid.*, p. 109: "A new book has just appeared, which challenges the kings of France to prove their divine institution by producing the treaty that the eternal father signed with them; the author of that book defies them to do so".

[80] *Ibid.*, pp. 157-8.

showed that the ministers used their authority to fatten their purses, procure mistresses, or simply enjoy villainy for its own sake.

Grotesque, inaccurate, and simplistic as it was, this version of political "news" should not be dismissed as merely mythical, because myth-making and unmaking proved to be powerful forces in the last years of a régime, which, though absolutist in theory, had become increasingly vulnerable in practice to the vagaries of public opinion. To be sure, the eighteenth-century French "public" did not exist in any coherent form; and insofar as it did exist, it was excluded from direct participation in politics. But its exclusion produced a political *naïveté* that made it all the more vulnerable to Morande's style of gazeteering. For instead of discussing issues, the "gazetier cuirassé" diffamed individuals. He buried Maupeou's reforms — probably the régime's last chance to survive by destroying some of the vested interests that were devouring it — in a torrent of mud-slinging. That the Maupeou programme would have benefited the common people did not matter to Morande, because he and his fellow hacks had no interest in reform. They hated the system in itself; and they expressed their hatred by desanctifying its symbols, destroying the myths that gave it legitimacy in the eyes of the public, and perpetrating the counter-myth of degenerate despotism.

Far from being limited to Morande's works, these themes became increasingly important in *libelle* literature as the Old Régime approached its finalé. *Le Gazetier cuirassé* merely set the tone for an outpouring of anti-government pamphlets that extended from the "Maupeouana" of the early 1770s to the "Calonniana" of the late 1780s. The most prolific producer of the latter was Jean-Louis Carra, an outcast from the closed circles of established science, who stated frankly that his efforts to damn the ministry had been provoked by the refusal of one of Calonne's pensions.[81]   Morande's motives

[81] See Carra's notes to his translation of John Gillies' *Histoire de l'ancienne Gréce* (Paris, 1787), i, pp. 4 and 11; ii, pp. 387-9; v, p. 387; and vi, p. 98. Carra produced an influential *"Mémoire"* attacking Calonne just before the opening of the Assembly of Notables in 1787 (it was reprinted in Carra's *Un petit mot de réponse à M. de Calonne sur sa Requête au Roi*, Amsterdam, 1787) and continued to pummel him in *libelles* like *M. de Calonne tout entier* (Brussels, 1788).   He also turned on Lenoir (Carra, *L'an 1787 : Précis de l'administration de la Bibliothèque du Roi sous M. Lenoir*, 2nd edn., Liège, 1788), because Lenoir had not only advised Calonne against giving Carra a pension but had also tried, with the help of some academicians, to get him dismissed from a subordinate post in the Bibliothèque du Roi, which was Carra's only feeble source of income: see the Lenoir papers, Bibliothèque municipale d'Orléans, MSS. 1421 and 1423.   Not surprisingly, Carra's pre-revolutionary pamphlets fairly sizzle with hatred of the literary patricians who *did* get the pensions, sinecures, and seats in the academy and of the *grands* who dealt them out.

had not been nobler.   He meant to make money, both by exploiting the market for sensationalism and by blackmailing the persons he libelled.

Did slander on such a scale, its crass motivation notwithstanding, amount to a call for revolution?   Not really, because the *libelles* lacked a programme.   They not only failed to give the reader any idea of what sort of society should replace the Old Régime; they hardly contained any abstract ideas at all.   In denouncing despotism, Morande cried out for liberty; and in fulminating against aristocratic decadence, he seemed to advocate bourgeois standards of decency, if only by contrast.[82]   But he did not defend any clear set of principles. He referred to himself as "*le philosophe cynique*"[83] and slandered everything, even the *philosophes*.[84]   The same spirit animated most other *libelles*; it was a spirit of nihilism rather than of ideological commitment.

Yet the *libelles* showed a curious tendency to moralize, even in their pornography.   The climax of one of Morande's obscene pamphlets about courtiers and courtisans came in an indignant description of Mme. DuBarry

> ... passing directly from the brothel to the throne, toppling the most powerful and redoubtable minister, overthrowing the constitution of the monarchy, insulting the royal family, the presumptive heir to the throne, and his august consort by her incredible luxury, by her insolent talk, [and insulting] the entire nation, which is dying of hunger, by her vainglorious extravagance and by the well-known depredations of all the *roués* surrounding her, as she sees grovelling at her feet not only the *grands* of the kingdom and the ministers, but the princes of the royal blood, foreign ambassadors, and the church itself, which canonizes her scandals and her debauchery.[85]

This tone of moral outrage was typical of the *libelles* and seems to have been more than a rhetorical pose.   It expressed a feeling of total contempt for a totally corrupt élite.   So if the *libelles* lacked a coherent ideology, they communicated a revolutionary point of view: they showed that social rot was consuming French society, eating its way downward from the top.   And their pornographic details got the point across to a public that could not assimilate the *Social Contract* and that soon would be reading *Le Père Duchesne*.

[82] See his implicit contrast of "bourgeois" and aristocratic morality and of England and France in *Le Gazetier cuirassé, op. cit.*, pp. 83-86, 171, and 173.

[83] *Ibid.*, p. 131.

[84] His victims included Voltaire, d'Alembert, and their companions in the salon of Mme. Geoffrin: see *ibid.*, pp. 178 and 181.

[85] Charles Thévenau de Morande (anonymously), *La Gazette noire par un homme qui n'est pas blanc; ou oeuvres posthumes du Gazetier cuirassé* (1784, "imprimé à cent lieues de la Bastille ..."), pp. 194-5.   See also the strikingly similar passage in *Vie privée de Louis XV, ou principaux événements, particularités et anecdotes de son règne* (London, 1781), iv, pp. 139-40.

This gutter Rousseauism — a natural idiom for the "Rousseau du ruisseau"[86] — may have been related to Rousseau's rejection of the culture and morality of France's upper classes. For the men of Grub Street saw Jean-Jacques as one of their own. In following his career, they could not only imagine the realization of their hopes but could also find consolation for their failures. *Débourgeoisé* like such typical *libellistes* as Brissot and Manuel, Rousseau had risen from their ranks into *le monde*, seen it for what it was, exposed élitist culture itself as the very agent of social corruption, and returned with his semi-literate, working-class wife to a humble existence in the neighbourhood of Grub Street, where he died pure and purged. The hacks respected him and despised Voltaire — Voltaire the "mondain", who had stigmatized Rousseau as a "poor devil" and who died in the same year, in the bosom of *le monde*.[87]

Is it surprising then that the writers whom Voltaire scorned as "la canaille de la littérature" should have moralized in the manner of Rousseau in their politico-pornography? To them the Old Régime was obscene. In making them its spies and smut-peddlers, it had violated their moral core and desecrated their youthful visions of serving humanity honourably in Voltaire's church. So they became rank atheists and poured out their souls in blasphemies about the society that had driven them down into an underworld of criminals and deviants. The scatology of their pamphlets — their frequent references, for example, to venereal disease passed on from the Cardinal de Rohan to the queen and all the great figures of the court during the Diamond Necklace Affair — communicates a sense of total opposition to an élite so corrupt as to deserve annihilation. No wonder that the government kept secret files on the *libellistes* and consigned the *libelles* to the bottom of its graduated scale of illegality, or that the very catalogues of them circulated secretly, in handwritten notes, like the list of "philosophical books" quoted above. The *libellistes* spoke for a sub-intelligentsia that was not merely unintegrated but beyond the pale and that wanted not to reform society in some polite, liberal, Voltairean way, but to overturn it.

There is a danger of using the word "revolutionary" too liberally and of exaggerating the ideological distance between the top and the bottom of the literary world in the Old Régime. The first *philosophes* were "revolutionary" in their fashion: they articulated and propagated a value system, or an ideology, that undermined the traditional

---

[86] "Rousseaus of the gutter", a term applied to Restif de la Bretonne in the eighteenth century and that fits many of Restif's Grub Street comrades.

[87] As an example of this widespread identification with Rousseau in opposition to Voltaire, see *Le Tableau de Paris, op. cit.*, xi, p. 186.

values Frenchmen inherited from their Catholic and royalist past. The men of Grub Street believed in the message of the *philosophes*; they wanted nothing more than to become *philosophes* themselves. It was their attempt to realize this ambition that made them see "philosophie" in a different light and to hold it up to the realities not only of society in general but also of the cultural world. The great *philosophes* had had a sharp eye for realities also, and their successors of the next generation may have been as realistic as the most hard-bitten hacks: nothing suggests that the view from the top is more distorted than the view from the bottom. But the difference in viewpoints was crucial — a difference of perspective not principle, of mentality not philosophy, a difference to be found less in the content of ideas than in their emotional colouring. The emotional thrust of Grub Street literature was revolutionary, although it had no coherent political programme nor even any distinctive ideas of its own. Both the *philosophes* and the *libellistes* were seditious in their own way: in becoming established, the Enlightenment undercut the élite's faith in the legitimacy of the social order; and in attacking the élite, the *libelles* spread disaffection deeper and more widely. Each of the opposing camps deserves its place among the intellectual origins of the Revolution.

Once the Revolution came, the opposition between the high and low life of literature had to be resolved. Grub Street rose, overthrew *le monde* and requisitioned the positions of power and prestige. It was a cultural revolution, which created a new élite and gave them new jobs. While Suard, Marmontel, and Morellet found themselves stripped of their income, Brissot, Carra, Gorsas, Manuel, Mercier, Desmoulins, Prudhomme, Loustalot, Louvet, Hébert, Maret, Marat, and many more of the old literary proletariat led new lives as journalists and bureaucrats.[88] The Revolution turned the cultural world upside down. It destroyed the academies, scattered the salons, retracted the pensions, abolished the privileges, and obliterated the agencies and vested interests that had strangled the book trade before 1789. Newspapers and theatres sprang up at such a rate that one

[88] For a striking account of a fortune labouriously built up by pensions and sinecures and then demolished by the Revolution, see the *Mémoires de l'abbé Morellet sur le dix-huitième siècle et sur la Révolution,* 2 vols. (Paris, 1921). Chapters v through vii in volume ii give a fascinating picture of an old veteran of the Enlightenment trying to communicate with young *sans-culottes,* who had no interest in the mid-century treatises he produced to prove the soundness of his principles but who wanted answers to questions like, "Why were you happy before the 10th of August and have you been sad since then"? (ii, p. 124). Morellet could not make sense of the *sans-culottes* any more than they could understand him: a *cultural* revolution separated them.

could even speak of an industrial revolution within the cultural revolution.[89] And in destroying the old institutions, the new élite meeted out a crude, revolutionary justice: Manuel took over the police department that had once hired him secretly for the suppression of *libelles*, and he published its archives in *libelle* form (carefully purging all references to his and Brissot's careers as police spies); Marat, a victim of academic persecution before the Revolution, led the movement that eventually destroyed the academies; and Fabre and Collot, frustrated actor-playwrights in the Old Régime, struck down the monopoly of the *comédiens du roi* and very nearly struck off their heads. In a sequel to his pre-revolutionary census, Rivarol interpreted the Revolution as the work of the status-hungry, surplus population of men who failed to "make it" in the old order.[90]

Of course the cultural revolution did not fit perfectly into the pattern of Rivarol's counter-revolutionary propaganda any more than it corresponded to Taine's counter-revolutionary history. Many of the old élite — even academicians like Condorcet, Bailly, Chamfort, and La Harpe — did not oppose the destruction of the institutions in which they had prospered. The literary hacks scattered in a dozen directions, supporting different factions in different phases of

---

[89] After the abolition of the monopoly of the Comédie française, 45 new theatres sprang up in Paris; 1500 new plays were produced between 1789 and 1799, 750 in the years 1792-1794, in contrast to the mere handful produced annually before the Revolution. These new plays (which seem to resemble those of the recent "cultural revolution" in China) may have derived more from the popular *foire* theatre and *drames poissardes* than from the Comédie française, which catered to aristocratic audiences and even had direct access to the king, thanks to its governing board, made up of gentlemen of the king's bedchamber. Perhaps the genres of Grub Street (the *libelle* type of pamphlet and the *Père Duchesne* type of newspaper) gained ground as the Parisian populace gained power: the *lumpen* intelligentsia certainly knew how to speak the language of the common people. Most striking of all was the revolution that the Revolution wrought in journalism. Only a few dozen periodicals, none containing much news, circulated in Paris during the 1780s. At least 250 genuine *news*papers were founded in the last six months of 1789, and at least 350 circulated in 1790. On the theatre, see John Lough, *Paris Theatre Audiences in the Seventeenth and Eighteenth Centuries* (London, 1957); Jules Bonnassies, *Les auteurs dramatiques, op. cit.;* and Beatrice Hyslop, "The Theatre During a Crisis: The Parisian Theatre During the Reign of Terror", *Jl. of Modern History*, xvii (1945), pp. 332-55. On the press, see Eugène Hatin, *Bibliographie historique et critique de la presse périodique française* (Paris, 1866); Eugène Hatin, *Histoire politique et littéraire de la presse en France* (Paris, 1859), esp. chaps. ii-viii; and Gérard Walter, *Hébert et le Père Duchesne* (Paris, 1946).

[90] A. Rivarol and L. de Champcenetz, *Petit dictionnaire des grands hommes de la Révolution* (1790). For a typical comment, see p. vii: "It is by a perfect agreement between the rejects of the court and the rejects of fortune that we have arrived at this general impoverishment which alone testifies to our equality".

the conflict. Some of them, particularly during the Girondist period and the Directory, showed that they wanted nothing more than to participate in a revival of *le monde*. And at least during the years 1789-1791, the Revolution realized many of the ideas propagated by the High Enlightenment. But the Revolution at its most revolutionary expressed the anti-élitist passions of Grub Street. It would be wrong to interpret those passions merely as a hunger for employment and a hatred of mandarins. The Jacobin pamphleteers believed in their propaganda. They wanted to slough off their corrupt old selves and to become new men, newly integrated in a republic of virtue. As cultural revolutionaries, they wanted to destroy "the aristocracy of the mind" in order to create an egalitarian republic of letters in an egalitarian republic. In calling for the abolition of academies, Lanjuinais put their case perfectly: "The academies and all other literary corps must be free and not privileged; to authorize their formation under any kind of protection would be to make them into veritable guilds. Privileged academies are always seedbeds of a literary aristocracy".[91]   From there it was but one step to Grégoire's injunction: "We must look for merit dwelling impoverished in basements and in seventh-storey garrets .... True genius is almost always *sans-culotte*".[92]   Perhaps the propagandists of the garrets functioned as the ideological "carriers" who injected the crude, Jacobinical version of Rousseauism into the Parisian *sans-culotterie*.[93]   Hébert certainly played that rôle — Hébert, who had rotted in obscurity before the Revolution and, at one point, had tried to persuade the Variétés to perform one of his plays only to get a job checking seat tickets in the *loges*.[94]

[91] *Réimpression de l'ancien Moniteur* (Paris, 1861), v, p. 439.

[92] Henri Grégoire, *Rapport et projet de décret, présenté au nom du Comité de l'instruction publique, à la séance du 8 août* (Paris, 1793).   See also the *Discours du citoyen David, député de Paris, sur la nécessité de supprimer les académies* (Paris, 1793), made during the same session of the Convention; the polemics between Morellet and Chamfort (S.R.N. Chamfort, *Des académies*, Paris, 1791, and abbé André Morellet, *De l'académie française ...*, Paris, 1791); and the debates on the cultural implications of the Revolution in the *Moniteur*, *op. cit.*, for example, vii, pp. 115-20 and 218-9; xvii, p. 176; xxii, pp. 181-4 and 191-3; xxiii, pp. 127-8 and 130-1.   The classic statement of the revolutionaries' hatred for the Old Régime's cultural élitism remains Marat's *Les charlatans modernes, ou lettres sur le charlatanisme académique* (Paris, 1791).

[93] Albert Soboul touches on this theme in *Les sans-culottes parisiens en l'an II* (Paris, 1958), pp. 670-3 and in "Classes populaires et rousseauisme", *Paysans, sans-culottes et Jacobins* (Paris, 1966), pp. 203-23.

[94] Gérard Walter, *Hébert, op. cit.*, chaps. i-ii.   See also R.-N.-D. Desgenettes (who knew Hébert as a starving hack writer before 1789), *Souvenirs de la fin du XVIIIe siècle et du commencement du XIXe siècle* (Paris, 1836), ii, pp. 237-54; and the description of the pre-revolutionary Hébert printed in a Robespierrist

It would seem to be necessary, therefore, in looking for the connection between the Enlightenment and the Revolution, to examine
the structure of the cultural world under the Old Régime, to descend
from the heights of metaphysics and to enter Grub Street.   At this
low level of analysis, the High Enlightenment looks relatively tame.
Voltaire's *Lettres philosophiques* may have exploded like a "bomb"[95]
in 1734, but by the time of Voltaire's apotheosis in 1778, France had
absorbed the shock.   There was nothing shocking at all in the works
of his successors, for *they* had been absorbed, fully integrated into
le monde.   Of course one must allow for exceptions like Condorcet,
but the Suard generation of *philosophes* had remarkably little to say.
They argued over Gluck and Piccini, dabbled in pre-romanticism,
chanted the old litanies about legal reform and *l'infâme*, and collected
their tithes.   And while they grew fat in Voltaire's church, the
revolutionary spirit passed to the lean and hungry men of Grub
Street, to the cultural pariahs who, through poverty and humiliation,
produced the Jacobinical version of Rousseauism.   The crude
pamphleteering of Grub Street was revolutionary in feeling as well
as in message.   It expressed the passion of men who hated the Old
Régime in their guts, who ached with the hatred of it.   It was from
such visceral hatred, not from the refined abstractions of the contented
cultural élite, that the extreme Jacobin revolution found its authentic
voice.

libelle attacking him, *Vie privée et politique de J.-R. Hébert* (Paris, Year II), p. 13:
"Without a shirt, without shoes, he only left the tiny room he rented on the
seventh floor in order to borrow some pennies from his friends or to pilfer them".
[95] Gustave Lanson, *Voltaire*, trans. R. A. Wagoner (New York, 1966), p. 48.

4. *Nobles, Bourgeois and the Origins of the French Revolution**

COLIN LUCAS

ONCE UPON A TIME, THE HISTORIANS OF THE FRENCH REVOLUTION laboured fraternally in the vineyards of the past. They were united in simple yet satisfying beliefs. In the eighteenth century, the French bourgeoisie had become aware of the increasing disparity between its wealth and social usefulness, on the one hand, and its social prestige and opportunities, on the other. Its way was blocked and recognition of its worth denied by a decaying class of parasitic, hereditarily privileged, noble landowners. Its vitality was further jeopardized by a monarchy not only committed to antiquated aristocratic values, but also incapable of giving the country that firm yet benignly restrained direction under which the initiative of men of business might flourish. The conflict of these elements produced the French Revolution. It was, furthermore, a deeper conflict between the progressive capitalist-orientated classes and the retrograde aristocratic classes. The French Revolution was won by the bourgeoisie, despite some interference from below, thus establishing the framework for the emergence of the capitalist economy and a class society and — *eureka* — the modern world. This, in capsule form, was the interpretation of the revolutionary crisis of the late eighteenth century favoured by the great authorities of the first half of this century from Jaurès to Soboul, each one giving to it a more or less explicitly Marxist tone according to his personal convictions.[1] But Marxist or non-Marxist, we were all united in the belief that we could not escape this groundswell of history.

This interpretation has been the subject of increasing debate among Anglo-Saxon historians ever since the publication in 1964 of the attack launched upon it by the late Professor Cobban in his Wiles Lectures of 1962.[2] A parallel, though apparently unrelated, debate

---

* I would like to thank Dr. John Roberts and my colleague Dr. I. Prothero for their perceptive criticisms of this essay in its final stages.

[1] Perhaps the clearest statement of this schema is to be found in A. Soboul, "Classes and Class Struggles during the French Revolution", *Science and Society*, xvii (1953), pp. 238-57: e.g., "The essential cause of the Revolution was the power of a bourgeoisie arrived at its maturity and confronted by a decadent aristocracy holding tenaciously to its privileges".

[2] A. Cobban, *The Social Interpretation of the French Revolution* (Cambridge, 1964).

has also been developing in France, where Monsieur Furet and Monsieur Richet in particular have been attempting to elaborate a more theoretical schema than Cobban's yet on basically the same lines.[3] Cobban's essential contribution to the historiography of the French Revolution was to question the notion of the bourgeoisie as a capitalist or even proto-capitalist class. He thereby questioned the whole nature of the Revolution. Cobban was a brilliant polemicist and his book displays both the qualities and the defects of this type of writing. He had an unerring eye for the weaknesses in the arguments of others; but they tended to capture his attention to the exclusion of all other considerations. His book, therefore, remained a very piecemeal affair, concerned primarily with destroying what he took, rightly or wrongly, to be a number of commonly accepted fallacies with only a relatively loose thread connecting them. Cobban made no attempt to produce any systematic construction to replace the whole edifice of interpretation, which he was very conscious of having undermined.[4] At most, he carved a few stones for a new façade. Thus, for example, he proposed a new definition of the revolutionary bourgeoisie, which he saw as a declining class of venal office-holders, yet he did not attempt to work out the structure of social conflict implied in such a view. He presumably believed this group to be but one element of the Ancien Régime bourgeoisie and he also suggested that the nature of the bourgeoisie was altered during the Revolution, yet he did not try to examine what the bourgeoisie was before the Revolution nor what the relationship was between the various component parts that he perceived. Above all, Cobban does not seem to have questioned the notion that a noble-bourgeois class conflict was the fundamental element in the genesis of the Revolution. He merely sought to alter one part of that proposition. In this sense, therefore, he retained a class interpretation of the French Revolution which did not stray too far from the classic mould.

Nevertheless, Cobban's remarks on the nature of the revolutionary bourgeoisie together with Professor Taylor's fundamental work on French capitalism in the eighteenth century have in fact brought into question the whole schema of the Revolution as the product of a conflict between nobles and bourgeois, as Taylor himself has

[3] D. Richet, "Autour des origines idéologiques lointaines de la Révolution française: élites et despotismes", *Annales E.S.C.*, xxiv (1969), pp. 1-23; F. Furet, "Le catéchisme de la Révolution française", *Annales E.S.C.*, xxvi (1971), pp. 255-89; C. Mazauric, *Sur la Révolution française* (Paris, 1970), pp. 21-113.

[4] A. Cobban, "The French Revolution, Orthodox and Unorthodox", *History*, lii (1967), pp. 149-59.

pointed out.[5]   For such an interpretation is necessarily based on the premise that there existed in eighteenth-century France two distinct and antagonistic classes of bourgeois and nobles. If, however, in our attempt to define the eighteenth-century bourgeoisie we can discover no such clear division, then it becomes extremely difficult to define a class conflict.   But, in that case, we have to decide why, in 1788-9, groups which can be identified as non-noble combatted and defeated groups which can be identified as noble, thereby laying the foundations of the political system of the nineteenth-century bourgeoisie; and why they attacked and destroyed privilege in 1789, thereby destroying the formal organization of eighteenth-century French society and preparing a structure within which the socio-economic developments of the nineteenth century might blossom. It is the aim of this essay to examine these questions in the light of recent research. It sets out to provide a constructed synthesis of the directions in which it seems to the author that French and Anglo-Saxon scholars have been moving in research and debate. It remains one man's point of view and its ultimate purpose is simply to suggest some hypotheses which may help to clarify, whether by assent or dissent, a few of the major problems of interpretation which currently beset the period of the revolutionary crisis of the late eighteenth century.

*   *   *   *

Generalizations about the socially predominant groups in eighteenth-century France must be made with considerable caution and many qualifications. There existed a regional diversity of which we are not as yet fully aware. Obviously, the structure, the internal relationships and the preoccupations of the society of any one area were moulded by the economic and occupational character of the environment in which it had evolved. It would be qualitatively different in an administrative or judicial centre, such as Toulouse, from a commercial or industrial centre, such as Beauvais. The condition, mentality and social prospects of the middle classes of a commercial centre of recent growth, such as Le Havre, would be different from those of their counterparts in one of long-established trade patterns, such as Montauban, and in one in decline, like Châteaudun. Equally difficult to equate would be the society of a seaport city like Marseille

[5] G. V. Taylor, "Types of Capitalism in Eighteenth-Century France", *Eng. Hist. Rev.*, lxxix (1964), pp. 478-97, and "Non-Capitalist Wealth and the Origins of the French Revolution", *Amer. Hist. Rev.*, lxxii (1967), pp. 469-96, especially p. 490.

with that of a small inland town, even one like Roanne much of whose trade emanated from Marseille. We have to consider the penny-pinching *avocat* in stagnant Bayeux as equally important socially in his own world as the successful wholesale merchant in prosperous Bordeaux was in his. Indeed, it is necessary to remember that the seaports and the few inland cities were not wholly typical of urban France, which was composed essentially of a large number of small towns, averaging from five to fifteen or twenty thousand inhabitants. The great majority of the deputies for the Third Estate, in the Estates-General, as in all the subsequent Revolutionary assemblies, came from this sort of background and brought with them the ambitions, fears, hopes, humiliations and prejudices of small town provincial life, which could never be completely obliterated by the capital city and by high political debate. The Ancien Régime experience of these men, moreover, was not necessarily a negative one, but often one of relative social pre-eminence in their own context. Indeed, in so far as the Girondins represented wealthy opinion in the provincial cities, their lack of success inside the Convention, despite their anti-Parisian stance, may perhaps be partially explained by the small town background of so many of the politically uncommitted men of the Plain. Certainly, among the members of the great Committee of Public Safety only Hérault de Seychelles and Collot d'Herbois came from a city; the others were men from towns like Arras, Clermont-Ferrand and Dôle. In 1789 Mirabeau noted that one of the most successful oratorical devices in the National Assembly "is to show the interest of the provinces in opposition with that of Paris".[6]

The orthodox approach to the upper strata of eighteenth-century French society has always been to stress exclusively the elements of disparity and division within them and to split them into two clearly defined and clearly antagonistic classes of nobles and bourgeois. Such an approach ignores all the elements that conferred on these strata a degree of homogeneity in some important respects. We may understand this without difficulty if, instead of peering so closely at the top of society, we stand back and attempt to view it as a whole. Whatever the distinctions and whatever the striking differences in wealth levels inside these strata, they achieved a certain common identity as a minority with disproportionate wealth in relation to the mass of poor Frenchmen. The primary articulation in Ancien Régime society was not the distinction between the privileged and

[6] Quoted by J. F. Bosher, *French Finances, 1770-1795* (Cambridge, 1970), p. 261.

the Third Estate; rather, it was between those for whom manual labour provided their livelihood and those for whom it did not.[7] Clearly this division, in common with all those in this society, was neither rigid nor absolute. It did not have the character of a boundary, but more that of a frontier with its attendant no-man's-land formed by transitional categories. The inhabitants of this zone were the artisans — the *sans-culottes* in Paris — the degree of whose penetration into the ranks of the lesser bourgeoisie can be determined by the extent to which trading activity had become preponderant in the combination of trade and manual production which characterized their state.[8] Moreover, some trades were more prestigious than others, either inherently so or because of local factors, and allowed those who exercised them to reconcile status with manual labour more easily than in the majority of cases.[9] For example, those engaged on luxury articles, such as the goldsmiths (*orfèvres*) or the wig-makers (*perruquiers*), derived status either from the value of their raw material or from the nature of their clientele.[10] This was a highly permeable frontier: the passport was basically the acquisition of a modest capital.[11]

There was, then, an important and real sense in which all levels of the bourgeoisie and nobility attained in very general terms a community of interest in face of the vulgar mechanic classes and of the vile and abject poor.[12] At the other end of the scale, the apparent simplicity of the distinction between privileged and unprivileged

[7] Cf. E. G. Barber, *The Bourgeoisie in Eighteenth-Century France* (Princeton, 1955), p. 15; M. Couturier, *Recherches sur les structures sociales de Châteaudun* (Paris, 1969), pp. 221-2; A. Daumard and F. Furet, *Structures et relations sociales à Paris au milieu du XVIIIème siècle* (Paris, 1963), p. 68.

[8] In this point resides the weakness of using professional categories as social categories. Not only can there be significant wealth differences between two carpenters or two stonemasons, but also significant functional differences. Cf. M. Thoumas-Schapira, "La bourgeoisie toulousaine à la fin du XVIIème siècle", *Annales du Midi*, lxvii (1955), pp. 315 and 318.

[9] One can suggest that the inferiority of surgeons (*chirurgiens*) to doctors (*médecins*), although clearly connected with their barbering, may also be imputable in part to the predominantly manual nature of their profession.

[10] Note how Chaumette, terrorist *agent national* of Paris, seems to have tried to substitute "jeweller" (*bijoutier*) for "shoemaker" (*cordonnier*) as his father's profession on his birth certificate: *Papiers de Chaumette*, ed. F. Braesch (Paris, 1908), p. 12.

[11] A calculation of the fortunes of the joiners (*menuisiers*) of Toulouse reveals an average of 1,000 *livres* for the masters, 600 for those companions who subsequently became masters, and 470 for those who did not: J. Godechot, "L'histoire économique et sociale de Toulouse au XVIIIème siècle", *Annales du Midi*, lxxviii (1966), p. 371.

[12] Richet, "Autour des origines idéologiques lointaines de la Révolution française".

is misleading. In reality no such absolute, horizontal division existed. Certainly trade was definitely inferior; certainly the hereditary noble was evidently superior. But between the two the permutations, the nuances, the ambiguities were infinite. \ The pursuit of ennoblement remained a realistic enterprise for the bourgeoisie of the eighteenth century.[13]/ The king continued to concede Letters of Nobility to honourable, successful and well-connected men.[14] Venal offices which carried nobility — particularly the office of *secrétaire du roi*, certain judicial posts, and municipal office in nineteen towns — could be purchased throughout the century. Privilege, which, in its origin, was the most tangible expression of noble social superiority, had long since been infiltrated by non-nobles. Fiscal exemption, the commonest form of privilege, could be acquired without particular difficulty by men of substance and even, in a partial way, by men of very little substance.[15] On the other hand, the eighteenth-century noble always paid some taxes — more indeed than the wealthy bourgeois of certain towns favoured by a history of bargains with the Crown — while, in practice, rich commoners benefited as much as nobles from the complaisance, deference or laxity of administrators and collectors of taxes.[16] Similarly, seigneurial rights were certainly not restricted to the nobility. They had become a merchandise possibly more readily obtainable than venal office. Fiefs and rights had been divided, subdivided, and shared out to such an extent that in some places it was impossible to know their origin. In 1781 22 per cent of the lay seigneurs in the *Élection* of Le Mans were non-nobles.[17]

[13] E.g. H. Carré, *La noblesse de France et l'opinion publique au XVIIIème siècle* (Paris, 1920), pp. 3, 12-14, and F. L. Ford, *Robe and Sword* (New York, 1965), pp. 208-9. Cf. J. G. C. Blacker, "Social Ambitions of the Bourgeoisie in Eighteenth-Century France and their Relation to Family Limitation", *Population Studies*, xi (1957), pp. 46-63, and P. Goubert, *L'Ancien Régime*, 2 vols. (Paris, 1969), i, pp. 145 ff.

[14] E.g. J. Meyer, *La noblesse bretonne au XVIIIème siècle*, 2 vols. (Paris, 1966), i, pp. 321-442.

[15] E.g. out of a total of 1,715 names on the tax rolls of Montargis in 1789, 852 were marked either as being exempt or privileged, or else as having a special status: B. Hyslop, "Les élections de la ville de Montargis en 1789", *Ann. hist. Rév. fr.*, xviii (1946), p. 125; cf. G. Bouchard, *La famille du conventionnel Basire* (Paris, 1952), pp. 91-2.

[16] C. B. A. Behrens, "Nobles, Privileges, and Taxes in France at the end of the Ancien Régime", *Econ. Hist. Rev.*, 2nd ser., xv (1962-3), pp. 451-75; M. Marion, *Histoire financière de la France depuis 1715*, 3 vols. (Paris, 1914-28), i, pp. 10-12.

[17] P. Bois, *Les Paysans de l'Ouest* (Le Mans, 1960), p. 378. But the regional variations were great; around Dieppe there was only one non-noble for thirty-six noble fief holders: M. de Bouard (ed.), *Histoire de Normandie* (Toulouse, 1970), p. 339.

Just before the Revolution, the Duc de Chaulnes sold his seigneury and viscounty of Amiens to a certain Colmar, a Jew and therefore definitely not noble, while the Polignacs' alienation of their seigneuries in the Velay around the beginning of the century was a veritable godsend for the socially ambitious wealthy of that region.[18]   In sum, between the privileged noble and the unprivileged commoner stood an important transitional category of indeterminate social mutants.   They were neither nobles nor commoners.   Indeed, almost everywhere except in Normandy, the appellation "noble" really meant a superior sort of non-noble; hence the birth certificate of the future Director Larevellière-Lépeaux stated that he was the son of "nobleman Jean-Baptiste de la Revellière, bourgeois of the town of Angers".[19]   How noble was a man whose office conferred on him personal nobility but who had not yet served the twenty years necessary to obtain the *lettres d'honneur* which declared that nobility now hereditary in the family?[20]   Was a man privileged or not when he possessed a fief, where he paid no taxes and levied seigneurial dues, and also non-noble land, where he paid both taxes and dues?   Of course, it had been stated as early as the Ordinance of Blois (1579) that possession of a fief in no way made a man noble. But, when taken with a certain life style and other similar attributes, it was an important element in helping to make a man appear noble. And in social promotion in this period, appearances were the first step towards reality.   In the 1780s an authority on jurisprudence complained that the usurpation of rank had got quite out of hand with men ennobled (*anoblis*) styling themselves in a manner reserved to lords of early fifteenth-century extraction, and commoners of good standing having themselves addressed as *marquis, comte, vicomte* or *baron*, and even passing themselves off as such in legal

[18] A. Young, *Travels in France*, ed. C. Maxwell (Cambridge, 1950), p. 8; G. Sabatier, "L'Emblavès au début du XVIIIème siècle", in P. Léon (ed), *Structures économiques et problèmes sociaux du monde rural dans la France du Sud-Est* (Paris, 1966), pp. 88-90.   Cf. *Cahiers de doléances du Tiers-Etat du bailliage de Rouen*, ed. M. Bouloiseau (Paris, 1957), i, p. xxix, on the dispersion of the seigneuries in the duchy of Longueville during the same period.

[19] A. Brette, "La noblesse et ses privilèges pécuniaires en 1789", *La Révolution française*, xxvi (1906), p. 102.

[20] Note, for example, how one inhabitant of Saint-Étienne, who at the beginning of the Revolution certainly considered himself, and was considered by others, to be a noble, was able to vote in the Year VI by arguing that his father had been a *secrétaire du roi* for only fourteen years and that therefore he himself could not possibly be noble: Archives Départmentales (hereafter A.D.), Loire, L 276, proceedings of electoral assembly at Saint-Étienne, Year VI.

documents.[21] More modest, but more commonplace, were the eighteenth-century families which had added the particle to their name,[22] and had acquired over a number of generations a surreptitious accumulation of partial recognitions of privileged status which allowed them to establish as a fact exemptions and privileges to which they had no real documented right. Provided that such a family was of some wealth, conformed to the standards of noble behaviour and married advantageously, it was sufficient for its members to claim indefatigably enough and for long enough a customary privileged position in order to obtain ultimately the Intendant's tacit acquiescence to their inclusion in some list of privileged persons, thus achieving irrefutable evidence of privileged status. A sustained effort of this kind by succeeding generations could finally be crowned either by the grant of Letters of Nobility or by an official decision ratifying explicitly or implicitly a claim to nobility.[23]

Jaurès sought to explain these anomalies as "a hybrid social force at the junction of the Ancien Régime and the new capitalism".[24] Obviously, such an interpretation alone was capable of safeguarding the concept of two distinct and antagonistic classes. In fact, however, it does not seem possible to discern a fundamental cleavage at this time between the bourgeoisie and the nobility. The middle class of the late Ancien Régime displayed no significant functional differences from the nobility, no significant difference in accepted values and above all no consciousness of belonging to a class whose economic and social characteristics were antithetical to those of the nobility.[25]

[21] Quoted by Carré, *La noblesse de France*, p. 14.

[22] 160 signatures on the Tennis Court Oath had the particle: Brette, *art. cit.*, p. 104.

[23] E.g. V. R. Gruder, *The Royal Provincial Intendants* (Ithaca, 1968), p. 130; F. Bluche, *Les Magistrats du Parlement de Paris au XVIIIème siècle* (Besançon, 1960), p. 95; G. Lefebvre, *Études Orléanaises*, 2 vols, (Paris, 1962-3), i, pp. 165-70.

[24] J. Jaurès, *Histoire socialiste, 1789-1900*, 12 vols. (Paris, 1900-8), i, p. 40.

[25] Taylor, "Non-Capitalist Wealth and the Origins of the French Revolution" *passim*. Cf. Godechot, "L'histoire économique et sociale de Toulouse", pp 363-74; Barber, *The Bourgeoisie in Eighteenth-Century France*, pp. 62-3; J. Sentou, *Fortunes et groupes sociaux à Toulouse sous la Révolution* (Toulouse, 1969), pp. 79-322, especially pp. 182-3. P. Léon ("Recherches sur la bourgeoisie française de province au XVIIIème siècle", *L'Information historique*, xxi [1958], pp. 101-5) believes that the division between the nobility and the bourgeoisie can be seen in the tax registers, provided that one recognizes a number of "enclaves" and operates a selection among the office-holders on the fringes of the Robe nobility. This sort of categorization (which is a fairly common approach to the problem) seems unrealistic in view of what we know about tax exemption; it is also extremely arbitrary, as indeed the author admits.

The commercial middle class of France at this time was not capitalist in one vital respect. The business of making money was subordinated to a non-capitalist social ideal, and social classifications and values did not depend upon a notion of productive force. The middle class accepted really without debate aristocratic values and sought to gain social approval by adhering to these standards. Social promotion required the abandonment of trade as soon as was financially possible. The consistent pattern of the eighteenth century, as of the seventeenth, was that commercial families placed their capital in land, in government and private annuities (*rentes*), and in venal office, all of which gave returns on investment in the order of 2 to 4 per cent, instead of seeking the higher returns on commercial investment.[26] These men were dominated by the social motive, not by the capitalist profit motive. They accepted that trade was by definition ignoble and dishonourable. If the corn merchant speculated on the misery of the times or if the cloth merchant risked his all in the chance of large profits from army contracts, it was in order that their progeny might the more quickly retreat into the social respectability of professional status and that, hopefully, they might themselves retire to live the life of noble idleness on revenues from land, government stock and private loans.[27]   Thus, in economic terms, nobles and bourgeois resembled each other to the extent that both sought to secure the greater part of their fortune in non-capitalist forms; at the same time, nobles indulged quite as much as wealthy commoners in proto-capitalist industrial and financial activities.[28] It seems difficult to perceive here the representatives of significantly different stages "in a complex set of socio-economic relationships, the one feudal, the other capitalist".[29]   Such fundamental divisions and their ensuing antagonisms did not properly begin to appear in France until the nineteenth century, possibly during the reign of

[26] But there were variations: both Bluche (*op. cit.*, p. 170) and R. Forster (*The Nobility of Toulouse* [Baltimore, 1960], p. 104), find returns of 5 per cent for the Parlements they study, while the government annuities (*rentes*) paid 5 per cent at most, as did private ones under the law at least.

[27] Cf. M. Vovelle and D. Roche, "Bourgeois, rentiers, propriétaires: éléments pour la définition d'une catégorie sociale à la fin du XVIIIème siècle", in *Actes du 84ème congrès national des sociétés savantes* (Paris, 1959), pp. 419-52; also Sentou, *op cit.*, pp. 191-2 and 253 on the connection between the *rentier* and professional groups.

[28] Taylor, *art. cit.*; G. Richard, "Les corporations et la noblesse commerçante en France au XVIIIème siècle", *L'Information historique*, xx (1957), pp. 185-9; Meyer, *La noblesse bretonne*, i, pp. 151-8.

[29] J. Kaplow, "On 'Who intervened in 1788?' ", *Amer. Hist. Rev.*, lxxii (1967), p. 498.

Louis-Philippe, and even then the socio-economic pattern described in this paragraph remained predominant among the entrepreneurial group.[30]

Hence, in the upper reaches of French society the great articulation was not between noble and commoner which, as I have tried to show, is an almost impossible division to demonstrate. It was between those who traded and those who did not. Of course, this dividing line, like all the others in this society, was neither absolute nor drawn horizontally across society. Each family made its own calculation of the amount of fortune necessary before severing its connection with the generating source of wealth in trade.[31] In the few great cities and seaports, with their opportunities for massive accumulation of wealth, oligarchies of trading families appeared, of such great wealth that social respect and even noble status could not be denied them.[32] Clearly, such men may be adduced as evidence of a capitalist *haute-bourgeoisie* in the classic sense; but the extent to which their careers are typical of the middle class as a whole is highly debatable and we shall refer later in this essay to other senses in which their situation may have been significant in the structure of this society. Moreover, in most cases, despite having been able to rise so high socially while in trade, even they quickly sought to take root among the landed nobility and retreated behind the discretion of intermediaries if they continued their business interests.[33]

In general it would appear true to say that above this frontier of trade — and always provided the possession of a level of wealth sufficient not to live meanly — there stood an élite whose internal distinctions could not destroy a common identity between its com-

---

[30] D. S. Landes, "French Entrepreneurship and Industrial Growth in the Nineteenth Century", *Jl. of Econ. Hist.*, ix (1949), pp. 45-61.

[31] There are of course countless individual examples, each with its own different permutation of the elements contributing to such a promotion; Taylor (*art. cit.*) presents some, as does O. Hufton (*Bayeux in the late Eighteenth Century* [Oxford, 1967], p. 61). A very clear example of a family in the act of transferring — marrying profitably, buying land and office, yet hesitating to abandon trade altogether — is provided by the future revolutionary Laurent LeCointre and his brother in the 1770s and 1780s: T. Lhuillier, "Laurent LeCointre (de Versailles)", *La Révolution française*, xv (1895), pp. 234-56.

[32] E.g. G. Richard, "A propos de la noblesse commerçante de Lyon au XVIIIème siècle", *L'Information historique*, xxii (1959), pp. 156-61. A royal decree of 1767 accorded the wholesale merchants (*négociants en gros*) the reputation of "living nobly" and some privileges.

[33] E.g. the complaint from Toulouse in 1773 that the moment a merchant obtained the ennobling office of *capitoul*, "he considers trading to be a thing very much beneath his dignity": M. Marion, *Dictionnaire des institutions de la France aux XVIIème et XVIIIème siècles* (Paris, 1968), v. "noblesse".

ponent elements.[34]   It was united, in the first place, by its control
of landed property, both directly as the landowning class and indirectly
through the exercise of seigneurial rights.   In the second place, the
tangible manifestations of social superiority — essentially fiscal
and seigneurial privilege — were becoming increasingly accessible
during the century to the majority of its members without regard to
their nobility or lack of it.   This is very clearly the message of the
difficulties which one encounters in trying to distinguish between
noble and rich commoner.   The third major element of unity is
that *in origin* the nobility of the late eighteenth century was no
different from those members of the élite who had not yet achieved
noble rank.   Already in 1660 an observer estimated that hardly 5
per cent of noble families could trace their lineage back to the medieval
feudal age.[35]   The great majority of the nobility of France dated
from the sixteenth, seventeenth and eighteenth centuries.[36]   They
were the product of that very same patient acquisition of social
pre-eminence upon which the non-noble élite of the later eighteenth
century was so ardently engaged.[37]   Most of the élite shared a
common origin in that, in the first instance, it was some measure of
wealth which had given them access to land and office.[38]   From
that base, there began the slow ascension through the devious channels
of a careful accumulation and permutation of a succession of progressively prestigious offices, of advantageous marriage alliances,
of inheritances and so on.[39]

[34] The notion of an élite was first examined in general terms by D. Richet,
"Autour des origines idéologiques lointaines de la Révolution française".
See also H. Luethy, *La banque protestante en France*, 2 vols. (Paris, 1959-61),
ii, pp. 15-25, and Goubert, *L'Ancien Régime*, i, p. 235.   Cf. the interesting
comment on such a view in Mazauric, *Sur la Révolution française*, p. 107.
[35] D. Bitton, *The French Nobility in Crisis* (Stanford, 1969), p. 98.
[36] A. Goodwin, "The Social Structure and Economic and Political Attitudes
of the French Nobility in the Eighteenth Century", in *XIIème congrès international des sciences historiques*, 5 vols. (Vienna, 1965), i, pp. 356-65; Gruder,
The Royal Provincial Intendants, pp. 177-80.   Cf. Bayeux in 1789, where five-
sixths of the noble families could not claim nobility before 1500; the nobility of
the majority of them was acquired during the seventeenth and early eighteenth
centuries: Hufton, *Bayeux in the late Eighteenth Century*, p. 41.
[37] E.g. the interesting comparison established by R. Bouscayrol, "Les
origines familiales et sociales de Romme et de Soubrany", in *Gilbert Romme et
son Temps* (Publications de l'Institut d'Etudes du Massif Central, Paris, 1966),
pp. 23-42.
[38] Cf. Lefebvre, *Études Orléanaises*, i, pp. 171-3; Sentou, *Fortunes et groupes
sociaux à Toulouse*, pp. 253-4; M. Bloch, *Les caractères originaux de l'histoire
rurale française*, 2 vols. (Paris, 1961-4), i, pp. 142-3.
[39] E.g. Bosher, *French Finances*, pp. 61-2, 69-71, 178, 278-84; Gruder,
op. cit., pp. 136-9, 142-66; Meyer, *La noblesse bretonne*, i, pp. 171-422, especially
pp. 349-61; Lefebvre, *op. cit.*, i, pp. 175-6.   A few spectacular careers are
detailed in Forster, *The Nobility of Toulouse*, pp. 24-6.   Cf. Couturier, *Recherches
sur les structures sociales de Châteaudun*, pp. 236 ff.

One may suggest that the confusion of the Ancien Régime social scene is largely due to the fact that the mechanisms of social ascension were extremely delicate. They demanded constant vigilance and a fine judgement. Although history records more prominently the success stories, the reality of a society can usually be seen much more clearly in its failures. The common story of failure in the Ancien Régime is that of a family which had miscalculated, had made an ill-timed exit from trade towards an insufficient capital and property basis, had failed to gain access to a proper professional clientele, and had compounded these errors by unfortunate marriages, unwise procreation, lack of cunning, and so forth.[40] Indeed, a close reading of even the standard success story suggests that the actual passage from commoner to noble status was almost incidental to the attainment of pre-eminence, for it guaranteed nothing. With the exception of the great aristocracy, whose position was unassailable, those noble families which did not continually strive to nourish their position stagnated or declined.[41] The nobility contained individuals of widely different wealth, prestige and power, ranging from those living more or less overtly on charity to men of great influence and vast estates.[42] At the end of the Ancien Régime, rank in the upper reaches of society was far too subtle a notion to be confined within the ungainly corsetry of nobles *versus* commoners. It depended above all upon a shrewd dosage of wealth, profession, family back-

[40] E.g. Sentou, *op. cit.*, pp. 238-40. See Daumard and Furet, *Structures et relations sociales à Paris au milieu du XVIIIème siècle,* p. 66, on the origin of Parisian domestic servants. Note also the 27 lawyers at Toulouse at the end of Louis XIV's reign who were too poor to be taxed and some of whom were even recorded as beggars: Thoumas-Schapira, "La bourgeoisie toulousaine à la fin du XVIIème siècle", p. 317.

[41] E.g. the father of the future revolutionary Prieur de la Côte-d'Or, who shattered the family's very promising position by his womanizing and his drunkeness: G. Bouchard, *Un organisateur de la victoire* (Paris, 1946), pp. 10 ff. Note the dilemma between ancient lineage and fortune which faced the parents of the Marquis d'Argenson when choosing a wife for their son: Carré, *La noblesse de France,* p. 38. Consider also the careful management of its financial affairs and its use of relatives and connections to help the son onwards and upwards by placing him at Court which characterized the provincial Parlementarian family of Dubois de Fosseux — Dubois himself listed the qualities of his bride in a significant order; "a very honest fortune, good expectations of an inheritance, pleasing features without being a beauty, and . . . an excellent character": L. N. Berthe, *Dubois de Fosseux* (Arras, 1969), pp. 53-60, 75.

[42] E.g. Meyer, *op. cit.,* i, pp. 21-7; Lefebvre, *op. cit.,* i, p. 184; Hufton, *Bayeux in the late Eighteenth Century,* pp. 41-56; Cobban, *Social Interpretation of the French Revolution,* pp. 29-32. A useful summary of recent work on the nobility is provided by A. Goodwin, "The Social Origin and Privileged Status of the French Eighteenth-Century Nobility", *Bull. John Rylands Library,* xlvii (1965), pp. 382-403.

ground, patrons and connections, title, privilege and office. Even the sort of people to whom one loaned and from whom one borrowed money counted, since in respectable circles these transactions seem to have taken place very much between people of similar status.[43] To take but one example, Bertrand Barère's father was a commoner and his mother a noble; his father acquired the seigneury of Vieuzac and enjoyed seigneurial rights, but could never aspire to nobility. Barère himself did have pretensions to nobility, but still jumped at the opportunity of marrying into an old-established noble family of the vicinity despite its impecuniosity.[44] Even within a body of men with common privileges, such as the Parlement of Paris, sharp contrasts existed between personal fortunes, between the scions of illustrious houses and those of no less ancient but undistinguished lineage, and so on.[45] The wealth of a financier was less ignominious than that of a merchant; the *avocat* tended to carry more weight socially in a small town than a *notaire* of greater fortune. Indeed, the bitter quarrels of precedence that enlivened provincial life throughout the eighteenth century were evidence less of friction over a strict social hierarchy than of ambiguity about social rank.

What I have said does not necessarily deny the existence of a "middle class" that was within the élite and that did not merely consist of the trading elements — these latter both stood outside the élite and played little direct part in the genesis of the Revolution. But until considerably more detailed research which does not postulate a "bourgeoisie" separate from and in contradiction with the élite has been accomplished, it is difficult to define it exactly. Above all, one may debate whether such a definition would be of major significance when there is little evidence that it possessed either a "class consciousness" or an alternative social structure. This argument does, however, deny the notion of two clearly defined and clearly antagonistic classes of nobles and bourgeois in eighteenth-century France and therefore denies the existence of a class conflict in the classic sense. It does not deny — and is not intended to deny — the existence of very real distinctions, divisions and antagonisms within this élite. Nor does it deny the existence of a social crisis, for, as H. R. Trevor-Roper remarked in quite a different context, "social crises are caused not by the clear-cut opposition of mutually exclusive interests but by the tug-of-war of opposite interests *within*

[43] E.g. Forster, *The Nobility of Toulouse*, pp. 117-9.
[44] L. Gershoy, *Bertrand Barère: a Reluctant Revolutionary* (Princeton, 1962), pp. 32-4.
[45] Bluche, *Les Magistrats du Parlement de Paris*, pp. 88-94, 132-3, 143-8, 237.

one body".[46]   It is quite wrong to consider that the upper reaches of late Ancien Régime society were static and decaying.   Any analysis confined to only a few decades will inevitably project a static image unless that period be one of actual crisis or revolution.   A wider context of a couple of centuries suggests that, on the contrary, this élite was the product of a process of evolution and that it was still evolving.

It is evident from the preceding pages that the nature of the nobility had been undergoing tremendous change since the end of the fifteenth century.   Indeed, the historian of the later Valois would not find unfamiliar our description of the ambiguity of the frontier between nobles and commoners, with its references to the escape from trade, venal office, usurpation, the adoption of the particle, ennoblement, and the purchase of fiefs, of elements of privilege and of nobility itself.   Noble complaints about the debasement of their estate sound very much the same whether written in the 1780s or the 1580s. The combined action of three major factors seems to have been responsible for this development: first, the financial difficulties of the late medieval and Renaissance nobility; secondly, the attempts of the emergent absolute monarchs to secure their power upon a service nobility; thirdly, the financial difficulties of these monarchs which prompted them to abandon ennobling offices into the possession of their incumbents and subsequently to resort to the downright sale of privileges and offices.   The great period of the transformation of the élite was unquestionably the seventeenth century.   It was in this period that the monarchy expanded its power and the business of its government enormously, and thus multiplied its officials and the machinery for the enforcement of its will; it was also the period when a great series of wars, undertaken on an unprecedented scale and in a time of economic instability, obliged the monarch to exploit office and privilege for revenue purposes.[47]   This double process, reaching its apogee under Louis XIV, accelerated the infiltration of the nobility by wealthy commoners which had been taking place during the sixteenth century.   More important perhaps, by encouraging its generalization, it finally rendered irrevocable the sixteenth-

[46] H. R. Trevor-Roper, "Trevor-Roper's 'General Crisis': Symposium", repr. in Trevor Aston (ed.), *Crisis in Europe, 1560-1660* (London, 1965), p. 114.
[47] Note how the concession of hereditary nobility to the members of the great law courts of Paris and the provinces coincided with moments of acute financial embarrassment — 1644-5, 1691 and 1704; there is a similar pattern in the sales of nobility: Marion, *Dictionnaire des institutions de la France*, *v.* "noblesse".

century encroachment on characteristically noble attributes by wealthy non-nobles.[48] Louis XIV in particular exploited every financial opportunity provided by office and privilege.[49] He even resorted several times to the direct sale of nobility, whereas neither of the eighteenth-century kings did more than sell the confirmation of nobility acquired in the normal ways. His extensive warfaring allowed commoners to enter the officer corps in relatively large numbers.[50] A man with wits enough to discover profit in the ruins of the economy and intelligence enough to further the extension of royal power could rise rapidly. In this sense, we may restore a dimension to Saint-Simon's much abused description of the Sun King's rule as the "reign of the vile bourgeoisie". Early in the seventeenth century, the famous jurist and political theorist Loyseau still based his work on the concept of a society divided into three separate estates. In the last decade of that same century the theorist Domat, whose writings influenced jurists for the next ninety years, was dividing society on a functional basis; the first rank, with honour, dignity and authority, he accorded to the prelates, high magistrates and military commanders, and in the second rank, endowed with honour but not dignity, he placed without differentiation — and this is significant in the context of this essay — the *avocats*, the doctors, the members of the liberal and scientific professions generally and also the "gentlemen" (*gentilhommes*).[51]

This, then, had been the hey-day of social promotion and, as a result, not merely was the composition of the nobility altered but also its traditional attributes diffused and its traditional functions adulterated. The situation in the later eighteenth century was simply the development of conditions already apparent in the second half of the seventeenth.[52] By the end of the Ancien Régime, the distinction between the Robe nobility and the Sword nobility, which had appeared so vital during the preceding two centuries, had become largely meaningless. Similar life styles, intermarriage, the parallel pursuit of military, judicial and administrative careers by the different sons of the same Sword or Robe family had abolished

[48] R. Mousnier, *La vénalité des offices sous Henri IV et Louis XIII* (Rouen, 1946), *passim*.
[49] Ford, *Robe and Sword*, p. 12.
[50] E. G. Léonard, "La question sociale dans l'armée française au XVIIIème siècle", *Annales E.S.C.*, iii (1948), pp. 139-40.
[51] R. Mousnier, *La société française de 1770 à 1789*, 2 vols. (Paris C.D.U., 1970), i, pp. 11-15.
[52] Cf. R. B. Grassby, "Social Status and Commercial Enterprise under Louis XIV", *Econ. Hist. Rev.*, 2nd ser., xiii (1960-1), pp. 19-38.

imperative to occupy it.[83] Its possession would constitute an important element in the maintenance of the pre-eminence acquired, which, as we have seen, demanded careful attention; it could benefit relatives, from whose progress in repute one would benefit oneself; it could afford a steady income since it could be leased out. Indeed, the only overriding incentive to sell such a venal office was to find the purchase money for a more prestigious one. As for those families lower down in the professional hierarchy, the same considerations applied.[84] The *notaire*, for example, would naturally see his practice as an indispensable element to be handed on to his descendants for the maintenance, let alone the improvement of their social situation. For the first half of the eighteenth century, at least, an atmosphere of pause descended on these groups while families digested, as it were, the seventeenth century, some waiting out their time in a necessary social purgatory, others repairing fortunes, yet others seeking to augment them. Thus, when the magistrates of the Parlement of Grenoble refused after 1762 to admit anybody who could not demonstrate four generations of nobility on the paternal side *unless* they were the sons of magistrates, they were at one and the same time ensuring the access to office of their own immediate circle and increasing the social promotional value of that office.[85] A significant echo of these attitudes and problems came from a group far advanced in the access routes to these prestigious positions when, in 1753, the *avocats* practising in the Parlement of Rennes, the most exclusive of all, decided not to admit to their ranks in future "persons of vile and abject condition . . . nor those whose fathers exercised a mechanic art or some other base estate and reputed as such".[86] Of course, although access to office and wealth were the most important elements in social status, they were not the only ones as I emphasized earlier in this essay. The other, less calculable elements of prestige really resided in the nature of a family's relations and connections, for a man was what he was

---

[83] E.g. Forster, *The Nobility of Toulouse*, pp. 103-6; Bluche, *op. cit.*, p. 135.
[84] Cf. Goubert, "Les officers royaux des Présidiaux . . .", pp. 59-63, 68-70.
[85] J. Egret, "Un Parlement de province à la fin de l'Ancien Régime", *Annales E.S.C.*, iv (1949), p. 340. The sovereign court of Alsace, with a non-noble intake of over seventy per cent, nevertheless operated a certain selection at the level of *conseiller* against too close a connection with trade precisely in order to raise the social rank of its members: F. Burckhard, "La bourgeoisie parlementaire au XVIIIème siècle", in J. Schlumberger (ed.), *La bourgeoisie alsacienne* (Strasbourg, 1954), pp. 151-72. Note also how those *avocats en Parlement* who were sons of Parlementarian judges had right of precedence over those who were not: Delbèke, *L'Action politique et sociale des avocats*, p. 95.
[86] Delbèke, *op. cit.*, p. 112.

accepted to be by those who counted. But, although this question is still far from clear, it does seem that even in this sense the eighteenth century may have seen a contraction of opportunity through the development of dynasties and closed groups of wealthy, respectable families contracting marriages among each other or else outside the locality, whether for fear of inferior alliances or for need of mutual reassurance through alliance with their own kind.[87]

Such a situation would not necessarily have produced a social crisis, if it had not been for the incidence upon it of the demographic and economic developments of the century. Of course, the poor multiplied more than anyone else largely because there were more poor to multiply. But the effects of the demographic explosion (an increase of the order of thirty per cent or more between 1715 and 1789) were also felt in the area under discussion. It was naturally an added stimulus to this phenomenon of colonization as worried fathers found themselves with an extra boy to establish without loss of honour and/or an extra girl to marry off advantageously but economically.[88] At the same time, of course, demographic factors contributed to increase the pressure for social promotion from the lower end of the élite. The economic prosperity of the eighteenth century was, however, far more potent as an aggravating factor. In the seventeenth century, economic uncertainty had operated in a sense as a social filter, for those who had managed both to get and to stay rich had done so in a fairly decisive fashion.[89] But in the eighteenth century, not merely were spectacular fortunes being made but also almost anyone with a modicum of business sense was acceding, at least between 1730 and 1770, to modest wealth in small town provincial France. In effect, this meant that an increasing number of families were able at this time to make the break from trade. The

[87] E.g. P. Goubert, *Beauvais et le Beauvaisis* (Paris, 1958), pp. 321 ff.; D. Ligou, "La bourgeoisie réformée montalbanaise à la fin de l'Ancien Régime", *Rev. d'hist. écon. et soc.*, xxxiii (1955), pp. 377-404; J. Kaplow, *Elbeuf during the Revolutionary Period* (Baltimore, 1964), pp. 87-8; Couturier, *op. cit.*, pp. 138, 140-1, 227-8; M. Bernard, "La municipalité de Brest de 1750 à 1790", *Annales de Bretagne*, xxxi (1915), pp. 114-6; G. Lefebvre, *Cherbourg à la fin de l'Ancien Régime et au début de la Révolution* (Caen, 1965), pp. 23 ff.

[88] Cf. Carré, *La noblesse de France*, p. 125; Hufton, *Bayeux in the late Eighteenth Century*, pp. 50-4; Forster, *op. cit.*, pp. 125-41. Note, however, a decline in the size of noble families at Toulouse after 1730. The Chevalier d'Arc, very much a spokesman for the poorer provincial nobility, wanted a system of exemptions, privileges, pensions, etc., for noble fathers with large families: Léonard, "La question sociale dans l'armée française au XVIIIème siècle", p. 146. In 1789, the Third Estate of Rochefort expressed similar demands for preferential employment for such men in their own Order: B. Hyslop, *French Nationalism in 1789* (New York, 1967), p. 37.

[89] E.g. Livet, *L'Intendance d'Alsace sans Louis XIV*, pp. 889-90.

bottom end of the élite and consequently the lower reaches of the promotional channels probably began to swell. At the same time, the greater noble families with large estates could benefit from the rise in land rents and in agricultural prices.[90]

Conversely, however, the economic prosperity of the century did not really affect the majority of established members of the élite to anything like the same degree. It was above all a commercial prosperity and they had, by definition, cut themselves off from it.[91] They were faced by an average price rise of 48 per cent between 1730 and 1788 without any equivalent increase in income. One effect of this was to stimulate the energy with which some noble and commoner holders of seigneurial rights indulged in the so-called "feudal reaction".[92] More important, it would have added a remunerative element to the phenomenon of colonization and would also have helped to attract men already noble to lower offices.[93] Those professional families, which with patient dexterity were rising through the channels of promotion, would thus be likely to encounter more competition for positions to which seventeenth-century precedent taught them to aspire. Of course, commoner families still continued to rise to ennobling high office through the traditional channels.[94] But it can also be plausibly argued that conditions generally may well have become more precarious for those provincial families which had long since abandoned trade and settled comfortably into the middle-rank judicial and administrative positions. For one can doubt whether a great many of them had land and wealth enough to do more than hold their own from traditionally acceptable sources of income, while the increase in numbers from below would have meant more competition for business. In the smaller provincial towns, the *avocats*, the *notaires*, the judges of the lesser courts, only achieved an adequate income by garnering together every available form of revenue.[95] Naturally, there always

[90] C-E. Labrousse, *Esquisse du mouvement des prix et des revenus en France au XVIIIème siècle*, 2 vols. (Paris, 1933), ii, pp. 444-5; Meyer, *La noblesse bretone*, ii, p. 715; Forster, *op. cit.*, pp. 27, 68 ff. and 175.

[91] Cf. the Chevalier d'Arc; "if . . . the price of the necessities of life increases in the same proportion as money, . . . those who do not trade, being unable to afford them, fall into indigence": quoted by Léonard, *art. cit.*, p. 144.

[92] But Doyle, "Aristocratic Reaction", pp. 114-20 [above, pp. 20-6], questions whether this "feudal reaction" took place.

[93] E.g. Meyer, *op. cit.*, i, pp. 159-63; Cobban, *Social Interpretation of the French Revolution*, p. 28. Cf. Dawson, *Provincial magistrates*, pp. 71 ff.

[94] E.g. Bluche, *Les Magistrats du Parlement de Paris*, pp. 96-8.

[95] E.g. Hufton, *op. cit.*, pp. 57-80.

existed a huge gap in terms of wealth and prestige between the mass of middle-rank lawyers and the great officers of the Parlements, the *Chambres des Comptes,* the *Cours des Aides,* and so on;[96] but it does appear that, in these ways, the established channels of social promotion within the law courts and the administration which led from the one to the other became progressively clogged. Even an *avocat* pamphleteering in favour of the Parlements in 1789 thought that the high Robe positions should be accessible to all citizens with a degree in law, a respectable income and good morals.[97] The monarchy contributed materially to this situation by failing to increase the number of venal ennobling offices and to multiply the number of its acts of direct ennoblement.[98] Indeed, on the contrary, the Crown seems to have tried actively to limit the amount of ennoblement by office.[99] Perhaps the great popularity of Necker among professional men should be attributed in part to the fact that the effect of his various attempts at reform during his period of office in the late 1770s would have been precisely to unclog and regularize some of these channels.[100] Certainly, the increase in prestige and business accorded to the *Bailliage* and *Présidial* courts by Lamoignon and the large number of new ones that he established very nearly succeeded in preventing the other echelons of the legal profession from adhering to the Parlements' resistance to the Edicts of May 1788.[101]

Notwithstanding these arguments, there is some evidence to suggest that the dynasties may have been releasing their hold on high judicial office towards the end of the Ancien Régime. It has been shown that of 462 new *conseillers* in the Parlements during the fifteen years before the Revolution, 266 did not come from traditional Parlementarian families—although it is true that the majority of cases were in the less prestigious of the provincial

[96] E.g. Sentou, *Fortunes et groupes sociaux à Toulouse,* p. 225, and Delbèke, *L'action politique et sociale des avocats,* pp. 92 ff.

[97] Delbèke, *op. cit.,* p. 96.

[98] Meyer, *op. cit.,* i, p. 420; M. Reinhard, "Élite et noblesse dans la seconde moitié du XVIIIème siècle", *Rev. d'hist. mod. et contemp.,* iii (1956), pp. 5-37. The latter author stresses that the legal profession was particularly neglected in the already small number of direct ennoblements. There were no large scale creations of venal office after the end of Orry's period as *contrôleur général* in the 1740s. Luethy, *La banque protestante en France,* ii, p. 18.

[99] Meyer, *op. cit.,* i, p. 232. The number of *secrétaires du roi* (the office was known as the "savonette à vilain" because it speedily washed away the stain of ignoble birth) was reduced not long after Louis XIV's death, and though it rose later in the century in answer to the Crown's financial distress, it never again reached the level of the Sun King's closing years.

[100] Bosher, *French Finances,* pp. 142-65.

[101] J. Egret, *La Pré-Révolution française* (Paris, 1962), pp. 281-90. This point is nuanced but not invalidated by Dawson, *Provincial magistrates,* pp. 145 ff.

sovereign courts.[102]   Such evidence does not, however, necessarily indicate a renewal of access through the traditional channels.   Indeed, it is clear that the best route to social promotion lay increasingly outside and in contradiction to the assumptions of these traditional methods.   The quickest passport to social pre-eminence was the acquisition of great wealth.[103]   The banker, the slave-trader, the wealthy planter, the financier, these men had no difficulty in entering the nobility.   They could afford the high cost of an office such as *secrétaire du roi,* which directly conferred hereditary nobility and which could be held jointly with other offices.   They could purchase fiefs and privileges liberally.   Their wealth made them attractive to the Crown and made their daughters attractive to established noble families.   A man like Danycan of Saint-Malo, who could settle a total of three million *livres* on his four children at their marriages during the first decade of the century, encountered few problems in having himself and his immediate descent absorbed into the particularly punctilious Breton nobility.[104]   Of course, this had always been one of the recognized channels of social promotion, and wealth had always been one of the requisites for access to the higher ranks of the élite.   In the sixteenth and seventeenth centuries, financial activity both on behalf of the Crown and independently had been capable of producing rapid social rewards.   But, until 1715, it had also been the most hazardous of social routes.   Not only did it involve a period of social ignominy despite wealth, not only was it fragile because of the minimal fixed investment so characteristic of entrepreneurial activity at this time, but it was also open to the dangers of the *chambres de justice,* by which the monarch tended to render his financial agents responsible for his embarrassment, and of *quo warranto* investigations into the titles of their nobility.[105]   But the Edict of 1715, which revoked all the ennoblements, privileges and exemptions conceded since 1689 (only to resell most of them shortly afterwards) and the attack on the great financiers by the *Chambre ardente* of 1716 were the last cases of these procedures. In the eighteenth century, such men were relatively immune from

[102] J. Egret, "L'aristocratie parlementaire française à la fin de l'Ancien Régime", pp. 6, 10.
    [103] Cf. Y. Durand, *Les Fermiers-généraux au XVIIIème siécle* (Paris, 1971), pp. 220-301, 372-83.
    [104] Meyer, *La noblesse bretonne,* ii, p. 960.   For comparison's sake, note that Toulousan high society considered 200,000 *livres* to be a very large dowry: Forster, *The Nobility of Toulouse,* p. 175.
    [105] Cf. Marion, *Dictionnaire des institutions de la France,* v. "noblesse", and Meyer, *op. cit.,* i, pp. 29-73.

anything but the snobbery of the *nobles de race*.   It seems likely that
many of those entering the higher offices of the judiciary from outside
the dynasties were men with this kind of background.[106]   Office
in the sovereign courts gave them respectability.   It gave them more
indeed, for the Parlement of Paris was one of the ways to the position
of *maître de requêtes* to whom the highest political, administrative
and diplomatic posts in the land were open.   This was the road
taken by men of great ambition, who rarely stayed more than four
years in the Parlement.[107]   Their practice in this respect contrasted
with the more orthodox habits of the traditional Robe families and
as they left the court they were probably replaced in large measure
by men of their own kind.   A recent study of the Intendants is
suggestive in this sense, for it shows that, although for the most
part they were consistently chosen from the Parlementarian milieu,
there was a marked decline during the century in the length of time
that their families had been in the traditional respectability of the
judiciary.[108]   Equally significant is the fact that as the position of
the tax-farmer, the financier, and the speculator became more
secure, so did the traditional Parlementarian dynasties begin to
contribute members to their ranks, while dynasties began to form
among the financiers and in the fiscal administration, where previously
families had only sought to pass through.[109]

---

[106] Egret, *art. cit.*, pp. 8-9. Cf. Barber, *The Bourgeoisie in Eighteenth-Century
France*, p. 114; Gruder, *The Royal Provincial Intendants*, p. 188, and Bluche,
Les Magistrats du Parlement de Paris, pp. 108-14. Note how this last author,
while arguing for the possibility of very rapid social promotion into the nobility
(two or three generations), nearly always mentions a direct connection with
finance in the cases that he cites. Of the Paris Parlementarians whose family
origins are known, exactly the same number stemmed from financiers who had
received Letters of Nobility as from lawyers who had been similarly ennobled,
while the nobility of half the total number of families had originated in the
purchase of the office of *secrétaire du roi*. This office, the favourite goal of
financiers etc., accounted for fifty-five of the eighty-four cases of ennoblement
in the eighteenth century (pp. 90-6). Bluche also gives examples, but no
statistical comparison of numbers, of the non-noble intake from the law,
finance, the wholesale trade and the royal household (p. 98).

[107] Bluche, *op. cit.*, pp. 62-8. Although Parlementarian prejudice operated
so far as the high posts within the court were concerned, it was less active
against the financial connections of postulants for the position of *conseiller*,
which was all that the men just passing through would need (*ibid.*, pp. 78-81).
This reflects perhaps a tacit recognition of the situation by the Robe families.

[108] Gruder, *op. cit.*, pp. 201-5.

[109] Bosher, *French Finances*, pp. 68-9; Carré, *La noblesse de France*, p. 9.
Cf. Barber, *op. cit*, p. 32, and G. Chaussinand-Nogaret, "Capital et structure
sociale sous l'Ancien Régime", *Annales E.S.C.*, xxv (1970), pp. 463-76. The
dynastic phenomenon was never, however, very marked: Durand, *Les Fermiers-
généraux*, pp. 379-81.

It has been calculated, however, that a man would need a fortune of one million *livres* before he could safely allow himself to be embraced by the restrictions of social promotion without this interfering with the progress of his fortune.[110] Few were those who had the talent, energy and opportunities to harmonize thus their economic and social ambitions. The achievement of such great wealth and swift promotion implied a move to the big city, preferably Paris, before whose unknown adventures the citizen of the small provincial town would hesitate.[111] He would find it difficult to resist the lure of immediate respectability in the local context, even though it involved the rejection of the generating source of wealth. But a man who thus engaged upon the traditional ladder had few chances of transferring to the fast track of finance before he had already risen high — only, for example, by purchasing one of the limited number of offices of *receveur particulier*, who was the treasurer of an *Élection*, after making profits on a receivership of the salt tax. More significantly, however, such a situation could not but further contribute to the growing sterility of the traditional channels of promotion. The judges of a *Présidial* or the officers of an *Élection* were thus likely to find themselves being hindered by unorthodox outsiders in their natural progression into the Parlements or the *Chambres des Comptes* or the *Bureaux des Finances*. In these circumstances, to say that the Parlement of Paris, for example, maintained a non-noble intake of about ten per cent throughout the century is to suggest that in real terms the accessibility of that court diminished during the period. It seems that, in the conditions of the eighteenth century, it is far less important to calculate how many people penetrated into the nobility than to see how they did it. The fact that the *anoblis*, to whom one would have expected the non-noble members of the élite to have been attached as symbols of what they themselves could achieve, were on the contrary widely disliked is perhaps evidence more of this situation than of the proverbial arrogance of the *parvenu*.[112] The mistrust of the capitalist financier displayed so markedly by the revolutionary assemblies may well have been the product of the experiences of the majority of their members with

[110] Chaussinand-Nogaret, *art. cit.*

[111] At Elbeuf, for instance, only one family achieved social promotion in this way between 1770 and 1789, despite the town's exceptionally rapid industrial expansion during the century, and even then its members do not appear to have spent much of the year there: Kaplow, *Elbeuf during the Revolutionary Period*, pp. 62-4, and *Histoire de Normandie*, p. 326.

[112] Cf. Meyer, *La noblesse bretonne*, i, p. 431; H. Sée, "Le rôle de la bourgeoisie bretonne à la veille de la Révolution", *Annales de Bretagne*, xxxiv (1920), p. 418; Lefebvre, *Études Orléanaises*, i, p. 208 (*cahier* of the *procureurs*).

their provincial town backgrounds. Finally, it is possible that the
falling price of venal office may have been a reflection of this situation.[113]   One must beware of a straight comparison between the
prices of the mid-seventeenth century and those of the mid-eighteenth.
The former were the inflated prices of a period of high mobility
expressing itself primarily in these offices; the latter were the
more regular levels of calmer conditions. As far as the eighteenth
century itself is concerned, although evidence is still fragmentary,
it is possible that this phenomenon affected above all offices in
courts whose business was declining.[114]   One can argue that it is
testimony to the increasing difficulties of the professional groups
needing both income and opportunity, that it is evidence of natural
adjustments inside the channels of promotion where the decline in
the business of an office — and hence, in the majority of cases, the
decline in its influence and prestige — meant its decline as a route
for social advancement. It is difficult to know how accurate a
general picture the Chancellor d'Aguesseau was drawing when he
bewailed in 1740 the lack of takers for judgeships at the *Sénéchaussée*
level, and contrasted this situation with "that almost incredible
avidity with which we have for so long seen them pursued";[115]
but one may argue that it is witness to the decline of the seventeenth-
century patterns of mobility. Certainly, there was always a very
close correlation between the price of an office and its security as a
social investment, as is shown by the fluctuations of even the prestigious Parlementarian offices later in the century, when the government
began to meddle with the structure of justice. It is significant that
the price of the office of *secrétaire du roi*, however, which was the
easiest entry point for those acceding to the nobility from outside
the traditional channels, suffered no set-back during the century.[116]

---

[113] Cobban, *Social Interpretation of the French Revolution*, pp. 59 ff.; Ford,
Robe and Sword, pp. 148 ff.
[114] Cf. Hufton, *Bayeux in the late Eighteenth Century*, pp. 7-8. Taylor,
"Non-Capitalist Wealth and the Origins of the French Revolution", p. 478,
says, "Generally speaking, an investment in office was an investment in standing". Couturier, *Recherches sur les structures sociales de Châteaudun*, pp. 231-2,
says that the price of office in the royal courts doubled between 1600
and 1660 and then began to collapse; he ascribes the decline to the increasing
pre-emption of business by the Intendant. It is not clear how typical this
chronology is.   [115] Quoted by Ford, *op. cit.*, p. 149, n. 7.
[116] E.g. W. Doyle, "Le prix des charges anoblissantes à Bordeaux au
XVIIIème siècle", *Annales du Midi*, lxxx (1968), p. 75. Note also that the
actual purchase price of many offices represented only a fraction of the total
outlay or costs, so that a study of the fluctuations of nominal prices alone
can be misleading: cf. P. Dawson, "Sur le prix des offices judiciaires à la
fin de l'Ancien Régime," *Rev. d'hist. écon. et soc.*, xlii (1964), pp. 390-2.

The problems which thus faced the professional men and the office-holders were not unlike those that faced another section of the élite, the lesser provincial nobility. Certainly, the poverty-stricken *hobereaux* were only a minority and most nobles managed their affairs with attention,[117] but these families had few opportunities to do more than hold their own financially, and the economic and demographic trends of the century made it even more difficult to do that. Whether from lack of initiative or from a scrupulous regard for the stricter conventions of noble behaviour, many such families had in the past confined themselves to landed property and the exploitation of seigneurial rights, not contending for office and at most putting their sons into the army, although this could be a costly business despite the existence of ten free military colleges and the *École Militaire* in the later years of the Ancien Régime. These men were the anachronistic paradox of the élite in its eighteenth-century form, belonging to its central and lower sections by fortune, prestige and life style, yet laying claim to the whole panoply of attributes which distinguished its highest echelons. Their opportunities for social promotion, in so far as it involved access to prestigious office and the establishment of alliances, connections and protections, were just as limited as those of the non-noble elements of the central and lower élite. Yet, their possession of nobility rendered them far more susceptible to a precise fear of social demotion than non-nobles of similar situation. Naturally, these men were resentful and suspicious of the great Court aristocracy and Parlementarian nobility, who had better access to prestige and profit and yet needed them less. Even the wealthier provincial nobles shared in this prejudice.[118] But more directly, the lesser nobles came into competition with those men whose station in life in all respects other than the possession of nobility was identical to theirs. In the small provincial towns where they spent the winter, they were confronted with the sons and grandsons of tradesmen able to buy the same sort of houses and land, the same sort of clothes and food, the same sort of seigneurial rights and fiscal exemptions.[119] With most of the tangible expressions of their superiority slipping into the common domain, such men were brought to emphasize their more intangible qualities, to insist upon those honours upon which no monarch had

[117] R. Forster, "The Provincial Noble: a Reappraisal", *Amer. Hist. Rev.*, lxviii (1963), pp. 681-91.
[118] Cf. Meyer, *op. cit.*, ii, pp. 863-912; Forster, *The Nobility of Toulouse*, p. 152; Lefebvre, *op. cit.*, i, p. 186.
[119] Cf. Barber, *The Bourgeoisie in Eighteenth-Century France*, pp. 75 ff.

ever bothered to set a price and to recall his low birth to the commoner.[120]   One seigneur in Burgundy even had his honorific privileges written into his rent roll (*terrier*).[121]   It was among the provincial nobility that the notion of derogation had always received the warmest support.[122]   These were the tensions that found expression in the increasing numbers of quarrels between nobles and commoners during the eighteenth century.   Moreover, often unable to compete in the arena of office-holding as much for lack of inclination as of training and capital, these men resented competition in areas which they considered to be their natural preserve, especially the medium-rank positions in the church and the army where impecunious younger sons could be honourably employed. It is in this context that the Ségur Ordinance of 1781 must be understood, for it was forced on the government by a provincial noble lobby against the advice of the great aristocracy and of the War Office.[123]   In 1789, the provincial nobility were not only unwilling to lose the revenue and status of the material privileges which the great aristocracy, socially and financially secure, were prepared to abandon; they were also intent on reorganizing access to prestigious and remunerative positions in their favour.[124]

In this sense, therefore, one may discern a form of "noble reaction" during the eighteenth century.   It was, however, peripheral to the major social problems of the period and, moreover, mild — almost timid — in comparison with the great inquests into nobility that could be used as evidence of such reactions in the sixteenth and seventeenth centuries.   Its importance was that it tended to affect most directly precisely those groups which were having difficulty in the traditional channels of promotion; it was an irritant expressed in the traditional terms most likely to impinge upon them, and it helped to prepare them to identify in a time of crisis the lack of social opportunity as the result of specifically noble exclusiveness. Yet, despite all these developments, it is doubtful whether one can talk of an open social crisis within the élite before 1788-9.   The

[120] Cf. Furet, "Le catéchisme de la Révolution française", pp. 268-9. Meyer, *op. cit.*, ii, pp. 611-2, refers to the great number of lawsuits concerning honorific rights.

[121] P. de Saint-Jacob, *Les paysans de la Bourgogne du nord au dernier siècle de l'Ancien Régime* (Paris, 1960), p. 248.

[122] Grassby, "Social Status and Commercial Enterprise under Louis XIV", p. 19.

[123] Six, "Fallait-il quatre quartiers de noblesse pour être officer à la fin de de l'Ancien Régime?", pp. 47-56.

[124] E.g. Lefebvre, *Études Orléanaises*, i, p. 193; *Cahiers du bailliage de Pont-à-Mousson*, ed. Z. Harsany (Paris, 1946).

expressed grievances of its central and lower elements during the last thirty years of the Ancien Régime were predominantly political and were directed against the system of absolute monarchy.[125] The eighteenth-century Bourbons were reforming monarchs, albeit spasmodically. Yet their reforms usually involved increasing royal authority and appeared for that reason to be acts of arrant despotism, while even their attempts to ensure more equitable justice could be seen as interfering with the independence of the judiciary.[126] Even the future reforming minister Turgot thought that Maupeou's reform of the Parlements was an act leading towards "legal despotism", while in 1788 a wealthy lawyer from Bordeaux was writing of "the need to repress the absolute power of the ministry which would have the monarchy degenerate into despotism".[127] Indeed, such political attitudes were another element of unity for the élite. In the main, the great nobles at Court and in the Parlements yearned for participatory politics, the lesser provincial nobles desired a system in which they could protect their interests, and the professional groups dreamed of a rational, utilitarian government which they thought they saw in classical Rome and which their studies of Roman jurisprudence in law school had taught them to admire.[128] All disliked the steady extension of central control over local affairs since 1660.[129] It was this attitude which produced the acquiescence of the "bourgeoisie" in the "aristocratic revolt" of 1787-8. The National Assembly inherited this struggle against absolutism. The great growth of political comment after 1770 may indeed have been a prime factor in rendering many elements of the élite aware of a common identity. This might be revealed by a closer study of the pre-revolutionary use of such terms as "nation" and "citizen", which may refer essentially to a political nation, socially definable,

[125] D. Mornet, *Les origines intellectuelles de la Révolution française* (Paris, 1933), pp. 243-58.

[126] E.g. the anger of a lawyer at Poitiers when the government, having put a man in prison on a *lettre de cachet* and thus provoked his bankruptcy, proceeded to accord him a safe-conduct on his release for long enough to allow him to escape his creditors — "where are we? In China, in Turkey, or in France?": *Correspondance de Félix Faulcon*, ed. G. Debien (Société des Archives historiques du Poitou, li, 1939), i, p. 205.

[127] W. Doyle, "The Parlements of France and the Breakdown of the Old Régime", *French Hist. Studies*, vi (1970), p. 435; M. Lhéritier, *Les débuts de la Révolution à Bordeaux* (Paris, 1919), p. 43.

[128] Delbèke, *L'action politique et sociale des avocats*, pp. 46 ff. Cf. Dawson, *Provincial magistrates*, pp. 180-1.

[129] E.g. A. Crémieux, "Le particularisme municipal à Marseille en 1789", *La Révolution française*, xxvii (1907), pp. 193-215; N. Temple, "The Control and Exploitation of French Towns during the Ancien Régime", *History*, li (1966), pp. 16-34.

and possibly somewhat analogous to the English seventeenth-century notion of "freeman".[130]

Above all, however, there seems to be very little evidence to suggest that the non-noble elements of the élite were contesting the validity of nobility as a social notion and questioning the system of privilege in a way that would indicate that they were developing a "class consciousness". Indeed, it would appear that right up to 1788 the overwhelming majority believed implicitly in the intrinsic value of a nobility, of noble standards, and hardly debated a system of privilege in which they largely participated or could reasonably aspire to participate.[131] Clearly, there were debates about the exercise of some forms of privilege, but their significance should not be over-emphasized. It would also be quite wrong to see the increasing demands for careers open to talent as incompatible with an acceptance of privilege and nobility. When a provincial lawyer from Loudun denounced venality of office, which put justice into the hands of incompetents, and hoped for the day when office would be distributed on grounds of merit, work and experience, he was essentially commenting upon the promotional difficulties which we have described.[132] One cannot deduce that he was also denouncing by implication the privileges and social prestige acquired by high judicial office. Other equally respectable provincial lawyers, like the future revolutionary Robert Lindet, could argue that, on the contrary, venality of office was a guarantee of impartiality, a safe-guard for the development of experience and talent against the interference of the despot.[133] Both of these arguments, moreover, were being clearly expressed sixty or seventy years before the Revolution.[134] The development of the Republican definition of virtue, mentioned earlier in this essay, was also basically an attempt to marry a desire for careers open to talent with contemporary conceptions of social superiority. Sébastien Mercier, recalling in the 1780s youthful reveries inspired by the classics, remarked that "it is painful to leave Rome, and to find oneself still a commoner

---

[130] Cf. B. C. Shafer, "Bourgeois Nationalism in the Pamphlets on the Eve of the French Revolution", *Jl. of Mod. Hist.*, x (1938), pp. 31-50; J. Godechot, "Nation, Patrie, Nationalisme et Patriotisme en France au XVIIIème siècle", *Ann. hist. Rév. fr.*, xliii (1971), pp. 481-501.

[131] Richet, "Autour des origines idéologiques lointaines de la Révolution française", pp. 12-13; E. L. Eisenstein, "Who intervened in 1788?", *Amer. Hist. Rev.*, lxxi (1965), pp. 77-103; Taylor, "Non-Capitalist Wealth", p. 492.

[132] Debien, *Correspondance de Félix Faulcon*, i, p. 276.

[133] A. Montier, *Robert Lindet* (Paris, 1899), pp. 2-4.

[134] Ford, *Robe and Sword*, pp. 121 ff.

of the rue des Noyers".[135]   Indeed, the notion of utility as a necessary element of nobility was not absent from traditional thinkers. That ultra-noble propagandist, the Chevalier d'Arc, for example, was arguing in the 1750s that the noble had to serve the state and that his only real privilege was the choice of the means, while in the later years of the Ancien Régime some of the higher ranks of the royal administration were developing a notion of the pre-eminence of the public interest over the private interest and were looking at venal office-holding with a critical eye.[136]   Obviously, these later years of the Ancien Régime did represent to a degree a softening-up period for the professional groups, as they did for the peasantry. The contraction of opportunity must have been becoming more sensible.   Moreover, such men must have been affected by the general economic malaise after 1770 in the sense that in a provincial town they would have been intimately connected with the trading community, where they would have their clients, neighbours and relatives.[137]   Yet, none of this was sufficient to make them identify nobility and privilege in general terms as a threat or an obstacle. Daniel Mornet found really no evidence to suggest that the "irresistible movement of opinion", which he perceived in the last two decades of the Ancien Régime, extended to any noticeable movement of respectable opinion against parasitic nobility and privilege.[138] On closer inspection, many of those whom one might claim as heralding the Revolution turn out to be a rather mangy collection of intellectual drop-outs, cranks and failures.[139]   On the contrary, perhaps the clearest statement of the position of the majority of the non-noble elements of the élite on the eve of the Revolution was the one made by the *avocats* of Nuits in Burgundy on the last day of 1788:

> The privileges of the nobility are truly their property. We will respect them all the more because we are not excluded from them and because we can acquire them: great actions, gallantry, courage, personal merits, offices, fortune even, all these are paths that lead us to them. Why, then, suppose that we might think of destroying the source of emulation which guides our labours?[140]

[135] Quoted by Parker, *The Cult of Antiquity and the French Revolutionaries*, p. 39.
[136] Léonard, "La question sociale dans l'armée française au XVIIIème siècle", pp. 147-8; Bosher, *French Finances*, pp. 125-41.
[137] E.g. Sentou, *Fortunes et groupes sociaux à Toulouse*, p. 223; Daumard and Furet, *Structures et relations sociales à Paris au milieu du XVIIIème siècle*, p. 79.   [138] Mornet, *op. cit.*, pp. 243-58, 431-9.
[139] R. Darnton, "The Grub Street Style of Revolution: J-P. Brissot, Police Spy", *Jl. of Mod. Hist.*, xl (1968), pp. 301-27, and "The High Enlightenment and the Low-Life of Literature in Pre-Revolutionary France", *Past and Present*, no. 51 (May 1971), reprinted as chapter 3 of this volume, pp. 53-87 above.
[140] Quoted by Egret, *La Pré-révolution française*, p. 352.

Should one see, therefore, in the economic crisis of 1788-9 the mobilizing factor which produced a "revolutionary bourgeoisie" in the same way that it produced a revolutionary peasantry? Obviously, the trading classes were badly hurt. But most historians agree that these groups were noticeably absent from the revolutionary process. Even though we may well believe that the professional groups expressed some of their grievances, it does not seem that the nature of these grievances would be essentially social in this context. More relevant is the fact that since wealth was an indispensable element of social status, any threat to it was a social threat as much as an economic one. Clearly, a bankruptcy would jeopardize the government annuities (*rentes*) and, significantly enough, the Constituent Assembly took great care to protect this form of investment. Similarly, the economic crisis threatened the payment of annuities served by private persons.[141] But these were really ancillary elements in the composition of the fortune of any member of the élite. The crisis did not affect his land; it may have endangered his revenue in the short term but it did not necessarily endanger his capital base. At all events, such considerations hardly provided an adequate stimulus to political activity in such a radical form.

Should one, therefore, agree with one recent historian in seeing the outbreak of revolution in France as essentially a political event?[142] In this context, the importance of the decision by the Parlement of Paris in September 1788 (largely endorsed by the second Assembly of Notables) that the Estates-General should meet in its form of 1614 has never been ignored.[143] But the nature of its significance has not perhaps always been exactly recognized. This decision polarized the component elements of the élite and crystallized their latent tensions by reintroducing from the early seventeenth century concepts of French society which, already obsolescent at that time, were by now totally erroneous.[144] The conditions demanded for entry into the noble electoral assemblies were far more rigorous than any that had been imposed for noble gatherings and lists during

---

[141] Cf. Vovelle and Roche, "Bourgeois, rentiers, propriétaires". But a great many official annuities were upon such bodies as provincial Estates, the church and town governments, and were less exposed to the consequences of a governmental bankruptcy, while it is far from clear that the private loans accorded by the élite groups were to commercial circles to any significant degree.

[142] [See additions to notes, p. 131 below.]

[143] E.g. Lefebvre, *Quatre-vingt-neuf*, p. 58.

[144] Sée, "Le rôle de la bourgeoisie bretonne", p. 410: "The really active campaign of the Third Estate begins in October (1788)".

the preceding century.[145]   The electoral procedure thus took on the aspect of a seventeenth-century type inquiry into nobility.   The frontier between noble and non-noble, which had been of diminishing importance, was suddenly and artificially reimposed.   The decision to separate the nobility from the Third Estate pushed the central and lower echelons of the élite down into the Third Estate.   It rent asunder what was essentially by now a homogeneous social unit, and identified quite gratuitously a section of that unit as irremediably inferior and to be confused not merely with the trading classes but also with the manual labourers and the vile and abject poor.   It is in this context that one must understand the apparent paradox of the fact that the leading voices at the national level against this decision in late 1788 were those of "liberal" nobles.[146]   As far as those who were directly affected by these measures are concerned, it needs no temerity to suggest that the *anobli* Le Chapelier, for instance, discovered his revolutionary vocation when he was excluded, despite his bitter protests, from the electoral assembly of the Breton nobility.[147]   But, in general, the position of the *anobli* was naturally somewhat ambivalent.   It was men further down in the channels of promotion who reacted most categorically to the situation.   At Rennes, to use examples from Brittany again, it was the *procureurs* of the *Présidial* who led the attack on the oligarchy of *anoblis* in the Municipality for refusing to endorse a demand for vote by head, and it was the *avocats* who organized the electoral campaign there, while at Saint-Malo and in most of the other Breton towns except Nantes the professional groups again took the initiative in the agitation.[148]   This was the situation in most of France.   In Provence, however, although the same direct effects of the decisions relating to the calling of the Estates-General are visible, the situation was somewhat different in that the polarization was already well under way by this

[145] Brette, "La noblesse et ses privilèges pécuniaires en 1789", pp. 97 and 124.
[146] Cf. Eisenstein, "Who intervened in 1788?"   Note also that only ten of the *General Cahiers* of the Third Estate thought that its representatives were sovereign and should ignore those of the privileged Orders: Hyslop, *French Nationalism in 1789*, p. 69.   The liberal noble Gouy d'Arcy wrote at the end of 1788, "What is an Order in an Empire?   It is an essential portion of the government, it is a fundamental class of society, and in both of these respects, there are only two Orders in France, the patricians and the plebeians": quoted by A. Decouflé, "L'aristocratie française devant l'opinion publique à la veille de la Révolution", in R. Besnier (ed.), *Etudes d'histoire économique et sociale du XVIIIème siècle* (Paris, 1966), p. 37.
[147] Meyer, *La noblesse bretonne*, i, pp. 436–8; Cf. Egret, *La Pré-révolution française*, p. 353.
[148] Sée, *art. cit.*

time.[149]   But, at root, a similar catalyst had operated, for the conflict took shape in the debate during the later months of 1787 over whether the provincial Estates of Provence should be re-established in the form of their last meeting in 1639, a debate which the Third Estate lost.   Once again, the lawyers had taken a leading part and continued to do so in 1788.

It was their experience of problems in social promotion which rendered many of the people thus implicitly demoted by the Parlement's decision so sensitive to such distinctions.[150]   This helps to explain why the traditional liberal professions provided so many of the leaders of the Third Estate movement at the local level during the winter of 1788-9.   This decision was all the more critical because it seemed to arbitrate definitively between two contradictory trends in recent comparable situations: it was all the more of a shock because the Estates-General were supremely more important than any of those situations and because this decision ran counter to the conceptions which the government had apparently been favouring. In 1787, following an earlier experiment by Necker in the Berry and a plan submitted to the Assembly of Notables by Calonne, Loménie de Brienne had established a three-tier structure of municipal, intermediary and provincial assemblies to handle some aspects of local government.[151]   Although a proportion of seats in all these bodies was reserved to the privileged orders, the system called for elections to the lowest assembly among the men of property on a tax franchise and for each assembly to designate to the one above it. Above all, there was to be no distinction by Order, voting was to be by head, and the Third Estate had double representation.   Moreover, the events at Vizille in the Dauphiné in July 1788 seemed to confirm this trend towards the unity of an élite of comfortable men of property. On the other hand, the decision of September 1788 echoed the most exclusive and antiquated formulas of representation which the government had conceded, by omission at least, to the renewed Estates of Provence.   Together these two events, reinforced in

---

[149] J. Egret, "La Pré-révolution en Provence", Ann. hist. Rév. fr., xxvi (1954), pp. 195-213.

[150] See the instruction given by the electoral assembly of the Third Estate of the Forez to its deputies to refuse to admit any of the distinctions of nobility which might humiliate the Third Estate.   Note also the great protests against the imposition of distinctively different costumes on the three Estates in April 1789; the Forezian deputies argued, significantly enough, that "the Third Estate's interest is that nothing should be innovated" (my italics).   Receuil de documents relatifs aux séances des Etats-Généraux, ed. G. Lefebvre and A. Terroine, 2 vols. (Paris, 1953-62), i, pp. 69, 76-82.

[151] P. Renouvin, Les assemblées provinciales de 1787 (Paris, 1921), pp. 79 ff.

December 1788 by the widely-read and extremely reactionary *Mémoire des Princes présenté au roi*, could appear as the final implementation of a threat long expressed. We do not yet possess a close study of the disputes between nobles and commoners during the years preceding the Revolution. But it is possible to argue that they usually arose because the nobleman acted in such a way as to suggest not merely that the respectable commoner was inferior socially, which in relative terms within the élite he obviously was, but that he was on a par with the vulgar mass. The nobleman who insisted on his precedence in church would certainly mortify the pride of the well-to-do commoner; but the nobleman who thrashed the son of a bourgeois was treating him as he would treat a domestic servant or a street porter — it was even worse when he had the job done for him by his lackeys.[152] This is of course an extreme example. The propagandists of the Third Estate in Brittany still remembered the reception of the demand formulated ten years previously that the provincial Estates authorize commoners to be admitted to the charitable institution for poor gentlemen, which they indeed had helped to subsidize.[153] "What, do they not have the poorhouses (*hôpitaux*), the workhouses (*maisons de force*), and the prisons?" a nobleman had inquired, thereby implicitly excluding all commoners from the élite and consigning them without distinction to those institutions which catered not merely for the honest though humble poor, but also for the vagabonds and beggars who stood outside society altogether. Of course, all this was very tame when compared with noble behaviour during the previous two centuries.[154] It is significant of the changing situation of the commoner elements of the élite that their sensitivity to this kind of attitude should have been such as to make them often the aggressors in violent quarrels.

This, then, was what Mallet du Pan was expressing in his oft-quoted observation — "The nature of the debate has completely

---

[152] Already in 1700 a wealthy merchant resented being described by any formula that might also be used of his tailor: Grassby, "Social Status and Commercial Enterprise", pp. 27-8. Note also the agitation over the militia during the century and Barbier's comment that it put the son of the wholesale merchant on the same level as servants, workers and shopboys: E. J. F. Barbier, *Journal historique et anecdotique du règne de Louis XV*, ed. A. de Villegille, 4 vols. (Paris, 1857-75), ii, pp. 353-4. Mornet, *op. cit.*, p. 436, cites some cases of such quarrels, but they are very uninformative, although army officers (and I have referred to their stress zone situation) figure rather prominently in the examples he has chosen.

[153] Meyer, *La noblesse bretonne*, ii, p. 1,114.

[154] E.g. E. Fléchier, *Mémoires sur les Grands-Jours d'Auvergne*, ed. M. Chéruel (Paris, 1856), *passim*.

changed. King, despotism, and constitution are now very secondary questions; the war is between the Third Estate and the other two Orders".[155]   In this sense, the doubling of the representation of the *Tiers* was a wholly irrelevant concession.   The revolt of the Third Estate was a revolt against a loss of status by the central and lower sections of the élite with the approval of those elements of the trading groups which were on the threshold of the élite.   It was this social group which became the "revolutionary bourgeoisie".   The *abbé* Sieyès became such an influential personality because he expressed precisely their aspirations.[156]   Under the rhetoric of his most celebrated pamphlet, *Qu'est-ce que le Tiers-état?* he was not in fact pressing the social and political claims of all those he defined as the Third Estate in the first chapter, but only those of the group which he called "the available classes of the Third Estate".[157]   In all his political writings, Sieyès conceived of society as composed essentially of two peoples, the property owners and the "work machines", and demanded the union of the property owners in defence of property against the poor.   He militated against the privileged orders because their existence prevented that union; from the beginning to the end of the Revolution he extolled the notables as a homogeneous social and political élite.   In 1789, the system of elections served this revolt for, whereas the direct election procedure for the First and Second Estates produced a faithful reflection of the stress zones within them, the indirect elections of the Third Estate not only eliminated the non-élite groups (and therefore the stress zones that their relations with the élite constituted), but also brought in a solid and unified group of professional men, that is to say precisely those who were the most directly affected by the contraction of the traditional channels of promotion.   Once the Third Estate had taken control in July 1789, the National Assembly abandoned the Ancien Régime structure of privilege with reluctance and considerable reservations in August.   It was hardly the act of an assembly of bourgeois liberating themselves from the restricting fetters of feudalism.   Indeed, the *abbé* Sieyès did all he could to reverse it.[158]   These men became the champions of an attack on privilege in part by the force of the logic of revolutionary politics in the context of the popular revolt of 1789.   But they also did so as

[155] Lefebvre, *Quatre-vingt-neuf*, p. 58.
[156] E. Sieyès, *Qu'est-ce que le Tiers-état?*, ed. R. Zapperi (Geneva, 1970), especially pp. 27-43.
[157] *Ibid*, p. 143: "les classes disponibles du Tiers-état".
[158] *Ibid.*, pp. 31-3.

a consequence of a number of confusions.   Obliged to become the leaders of the Third Estate, they presented their own grievances as those of the whole of the Third Estate.   Certainly, they expressed hostility to the nobility, but their grievance was one of political and social definition in the precise context of 1788-9.   However, the mere fact that they did express this hostility encouraged the peasantry, initially at least, to identify privilege predominantly with the nobility rather than with the élite as a whole and to confuse the grievances of the "revolutionary bourgeoisie" with its own.[159]   It was this which enabled the revolutionary behaviour of the representatives of the Third Estate to find support among the protest movements of the vile and abject sections of the community, which were not their natural allies.   Furthermore, in 1788-9 the circumstances and background which have been elaborated in this essay allowed the "revolutionary bourgeoisie" to identify, erroneously and in general terms, the Ancien Régime nobility as an exclusive group threatening its social position, while the political developments of the early days of the Estates-General incited it to confuse this conception of the nobility with the system of absolute monarchy, and to see the two as interdependent and as allies.   But such a thought-process necessarily imposed the identification of the nobility as a distinct social group, which, as we have seen, was an unrealistic enterprise; the easiest solution to this paradox was to indulge in another confusion and to identify the nobility by the traditional system of privileges which had originally been specifically noble attributes.   Thus, spokesmen of the Third Estate could quite happily refer to the first two Estates as the "privileged Orders", forgetting that they themselves were in many cases at least partially privileged.   It was for this reason that the attachment of the "revolutionary bourgeoisie" to that system of privilege, in which they themselves participated, was weakened.   In mid-1789 the combination of the counter-offensive of the Ancien Régime and anti-privilege pressure from below brought the revolutionary leaders to jettison privilege.

However, the true sense of the rejection of the Ancien Régime system of privilege by the "revolutionary bourgeoisie" was revealed by the Constitution of 1791.   In this document, this assembly of men from the Ancien Régime élite redefined that same élite in such

[159] Cf. Lefebvre, *Études Orléanaises*, i, p. 73: "The wealthy peasants (*laboureurs*) and the artisans only spoke out frankly against the seigneur . . . The hostility towards traders and members of the liberal professions, and more generally towards all town dwellers, which indubitably existed, does not transpire . . .".

a way that it could never be divided again by artificial distinctions within it. The characteristic of élite status was recognized to be the control of landed property. The tangible attribute of élite status was defined as access to public office and the political control of the country. This is the sense of a Constitution which made every public position elective and largely confined eligibility to men of some substance expressed in property. The Thermidorians and the Directorials reasserted these same conceptions of politics and society far more explicitly and successfully, as the surviving Jacobins, not to mention Babeuf, clearly understood.[160] The Constitution of 1791 in no way implied a rejection of the Ancien Régime nobility, for it was comprised within this definition as much as were wealthy non-nobles. It was merely because some noble elements chose rather vociferously not to participate that the Revolution was made to appear as a revolt against the nobility as a social class. In the same way, the technical detail of the ordering of the Estates-General, while crystallizing the tensions of the Ancien Régime, also forced them to be expressed in terms which can easily be taken as those of a conflict between nobles and bourgeois, a conflict which did not exist in any very meaningful sense in the eighteenth century. Nevertheless, the redefinition of the élite by the Revolution was indubitably of fundamental importance. Although nobility as an institution was only momentarily abolished and Napoleon was indeed to reinforce it in a certain sense, the revolutionary crisis did result in the emergence of an élite defined in terms of landholding and function, with the hereditary element confined to the simple passage of wealth and its advantages from one generation to another in a family. The Revolution did therefore provide a social framework within which the acquisition of nobility was to be increasingly irrelevant and which allowed élite status to develop into the attribute of men of wealth however acquired and however expressed. In this sense, we may say that the Revolution made the bourgeoisie even if it was not made by the bourgeoisie.

[160] Cf. I. Woloch, *Jacobin Legacy* (Princeton, 1970), especially pp. 155-6. But note the social assumptions expressed by the Jacobin Garnerin in the middle of Year II when he denounced speculation by the Jews; "There are some among them rich to the tune of fifteen or twenty millions' worth of assignats, and who do not have a sou's worth of landed property": Véron-Réville, *Histoire de la Révolution française dans le département du Haut-Rhin* (Paris, 1865), p. 194. R. Marx, *Recherches sur la vie politique de l'Alsace pré-révolutionnaire et révolutionnaire* (Strasbourg, 1966), *passim*, contains interesting illustrations of the practice of this situation at all levels throughout the Revolution. Cf. Cobban, *Social Interpretation of the French Revolution*, pp. 81 ff.

ADDITIONS TO NOTES, 1976

[61] For a slightly different emphasis see the recent article by Norman Hampson, "The French Revolution and the Nationalisation of Honour", in M. R. D. Foot (ed.), *War and Society* (London, 1973), pp. 199-212.

[71] This argument was based on G. Six, "Fallait-il quatre quartiers de noblesse pour être officier à la fin de l'Ancien Régime?", *Revue d'hist. mod.*, iv (1929), pp. 47-56, and Reinhard, "Elite et noblesse", p. 10. It has, however, been invalidated by David Bien's article referred to below in note 75.

[75] This paragraph is now shown to be unsound by D. D. Bien, "La réaction aristocratique avant 1789: l'exemple de l'armée", *Annales E.S.C.*, xxix (1974), pp. 23-48, 505-34. This important article demonstrates that commoner entry into the officer corps was never as great as had been previously believed. The Ségur Ordinance was aimed at the scions of wealthy *anobli* families, for its promoters wanted a professional officer corps drawn from "army families", which was what most families of *noblesse de race* could claim to be. However, Professor Bien does not believe this to be evidence of a wider "aristocratic reaction", while his important calculations of the number of commoners acceding to all ennobling offices tend to support the arguments put forward elsewhere in this essay.

[78] The hierarchy of the law courts in terms of prestige and wealth is elaborated in P. Dawson, *Provincial magistrates and revolutionary politics in France, 1789-1795* (Cambridge, Mass., 1972), chaps. ii and iii. Pp. 101-9 especially provide clear illustration of the social promotional mechanisms of these offices. Unfortunately, this book appeared too late for my essay to profit from its wealth of material.

[142] Taylor, "Non-Capitalist Wealth", p. 491; see also the tentative elaboration of this view in his article "Revolutionary and nonrevolutionary content in the *cahiers* of 1789", *French Hist. Studies*, vii (1972), pp. 479-502.

5. The Survival of the Nobility During the French Revolution*

ROBERT FORSTER

"THE WHOLE DEVELOPMENT OF FRENCH SOCIETY", WRITES PROFESSOR Cobban, "appears in a different light if we recognize that the Revolution was a triumph for the conservative, propertied, landowning classes, large and small".[1] How new this conclusion is or what is meant by "conservative" are not at issue in this article.[2] The question here is the "triumph" of the "large" landowners.

Before the Revolution the largest landowners in France were the nobles. Representing perhaps one per cent of the total population, the Second Estate owned about one quarter of the soil directly, with seigneurial claims over considerably more.[3] Small enough by English standards, the individual holdings of a French nobleman (five to ten *métairies* of 40 acres each) were substantial when contrasted with the holdings of the average commoner, whether a peasant cultivator or a proprietor *non-exploitant*.[4]

Did the Revolution actually benefit these nobles, at least as landlords? The question is not so absurd as it may at first appear. Many nobles escaped the effects of anti-noble legislation by remaining discreetly on their domains, and their names begin to re-emerge among the prefects of the Empire and the "notables" of the Restor-

---

* This is a revised version of a paper presented to a meeting of the American Historical Association in December 1965.

[1] Alfred Cobban, *The Social Interpretation of the French Revolution* (Cambridge, 1964), pp. 169-70.

[2] Marcel Marion wrote in 1908: "The sale of national land thus greatly contributed to form or to strengthen that mass of landed proprietors, large, middling, but, above all, small that have dominated France in the nineteenth century...". M. Marion, *La vente des biens nationaux* (Paris, 1908), p. 419. Cobban has, however, shifted the emphasis from "small" to "large". This *is* new.

[3] Georges Lefebvre, *The Coming of the French Revolution*, trans. R. R. Palmer (Princeton, 1947), p. 114. Franklin Ford, *Robe and Sword* (Cambridge, Mass., 1953), pp. 29-31. For a regional summary of noble landholdings, see G. Lefebvre, "Répartition de la propriété et de l'exploitation foncières à la fin de l'Ancien Régime", *Etudes sur la Révolution française* (Paris, 1954), pp. 216-8.

[4] C. E. Labrousse, *Origines et aspects économiques et sociaux de la Révolution française, 1774-1791* ("Les Cours de Sorbonne", n.d.), i, p. 29. Labrousse estimates the average noble holding at 150 hectares (370·7 acres). Only a few non-noble proprietors might attain this figure. These would usually be merchants of the port cities. See H. Robert, *Les trafics coloniaux du port de La Rochelle au XVIIIe siècle* (Poitiers, 1960), pp. 190-8 and *passim*.

ation and after.[5] Cobban broaches the issue somewhat more cautiously when he states that "it would be interesting to know to what extent, in different parts of the country, the noblesse kept its lands during the Revolution, or regained them after temporary loss".[6]

There is, however, more to the question of noble survival than the immediate impact of Revolutionary legislation on the economic position of the nobility. The Revolution accelerated a change in attitudes, among nobles as well as non-nobles, that irrevocably dislocated the hierarchical society of the Old Régime. Even if Comte de Villèle could have reconstructed the landed aristocracy with the famous indemnity bill of 1825, it was impossible to recreate the habits and mores to sustain it. In the light of Professor Cobban's recent book this point is worth restating.[7] Therefore, I propose to review what we know about the fate of noble fortunes during the Revolution and to insist that this economic material be related to more subtle changes, both legal and psychological, that affected the social and economic position of the nobility in the nineteenth century.

I

The first economic blow against the nobility was delivered on the night of 4 August 1789. Historians have been so interested in the burden of seigneurial dues on the peasant that they have often failed to consider what portion of noble revenues the dues represented. Curiously, the text-book generalization that the dues were not burdensome on the peasants and yet furnished the nobility with the bulk of their revenues dies hard. The fact is that in some regions the dues represented only a small supplement to noble income while in others they might compose over half the receipts from the land. Near Toulouse, Bordeaux, and Le Mans, they represented only 8, 5, and 8 per cent respectively, while in Aunis and Saintonge they amounted to 63 per cent of noble landed income.[8] Consider the plaintive

[5] Local studies are beginning to extend into the Restoration, making use of electoral-college lists. See Pierre Bouyoux, "Les 600 plus imposés du département de la Haute-Garonne en l'an X", *Annales du Midi*, lxx (1958), pp. 317-27.

[6] Cobban, *The Social Interpretation*, p. 87.

[7] Cobban plays down the importance of the change in the type of landlord brought about by the Revolution. "It was, of course, *to some extent* a different class and type of landowner from that of the ancien régime, . . .": Cobban, *The Social Interpretation*, p. 89 (Italics mine). Cobban hardly labours this crucial point.

[8] See my *Nobility of Toulouse in the Eighteenth Century* (Baltimore, 1960), p. 38, and "The Noble Wine Producers of the Bordelais in the 18th Century", *Econ. Hist. Rev.*, 2nd ser., xiv (1961), p. 23; Paul Bois, *Paysans de l'Ouest* (Le Mans, 1960), pp. 400-1; the figure for Saintonge is based on 18 noble leases. Archives Départementales (Charante-Maritime), Q-287.

words of Marquise de La Tour du Pin: "We never recovered from the blow to our fortune delivered on that night".   According to the marquise, property returning nothing but seigneurial dues "was very much in usage in the south-west part of France" (Quercy, Saintonge).[9] Wherever the *champart* (*terrage, agrière*) or *dîme inféodée* were collected the seigneurial dues were not negligible.   In Northern Burgundy even the *cens* became a regular five per cent rent on the land.[10] Chateaubriand tells us that Combourg was "rich in seigneurial rights", yielding 70,000 *livres* one year from the *lods et ventes*.   After abolition of these rights Combourg returned less than 10,000 *livres*.   There is now good reason to believe that Chateaubriand's estate was typical of the large seigneuries in Britanny.[11]

For some nobles, then, the abolition of seigneurial dues was a heavy loss and it seems that compensation payments provided by the laws of the Constituent Assembly were few.   Peasants simply refused to pay dues after 1791.   True, in cases where share-cropping was involved, there is some evidence that the dues were converted into supplementary rents.[12]   But this could not be done in the case of the ordinary *censitaire* whose dues had made up the bulk of seigneurial income.   Moreover, the abolition of the seigneurial system meant more than a loss of income to the nobles.   It is often forgotten that seigneurial rights had been an effective aid to noble domain-building. *Cens* arrears could no longer be employed to create indebtedness and prepare for foreclosure.   Nor was it any longer possible to exercise the right of option in order to force sales.   The rights of *triage* and *terre abandonnée* were not only abolished; village communities and individual peasants attempted to retrieve their lost lands with some success.   Furthermore, seigneurial justice should not be characterized as a defunct institution before 1789.   In the eyes of the average

[9] La Tour du Pin, Marquise de, *Journal d'une femme de 50 ans, 1778-1815* (Paris, 1913), i, pp. 199-200.

[10] Pierre de Saint Jacob, *Les paysans de la Bourgogne du Nord au dernier siècle de l'Ancien Régime* (Paris, 1960), pp. 439 f.

[11] François-Réne de Chateaubriand, *Mémoires d'Outre-Tombe* (Paris, 1846), i, p. 73; George Collas, "Dix ans au château de Combourg", *Annales de Bretagne*, xxxv (1921-3), pp. 30-1. Cf. Jean Meyer, *La Noblesse Bretonne* (Paris, 1966), ii, pp. 651 f. for a discussion of the composition of noble revenues in Brittany. Seigneurial dues "often" represented over 50 per cent of landed income, especially on large seigneuries such as those belonging to the Duc de Penthièvre or certain members of the *Parlement* of Rennes.

[12] A striking example of this was the conversion of the *dîme* in the share-cropping contracts with the salt-makers on Oleron into a supplementary rent: see M. Delafosse and C. Laveau, *Le commerce du sel de Brouage aux XVIIᵉ et XVIIIᵉ siècles* (Paris, 1960), p. 32; P. Massé, "Survivances des droits féodaux dans l'Ouest (1793-1902)", *Annales historiques de la Révolution française*, no. 181 (1965), pp. 269-98.

villager of the Old Régime it gave the seigneur a status and a power
that made him much more than just a landlord.   The *seigneur-
justicier* represented local authority, and in ordinary property cases it
was wise for the half-literate peasant to remember it.[13]   This
institution was now gone.

The Constituent Assembly also abolished all tax privileges.   What
did this mean to a country nobleman with an income of 10,000 *livres*?
Whereas the *vingtièmes* and capitation scarcely claimed more than five
per cent of his net income, the new *contribution foncière* extracted
close to sixteen per cent, and it was enforced.[14]   During the Revolutionary decade, the resident nobleman was also called upon to
contribute considerable sums to the Patriotic Gift, the "*Quart*", the
Forced Loan — opportunities to demonstrate loyalty to the new
régime that no *ci-devant* should forego.   But above all, it is too easy
to underestimate the blow that fiscal equality dealt to noble prestige.
The *gentilhomme* was now a *taillable*.

The abolition of the venality of office was perhaps less of a financial
loss than is usually assumed.   Office-holders received compensation
early in the Revolution.   Although the payment was in *assignats*,
there is no reason why the paper could not be used to buy church
land or at least pay taxes and debts. Surely, most of the fifty-five
noble purchasers of church land in the department of Vienne paid in
assignats.[15]   On the other hand, the abrupt demise of the *parlements*
was a large chip out of the judicial shield of the noblesse.   Not even
the appellate courts of the Restoration would be quite so kind to
gentlemen in distress, financial or otherwise.

II

How much noble land was expropriated and sold by the Revolutionary governments?   To answer this we must first know what
proportion of the Second Estate emigrated.   According to Greer,
16,431 nobles appear on the list of émigrés for all of France.   This
represents eight per cent of the order if we accept 200,000 as the best
estimate of the total number of nobles — men, women, and children.
Thirty-five per cent of the noble émigrés (5,695) were army and naval
officers while only fifteen per cent (2,506) were women and only 0·5
per cent (872) were former members of the *parlements*.   Greer also

---

[13] See Marc Bloch, *Les caractères originaux de l'histoire rurale française*
(Paris, 1952), pp. 131-55.
[14] Jacques Godechot, *Les Institutions de la France sous la Révolution et
l'Empire* (Paris, 1951), p. 135.
[15] *Ibid.*, p. 167.

notes that noble emigration was remarkably consistent in number throughout all the departments.[16]   It might be assumed, therefore, that the typical noble émigré was a man in the prime of life with some military aspirations who would maintain the honour of the family by joining the Princes abroad.   The comment of Madame des Escherolles supports the impression that much more than eight per cent of noble *families* were touched by the emigration:

> Everyone who was noble and loyal to his king felt he was performing a duty. This decision was quickly made.   One could see old military men, peaceful people, and heads of families respond to this high-minded appeal, and without hesitation, leave the comforts of the foyer for the painful and adventurous life of a simple soldier . . . It was very difficult to resist the pressure of public opinion . . . One must leave or be dishonored.[17]

Assuming that one third of the nobility represented children under twelve who did not emigrate and that one half of the remainder were women, there would be about 66,000 noble males over twelve in France in 1789.   According to Greer, 13,925 of these emigrated or 21 per cent, if one accepts the total above.   An intelligent guess might be that 1·5 male nobles emigrated per family.   This would suggest that almost 10,000 noble *families* (and their property) were affected by the emigration, that is, about one noble family in four.   Moreover, those who did not emigrate were likely to be among the poorest members of the order.

Better evidence for this assumption that a large portion of the nobility was affected by the laws against émigrés may be taken from the indemnity of 1825.   Among 130,000 émigrés of all classes, 25,000 received indemnification for their lost property.   Lacking a complete analysis of all departments, we have nonetheless some suggestive samples.   In the Côte d'Or 64 per cent of the 260 émigrés indemnified were nobles; in the Meuse 57 per cent of 426.   Even in the Doubs, which had an unusually high peasant and clerical emigration because of the insurrection there, 32 per cent of 442 indemnified were nobles.   When one adds to this sampling the fact that 150 peers received indemnities, André Gain's conclusion that the "majority of the dispossessed were nobles" seems convincing.[18]   Would it be legitimate to conclude, then, that at least 12,500 noble *families* (50 per cent of the 25,000 indemnified) lost some land in the Revolution ?

[16] Donald Greer, *The Incidence of the Emigration during the Revolution* (Cambridge, Mass., 1951), pp. 84-5, 112.

[17] Alexandrine des Écherolles, *Une Femme Noble sous la Terreur* (Paris, 1879), pp. 12-13.   See also Comtesse de Genlis, *Mémoires*, ed. F. Barrière (Paris, 1856), p. 285, for substantially the same observation about the dishonour of delayed emigration.

[18] André Gain, *La Restauration et les biens des Emigrés* (Nancy, 1929), ii, pp. 211-4, 454-76.

Gain's monumental and too often neglected study of the indemnity of 1825 draws another important conclusion from the distribution of the indemnity.   Each department had from five to fifteen large indemnities (over 225,000 francs) suggesting to Gain that "the large proprietors were always among the fugitives".[19]   This means that the wealthiest landlords were struck by expropriation and a large part of their lands sold.   Consider Gain's list of compensation for 122 peers. These include the largest noble estates — the vineyards of Richelieu in the Médoc (465,000 francs), the domains of La Tremouille on the Sarthe and on the Aisne (439,894 francs), of Montmorency-Laval outside of Paris (529,128), of Choiseul-Stainville in the Jura (765,988) for a total of fifty-one million francs capital or an average of 420,000 per peer!   Such a capital represents about 23,000 *livres* landed income in 1790.   The thirty-one largest indemnities (over one million francs each) were *all* awarded to nobles, from the Duc d'Orléans (12,704,691) down to Mlle. da la Frezelière (1,000,370). Altogether, 842 indemnities of more than 225,000 francs each were awarded, most of them to nobles.[20]

According to Gain, then, the large noble landlords in 1789 were hard hit by expropriation.   Yet, having accounted for some 150 *grands seigneurs* and several hundred more "large" noble landlords, what about the rest of the 12,500 families who lost some land?   One would hope to find the statistical answer in the numerous local studies of *Documents relatifs à la vente des biens nationaux*.   Unfortunately for this purpose, these studies are very disappointing.   Georges Lefebvre revealed no small measure of irritation with most of these publications when he said that "no attempt has been made, and it is of capital importance, to establish the division of land among the different social classes statistically".[21]

Given these limitations and after a cursory examination of ten regions, the following conclusion can be drawn.   In the district of Sens (89 parishes) and in the departments of the Sarthe, Haute-Garonne, Ille-et-Vilaine, and Eure noble losses were "light", even minimal.   In the district of Vire (two cantons) and the departments of the Nord, Côte d'Or, and the Gironde noble losses were "heavy", perhaps a third of their original holdings if the Nord is typical.   For the tenth region, Saintonge, my estimate is based on only twenty

[19] *Ibid.*, ii, p. 193.
[20] *Ibid.*, ii, pp. 191-2, 223.
[21] Georges Lefebvre, *Etudes*, p. 226.   Marc Bouloiseau outlines the relevant sources and method for a systematic statistical study of émigré property in his recent handbook, *Etude de l'émigration et de la vente des biens des émigrés* (Paris, 1963).

noble families whose land was divided under the émigré laws of the Directory. These nobles lost 23 per cent of an average net fortune of 88,000 francs. Given the modesty of these fortunes, such losses must be considered heavy. Thus, in five regions the losses of noble land were almost negligible, while in five other regions of roughly the same area the losses were appreciable.[22]

The impact of the laws against noble émigrés depended on a variety of local factors. The local Revolutionary administration was apparently vigorous and efficient at Bordeaux, but slow and negligent at Toulouse. Moreover, the vineyards of Bordeaux lent themselves more readily to division and sale than did the more compact *métairies* of the Toulousain. Most important, a recently thriving commercial port provided a good market for national land, while bureaucratic, conservative Toulouse lacked commercial capital. Thus Marcel Marion concludes his study of the Gironde by asserting that the "spoliation of the émigré nobility was almost total", while Pierre Bouyoux tells us that one quarter of the 600 wealthiest "notables" at Toulouse in 1802 were descendants of old noble families and that almost all of the former Parlementary and municipal nobles (over 200 more) were among them.[23]

The most important category of land restored to the noble émigré was forest. Confiscated forests were not divided into small lots and sold but kept by the Revolutionary government as national domain.

[22] For a general treatment see Georges Lefebvre, "La vente des biens nationaux", *Etudes sur la Révolution française* (Paris, 1954), pp. 223-45. For the district of Sens, A. Gain, *La Restauration et les biens des émigrés*, ii, p. 186, based on C. Porée, *Documents relatifs à la vente des biens nationaux dans le district de Sens* (Auxerre, 1912). For the district of Vire, also Gain, ii, p. 423, based on C. Nicolle, *La vente des biens nationaux à Vire* (Vire, 1923). For the Gironde, Marcel Marion, *La vente des biens nationaux* (Paris, 1908). For the Sarthe, Paul Bois, *Paysans de l'Ouest* (Le Mans, 1960), pp. 309-38. For Haute-Garonne, H. Martin, *Documents relatifs à la vente des biens nationaux, district de Toulouse* (Toulouse, 1916, 1924) and P. Bouyoux, "Les 600 plus imposés du département de la Haute-Garonne en l'an X", *Annales du Midi*, lxx (1958), pp. 317-27. For Ille-et-Vilaine, Rébillon et Guillou, *Documents relatifs à la vente des biens nationaux, Districts de Rennes et de Bain* (Rennes, 1911) and E. Tanguy, "L'Emigration dans l'Ille-et-Vilaine", *Annales de Bretagne*, xxi (1905-6), pp. 160-5. For Eure, J. Vidalenc, *Le Département de l'Eure sous la monarchie constitutionnelle 1814-1848* (Paris, 1952), pp. 363-72. For the Nord, G. Lefebvre, *Les paysans du Nord* (Lille, 1924), pp. 414-545 and G. Lefebvre, *Etudes . . .*, pp. 241, 237. For Côte d'Or, Archives Départementales (Côte d'Or), Q-403 for a list of dispossessed proprietors, including 57 identifiable nobles, 39 of whom suffered heavily (50 to 1,000 "sales"). For Saintonge, Archives Départementales (Charente-Maritime), Q-248, 249. These nobles lost part of their estates under the law of *présuccession*, 9 Floréal An III (April 28 1795).

[23] Marion, *La Vente des biens nationaux*, p. 208, pp. 391-3; Bouyoux, "Les 600 plus imposés", p. 323.

As a result, they could be restored to their original owners intact in 1814.[24] Thus the family Saulx-Tavannes recovered over 5,000 acres of woodland north of Dijon, and the Comte d'Artois regained some 25,000 acres of forest scattered from the Ardennes to Poitiers.[25] No doubt noble landlords of heavily forested areas in Burgundy, Brittany, and Nivernais survived expropriation much better than owners of grainland and vineyard. Large noble holdings of forest in the Sarthe may help explain the extensive reconstitution of noble domains in that department between 1800 and 1830.[26] Similarly, in the district of Sens one third of the sequestered noble land was woodland and was returned in 1814.[27] The largest noble landowners remaining after the Revolution were likely to be owners of forest.

A certain amount of lost land was also bought back by noble families either through their agents during the emigration or openly after Brumaire. Precise statistics are again limited.[28] The most striking case is the Sarthe where the nobles lost about 100,000 acres and repurchased (or at least regained) the entire amount by 1830.[29] No doubt, by a combination of shrewdness and patience, by the loyalty of agents and *fermiers*, and by profiting from the insecurity of the new owners, the émigré nobles reconstituted a part of their original holdings. Another article could be devoted to the various subterfuges employed by the nobility to retain or retrieve their land.

On the other hand, one hears less about those who failed to regain their alienated property. Madame des Echerolles tells us of her father's futile efforts to deal with the new owners and comments:

> Many émigrés, more fortunate than ourselves, regained a *part* of their land; by strict economy and great activity, they found the means to pay the debts contracted for the repurchase of their homes . . . There were families destined to go under; ours never came back. All our efforts to keep ourselves afloat were in vain.[30]

[24] Gain, *La Restauration*, i, p. 156; Marion, *La Vente des biens nationaux*, p. 368.

[25] For Saulx-Tavannes, Arch. Dép. (Côte d'Or), Q-1117-1118. For Artois, P. Lefranc, "Les propriétés privées de Charles X dans la Vienne, vicissitudes et procès", *Bulletin de la Société des Antiquaires de l'Ouest*, vii (1964), p. 527.

[26] P. Bois, *Paysans de l'Ouest*, pp. 331-3.

[27] Gain, *La Restauration*, ii, p. 186.

[28] In the Nord, the *nobles* lost 75,000 acres and repurchased 17,500; in the Côtes-du-Nord the émigrés lost 24,000 acres and repurchased about 12,000; in the district of Rouen the émigrés lost 5,000 acres and regained 3,000: Lefebvre, *Etudes* . . . , pp. 237, 244; Gain, *La Restauration*, ii, p. 422.

[29] Bois, *Paysans de l'Ouest*, pp. 313-23.

[30] Echerolles, *Mémoires*, p. 403 (Italics mine.)

III

Repurchasing usually required borrowing. For many provincial nobles such new debts were no small burden when added to the recent financial strain of emigration. A well-to-do *anobli* such as Depont des Granges at La Rochelle might repurchase the confiscated part of his estate for 60,000 francs (half in silver) immediately after it was offered for sale in 1797. A military officer such as Comte de Saint-Mendé, buying back his land parcel by parcel in the heart of Saintonge, found himself increasingly hounded by creditors and lawsuits after 1830.[31]

This leads us to the general question of noble indebtedness. Although it is customary to regard the French nobility as chronically in debt even before the Revolution, this was not necessarily true. Even the generalization that court nobles were wastrels, *robe* nobles thrifty, and provincial military nobles impoverished requires more investigation. The picture is complicated by the fact that nobles lent money to other nobles so that it is difficult to know if the nobility as a whole was a creditor or debtor class before 1789. For our purposes it might be more useful to consider the noble as both lender and borrower. Since it was usually difficult to convert investments quickly into coin or even to transfer them for various legal and technical reasons during the Old Régime, even noble families with ample resources had to resort to borrowing when large sums of capital were required for dowries, portions, or building. A nobleman's account book in 1789 almost invariably included interest income from loans extended as well as interest charges for loans contracted.

Although creditors in general improved their legal status as a consequence of the Revolution and Napoleon, it is not certain that the rural creditor, most frequently a noble landlord, profited from this improved legal position. True, the peasant debtor was largely unsuccessful over the long run in identifying the *rente foncière* with seigneurial dues and hence abolishing both without compensation. But the Revolution did authorize the amortization of this "non-feudal" type of *rente*, permitting many peasants to repay the capital in *assignats*. The proprietor who lent his share-cropper livestock fared even worse. Customarily, the lease (*bail à cheptel*) evaluated the livestock or ploughteam in *livres* and provided for a return to the proprietor at the end of the lease of either the livestock or its capital

[31] Arch. Dép. (Charente-Maritime), Q-250, 301 (Depont); E-374-375 (Saint-Mendé).

value. Before the Revolution, the clause was practically meaningless since few *métayers* could amass even a few hundred *livres* capital. After the *assignats* were offered in payment for grain at inflated prices, however, there was a real opportunity for the share-cropper to secure the livestock for a nominal sum, thereby considerably increasing his independence at the expense of the proprietor. Pierre Massé, the first historian to explore this problem intensively, concludes:

> The livestock lease, like the *rente foncière*, was liquidated to the profit of the *métayer*. The proprietor succumbed to a double hæmorrhage which could become a mortal danger to him.[32]

For this breed of rural creditor, then, the Revolution was far from beneficial. And lacking many alternative investment outlets, the provincial nobleman was most likely to be this kind of creditor. The Parisian noble, no doubt, had wider investment opportunities, including easy access to fresh issues of government *rentes* and even entry into overseas commercial ventures about which we still know too little. There is no doubt, however, that the loss of two thirds of his income from government *rentes* caused by the "consolidation" of the public debt in 1797 gravely undercut a noble who had large investments in government *rentes*.[33] Income from government securities which once covered interest payments on debts evaporated.

It might first appear that the Revolution aided the noble debtor. Many could and did pay off their obligations in depreciated *assignats*. Others profited from their own uncertain future as émigrés to have agents liquidate their debts at a discount. Still others who emigrated hoped to escape their creditors altogether, and upon return to France after Brumaire looked forward to a general moratorium on all debts.

Such a moratorium was not to come, however. Neither the Empire nor the government of the Restoration had any intention of hurting creditors and frightening potential sources of public funds. In fact, the Napoleonic Code had strengthened the legal position of the creditor not only by legalizing interest and publicizing mortgages, but by enforcing constraints on debtors, including "bodily seizure".[34] Noble émigrés returning to France after the amnesty of 1801 were often besieged by creditors, now operating openly and frequently in

---

[32] P. Massé, "Les amortissements de rentes foncières en l'an III", *Annales historiques de la Révolution française*, no. 165 (1961), p. 380 and *passim*.

[33] The actual losses are best traced in the account books of individual noblemen. See, for example, the accounts of Depont des Granges at La Rochelle, Arch Dép. (Charente-Maritime), E-484, 475; Q-250. The history of the public debt has yet to be written.

[34] Godechot, *Les Institutions*, pp. 448, 565. See Articles 530, 1265-1270 of the Civil Code.

consortiums. In 1804, one seigneur of Varennes, who had otherwise survived the vicissitudes of the Revolution by a combination of luck and manoeuvre, was pursued by a *société* of fifty creditors ranging from hat-makers and tailors to bakers, masons, servants, and even day-labourers claiming a total of 32,000 francs, most of it borrowed twenty-five years before. There was no possibility of further delay. By the end of the year, the former seigneur of Varennes sold his principal domain at auction.[35] Somewhat higher in the social scale, the Comte de Roure was imprisoned at the request of his creditors, while the Duc d'Havré, one time Ambassador to Madrid, after a prolonged lawsuit with the heirs of his land agent, was condemned by a Restoration court of appeals to pay 80,000 francs to his creditors.[36]

In 1793 the government had assumed the debts of émigré noblemen whose property had been sequestered, inviting creditors to enter their names on the "Great Book of the Public Debt" and settle with the State. Very few creditors accepted this offer either because of negligence, or because of fear of repayment in paper, or in the hope of better terms later. Their long wait was not in vain. After 1 January 1820, the last stays restraining the collection of émigré debts expired and nobles who returned with the Princes were now liable to pursuit. The decade of the 1820s, sometimes characterized as the last "feudal reaction", saw many a noble summoned before a debtor's court without any special consideration for his rank.[37]

Ironically, the heaviest blow came with the indemnity bill of 1825. The new law provided that all obligations and liens on émigré property, many dating back thirty-five years, were to be deducted from the indemnity by the government. The government even deducted perpetual rents due to religious orders that had been abolished. The administration of the Comte de Villèle, a thrifty country gentleman from Toulouse, indemnified the émigrés for their lost land (though not for their lost *rentes*, seigneurial rights, household furnishings or jewellery) and at the same time made them responsible for *all* their debts. If the indemnity was insufficient to cover the debts, the creditor was authorized to pursue the noble debtor without further delay. According to Gain, creditors flocked in from all sides.[38]

This is not to say that many nobles did not weather this storm as they had so many others. Even the peers with their prodigious debts

[35] Pierre Massé, *Varennes et ses maîtres: Un domaine rural de l'Ancien Régime à la Monarchie de Juillet (1779-1842)* (Paris, 1956), pp. 113-4.

[36] Gain, *La Restauration*, ii, p. 253.

[37] *Ibid.*, ii, p. 252.

[38] *Ibid.*, ii, pp. 253-4.

in absolute figures ended with a substantial balance. In the Meuse only sixteen émigrés out of 393 found that their debts exceeded their indemnities, while in frugal Toulouse out of 103 indemnified nobles only thirteen had any debts at all.[39] Nevertheless, the climate of creditor-debtor relations had changed; the law now stood decidedly behind the creditor.

Having surveyed a number of the components of noble income, one is still left with a rather ambiguous, imprecise picture. Some speculation is in order. If we accept the incomes of the nobility of Toulouse in 1789 as typical of the provincial noblesse, we find that of an income of 8,000 *livres*, about 5,000 came from the land, 2,000 from *rentes* (public and private), and about 1,000 from *gages, épices,* and *pensions.* A conservative guess might be that in 1830 the landed income (adjustment made for inflation) had fallen to 4,000 francs, the *rentes* to 1,000 francs (most of this from the indemnity), and royal pensions to 200 francs. We shall even assume that interest on debts remained unchanged, though there is every reason to believe that indebtedness increased. This would mean that our hypothetical provincial nobleman would have lost perhaps only a fifth of his land, but as much as one third of his income because of the laws and events of the Revolution. Parisian nobles, omitting some 150 families of *grande noblesse,* were probably even harder hit because of their preference before 1789 for *rentes* on the *Hôtel de Ville* and the Clergy of France, both reduced by two thirds after the consolidation of the public debt in 1797.[40]

Until the research project on émigré property recently launched by Marc Bouloiseau reaches fruition, statistical speculations such as the one above are hardly more than informed guesses. Even after a statistical average has been determined, individual case histories will seem more real. As for the nobles at Toulouse, a fragmentary police report in 1808 lists nine noble proprietors of whom seven are qualified as "riche et tranquille" while the two remaining are described as "having lost almost all of their land in the Revolution".[41]

[39] *Ibid.*, ii, pp. 267-70.
[40] "I am beginning to think like all the rich people of Paris. There is not one who wants land. Most of them have only shares or *rentes* on the *Hôtel de Ville*": Arch. Dép. (Calvados) E-2, Marquis de Longaunay to Comte de Longaunay, 1 Dec. 1736. Mr. Rock Ley, an undergraduate student at Dartmouth College, found this letter in the archives at Caen. See also François Bluche, *Les magistrats du Parlement de Paris au XVIIIe siècle, 1715-1771* (Paris, 1960) on the number of *robe* nobles who invested largely in *rentes* rather than land.
[41] Archives Municipales (Toulouse), Series S-Emigrés, Register 245. Amnisties.

However, in order to answer the question of noble survival in the larger perspective of social prestige, it may not be necessary to have precise statistical data on noble fortunes before and after the Revolution. It can be demonstrated that even those shrewd, frugal and fortunate provincial nobles from such royalist strongholds as Toulouse or the Vendée "lost" the Revolution.

IV

Under the Napoleonic Code the amount of property a father could will to any one of his children was strictly limited. This *quotité disponible* amounted to one third of the family fortune when there were two children, one quarter when there were three children or more. The rest had to be divided equally. Unless the number of children could be restricted to two nothing approaching the old "right of the eldest" could be maintained.[42]

Villèle was certain that the abolition of the "right of the eldest" was the cause of the fragmentation of large property, disorganizing the family at each new generation. The first minister's correspondence with Prince Polignac makes clear that Villèle associated *grande propriété* with noblesse and that his proposal to modify the inheritance law in favour of one heir was part of an effort to reconstitute a landed aristocracy. What is even more revealing is Villèle's observation about a change in noble mores:

> Of twenty well-to-do families, there is scarcely one who employs its option [under the Code] to favour the eldest or any other of its children ... *The bonds of subordination are so loosened everywhere* that in the family the father thinks he must coddle his children. The evil is in our mores, so influenced are we still by the Revolution.[43]

When Villèle defended his proposed legislation before the House of Peers, he supplied some significant statistical information. Among 7,649 inheritances in 1825, 6,568 were settled without any will at all, and only 59 legators had made use of the *quotité disponible* to favour one of the children. Such habits, asserted Villèle, would make France a nation of "well-to-do beggars" in a few generations.[44] The reaction of the liberal press was to be expected; the strong opposition of the nobility was not. Villèle's mild amendment to the inheritance law was voted down by the Peers, 120 to 94, having been assaulted on the floor by such venerable aristocrats as Duc de Broglie:

[42] Philippe Sagnac, *La législation civile de la Révolution française* (Paris, 1898), p. 350. See Articles 896 and 913 of the Civil Code. See also B. Schwartz, ed., *The Code Napoleon and the Common Law World* (New York, 1956), p. 140.
[43] Villèle to Polignac, 1 Oct. 1826, quoted in Jean Fourcassié, *Villèle* (Paris, 1954), p. 323 (Italics mine.)   [44] *Ibid.*, pp. 322, 325.

This is not a law but a declaration of principles . . . a manifesto against the present state of society.   The right of primogeniture is the foundation of an inequality of conditions, it is pure privilege, . . . It is a social and political revolution, a revolution against the Revolution accomplished in France forty years ago.[45]

The vehemence of Broglie's remarks may not have been typical of the nobility of the Restoration, but equality of treatment of children had made converts in all classes of society.   Philippe Ariès in his study of childhood since the Middle Ages makes an interesting case for the decline of the patriarchal "house" and the increasing attention given to sentimental ties within the family in the eighteenth century. And he cites Villèle's correspondence as evidence of the change even in noble families.[46]

Villèle deplored other changes in noble mores as well.   Where were the old *moeurs agricoles*?

No one wants to live in the countryside on his land; all our *gentilshommes* are turning themselves into bourgeois by spending six or nine months in town in order to enjoy social life, comforts, and the facilities to raise and place their children.   They are not rich enough to have all this in the country.[47]

Admitting the timeless quality of this complaint, does it reflect a change in habits, an urbanization, preventing the nobles from using the indemnity of 1825 to repurchase their old domains ?   Other more materialistic reasons can be advanced — the five-year payment schedule for the indemnity, the poor market for the new government bonds, the resistence of the now reassured owners of national land.[48] Perhaps as Gain suggests, the provincial noble, obliged to hide and retrench during the Revolutionary generation, had acquired a new outlook.   Many nobles seem to have exchanged château life for the apartment in town, reduced the expenses of a large household, and escaped the land tax and the details of estate management by drawing more and more of their income from 3 per cent bonds.[49]   In any case, the nobles of the Restoration were becoming slowly and almost imperceptibly *rentiers* instead of landlords.

If attitudes and living habits were changing among nobles, attitudes towards them were also changing.   Surely there was less contact between the rural community and the noble *rentier* or the noble owner of thinly-populated forest, and less contact meant less local

[45] G. de Bertier de Sauvigny, *La Restauration* (Paris, 1955), p. 525.
[46] Philippe Ariès, *Centuries of Childhood*, Eng. trans. (London, 1962), pp. 372-3.
[47] Gain, *La Restauration*, ii, p. 419 n: Villèle to Polignac, 31 Oct. 1824.
[48] *Ibid.*, ii, p. 426; Marion, *La vente des biens nationaux*, pp. 388-91.
[49] Gain, *La Restauration*, ii, pp. 427-8.

influence for the nobility.   Furthermore, peasants were less docile after the Revolution.   The daughter of the Marquis des Echerolles recalled the "avidity of the lower classes" especially after the Terror. She was shocked when she overheard her father's share-croppers say that they wanted ownership of the land they worked.[50]   And in 1822, in the foothills of the Pyrennees south of Carcassonne, a group of villagers petitioned the prefect, protesting against the management of community finances.   One sentence read:

> The undersigned regard Monsieur de Fleury only as their mayor . . . and not as their former seigneur armed with feudal power and arbitrary dispenser of the product of their sweat.[51]

*   *   *   *

The cumulative effect of the abolition of the seigneurial system, tax privileges and venal office, the large inroads of expropriation, increased vulnerability of the noble whether as creditor or debtor, and a new inheritance law struck hard at the economic underpinnings of the nobility.   Important as these blows were, however, the fundamental change in attitude that lies behind them was to act as an even more powerful corrosive in the course of the nineteenth century. Villèle had sensed this change a generation before de Tocqueville. The "bonds of subordination" both within the noble family and throughout the entire society had been "loosened".   By 1825 the erosion of the hierarchical society upon which hereditary aristocracy rested was far advanced.

This is not to say that the social hold of the nobility on the countryside disappeared abruptly after 1800 or even after 1830.   For many small peasants, "Monsieur le Marquis" remained a local "notable" and a man with whom to reckon even in the Second Empire.   But it does mean that the gradual disintegration of noble properties and of local noble pre-eminence began with the Revolution of 1789. A sub-prefect of Loire-Inferieure, not the most dynamic of departments, could write in 1853:

> The peasant who sixty years ago owned nothing is today everywhere a landlord.   Henceforth his interest prevails over old traditions . . . They [the peasants] are happy to reach municipal office which gives them some authority over the descendants of their own lords.   The influence of the nobility in the countryside received a first blow in this way.[52]

[50] Echerolles, *Mémoires*, p. 285.

[51] René Descadeillas, *Rennes et ses derniers seigneurs, 1730-1820* (Toulouse, 1964), p. 199.

[52] F(ic) III, Loire-Inf. 8, sub-prefect, Ancenis, 28 Feb. 1853, quoted in Theodore Zeldin, *The Political System of Napoleon III* (London, 1958), pp. 166-7.

To be sure, Professor Cobban's "conservative landowning classes" had benefited from the Revolution. But an emerging society of self-confident, tenacious, middling and small landlords was not the aristocratic landed society of the Old Régime.[53] Whoever won the Revolution, the noble landlord lost.

[53] By "middling", I mean between 25 and 100 acres; by "small", I mean under 25 acres. Cf. C. E. Labrousse, "The Evolution of Peasant Society in France from the Eighteenth Century to the Present" in E. M. Acomb and M. L. Brown, eds., *French Society and Culture since the Old Régime* (New York, 1966), pp. 47-53, 59. It might also be argued that the French Revolution was a victory for subsistence farming over commercial agriculture, but this is a separate issue.

6. *Women in Revolution, 1789-1796*[1]

OLWEN HUFTON

THE HISTORY OF WOMEN IN THE FRENCH REVOLUTION HAS RECEIVED at best limited attention. If Marie Antoinette, Madame Roland and Claire Lacombe have inevitably found their biographers and hagiographers, the ephemeral *clubs des femmes* their panegyrists and their critics,[2] and the *tricoteuse* has been pushed into a respectable place in the most luxurious of pictorial histories,[3] the attitudes of working women and their revolutionary experience remain an enigma, conceded but passing reference even in works concerned exclusively with the attitudes and activities of the working classes. Yet their rôle was both unique and important and their attitudes demanding of consideration. This short study is an attempt to begin to redress something of the balance by isolating a type of woman on whom information abounds, the working woman of the towns; the sort of woman the *sans culotte* most likely went home to, the sort of girl the married soldier at the front most probably left behind; the woman of the bread riots, of the revolutionary crowds, the "mother heroine" figure of the *fêtes nationales,* carrying her banner with the proud device, *"J'ai donné un (deux, trois, quatre, cinq, six) citoyen(s) à la*

---

[1] This work was undertaken in response to a request for a paper on this topic by the history society of Balliol College, Oxford in 1969. It makes no claim to be anything other than a preliminary discourse on an immense topic. It perforce leans most heavily on my knowledge of Bayeux during the Revolutionary period and in particular on material found in Arch. Dépt. Calvados L. *Registres du bureau de district de Bayeux*; LX *Assistance*; LM *Police*; and on parallel material in the Arch. Dépt. du Côte d'Or and of the Doubs to which pointers were given in G. Langeron, *Le Club des Femmes de Dijon pendant la Révolution* (Dijon, 1929) and H. Perrin, "Le club des femmes de Besançon", *Annales Revolutionnaires,* ix and x (1917-18), pp. 629-53, pp. 37-63, pp. 505-2, pp. 654-72. Both these studies were undertaken while Mathiez was professor in Dijon and range wider than the titles would suggest. The references to the economy of the poor of eighteenth-century France are largely based on the Arch. Dépt. of the Aveyron, Haute Loire, Indre et Loire, Loir et Cher and the Lozère, série Lx, *Assistance.*

Much of the inspiration for the work was found in R. C. Cobb, "Quelques Aspects de la mentalité révolutionnaire (Avril 1793 — thermidor an II)" in *Terreur et Subsistances 1793-5* (Paris, 1965), pp. 3-53 in which the attitudes, enthusiasms and preoccupations of the *sans culotte* are so imaginatively outlined that the task of giving such a flesh and blood individual a wife was much lessened. It is to be regretted that when this piece was written Mr. Cobb's *The Police and the People* (Oxford, 1970) which opens up so many other avenues for pursuing women in Revolution had not been published.

[2] The general bibliography on this currently fashionable subject is found in M. Cerati, *Le Club des Citoyennes Républicaines Révolutionnaires* (Paris, 1966).

[3] F. Furet and D. Richet, *The French Revolution* (London, 1970), p. 208.

République" (I have given a citizen to the Republic) and ultimately the worn-out, disillusioned, starving hag who sank to her knees in the Year III to demand pardon of an offended Christ.

To appreciate the nearness of women to the Revolution one must understand their rôle in the family economy, an appreciation crucial to our theme. One must start with the recognition that the family economy of the working classes, whether in town or country, was their natural economy: the family needed the work of each of its component members to support the whole. Hence, in a rural context, the man who had sufficient land to provide for the wants of his family had sufficient to employ that family. In the event of his not having enough, he or his family or both must seek an alternative source of income. In the case of the towns this was doubly true, for nowhere could the wage-earner, unless he practised some highly specialized craft, expect to earn more than he needed for his own personal maintenance, the rent of a shelter and possibly the upkeep of one child — a fact which the *Comité de Mendicité* spelt out in 1790 for all who cared to read its debates.[4] Once this has been recognized, then the importance of the earning capacity, the labour and the sheer ingenuity of women and children becomes readily apparent. They were expected by their efforts to make a contribution and an important one to the family economy. Female labour can be easily categorized: for the unmarried, domestic service where payment was largely in the form of food and shelter but where a girl might raise enough to purchase the sheets and household linen which commonly constituted the dowry of the working girl; for the married, domestic industry in the form of spinning wool and cotton and the manufacture of lace.[5] The last employed the largest numbers at least in Northern and Central France and in country as well as town. The value of lace lay almost entirely in the handiwork, for the quantity of linen or

[4] C. Bloch and A. Tuetey, *Procès Verbaux et Rapports du Comité de Mendicité de la Constituante* (Paris, 1911), p. 77: "un homme valide peut gagner au delà de ses besoins et faire subsister deux ou trois individus avec lui" ("a healthy man can earn more than his needs and can give subsistence to two or three people in addition to himself"); but on p. 379, an older and wiser *Comité* admitted that a man paying tax equivalent only to the proceeds of one day's labour (about a fifth of the work force) could not do as much as that.

[5] The lace industry as a massive employer of women and girls has been strikingly neglected in standard economic histories such as E. Levasseur, *Histoire des classes ouvrières et de l'industrie en France avant 1789* (Paris, 1900-1) or P. Léon, *Economies et Sociétés Préindustrielles* (Paris, 1970). On the massive numbers employed in the *généralité* of Caen, J. C. Perrot, "L'Industrie et le commerce de la dentelle dans la region de Caen", *Actes du 81e Congrès des sociétés savantes, 1956* (Caen, 1956), pp. 215-37. Unfortunately his study stops in 1792.

silk thread involved was slight and no expensive equipment was needed. Highly dependent upon the dictates of fashion, a luxury industry with an aristocratic and an international clientèle, it was on the eve of the Revolution, the most flourishing female industry in France even if the lacemaker only received a pittance for labours which would ultimately take her sight.   In towns, women made up the bulk of the garment trades — seamstresses, milliners, corset-makers, embroiderers, ribbon-makers, glove-makers and so on — and lastly, in any community, poor women, the lowest cipher on the employment market, performed the heavy and distasteful tasks such as load carrying. Nothing was too menial. They carried soil, heavy vegetables to and from market, water, wood — anything.[6] In the large cities, they found employment as rag sorters, cinder sifters, refuse collectors, assistants to masons and bricklayers — one can so easily multiply the examples. Where work could not support the family, then the mother had to have recourse to ingenuity. She taught her children how and where to beg or hired them out for a minor fee to other women who wanted to elicit pity at markets and fairs by the appearance of a large family or trailed her infants round from door to door with long and pathetic stories.[7]   She had a whole legacy of mendacity to bestow if nothing else: the children of Rodez, Richeprey, Necker's empissary in the Rouergue declared, are taught individual hard-luck stories by their mothers to impose on the passer-by to demonstrate a special claim to assistance.[8]   In the salt court of Laval alone, 2,000 women, mothers of families, were brought to trial annually for petty salt smuggling between Brittany, an area of free salt, and the Maine, against a mere 150 of the opposite sex.[9] The importance of the mother within the family economy was immense; her death or incapacity could cause a family to cross the narrow but extremely meaningful barrier between poverty and destitution.

A contemporary feminist, Madame de Coicy, concerned to draw the attention of middle-class and aristocratic women to their subservient position in the household, emphasized the equality achieved within the working class home of the mother of the family

[6] Mercier, *Tableaux de Paris* (Amsterdam, 1782), "Les portefaix".

[7] O. Hufton, "The Rise of the People", in *The Eighteenth Century*, ed. A. Cobban (London, 1969), pp. 297-8.

[8] *Journal des Voyages en Haute Guienne de J. F. Henry de Richeprey* (Rodez, 1952).

[9] A. Calléry, *La Fraude des Gabelles sous l'ancien régime* (Paris, 1882). Also Arch. Nat. AD IX 426 on similar practices in Touraine and Arch. Dépt. Ille et Vilaine C 3475 on the Vitré area.

because of her important participation in the family economy.[10]
Indeed one might, considering the importance of her rôle, go further
than Madame de Coicy, and claim for her social supremacy within
the limited context of the family. Restif in *La vie de mon père* has
painted a patriarchal society but it is comfortable landowning society
which is thus depicted. In its lower echelons society was far from
being so. The strains involved in keeping a family together were
immense. Poverty is an acid: it corrodes or dissolves human
relationships. But it was easier for a father to opt out than for
a mother to do so — easier for him to return home via the *cabaret*
suitably anaesthetized with cheap alcohol to the squalor of home and
hungry children and easier for him as well to clear off altogether, to
turn temporary migration into permanent disappearance, or in the
words of the Curé d'Athis, "They lose heart: they weary of the strain of
keeping a family on a wage barely adequate for one person and having
done so they gather their few remaining garments into a bundle and
hit the road, never to be seen again by their families".[11] The divorce
lists of the Revolution confirm just this factor: in Metz, for example,
268 women sought divorce, with, for working women, separation as
a result of the disappearance of their husbands in times of economic
stress as the most usual cause.[12] The results of the inquiry conducted
by the bishops into the state of their dioceses in 1740 and 1770-4 are no
less explicit: I am overwhelmed, wrote the *curé* of Bort, near Clermont,
with women who come to me not only beseeching bread but accusing
their husbands of threatening them that if they do not let the youngest
children perish they will leave them and that alone they can manage
but that even working all day they cannot feed their families;[13] while
a *curé* of Tours described a hierarchy of hunger in which he referred
not merely to rich and poor. Women, he said, are not the first to die
but they feel the pangs of hunger first because they deprive themselves
to feed husband and children, and he made the inevitable and lengthy
comparison with the pious pelican of the *adoro te* who gave her blood
to feed her young.[14] This is not to say that women did not drink,
thieve, lie, prostitute themselves, indulge in every criminal practice one

[10] Mme. de Coicy, *Les femmes comme il convient de les voir* (Paris, 1785), p.4.
[11] Arch. Dépt. Calvados, H. Suppl. 1308.
[12] J. L'Hôte, "Le divorce à Metz sous la Révolution et l'Empire", *Annales de l'Est*, 5th ser., iii (1952), pp. 175-83; the figures offered for Toulouse by S. Maraval, *L'introduction du divorce en Haute Garonne* (D.,E. S. Toulouse, 1965) demonstrates a similar phenomenon.
[13] Arch. Dépt. Puy de Dôme C 897.
[14] Arch. Dépt. Indre et Loire C 304.

can think of, but that in general they clung more devotedly to their families and that this was widely recognized.

Indeed in time of dearth the importance of the mother within the family grew beyond measure. It was not merely that her deviousness, her relationship with baker, pawnbroker and priest became more important than before[15] — there was no laicized parish rate as in Protestant countries and the poor had to depend on the voluntary alms of the faithful administered by the *curé* — nor just her assiduity in rooting out what food there was but that when all else failed it was she who had the right to spill over into riot, not the father of the family.   By the end of the *ancien régime* this was tacitly not openly expressed: indeed one perhaps has to go back to Aquinas for the last discourse on the right of a starving mother to thieve bread for her young; but it certainly was, under certain circumstances, permitted to her to do so with impunity.   She had to do it collectively and it evidently had to be a very abnormal year.   The sort of women who were punished after a bread riot up to and including 1789 were those who in the course of rioting had destroyed property or shown themselves violent towards persons.   It was this criterion which allowed administrators usually to pick out a handful for punishment — not that their share of the pickings were any greater.   She also had to be doing it for her children, though it was rare to see a grandmother called before the courts either.[16]   I am not saying that men were never involved in bread riots — indeed during the Revolution they were markedly so — but that predominantly the bread riot was female, or rather maternal, terrain.   One can make further generalizations about the women involved in these riots.   In Bayeux, Troyes and Orléans those arrested in 1789 did not, with one exception, appear on the lists of those in those particular towns given an annual subvention by the *bureaux de charité,* so they were not paupers but women who in normal times could manage, proud women who were not counted among the destitute and who were fighting to remain so and to hold their families together.[17]   There is little doubt the most

[15] Often *bureaux de charité* dealt directly with the mother of the family and it was her piety, thrift and readiness to work hard if she was able which were the conditions for relief being given: Arch. Dépt. Lozère, J 570 *bureau de charité de Florac*; E 1000 *bureau de charité de Villefort*; GG 12 *bureau de charité de Saint Etienne Vallée Française.*

[16] Even after the bread riots of the Year III, administrators were reluctant to imprison women who had been violent but who had babies at the breast: Arch. Mun. Bayeux, *Registres des délibérations du corps municipal, 2-3 floréal an III.*

[17] Arch. Dépt. Calvados C 2643 and C 955; Arch. Mun. Rodez Cité BB 9 CC 318, "Femmes prévenues et condamnées pour sédition"; Bibliothèque Municipale Orléans MS. 585, "Evènements arrivés à Orléans de 1788 à 1804", cited briefly in C. Bloch, "Les femmes d'Orléans pendant la Révolution", *Révolution Française,* xxix (1902), p. 62-3.

significant social division of the *ancien régime* was quite independent of order or class but lay between those who could make the proud claim, "There is always bread in our house" and those who could not; and within those who could not, those who could claim there was adequate in normal times and those who had fallen below. That the latter were recruited from the former there could be little doubt and that most were recruited in times of dearth when prices rose and the family parted with what little property it had to buy bread and probably ran into debt seems equally axiomatic. The woman of the bread riots owed her intensity to her appreciation of the need to stay on the right side of the line between poverty and destitution. She lived constantly on her nerves but for her there was a worse state — it might be called living on her wits, on the caprice of voluntary charity.[18]

It is with the type of woman who had to struggle to stay on the right side of the line that one is mainly concerned — though the destitute should not be forgotten: they comprised after all a fifth of the total population of France in 1790; but the destitute were not protesters, not rioters. The line between poverty and destitution was a psychological as well as a physical boundary, on the other side lay passive demoralization, the point at which the poor gave up and expected nothing.

The bread riots of the French Revolution then, whether the march to Versailles on 5-6 October 1789 or, to a less extent, the *journées* of Germinal and Prairial of Year III were *par excellence* women's days. Where bread was concerned this was their province: a bread riot without women is an inherent contradiction. How much they understood of the political implications is more open to speculation. Between October 1789 and Germinal Year III a lot happened to them however which was strongly to influence what ensued. It is their revolutionary experience in so far as it can be examined collectively that must now be outlined. Where did the Revolution impinge on the family economy of the poor: how did it alter the often delicate balance between poverty and destitution: and how far did these issues affect the attitude of women to Revolution?

[18] The line between poverty and destitution, between *pauvreté honnête* and *indigence,* was one to which moralists, physiocrats and administrators alike made constant reference. The first condition was to physiocrats and administrators inevitable (Bloch and Tuetey, *op. cit.,* pp. 315-16) and to moralists like St. Vincent de Paul, even virtuous; only the second condition was to be feared because of the misery and degeneracy it entailed. The aim of both *ancien régime* and revolutionary administrators was to prevent the merely poor slipping into the ranks of the indigent. O. Hufton, "Towards an Understanding of the Poor of Eighteenth-Century France", in *French Government and Society 1500-1850: Essays in Memory of Alfred Cobban,* ed. by J. F. Bosher (London, 1973), pp. 145–65.

In answering these questions it is difficult, given the research that remains to be done, not to be stranded between broad vapid generalizations on the one hand and a multiplicity of particularities on the other. One must at the same time distinguish between long term trends and sharp immediate results: not everything which seemed so blatantly obvious in 1795 had been so in 1790. No one had any conception then, and the question needs exploring much further, of the extent to which the economy of the poor was bound up with the abuses, institutions and society of the old régime. One does not know yet what happened to the 200,000 Breton families who had lived by salt smuggling when the *gabelle* was abolished. Cities such as Toulouse, Dijon, Rouen, Montpellier, Bayeux or Angers made cogent complaints of the disappearance in each case of hundreds of thousands of *livres* with the destruction of *parlements, états,* and the wealth of the church; money spent on consumer goods, as workmen's and servants' wages and as charity, and at least in one of these cases the laments were justified and it is clear that the economy of whole cities could be jeopardized if they were dependent upon *ancien régime* institutions.[19] If a veil of ignorance as yet persists here, one can state more categorically the almost uniform drying up of luxury industries, many of them the preserve of women — partly due to the emigration of a wealthy clientèle, partly to the suspension of international trade and partly to the emergence of much more austere fashion. The lace industry, for example, depended on fichus, cravats, ruffles, petticoat edging, the paraphernalia of a girl on a swing in a *fête galante*. The economy of the working population of Le Puy, Chaise Dieu in the Massif, innumerable Norman towns and several in Flanders simply collapsed: hence the Norman and Velay lace riots of the Year II.[20] Velvet, silk brocade,

[19] The dependence of a city on the wealth of the church is pointed to in J. McManners, *French Ecclesiastical Society under the ancien régime, A Study of Angers in the Eighteenth Century* (Manchester, 1960), pp. 103-28; and O. Hufton, *Bayeux in the Late Eighteenth Century* (Oxford, 1967), pp. 271-83. The dependence of a city on *ancien régime* institutions destroyed by the Revolution is shown in D. Higgs, *The Ultra-Royalist Movement at Toulouse under the Second Restoration* to be published shortly by Johns Hopkins. Arch. Dépt. Côte d'Or C 3687 *Dénombrement des citoyens de la ville de Dijon* shows that out of a population of some 21,000, 1,800 were directly employed full-time as servants by the church and court officials. This is without counting the lesser officials of minor courts, wig-makers, barbers and tradesmen dependent upon the business of the courts.

[20] On the dependence of certain regions on the lace industry before the Revolution, J. C. Perrot, "Le commerce et l'industrie de la dentelle dans la généralité de Caen à la fin de l'ancien régime", *Actes du 81e Congrès National des Sociétés Savantes, 1956)*, (Caen, 1956), pp. 215-17; V. Thuvenon, "La dentelle du Puy, la situation présente, son avenir", *Bull. Soc. Acad. du Puy,* vii

ribbons, embroideries — all these ceased to command a clientèle. In the classical gown alone is succinctly expressed the decline of at least five industries. Straight, austere, untrimmed by lace or ribbon, made of lawn, cambric or wool over a straight shift, it hid the waist and even put the stay maker out of business.[21]

The second categorical statement that can be made is that ultimately when dearth and disease came in 1794 all the poor were to be affected by the total failure of French Revolutionary legislation on poor relief.[22]

This legislation was to be the culmination of the enlightenment, the creation of a social utopia in which the poor were to be legislated away. Reduced to its simplest what was aimed at was: the assumption of the property of the *hospices* which catered for the old, the sick and the orphaned as *biens nationaux* and the direction and financing of them by the state; the total abolition of almsgiving, and *bureaux de charité* and the creation instead of work projects to employ the able-bodied poor at wage rates slightly below those current in the particular locality, that is work for the unemployed adult male; lastly, an annual subvention to the fathers of large families based on the numbers and age of the children. On paper it was at the time unparalleled in the history of philanthropy but those who drew it up neither had an idea of the numbers or kinds of people involved — they imagined a problem of unemployment, not a problem of the living wage; nor had they any conception of the value of the property of the *hospices* — they imagined it was huge and that just as the property of the church would allow the financing of the constitutional clergy, so the assumption of hospital property would go a good way to financing both the new

(1922), pp. 1-34. On the collapse of the industry after 1793, Hufton, *Bayeux* . . . , pp. 241, 248; Thuvenon, *op. cit.*; and *Recueil des évènements qui ont lieu au Puy et aux environs depuis l'an 1775 jusqu'en 1815* (Le Puy, 1931), p. 322.

[21] At Bayeux the lace-makers viewed the coronation of the Empress Josephine as heralding the first real break the industry had had since the end of the *ancien régime* in heralding the advent of a court with more sumptuous clothing which others would wish to copy.

[22] The historiography of this failure is extensive but scattered. There is no overall adequate study. L. Lallemand, *Le Révolution et les Pauvres* (Paris, 1898), is largely concerned with legislation as is M. Bouchet, *L'Assistance publique en France pendant la Révolution* (Paris, 1908). But there are innumerable local studies: e.g. E. Chaudron, *L'Assistance Publique à Troyes à la fin de l'ancien régime et pendant la Révolution, 1770-1800* (Paris, 1923); M. Accapias, *L'Assistance Publique dans le Puy de Dôme sous la Révolution* (Clermont Ferrand, 1933); J. Dubois, *L'Assistance dans le district de Bar pendant la Révolution* (Paris, 1930); Hufton, *Bayeux* . . . , pp. 236-49; J. Adher, *Recueil de documents sur l'assistance publique dans le district de Toulouse 1789-1800* (Toulouse, 1918); P. Rambaud, *L'Assistance publique à Poitiers, jusqu'en l'an V* (Paris, 1912); X Renouard, *L'Assistance publique à Lille de 1527 à l'an VIII* (Paris, 1912); etc.

hospices and the work projects.   Two years were spent in compiling
some sort of reliable figures but when this was realized, it became
apparent that the issue was not mainly unemployment but the
subvention of huge numbers of women and children, figures so
immense that the *comité* saw that it did not have the means to
cope.   Even before the war came to reduce government finances to
havoc, the government tacitly admitted failure in this respect.   The
net result was that the traditional methods of according relief were
destroyed without any substitute.   Moreover, in its need to raise
money in 1795 the government assumed the property of the *hospices,*
and the hospitals were made totally dependent upon the state just at
the time when the war was demanding every penny the government
could muster; many, especially in small towns, were simply obliged to
close and that on the eve of the epidemics which chronic malnutrition
inevitably brings in its wake.   The frail safety valves of a society
facing dearth were taken out.

Lastly, there was of course inflation and dearth which in some areas
prevailed even with the maximum and certainly existed when it was
withdrawn.   Inflation and dearth which were to place a strain on the
family economy of the poor in the traditional way and to demand that
the women of the poor play their accustomed rôle but in circumstances
which were markedly changed.

All these facets were glaringly apparent by the Year III but no one
could have envisaged them in 1789.   Indeed to do so is to pass from
winter to winter without considering spring, summer and autumn.
It is to imply that right from the beginning all looked bleak for all the
poor: they did not necessarily, why should they, identify their fate
with cleric and *émigré*, *parlement* and *états*.   They did not
necessarily see that they had any common interests with the indigent
and destitute — quite the reverse.   The hand that gave to some,
under the *ancien régime*, or any régime, invariably took from someone
else.   The Trappist monastery of Bonnecombe near Flavin in the
district of Rodez was in the habit of dispensing 300,000 *livres*' worth
of bread annually to the destitute of the area but the grain used was
drawn from the tithe paid in the main by the little landholders of the
area.[23]   Now the destitute lost their bread and the little landholders
retained a share of the crop which they much needed.   The bishop
of Mende usually accorded an annual 10,000 *livres* in bread to the
destitute of the town but much of this came from tithe and
seigneurial rights paid by the poor in the country.[24]   It all seemed and

[23] Arch. Dépt. Aveyron 5L236 *Assistance Publique.*
[24] Arch. Dépt. Lozère, H. 495.

it all was incredibly complicated.   It is not surprising that administrators of towns, districts and departments spoke half of the time in the future or conditional tense: when lists had been compiled, when estimates had been submitted and approved, if old régime officials would speedily turn over the information which they had at their disposal, if the government would accept a temporary or provisional estimate while a more accurate one was drawn up — then such and such a thing could be done.   It was merely a question of waiting: the period was one of adjustment: Rome was not built in a day.   In the meantime indirect taxes had gone for good; there were two good harvests and bourgeois ladies (as opposed to aristocratic ones who had done the same thing in the eighteenth century but under another name) formed *clubs des femmes* whose function was to collect voluntary alms (the government pretended not to notice) to help the destitute until new legislation was implemented.   The *club des Amies de la Verité et de la bienfaisance* of Dijon formed in 1791 is utterly typical.[25] The wives of department and district authorities and town officials met every Sunday; gave the populace an example of attending the mass of a constitutional priest and swore not to employ a servant or purchase from a shopkeeper or dressmaker who favoured a non-juror; and they ran lotteries to help families suffering from temporary dislocation and who might have cause to regret the old régime.   One cannot as yet draw a clear picture of the working woman in 1790-1.   In Bayeux, in Orléans, there are sporadic references in 1791 to women forcing *assignats* upon peasants at the market who reluctantly exchanged their produce for paper money,[26] but the image is shadowy, unclear: she is a thing of bits and pieces.

In 1792 she emerges in anger at the interruption of supplies, particularly milk, which the country failed to deliver to the town,[27] and increasingly her voice is heard as the protagonist of price fixation. From mid-1792 local attempts were made to stabilize prices and in Lyons and the large cities of the east, Besançon, Chalons, Vesoul, the impetus came from the local *club des femmes* whose recruitment expanded in the course of that year and changed rapidly in character from the rather precious early women's associations.   Until they were forcibly closed by the Convention about a fortnight after the elimination of the Hébertistes, this was the common platform of the

[25] Langeron, *op. cit.*, pp. 11-13.
[26] Arch. Mun. Bayeux, "Registres des délibérations du corps municipal", September 1791; G. Lefebvre, *Etudes Orléanaises* (Paris, 1963), ii, pp. 53-5.
[27] Arch. Mun. Bayeux, "Registres des délibérations du corps municipal", July, 1792; Arch. Comm. Troyes, D4 fol. 72 23 January 1793.

clubs des femmes and "any other business" was confined to the war effort.   Indeed it is with the war in the spring of 1792 that one really gets an indication that women had come to have an emotional investment in the Revolution and an intense one at that.   Something of this investment is reflected in the tons of household linen — often the main assets of a working class family, the woman's dowry intended to last for life — which were sacrificed as bandages for the wounded. Chalons gathered together 20,000 pounds of sheets for this purpose; Bergerac in the Dordogne ran a close second and when the deputy of the area asked the Convention for a public expression of thanks he was told that instances of such patriotism were too common for special mention.[28]   Women of Pontarlier, a frontier town, contributed their wedding rings — the most pawnable piece of property any woman had — to clothe volunteers; in Besançon street walkers and women who had toiled all day turned up when they had put their children to bed to knit stockings for the soldiers at the front.[29]   In the summer of 1792 when war fever ran high, innumerable addresses were drawn up and sent to the Assembly wherein women stressed their patriotism and swore to feed their children the right sort of milk: the milk of "bons principes, amour de la constitution, haine des tyrans" ("good principles, love of the constitution, hatred of tyrans"), or more specifically hatred of the Austrians, and the Piedmontese, milk of liberty and equality, or the uncompromising mixture on which the mothers of Clermont swore to nourish their young "un lait incorruptible et que nous clarifions à cet effet avec l'esprit naturel et agréable de la liberté" ("a milk we shall purify with the natural, sweet spirit of liberty").[30]   Moreover and much more significantly, they undertook personally to conduct the internal war while their husbands and sons went to the front: the war against traitors at home and not only actual traitors but potential ones, the children of traitors.   On the outbreak of war against Austria the women of Lons le Saulnier, Mâcon and the Côte armed themselves with pitchforks and pans and declared they would defend their homes and children in the absence of their men, and if their men were defeated (the Legislative took exception to the implication) then they would make a last stand.[31]   The women of the district of Tarbes in

[28] Moniteur no. 99, 29 Dec. 1793; no. 130, 10 Pluviôse Year II.
[29] The club at Besançon was in fact expressly formed to cope with the war effort: Perrin, *op. cit.*, p. 634.
[30] *Adresse des citoyens de Clermont Ferrand à l'Assemblée Législative*, cited by M. Villiers, *Histoire des Clubs des Femmes et des Légions d'Amazones* (Paris, 1910), p. 72.
[31] A. Laserre, *La participation collective des femmes à la Révolution Française* (Paris, 1906), p. 281.

the summer of 1792 armed themselves with kitchen knives and their children with ladles and set out to meet the Spanish. The women of Port en Bessin erected coastal defences lest the English should take them unawares.[32] As early anticipated victory turned into early defeat, antipathy turned more and more against those suspected of internal conspiracy. There is little to equal in hatred and vindictiveness the venom poured out by women on fleeing priests and the relations of *émigrés*. September 1793 saw a spate of professions and declarations, a popular theme "Comment peupler la terre avec d'autant de Marats" ("how to people the country with so many Marats") wherein women volunteered to breed little spies who would report on their playmates who were not being brought up on principles of *civisme* so that these unpatriotic mothers and children could be not corrected but *exterminated* and France's progeny could hence be purified.[33] Old ladies called out in Lady-Macbeth-type language that children at the breast of a traitor should have their brains dashed out. When Pourvoyeur, a police official, spoke in the Year II of the bestialization of women and compared them to tigresses and vultures anxious for blood, the language seems rather strong but the evidence to support it is not lacking.[34] Citoyenne Defarge, *tricoteuse*, the one stock image on which anyone can draw of women in Revolution, the hag knitting stockings for the war effort as the internal conspiracy is annihilated before her eyes, is a grim expression of the same thing and she is undoubtedly real.[35] In every outward manifestation in 1793 women were more frenzied, more intense, doubly gullible, doubly credulous, doubly vindictive and the only exception to this is that they were less publicly garrulous than their men — but here it may merely be a question of lack of opportunity.

But how far was all this emotion a cover for the uneasy realization that circumstances were rapidly deteriorating? How far was she transferring her discontent, seeking some scapegoat, some acceptable explanation for the suspension of trade, the drying up of luxury industries, the very evident economic dislocation which was by now only too visible? Initially war can seem to unite a society in opposition to a common enemy and anticipated victory can too

[32] Villiers, *op. cit.*, p. 105.
[33] Arch. Nat., C 262 no. 580.
[34] Arch. Nat. W 191, Report of 26 Pluviôse Year III. Pourvoyeur found repellent the presence of women at executions "C'est étonnant à quel point les femmes sont devenues féroces. Elles assistent tous les jours aux exécutions". ("It is astonishing how ferocious women have become. Every day they are present at executions".)
[35] Visual evidence of this is found in Furet and Richet, *op. cit.*, p. 208.

often seem the panacea to current economic problems. Both respects are deceptive: the last doubly so. The unity involved at a national level is a dissolvent at a personal level. War strikes at the family: it takes fathers and sons and what death does not destroy can be left to the effect of a long separation. This was certainly the hard lesson of the French Revolution. Moreover, the *sans culotte* was not too generous in sharing his new-found political importance: as the backbone of the local *sociétés populaires*, his evenings in the autumn of 1793 and the winter of 1794 were spent outside the home, in endless verbal demonstrations of patriotism and gratitude for liberty.[36]. The *sans culotte*, Chaumette said when he dissolved women's clubs in October 1793, had a right to expect from his wife the running of his home while he attended political meetings: hers was the care of the family: this was the full extent of her civic duties.[37] Others have lingered on the pride of the *sans culottes* in his new-found importance in *société populaire*, section or as a professional revolutionary on commission, but in the meanwhile what was happening to his wife in isolation; how did she respond when he returned drunk on dubious alcohol and the vocabulary of liberty? Obviously the *sans culotte* in his home is a somewhat closed book, but at least one can know that the wife was steadily accumulating experience which was to sour her on the Revolution and all it stood for; that she was to turn against it sooner and with far greater intensity than her man, and in a way which was totally original, totally hers. In 1794 and even more so in 1795 she was to be confronted with the sort of crisis which was to try her particular rôle in society: with a famine which as usual was to hit her strikingly in her family and in her own health.[38] It was to confront her with watching the unit she fought to maintain spilling over into the ranks of the destitute. While her husband was still talking she in some areas had joined the food queues and the minute she did that her loyalty was potentially suspect. For a time it might well intensify her hatred of the internal conspiracy: nourish her

[36] Most *sociétés populaires* did not welcome women or, if they admitted them, did not allow them to speak: Villiers, *op. cit.*, p. 109.

[37] Cerati, *op. cit.*, p. 173-4; on the political machinations behind this closure, S. H. Lytle, "The Second Sex (September, 1793)", *Jl. of Modern History*, xxvii (1955), pp. 14-26.

[38] The point at which food crisis was experienced varied considerably. The artificial food shortage of the Year II provoked by peasant hostility to the maximum and the deflection of food supplies to feed the armies meant that the incidence of hardship varied whereas in the Year III real famine took over and suffering was generalized. The priorities of the Jacobin government and the problems of supply are cogently illustrated in Cobb, *Terreur et Subsistances, 1793-5*. Broadly speaking, the more important and larger the city, the better its chances of adequate provisioning.

antipathy towards malevolent land-owners intent upon starving the people for their own gain by this artificial dearth and hence increase the violence of her disposition. But her nerves, her patience, her physical strength were already being stretched. At what point would she turn against the administration for its failure to cope? Some evidently were put more to the test than others. If the maximum in 1794 largely worked in Paris and ensured basic food at a reasonable price, the same could not be said for the little towns and villages of Normandy, for example, where the reluctance of the peasantry to turn over their food at a fixed price coupled with a deflection of resources to feed the troops in the Vendée and the great gaping mouth of Paris put women into food queues from February 1794 while the black market thrived.[39] When real famine came with the failure of the harvest of Northern France and the great wheat belt later that year she had already been struggling for eight months to keep her family fed and that in a totally inadequate fashion. The death toll of 1795-6 was the result of *cumulative weakening* — not just the shortage of one year. The lifting of the maximum in December 1794 and the rocketing of prices only universalized a problem which in some areas was already advanced.[40] By May 1794, seven months previously, the women of Masannay were already demanding the annihilation of people over sixty in order to increase the ration for the young.[41] The first lace riots had already occurred in the Velay, and the women of Le Puy (if not the men who lived off them) were already identifying the cessation of the lace industry with the disappearance of the Church.

The woman had both to procure the food and to cook it; all her husband had to do was eat what she prepared and judge whether he was hungry or not. What she got was often the result of *hours of*

[39] Examples of small towns which felt hardship from mid-1794 were Bayeux, Hufton, *op. cit.*, pp. 219-25; and Honfleur, R. C. Cobb, "Problèmes de subsistance de l'an II et de l'an III. L'example d'un petit port normand. Honfleur, 1794-5", *Actes du 81e Congrès des Sociétés Savantes* (Rouen-Caen, 1956). An example of a city experiencing grave difficulty from the beginning of 1794, if not earlier, is Troyes (Chaudron, *op. cit.*, pp. 239-44), perhaps because of its proximity to the army on the frontier. Certainly small towns whose interests had been sacrificed to the larger cities had little ease from the Jacobin policy of price controls and hence little nostalgia for the maximum.

[40] Lefebvre, *Etudes Orléanaises*, vol. ii, p. 294 offers an excellent instance of a large city where the suppression of the maximum was the beginning of major troubles.

[41] Villiers revelled in this kind of story, *op. cit.*, p. 123, but similar instances are not difficult to find: e.g. Le club des femmes de Gevrey Chambertin, "Famille et clocher", *Bulletin paroissial de Gevrey Chambertin*, no. 187 (Dec. 1962).

waiting. She stood in the endless queues, each one a hotbed of discontent hoping that when her turn came something would be left and even then her troubles were not at an end. Often what she was confronted with was beyond her knowledge or resources to prepare. Rice was first introduced to Normandy at this time. Some did not have the fuel to boil it; others did not know that it required boiling and merely soaked it in water — what both tried to eat was a hard gritty substance in no way digestible. Then there were the queues for which the only reward was a ration of salt fish which had already begun to go off with the rising temperature of the summer months and which when boiled yielded a stench like ammonia.[42] Just what of all this was a fit meal for a child? Even if the food ration consisted of vegetables, turnips or swedes, fears were not totally allayed for a pure vegetable diet was associated in the popular mind with the advent in children of summer diarrhoea which was a heavy killer of the young. And when malnutrition hardened into real starvation in 1795, when the government had abandoned price fixation and could be identified with the hardship, and when obviously the rich were still well fed, when the family's small saleable possessions had either been disposed of or dumped at the *mont de piété*, and when the riots of Germinal and Prairial had failed to bring relief, then the usual "sexually selective" manifestations of dearth became apparent. It is perhaps unnecessary to recall the classical manifestations of famine: the death of the weakest, the young and the aged, the increases in the number of miscarriages and the number of still births — but one should bear in mind that the latter are the fate of women, that the whole female body is a grim metering device registering degrees of deprivation. A premature termination of pregnancy or infertility through malnutrition are the best things under these circumstances to be hoped for: better than knowing that one is carrying a dead child, motionless within one or that if one gives birth one will not have the milk to feed it. The mothers of Caen in 1795 were allaying the cries of their new born children with rags dipped in water[43] — that way they did not take long to die. Then there was watching one's children grow too feeble to cry. The *silence* of the hungry household was something that struck St. Vincent de Paul in 1660 but it also moved observers in 1795.[44] And in Rouen, in Bayeux, in Troyes the female

[42] On the diet of the poor of Rouen in this period, Cobb, "Disette et Mortalité, La crise de l'an III et de l'an IV à Rouen", *Terreur et Subsistances*, pp. 309, 339-40; Hufton, *Bayeux*, p. 234.
[43] Arch. Nat. F^ic III Calvados 7.
[44] *Ibid.*: report of 20 Brumaire An IV.

death toll was far higher than the male — for the reasons suggested by the *curé* of Tours some twenty years previously.[45] If death usually came to the adult from a minor disease playing on a weak body, the chances of confining that disease within the hospitals was non-existent. Even under the *ancien régime*, these were fairly frail institutions catering only for the poor urban sick but the nominal absorption of their property in the Year II by the government and the suspension of payments to them meant that except in the large cities where departmental authorities stalled on putting the property up for sale, the hospitals just closed: ceased to operate. Indeed, 1795-6 became legendary not only for the hardness of the times but for the total lack of any organs of public relief. The mayor of Toulouse in 1816 challenged a group of petitioners about the inadequacy of poor relief with the words: do you prefer the charity of the *philosophes?* He needed to say no more: *la charité des philosophes* was no charity.[46]

There can be no over-emphasizing that the revolts of Germinal and Prairial mark that frontier, that psychological watershed, that last weapon in the armoury — whichever metaphor one chooses to express the final woman's protest before watching herself and her family spill over into that silent twilight world of the weak and the worn out which is so difficult to fathom because so largely inarticulate: it was her last defence of her human relationships. One can perhaps discount the accompanying cries of *vive le roi*, or the Parisian one for the days of Robespierre, the rivers of blood and the time of cheap bread or the Bayeux one of "quand le bon Dieu était là nous avions du pain" ("when God was there we had bread"), as more an expression of opposition to the present than hankering for the past; though one should take more seriously the women's cries for peace in Rouen and even more in the frontier towns of the East like Besançon and Vesoul where war fever had run so high in 1792. The cry for peace was one for normalcy: to call a halt — their great grandmothers had done the same in 1709 under exactly the same physical conditions.

The aftermath of Germinal had been indicated in terms of suicides,

[45] The death toll of children was of course the highest of all. On the situation in Rouen, Dieppe and Havre, see Cobb, "Disette et Mortalité...", pp. 339-42; the death rate at Bayeux rose overall by some 30% but that of adult males was scarcely affected: Hufton, *Bayeux*, p. 235 and Arch. Dépt. Calvados, Etat Civil, Bayeux, Registres 32 and 33; similarly in the case of an overall rise of some 35% at Troyes, Arch. Dépt. Aube 40H.

[46] D. Higgs, "Politics and Charity at Toulouse, 1750–1850", *French Government and Society 1500-1850: Essays in Memory of Alfred Cobban*, ed. by J. F. Bosher (London, 1973), pp. 191-207. According to Dr. Higgs the failure of the Revolution to make any provision for the poor, and the pauperization of the once proud and independent was a fact much capitalized by Restoration governments.

the daily occurrence of women and children fished out of the Seine, economically and emotionally bankrupt,[47] but one might more profitably linger on another aspect: the revival of popular catholicism, perhaps one of the most striking characteristics of popular history in the last five years of the eighteenth century and one in which the rôle of women was decisive.

The intensity of religious fervour that emerged from 1792 was without parallel in the eighteenth century. Much remains to be explored of the quality of religious belief under the *ancien régime*: indications point to a general formal adherence to the faith without the existence of any marked degree of fervour and of areas where even formal adherence was diminishing — perhaps that most particularly in the cities which attracted the rural immigrant and where the pattern of religious worship was most easily eroded.[48] Certainly anti-clericalism could always find popular support in the towns perhaps because here the wealth of the higher clerics was most conspicuously on view. Moreover the anti-clericalism which surrounded the implementation of the civil constitution of the clergy was an end in itself: it was not part of a wider movement, part of a programme for the achievement of religious purity. Latreille noted the falling off of observance in the towns from mid 1791 when clerics became involved with the pros and cons of oath-taking and the framework of religious worship became clouded.[49] Without doubt, the equation of "non-juror" with "traitor", the result of the panic surrounding the outbreak of war, made the non-juring church the object of popular violence in which women undoubtedly played their part.[50] The constitutional church never secured any widespread loyalty and a couple of years' absenteeism from worship was the background to the image breaking and desecration of places of worship in which women were often predominant during the

[47] Cobb, "Disette et Mortalité", p. 315 and the footnote; G. Duval, *Souvenirs thermidoreans* (Paris, 1843), and R. C. Cobb, *The Police and the People* (Oxford, 1970), pp. 161-2.
[48] This is a line of research on which much work is heralded in the imminent future (*Annales, E.S.C.*, xxv, 1970, "*Enquête Ouverte*".) in response to suggestions made by G. Le Bras, *Études de Sociologie Religieuse* (Paris, 1955), 2 vols. in which pointers to a decline in religious fervour in the towns at the end of the *ancien régime* are indicated; vol. i, pp. 51, 68; they are also made in P. Deyon, *Amiens, Capitale Provinciale* (Mouton, 1967), p. 425 and *Histoire de Bordeaux*, vol. iv (Bordeaux, 1968), pp. 140-1.
[49] A Latreille, *L'Eglise Catholique et la Révolution française* (Paris, 1964), p. 108.
[50] E. Sévèstre, *La Déportation du clergé orthodoxe pendant la Révolution* (Paris, 1915), p. 192; Uzureau, "La Déportation ecclésiastique dans le Calvados, 1792", *Revue Catholique de Normandie* (1931).

Jacobin period.[51]   In short, the women of this study could feel they had actively participated in the disintegration of the Roman Catholic Church: they had done enough to feel guilty, and the existence of this guilt is crucial to an appreciation of why, in 1796, women ended up on their knees and from then on worked wholeheartedly for the restoration of formal religion within France, the Roman Catholic religion of the *ancien régime*, but endowed with a new vigour from below.[52]

When Citoyenne Defarge, ex-*tricoteuse*, put down her needles and reached for a pair of rosary beads, an image to linger on if ever one was, she had to search out her priest and even force the opening of a church.   From late 1795 onwards, even in cities which had demonstrated the most intense anti-clericalism, like Paris, this is exactly what women did.   They brought back the formal worship of God.   Nor can this be shrugged off superficially as both Aulard and Mathiez did in terms of women turning from the *fanatisme* of their particular clubs to the *fanatisme des prêtres*.   This is only a half truth. They were not trying to revenge themselves on the Revolution.   The cycle of dearth, disease, devotion is a common enough one: one has only to think what fruitful ground the hardship of 1816 would provide for the priests of the mission, but in 1795 there was something extra, contrition.   The catholicism of 1795-onwards was the visceral kind: it owed its strength to the rigours of the times, the imminence of death from disease or undernourishment, disillusionment, shame, failure, the sense of contrition which sought as solace the *confiteor* and the *viaticum* and as such the sort of expiatory religion which defies rooting out.   Women at Vidouville, in the Calvados, queued to have their tongues scraped free of the contamination of the masses of a constitutional priest and ensuing blasphemies;[53] the wife of a fishmonger of St. Patrice, also in the Calvados, scrubbed out the parish church which her husband had bought for a song as national property to use as a fishmarket and which probably represented his one solid gain from the Revolution, and she and the women of the parish

[51] Perrin, *op. cit.,* pp. 636, 649.   In Besançon a midwife, a traditionally anti-clerical figure, led an attempt to lynch a non-juror: Bisson, *Histoire Eccléasitique du diocèse de Bayeux pendant la Révolution,* p. 20.

[52] On the return to religion of townswomen: C. Bloch, *Les femmes d'Orleans . . . ,* p. 66; R. Patry, *Le régime et la liberté des cultes dans le départment du Calvados pendant la première séparation, 1795-1802* (Paris, 1921), p. 60; Hufton, *Bayeux,* pp. 262-4; M. Reinhard, *Le départment de la Sarthe sous le Directoire* (Paris, 1935); Cobb, "Politique et Subsistances au Havre", *Terreur et Subsistances,* p. 251.

[53] Bibl. Chanoine Deslandes, Bayeux: correspondence of the episcopal vicars, an V - an VII.

handed it back to a non-juror emerging from exile while her husband couched an impotent letter of protest to an equally impotent departmental authority.[54]   The women of Coutances fought with each other over whose babies should be baptized first and the priest in question resolved the problem by a personal estimate of which ones were likely to be dead before he reached the end of the queue; he misjudged in two cases but he sprinkled water notwithstanding on their little corpses.   No government could hope to eradicate a church drawing on emotions which ran as deep as this: there was certainly nothing so fundamental in circulation in the last fifty years of the *ancien régime*. Such a movement had its vicious aspects.   It was an essential accompaniment of the White Terror, as in the diocese of Le Puy where women sought out local Jacobin leaders, clawed them to death or perhaps ripped them limb from limb while the churches of that most clerical of cities were triumphantly reopened.   But oftener the return to religion was quieter, less obtrusive, more symptomatic of the desire for a return to a way of life remembered.[55]

Women perhaps turned to the church too for another fundamental reason: revolution, war, famine — these are the dissolvents of the family while the church stood at least for its integrity, its sanctity; the hallowing of birth, marriage, death; the cement of something much more intrinsic than the social system.   When the cards were down and the scores chalked up, what really was the cumulative experience of the working woman from 1789-95?   How else could she assess the Revolution except by examining her wrecked household; by reference to children aborted or born dead, by her own sterility, by the disappearance of her few sticks of furniture, by the crumbling of years of effort to hold the frail family economy together and what could her conclusion be except that the price paid for putative liberty had been far too high?

[54] Arch. Dépt. Calvados, "Comptes décadaires", 19 Thermidor Year V.
[55] There was of course nothing incompatible in violence accompanying a religious revival.   On women in the White Terror and personal vendettas transmitted by them down the generations, Cobb, *The Police and the People*, p. 146.

7. The Justices of the Peace of Revolutionary Paris, September 1792–November 1794 (Frimaire Year III)*

RICHARD M. ANDREWS

Despite the salary, recruitment for the office of justice of the peace was democratized only very slightly in 1793. The office remained a monopoly of the upper levels of the petty bourgeoisie. It required of its aspirants a certain legal culture, and this was not an attribute of genuine *sans-culottes*. The justices of the peace were recruited generally among men of the legal profession from the Old Régime who had embraced the popular cause since the Revolution.[1]

IN THIS SEEMINGLY LUCID AND TOTALLY CONFIDENT STATEMENT, OF the sort that frequently mars the immense work of exploration and discovery achieved in the *Sans-culottes parisiens en l'an II*, Albert Soboul passes social and political judgement on the justices of the peace of Revolutionary Paris, and in doing so presents most of the ultimate, vital problems, difficult and unsolved, concerning the men who formed the political élites of the Paris Sections. What did "democratization" mean in the political life of the Sections and in the composition of their institutions? How can it be measured? And a statement of such pseudo-precision as the "upper levels of the petty bourgeoisie", which falsely suggests both that such razor-sharp demarcations existed in the social structure of Revolutionary Paris and that its author has their evidence in his line of vision, merely complicates the task of unravelling the very complex and incessantly moving fabric of late eighteenth-century Parisian life. As for the "genuine *sans-culottes*", there is no more elusive and mystifying phrase than this, either in the language of the Revolutionary generation itself or in that of its subsequent historiography. Finally, there is the supremely difficult question of the motives and behaviour of the official élites of the Sections and in their multiple relations with the labouring classes, a question so blithely veiled by the assurance that most of the justices of the peace, at least, were barristers "who had embraced the popular cause".

* This essay is extracted from a general study of the Section personnel of 1792–Year II, entitled "Political Élites and Social Conflicts in the Sections of Revolutionary Paris, 1792–Year III", (unpublished Univ. of Oxford D.Phil. Thesis, 1970).

[1] Albert Soboul, *Les Sans-culottes parisiens en l'an II. Mouvement populaire et Gouvernement révolutionnaire, 2 juin 1793 — 9 thermidor an II* (Paris, 1959), p. 604.

The *justice de paix*, the institution and its personnel, has been almost completely ignored by the historians of Revolutionary Paris. The purpose of the institution, set forth in the legislation of 1790-1 which created it, was explicitly and intentionally non-political. Of all Section offices, it was perhaps the least subject to governmental pressure and control. This institution, with that of the police commissioner, was one of the two most durable of local offices created by the Revolution, an office whose life-span stretched from the censitary régime of 1790-1 through the Empire and beyond, and in comparison with which civil and revolutionary committees were quite evanescent. Yet, for all its unobtrusiveness, its apparent banality, its seeming remoteness from the exhilarating rush of crowds in the streets, of vast "popular movements", from the marches and counter-marches of the Parisian Revolutionary Army, and from the swirling dialectic of "reactionaries and *sans-culottes*", the *justice de paix* was a totally revolutionary institution, a radical breach with the past, in conception, structure, and implications for local collective existence. It was one of the fundamental institutions of Section life, one through which the specific social character, the daily and *de facto* autonomy of a Quarter was expressed and preserved. Unlike police commissioners, whose principal "clients" were transients, outsiders, and elements peripheral but threatening to the life of a Section, the justices dealt with all groups of the resident and voting population in a range of vital matters which gave them possibilities for enjoying deep and intimate power. They had to maintain coherence and discipline in the social life of a Section, and they dealt constantly in subtle relations of domination and servitude.

For these reasons, the *justice de paix* commands the attention of any historian who wishes to penetrate the internal life of the Paris Sections. The functioning of the institution, the daily operations of the justices and their assessors, await their historian. Although relatively few records have survived from 1793-Year II, there are, in the *Archives départementales de la Seine*, dense series from the tribunals of about twenty Sections and their corresponding *arrondissements* covering the period 1795-1815. Any historian of Parisian social life during this period, of relations within families, workshops, businesses, and between social groups at odds in every sphere of urban life, any historian who wishes to explain how the legal and social power of the propertied classes was maintained in the great City, will have to mine this ore.

This essay, concentrated on the personnel of the institution, on the justices, their recording secretaries and assessors, from 1792 through the Year II, and on their relations with political groups, forces, and crises in Section life during those years, may prepare some of the terrain for those who undertake to study the institution itself.   This was one of the most sophisticated institutions through which the Parisian bourgeoisie preserved its social order, and its magistrates of the Directory and Empire surely must have learned much from the experience of their predecessors in 1792-Year II.

The legislators who created the office intended that its personnel should transcend all forms of partisanship within their jurisdictions. They also quite publicly intended that the office should be held by men of a certain temperament and moral character: the legislators of the Constituent Assembly were far more interested in a certain type of bourgeois patriarch than in those whose basic claim to the office was a "legal culture", however brilliant.   Through examining the justices, one can see the refraction of these legislative intentions, or their outright perversion, in the mentality and priorities of the Parisian voters and militants who elected and dismissed or imprisoned these men in 1792-Year III.   And through this refraction and perversion of legislative intentions, one can also glimpse the virility and tenacity of localism in Revolutionary Paris, of Quarters determined to choose men who would reflect their social and civic character.   The careers of the justices — how they came to the office, their tactics of survival once there, how they left the office and their subsequent fates — can also suggest the nature and depth of political conflict throughout the City.   The route to any understanding of the place of the revolutionary committees in the Section régime of 1793-Year II, and of the local meaning of their Terror, passes through a scrutiny of justices of the peace, police commissioners and civil committees, and not simply from one "popular thrust" and insurrectionary *journée* to another.

"The *justice de paix*!   The very phrase generates enthusiasm; it warms the heart"!   Enthusiasm and confidence, these were the sentiments shared by the deputies of the Constituent Assembly who created the institution in 1790, sentiments expressed by Prugnon.[2] The nation-wide desire for local self-government and the equally powerful desire for some form of uniform but local justice, paternalistic and equitable, which would both serve the poor and minimize litigation, these were the sovereign moral forces presiding at the creation of the justices of the peace in 1790-1.   Thouret, spokesman

---

[2] Cited by Edmond Seligman, *La Justice en France pendant la Révolution* (Paris, 1913), i, 302.

for the Constitution Committee, sketched the original contours of
the institution on 14 October 1790:

> We must enable the justices to settle the disputes referred to them by simple,
> rapid and inexpensive means, by means which will lead to a judgement
> without creating the impression that a formal proceeding has taken place;
> to do this, we must set aside all those precedents created by the complicated
> system of Old Régime justice . . . .[3]

Here, there was large unanimity among the deputies. The debates
were brief and the institution was constituted by laws of 16 August
and 14 October 1790. The first "generation" of justices was
elected in November and December 1790 in villages, cantons and
urban Sections throughout France.

The institution was to be as stable as possible, and the office of
justice, something of a genuine vocation. The justices were elected
for a term of two years and could be re-elected; a justice who abandoned the office or who could not complete his term was to be immediately replaced by a new election, and should this be momentarily
impossible, the first of his six assessors became temporary, acting
justice. Justices had to be thirty years of age and eligible for district
offices. To protect the civil "purity" of the office, no justice,
recording secretary (*greffier*) or assessor could be concurrently an
officer of municipality, district or *département*, and none could
exercise concurrently the professions of barrister, solicitor, private
recording secretary, notary, process-server or tax collector. The
justices were to have no specific hours for audiences. A sort of flying
squadron of legal order and social peace, they were to be permanently
available, even to judge, arbitrate, and conciliate in homes, cafés,
wine-shops, ateliers, on the streets, at the very sites and moments of
disputes. And they were well paid, 2,400 *livres* a year, a salary raised
by the Convention on 8 June 1793 to the sum of 2,700 *livres*. They
and their recording secretaries could also charge small sums, up to
three *livres*, for such operations as notification of judgements, preparation of documents, placing and raising of seals. A justice could not
manipulate his office as a sinecure; if he was absent from his functions
for more than eight days at a time, for any reason, his salary went to
the assessor who replaced him as acting justice.

Each justice was assisted by a recording secretary, a process-server
(*huissier*) and six assessors. Together, they formed the *bureaux de
paix*. The recording secretary, an extremely important figure since
he was responsible for procedure, documents, and maintaining the
integrity of legal form, and the process-server were both appointed

---

[3] *Ibid.*, i, p. 181.

by the justice and could be dismissed by him. Recording secretaries were subject to the same restrictions as justices but were paid considerably less, only 800 *livres* a year, which was raised to 950 *livres* by the Convention in June 1793. The six assessors were elected for a term of two years and they were not salaried. Their service was by rotation; two assessors had to be active constantly, but only for two-month periods each. And the institution was to be highly visible, in symbols of the authority and inviolability of its officers; justices when in public or in their offices were to wear a large oval medallion bearing the inscription "The Law and Peace" in white letters, on a blue ground with a red border, and the process-servers on their rounds were to carry a special white baton.[4]

Parties to disputes before a justice of the peace could not have legal counsel. These were to be frank, direct confrontations, insulated from the divisive eloquence of men of the law. One of the institution's principal commentators, the barrister Antoine Colin, succinctly expressed the reason for this prohibition: "Under the new régime as before, the professionals of the law are interested only in litigation. By exaggerating the claims of the disputants, they would prevent conciliation and thus defeat the essential purpose of the institution itself".[5] And this adjudication was practically gratuitous; justices were entitled to levy a maximum of twelve *livres* for the total costs of procedure and judgement. Originally, justices had no coercive powers, although they could summon a defendant against whom a complaint had been made and if the defendant refused to appear within a fixed period of time they could give judgement by default which was not subject to appeal.

[4] *Archives parlementaires*, xviii, 104-10; xix, 605, 610-14; lxvi, 164. At the end of August 1792 the Legislative Assembly conceded that justices could hold office in the administrations of municipalities, districts and Departments, a concession made in recognition of the fact that there were several newly elected justices among the members of the Insurrectionary Commune of Paris, and also because of the scarcity of qualified candidates for administrative offices in rural areas. And under the republican régime, from 16 September 1792, the age of eligibility for the office of justice was reduced to twenty-five. Finally, on 8 Nivôse Year II, the Convention decreed that henceforth justices and recording secretaries would no longer be elected or dismissed by their Sections, but by the municipalities in cities and by the district administrations in rural areas, under the surveillance and ultimate authority of the Committee of Public Safety. See *Archives parlementaires*, xlvii, 499; l, 60 and Soboul, *op. cit.*, p. 604. Since this essay was written, an excellent, detailed description of both the nature of the *justice de paix* and the richness of the institution's records has been published: Nicole Felkay, "Notes sur les fonds des justices de paix, 1791-1830", *Annales historiques de la Révolution française*, 1970, pp. 530-49.

[5] Antoine Colin, *Réflexions sur quelques articles du Code de police correctionnelle* (Paris, 1792), p. 23. British Museum (cited hereafter as Brit. Mus.), F.R. 224 (18).

This was pre-eminently the civil justice of the poor. Any claim for damages or dispute involving one hundred *livres* or less had to be decided by the justice of the peace, and without possibility of appeal to a civil court in cases of sums under fifty *livres*. It was also designed to prevent ligitation, to keep disputants out of the civil courts: parties to disputes involving more than one hundred *livres* had to resort first to the conciliatory authority of the local justice, but at their own risk, for in these cases a justice could fine a plaintiff up to sixty *livres* should he judge the claim unfounded; only if one or more of the parties refused the settlement offered by the justice could the case be brought, by the disputants themselves, before a civil court.

The competence of a justice was vast, and specifically embraced the following types of actions: claims for damages, conflicts of interest between landlords, lessees, *principaux locataires*, and tenants over rents and occupancy; wage disputes between employers and workers or domestic servants, as well as complaints by employers of non-execution of engagements by employees; complaints involving "verbal injury, brawls and assaults" which were not made to police commissioners; the placing and raising of seals on property; family justice and guardianship. Here then, were most of the points of chronic tension in the life of any community. Justices were called upon to preserve the structure of private property, and within it, to conciliate disputes between those who owned and lived off property and the property-less who supported them. They were responsible for maintaining the social organization of production, for maintaining the relationship between those who bought labour and those who sold it. They dealt with the very thorny, explosive matters of insults, threats, "moral assassination" and actual violence among a people and during a period much given to sanguine emotions, and in Paris, the densely populated city whose residents were condemned to live in such close proximity to each other and where such outbursts had to be appeased and their damages repaired if bare, daily order was to be preserved in a residential building, at a work-site, on a street. They were privy to the secrets of the basic unit of eighteenth-century French society, the family, and responsible for bolstering its moral unity and preserving its social continuity.

Justices, recording secretaries and assessors also formed "offices of charitable jurisprudence", obliged to provide the poor with free legal advice and even to arrange counsel for them among the public defenders which proliferated in Paris after 1789. Dispensers of "charitable jurisprudence", they were magistrates defending the rule of law itself and on its first line of defence, against the frustration, desperation and resentment of the poor and illiterate, against impulses which could lead to summary, "popular" justice and vengeance. However benevolent and sentimentally generous this rôle may seem, it was, one suspects, a more subtle and effective means of social control than those used by police and revolutionary commissioners. In fact, greater legal knowledge and general sophistication were required of competent justices than were required of equally competent police and revolutionary commissioners, for these latter officials enforced a comparatively accessible criminal code or set of laws and directives concerning suspects, and they were aided by the tribunals and the great Committees of Government which had the responsibility for final decisions in all cases. The justice of the peace stood alone. For him to refer a case to the judgement of the courts was an admission of failure. He and his associates had to interpret and apply decisively a fluid mass of civil statutes and decrees, many of them contradictory, which were continually being voted, modified and repealed by the legislatures of the Revolution. Justices were not even provided with dispatches of laws and decrees until after 5 August 1793. Until then, the assiduous justice (or his recording secretary) had to read the *Moniteur* every day; he knew the high politics of the Revolution and its movement on a national scale.

It is not mere coincidence that among those justices who in 1792-Year II were genuine political leaders in their Sections, who had real power among the labouring *sans-culotterie*, most — such as Mathias Hû in the Panthéon-Français, Florentin Phulpin in the Arcis, Pierre-Nicolas Letellier in Bondy, Mathurin Bouin in the Marchés, Jean-Marie Martin in the Gravilliers, Toussaint Wisnick in the Maison-Commune, Pierre Blandin in the Lombards, and Joachim Ceyrat in the Luxembourg — exercised their office in Sections with high proportions of poor or barely literate citizens. Here and there, one can glimpse the social geography and roots of the power enjoyed by these justices, as well as its dangers. In a letter to the Legislation Committee of the Convention in Germinal Year II, Pierre-Nicolas Letellier of Bondy sketched some of the complex social and moral terrain in which a justice, and particularly a justice in the Faubourgs, had to manoeuvre:

My Section is composed for the most part of labourers of all sorts and vegetable gardeners; disputes between them usually involve only very small, but very precious, sums of money. I am often obliged to ask them to choose arbitrators, to estimate, for example, the value of a crop of vegetables or the average rate of pay of labourers in a certain trade, at a certain time. Since each citizen has the right to choose his own arbitrator, the vegetable gardener chooses another vegetable gardener and the labourer, another labourer from the same trade, and I am forced to render a judgement.[6]

[6] Archives nationales (cited hereafter as A.N.), D III 253, *liasse* 21.

Florentin Phulpin, who had masses of coal heavers, water carriers and dock labourers among his clientele in the Arcis, could exclaim, in complaining to the Committee of Decrees in Pluviôse Year II, that since 14 Frimaire he had not received the daily dispatch of laws and decrees:

> These consignments are vital to me, since my Section is populated by uneducated *sans-culottes* who come to me constantly with their personal disputes. In my office, these disputes are settled without summations and charges; during my eighteen months as justice there have been only twenty-seven summations and I am certain that each day I settle at least thirty disputes. [7]

In the Marchés, Mathurin Bouin used the full range of his authority, legal and extra-legal, to spare the families of volunteers having to pay rents which they could not afford to pay while their breadwinners were with the armies. [8]

The revolutionary circumstances of 1792-Year II which widened the possibilities for influence and power available to these justices among the *menu peuple*, also made them vulnerable in the Year III. The merchants and landlords who imprisoned the "terrorist" Mathurin Bouin in Prairial Year III as an "anarchist" and subverter of property had not forgotten that the justice of the peace Bouin had defended the families of volunteers against the lawful exactions of their landlords, and when the Thermidorian bourgeoisie of the Fontaine-de-Grenelle poured out its hatred of the justice Balthazard-Marie Laugier, one of the Jacobin leaders of the Section, in the proscription session of 30 Pluviôse Year III, one voice in the assembly, that of someone against whom Laugier had rendered a judgement, shrieked at him, "Thief! You wanted to confiscate and sell all my furniture"! [9]

It is also not coincidence that most of the prominent justices of 1792-Year II were articulate, consequent Jacobins. In its paternal stance towards the poor, its purpose of reducing tensions and conciliating differences within the social ranks of the "Third Estate", of upholding the legal order elaborated by the Revolutionary bourgeoisie, the *justice de paix* embodied Jacobin ideology and political strategy. And these Jacobin justices, at the same time magistrates of social peace and combative political militants, themselves embodied the ambivalence and contradictions of both Jacobinism and the *justice de paix* in a situation of revolutionary crisis.

The institution had an intense propoganda, a series of highly publicized images of the ideal justice: he is a patriarch, charitable,

---

[7] A.N., D XL, 27.
[8] A.N., D III 253, *liasse* 17.
[9] Archives départmentales de la Seine (cited hereafter as A.D.S.), 2AZ 259.

knowing and firm, who transcends partisanship although constantly dealing with its most extreme forms; he is a daily architect of social unity, imposing reason on emotional chaos; he is the "tutelary angel of the Quarter".[10] In 1793-Year II the official imagery was the same as it had been in 1790-1, and it was perhaps best expressed by Sylvain Bailly, mayor of Paris, when he addressed the first "generation" of justices assembled at the *Hôtel-de-Ville* to take the Constitutional Oath in January 1791:

> Magistrates of the people, it is you who will always stand by the people to educate and to guide them . . . . Apostles of peace in the midst of your fellow citizens, you shall strengthen all the bonds of cohesion among them. In protecting family unity, you will serve public morality and in preserving harmony among individuals, you will lay the foundations of public harmony.[11]

In the evening of 2 September 1792, a citizen of the Section Luxembourg burst into the meeting of its general assembly to announce in horror that the priests incarcerated at the near-by *Carmes* were being massacred, and Joachim Ceyrat, the Section's recently elected justice of the peace who presided over the assembly, icily replied: "What? You mean to say that the job is not finished yet"?[12] But it was not Jacobin justices like Ceyrat, "men of 10 August" or *sans-culottes* of 1793-Year II, who degraded the ideal of this office by politicizing it; this was begun by the friends of Sylvain Bailly, the *constituants* who created the institution.

On 19 July 1791, two days after the "massacre" on the *Champ de Mars* and in a psychological climate of defensive panic, the Constituant Assembly forced police responsibilities upon the justices of the peace, making them agents of political repression. The formidable "law of correctionel police" voted then stipulated that those arrested for "offending public morality", damaging property, theft, fraud, gambling, violence or insults against persons, troubling the exercise of religious cults, and, most importantly, for any seditious statements or actions which in any way trouble "social order and public tranquillity", including provocation to insurrection, riot or "tumults and illegal gatherings", were to be arraigned, without legal counsel, before the local justice of the peace who was made responsible for deciding if there would be prosecution by the criminal courts. And justices were also empowered by this law to order arrests.

The "insulation" of the justices of the peace was torn away by

---

[10] This expression was used by Antoine Colin, *op. cit.*, p. 18. See also J. Barbier, *Réflexions sur la justice de paix* (Paris, 1792). Bibliothèque Nationale (cited hereafter as B.N.), Lb40 1798.
[11] Cited by Seligman, *op. cit.*, i, p. 356.
[12] A.N., D III 254, *liasses* 12 and 13.

this law and the uses to which it was put by royalists and constitutional monarchists during the bitter prelude to the Insurrection of 10 August 1792. On 26 June, the Court gathered some twenty pro-monarchist justices into a "central committee of justices of the peace" which began the pursuit of those deemed responsible for the seditious *journée* of 20 June, and particularly of the Municipal officers Petion and Manuel, and Santerre, the Commander-in-Chief of the Paris National Guard. The personnel of the *justice de paix*, like that of most Section offices, had been embroiled in that conflict between monarchists and "patriots" which wracked Paris in the spring and summer of 1792, and one of the first actions of the Insurrectionary Commune, on 11 August, was to suspend all the incumbent justices. On the 15th it ordered the Sections to elect justices and the Convention ratified these decrees on 22nd September when it ordered a general renewal of administrative and judicial personnel.[13] By the end of September, most Sections had elected new justices, and although the Convention gave them the option of re-electing justices "who had deserved well of the nation", only seven of the forty-eight chose this option.

The Convention never formally annulled the police powers forced on the justices by the law of 19 July 1791, although in October 1792 twenty-three newly elected Paris justices petitioned the Convention to relieve them formally of these "odious responsibilities" and thereby resurrect in its original purity an institution "dedicated to promoting friendship and concord among citizens".[14] But, as with much of the legislation of the Constituent Assembly and the legal apparatus of the Constitution of 1791, the police rôle of the justices was simply not performed by most of them in Paris after 10 August 1792, nor did the Convention demand that it be performed. Henceforth, police commissioners generally carried out the tasks which had been foisted on justices of the peace by the law of 19 July 1791. Under the republican régime, the institution returned, *de facto*, to its original purposes, but it had been invaded by politics, and henceforth its stability would depend on local rhythms of political conflict.

Fifty-eight of the sixty-five justices who served between September

---

[13] The text of the notorious *loi de police correctionnelle* is in *Archives parlementaires*, xxviii, 420-33. On the "central committee" at the Tuileries, see Seligman, *op. cit.*, i, pp. 126-30. For an example of highly effective use of justices of the peace as agents of repression of a popular movement, see my "L'assassinat de Jean-Louis Gérard, négociant lorientais (15 septembre 1792)", *Annales historiques de la Révolution française*, 1967, pp. 309-38.

[14] *Pétition des Juges de Paix de la Ville de Paris à la Convention nationale* (Paris, 1792), p. 2. Brit. Mus., F. 570 (19).

1792 and Frimaire Year III entered the office either in the general renewal in the aftermath of 10th August or in 1793-Year II: in only seven Sections was the transition from the censitary to the republican régime effected without replacement of the justice of the peace. The great renewal, the one which was a genuine watershed in the social and civic history of this institution from its creation in 1790 until the purges of Germinal-Prairial Year III, took place in August-September 1792. From then until at least Frimaire Year III, the office was stable, held by the same man, in thirty of the forty-eight Sections. Of these thirty justices who served their two-year terms, twenty-six were new men who entered the office through the Insurrection of 10th August, and managed to survive the successive political conflicts of 1793-Year II until at least the purges in the spring of the Year III. For at least twelve of these thirty (and eleven of the twenty-six "new men" of 10th August), the price of survival in office in 1793-Year II was dismissal and imprisonment in Germinal-Prairial Year III, as Jacobin militants, accomplices of revolutionary committees, and partisans of the régime of the Year II.

In seventeen Sections, the justices elected or re-elected in the renewal of August-September, 1792 were replaced in 1793-Year II.[15] Only two of them resigned. Two others, J. Roulleau (Marais) and Nicolas Mathieu (Piques), were dismissed and imprisoned by the government during the Year II and on charges of fraud and peculation. The remaining thirteen were all engulfed in the conflicts and upheavals within their Sections in 1793-Year II, dismissed and in most cases imprisoned as "royalists", "moderates" or "aristocrats".[16]

Only eighteen of these sixty-five justices entered the office in 1793 or during the Year II. These were the *sans-culotte* justices of the peace, who owed their tenure of office to the dismissal and political imprisonment of their predecessors in the "regeneration" battles of 1793 and to the interventions by the Committees of Government in the faction conflicts within their Sections during the Year II. Most ascended to office through their favour with the revolutionary committees of their Sections, and at least six of these eighteen were dismissed and imprisoned as terrorists either in the aftermath of the 9-10 Thermidor or in Germinal and Prairial Year III.

The personal and political attrition was very intense among these

[15] It is uncertain if Louis Houet, justice of the Section Lepeletier during the Year II, had been retained from the censitary régime or elected after 10 August 1792; this is the only Section without a dossier in A.N., D III 253 or 254.

[16] On the case of Roulleau, who had also run foul of the Section's revolutionary commissioners, see A.N., D III 254, *liasse* 4 and A.N., F7* 2496, f. 12. On the case of Mathieu, see A.N., BB3 56 and A.N., D III 253, *liasse* 21.

sixty-five justices of September 1792-Frimaire Year III. At least thirty of them came to know the interior of political prisons either in 1793-Year II or in the Years III and IV. The political reality of this office in the Paris of 1792-Year III was far removed from the pacific and benevolent anticipations of Prugnon and his colleagues ("The very phrase warms the heart!"), although its social composition during this period did indeed approximate to the intention of the Constituent Assembly. The paradox was only superficial: the same process which, beginning in the summer of 1792 and continuing through the Year II, opened the office of justice to practically all categories of the Parisian bourgeoisie also, and simultaneously, drew it into the vortex of the conflicts within the ranks of this bourgeoisie, transforming it into a prize and a weapon.

The *justice de paix* of September 1792-Frimaire Year III was the "monopoly" not of the "upper levels of the petty bourgeoisie", but of the full range of the Parisian bourgeoisie, in nearly all the diverse expressions of its social personality.[17] The democratization of the office which began in the aftermath of the 10th August continued through 1793-Year II, and in the two senses in which general Paris politics were democratized during this period. In the passage from the censitary to the republican régime there was a radical change in recruitment for the office. The monopoly of Old Régime professionals — former solicitors, barristers and magistrates of royal courts — was broken and the office was opened to practically every segment of the Parisian bourgeoisie, to the artisan trades, manufacturing, commerce, the liberal professions, including the most modest, as well as to certain men who had no careers other than those created by the Revolution. By the end of the Year II, the staffing of the institution was symmetrical to the general social pattern of local leadership in Paris, and it bore no resemblance to the composition of the *justice de paix* on the eve of 10 August 1792. In several Sections, although not in most, the new recruitment also meant a clear devolution of authority in class terms, but on a metropolitan scale the staffing of the office of justice never became socially uniform or settled at any discernible class level. This expansion of social recruitment was an affirmation of localism, of the primacy of the

[17] The principal sources for the study of the institution's personnel during this period are the dossiers on the justices and their *bureaux de paix* which were compiled in Frimaire Year III by the Legislation Committee of the Convention, in A.N., D III 253 and 254; the lists of civil personnel of the Sections compiled in Vendémiaire Year III, in A.N., Flb II Seine, 18; the *Almanachs*, royal and national, for 1792-Year II; and the various police and political records which appear in subsequent footnotes.

Quarter in selecting men who would reflect its character; in this sense also, the *justice de paix* was politically democratized after the Insurrection of 10th August. By the end of the Year II, the institution was thoroughly local in its social character; its responsibilities were assumed by men as socially diverse as the Parisian bourgeoisie itself, men whose diversity corresponded to the geography of this bourgeoisie and whose election to office expressed its collective vitality and self-confidence. In 1792-Year II, the essential qualifications for the office were no longer "external", professional experience of royal courts, certified knowledge of the law, expertise in manipulating the formulas of government, but now "internal," roots, productivity, identity, "place" within the social and political life of a Section.

In Paris and until the Insurrection of 10th August, justices were indeed generally recruited among "men of the legal profession of the Old Régime" but hardly among those who in any sense had "embraced the popular cause", at least in the judgement of the democrats who ejected all but a very few of them from office in the immediate aftermath of the Insurrection and then imprisoned many as royalists in 1793-Year II. At least twenty-six of the forty-eight justices in office at the time of the Insurrection were professionals of the law.[18] These were not fledglings of the bar; there were no explicit solicitors and only one recent graduate of the Faculty among them. Many, if not most, were figures such as Jean-Baptiste Jossier (Gravilliers), former advocate of the *Cour des Aides*, Étienne de la Rivière (Pont-Neuf), former advocate of the *Parlement* of Paris, Sanson Duperron (Bon-Conseil), former advocate of the Royal Council, Antonie-Joseph Thorillon (Finistère), former prosecuting attorney at the *Châtelet*, or Nicolas-Alexandre Herbault (Marchés) and Nicolas-Vincent Légier (Postes), both former prosecuting attorneys at the *Parlement* of Paris, men who had known substantial careers with suppressed royal courts and jurisdictions and who found an ideal transitional employment as justices of the peace.[19] The office was well-paid, and because of its prestige within Section politics it practically guaranteed its incumbent admission to the electoral assembly of the Paris

---

[18] *Almanach royal*, 1792. These twenty-six are of the thirty-three justices of 1792 who have been socially identified. Among the remaining seven, there were two wholesale merchants, one merchant-tradesman, one business agent, two former notaries, and a former private secretary to the count of Artois.

[19] On Jossier, see A.N., F7 4757, d. Jossier. On Étienne de la Rivière, one of the most prominent of the monarchist justices, see A.N., BB3 52, d. Delarivière. On Sanson Duperron, Thorillon, and Herbault, see *Almanach royal*, 1792, pp. 373-74, 398. And on Légier, see A.N., F7 4584, d. Bachelard.

département, where he could manoeuvre for the judge's chair of a civil or criminal tribunal, an executive position in the administration of the *département*, or even a deputy's seat in the national legislature. The price exacted, and particularly after the crisis of Varennes, was loyalty to the censitary régime and to its monarchy; in June 1792 over twenty of these monarchist justices, most of whom were among the professionals of the law, paid this price in full at the *Tuileries*, in the "central committee of the justices of the peace".

Men of the legal profession generally accounted for a far greater portion of the Parisian élite in 1789–92 than they did after the 10th August, but their numbers were diminished and their influence eclipsed after the Insurrection more rapidly and dramatically in the case of the *justice de paix* than in that of any other Section institution. Of the forty-two justices who have been socially identified in the "generation" elected or re-elected in late August and September 1792, only eight were men of the law, and of the twenty-six new men in this group, only four. Two of the barristers retained from the censitary régime had more than professional claims to office. Claude-Louis Thuillier in the Théâtre-Français, who was sixty-seven in 1792, held his office from its creation in 1790 until at least Frimaire Year III in a Quarter where he had resided since long before 1789, and where men of the law and related liberal professions composed much of the indigenous social élite as well as the successive political élites from 1789 to the Year III; he had also been a member of the permanent committee of the District of the Cordeliers, with Georges Danton and Camille Desmoulins, and joined the Jacobin Club in the early years of the Revolution. In Molière-et-Lafontaine, Claude Lefrançois, a former prosecuting attorney at the *Châtelet*, remained justice from 1791 until at least Frimaire Year III; here, men of the law, bureaucracies and finance dominated Quarter and Section before and during the Revolution.[20] The barristers Pierre-Étienne Patris in Ponceau and François-Marie Botot in Temple were both re-elected in Sections where conservatives were still strong in September 1792; in September 1793 they would be swept from office and replaced respectively by a decorative painter and a former barrister's clerk, when these conservative blocs were smashed. The four men of the law who entered the office in the aftermath of the Insurrection entered as "patriots". Only Jean-Antoine Buquet (Cité) had enjoyed a substantial legal career under the Old Régime. As for the extremely supple barrister Nicolas Chépy (Louvre), he had been installed in

[20] On Thuillier, see A.N., D III 254, *liasse* 21; and on Lefrançois, see A.N., D III 253, *liasse* 20.

the Quarter of the Louvre, in an apartment on the place du Chevalier-du-Guet, since well before 1789, and from the outbreak of the Revolution through at least the Year II he was a figure in the Section's militant élite and a member of the Jacobin Club from December 1790 until Brumaire Year III. Charles Pointard was a simple advocate who replaced one of the most active pro-monarchist justices of the "central committee", J. Fayel, and during his tenure of office (until at least Frimaire Year III) he was the very type of the discreetly non-political justice in an intensely political Section, the Droits-de-l'Homme. One doubts that J. B. Lessore (*sans-culotte*) was an established barrister; he was only thirty in 1791 when he accepted the ill-paid office of recording secretary to the justice of the peace, the office from which he was promoted justice in late August 1792.[21]

Fifteen of the eighteen men who entered the office in 1793 or during the Year II have been socially identified, and only two of these *sans-culotte* justices were men of the law. J.–B. Dournel (Temple) and Sylvain Lardy (Panthéon-Français) were both young men from the lowest ranks of the profession, from dubious careers which had been abandoned for more lucrative Revolutionary office.[22]

The social physiognomy of the institution during this period resembled that of the City's general élite, relatively successful artisans, tradesmen and merchants allied with the prolific liberal professions of office employees, various functionaries and bureaucrats, private tutors, as well as with those who lived off properties, and a handful of genuine *dégringoleurs* who depended utterly on the Revolution for a career. The largest single group among the justices of September 1792-Frimaire Year III were the eighteen artisans, tradesmen, manufacturers and merchants, followed by ten men of the legal profession, seven various office employees and bureaucrats, four professional process-servers and two recording secretaries, four educationalists (two private tutors, or *instituteurs*, one professor at at the "Collège des Quatre-Nations", and one boarding-school master, or *maître de pension*), two rentiers, one business agent, one former chief clerk to a notary, one priest, one medical doctor, one land surveyor, one artistic painter, one former private secretary to a noble family, and finally, one total revolutionary with no occupation.

Through the Insurrection of 10th August, the recruitment of

---

[21] On Buquet, see A.N., Flb II Seine, 18. On Chépy, see A.N., D III 253, *liasse* 21 and A.N., F7 4645, d. Chépy. On Pointard, see A.N., D III 254, *liasse* 4. And on Lessore, see A.N., D III 254, *liasse* 20.
[22] Ob Dournel, see A.N., D III 253, *liasse* 26 and D III 256⁴, *liasse* 9. On Sylvain Lardy, see A.N., D III 239, *liasse* and D III 254, *liasse* 15.

assessors shifted in the same social directions as did that of justices. Of the 266 assessors in office on the eve of the Insurrection, 189 have been socially identified. The dominant group among them were the sixty-eight men of the law (fifty-three persons qualified simply as *hommes de loi*, six definite barristers, one solicitor, two former counsels to the *Châtelet*, one former counsel to the *Chambre des Comptes*, one former prosecuting attorney at the *Châtelet*, one former prosecuting attorney of the Grand Council, one former advocate of the *Chambre des Comptes*, one former judge-advocate of the Chancellery of the *Parlement*, and a former President of the *Cour des Monnaies*), followed by thirty-seven artisans, tradesmen, merchants and entrepreneurs, many of whom were retired (and of whom only nine were of the building and associated trades and eight of the luxury crafts, two of the most dense social groups among the assessors and general Section personnel of 1793-Year II), twenty wholesale merchants (*négociants*), most of whom were retired, twelve rentiers, eleven notaries, twenty-three men of diverse liberal professions, eight former magistrates of Old Régime bureaucracies or *corporations* (four former directors of the General Tax Farm, two former Judge-Consuls of the Paris guilds, one former general superintendent of road taxes, and one former chief magistrate or *échevin* of the *Hôtel-de-Ville*), only two employees in national bureaucracies, and one former valet.

Approximately two-thirds of these pre-10th August assessors were replaced in the six weeks following the Insurrection, and nearly half of the men elected to succeed them were still in official service at the end of the Year II. Between September 1792 and Frimaire Year III about five hundred men served as assessors, and 375 of them have been identified socially. Artisans, tradesmen, merchants and manufacturers were now the dominant group in the *bureaux de paix* of Revolutionary Paris, accounting for 228 of these 375, and among them were 110 artisans and manufacturers. Within this group there were forty-eight men of luxury crafts and commerce, forty-seven of the building and associated trades (in addition to nine architects), thirty-eight food and drink tradesmen (in addition to seven vegetable gardeners) of whom only four were definitely wholesale dealers, thirty-four of clothing and fabric manufacturing and commerce, and only nine explicit wholesale merchants. None were of the ambulant trades of the street, and the general social level of those involved in production seems to have been relatively high; at least twenty per cent had been employers or entrepreneurs as of 1790-1. Before the Insurrection, men of the legal profession accounted for at least 35·5 per cent of the assessors; in 1793-Year II they represented only nine per cent. And also in sharp contrast to the *bureaux* of 1791-2, in 1793-Year II there was a bloc of twenty-six employees of government or municipal bureaucracies (who were distributed among seventeen Sections), and there were only nine men living on pensions from the suppression of their employments in Old Régime bureaucracies and *corporations*. The remainder of the assessors of 1792-Year II were scattered among a gamut of vaguely liberal professions which, with the possible exceptions of an ex-infantryman, a riding and dancing master, a door-keeper and an actor, were both banal and respectable.

In 1793-Year II, the social distribution of the assessors corresponded to the geography and structure of the Parisian bourgeoisie. The assessors in the Sections of the Faubourgs were drawn largely from the building and associated trades, those in the Sections of the Halles and the rue Saint-Denis from commerce in food, drink, garments and the working of fabrics, those of the two Sections of the *Isle de la Cité* from the crafting of gold, silver and jewels, those of the Sections of western Paris from luxury commerce, the law, bureaucracies and finance, those of the Sections of the Latin Quarter and the *Montagne Sainte-Geneviève* from education, printing, publishing and the crafting and retailing of medallions and engravings.[23]

In the Paris of 1792-Year II, the lack of a "legal culture" did not prevent artisans, tradesmen and manufacturers from holding the office of justice of the peace. But the Section régime of those years, for all its political flux and putative anarchy, was sophisticated in vital matters and did maintain a subtle check on the possibilities of incompetence or disruption in the operation of the institution, possibilities which were created by the expanded social recruitment of justices. This check is discernible in the social recruitment of recording secretaries, the officers responsible for correct procedure, the precise manipulation of legal formulas, and the preparation of documents. There were seventy of them between September 1792 and Frimaire Year III — a figure predictably symmetrical to that of the justices during the same period, for justices appointed their recording secretaries and in all but a few cases the replacement of a justice, for political or other reasons, entrained that of his recording secretary. Fifty-two have been socially identified. At least thirty-two of them had some certified, professional capacity for this activity,

---

[23] The information concerning the assessors of 1791-2 has been drawn largely from the *Almanach royal*, 1792; that concerning the assessors of 1792-Year II has been drawn from the *Almanachs* for 1793 and Year II, the lists of civil and judicial personnel in A.N., D III 253, 254, Flb II Seine, 18, and the dossiers of employers in A.N., F30 115 to 159.

the eight former barristers' clerks, eight professional *huissiers*, five professional recording secretaries, five former clerks to notaries, three former clerks in Old Régime bureaucracies, two former advocates, one book-keeper and one ex-notary.   Most of these men were in their thirties when they were appointed, eager if not desperate for the office, and assiduous once there.   It is hardly surprising that most of the archly political justices of 1793-Year II, those who devoted at least as much energy to militancy as to the rôle of justice, chose their recording secretaries from within this group, and of the eighteen artisan, tradesmen and manufacturing justices at least twelve did so. The majority of these thirty-two came either from the debris of Old Régime institutions or from the lower ranks of the legal and notarial *cléraille*.   Their very social dependence guaranteed the institution a certain stability in operation and bred that political conformity which characterized most of the recording secretaries of 1792-Year II. Most of these thirty-two were spoken for in the dry, precise autobiographies of Frédéric Fariau (Marais), "former clerk of the commissioner Desrosiers at the *Châtelet*, recording secretary of the justice of the peace since the suppression of the *Châtelet*", of Jean-Charles Gavot (Invalides), "clerk of the Paris Bar until the end of 1790, and recording secretary since then", and in the language employed by the civil committee of the Section Popincourt in Frimaire Year III when it recommended the former recording secretary Pierre Varin for appointment as police commissioner: ".... Far more than the other candidates, who are all artisans, he has a flair for paper-work and procedure, and he knows the correct forms for conducting interrogations and keeping records; furthermore, he needs and wants the job far more than the others do".[24]

They could be the mainstays of their *bureaux*, but in the tense and partisan atmosphere of 1793-Year III the price of survival in office paid by many of these recording secretaries was the contempt of their

[24] A.N., D III 254, *liasse* 9 (Fariau); D III 254, *liasse* 21 (Gavot); D III 251-2, *liasse* 2 (Varin).   All but a very few of these recording secretaries of 1793-Year II were rather self-effacing functionaries, men without civic or personal salience.   The dramatic and singular exception was Pierre Vergne of the Section Lepeletier, an authentic militant who was simultaneously a revolutionary commissioner and recording secretary during the Year II. According to the Section's authorities of the Year III, "Vergne avoit un caractère qui lui étoit particulier; rencontroit-il un vieillard septuagenaire? Il s'écrioit, 'Voila un bougre bon à guillotiner; il est riche et vieux, et puis que fait-il sur la terre'?"   ("Vergne was a rather singular personality.   If he encountered an elderly man of seventy, he would shout: 'There's a customer for the guillotine!   He's old and rich, and besides, what on earth is he good for?'") A.N., C 336, *liasse* 1570, f. 23.

fellow citizens.   And this contempt could lead to proscription, as in the case, among several others, of Jacques-Charles Rousselet, a former barrister's clerk and the recording secretary of the Marchés from 1791 until the spring of the Year III:

> This recording secretary is a chameleon!   An aristocrat before the Revolution [for a time Rousselet had been a baillif and process-server at Choisy-sur-Seine], then a great friend and partisan of the Monarchy and the Constitution of 1789, and since the 10th August, an ultra-revolutionary democrat and *enragé*, a vociferous supporter of the cannibalistic politics of the anarchists and terrorists, today [Frimaire Year III] he is a perfect moderate and, as always, in order to keep his job.[25]

There were eight recording secretaries during this period who had been, or remained, artisans, tradesmen or merchants.   Their appointment to office was in every case blatantly political, the fruit of common militancy in general assembly or popular society with the reigning justice, and five of these appointments were made when general recruitment for Section offices was most elastic, in the late summer and autumn of 1793.   And yet even then, and in six of these eight situations, the respective *bureaux* were insulated against the possible incompetence of these recording secretaries by the fact that the justices who appointed them were men of the pen and verb by profession, whether ex-bureaucrats, educationalists or notaries.

At least in the social character of its personnel, in 1793-Year II this institution came much closer to the *constituants'* ideal of it — that it should be an immediate expression of local life, with a minimum social and psychological distance between its officials and the community which they served — than it had before the 10th August, when it was a prize among many for those armed with a legal culture. Most of the justices of September 1792-Frimaire Year III were men in their social and biological prime, with a local identity established either before the Revolution or through militancy during its course.   The ages in 1792 of thirty-seven of these sixty-five are known: the average was forty-four.   There were only two young men, aged twenty to thirty, and a solid group of twelve biological patriarchs, aged fifty to seventy, and separating these extremes, fourteen men aged thirty to forty and nine aged forty to fifty.   For many of them ascension to the office of justice was a translation into the local, political realities of 1792-Year II of a social importance and personal or family status acquired long before 1789.

J.-E.-A. Lebrun of the Croix-Rouge was sixty when he was elected justice in 1791, and had lived for forty years in the Quarter.   His was one of the great commercial families of the Croix-Rouge, and

[25] A.N., D III 253, *liasse* 17.

J.-E.-A. Lebrun himself one of the Quarter's genuine and perennial notables: the son of a rug merchant, he and his younger brother Joseph directed the rug business on the rue de Sèves which employed several of J.-E.-A. Lebrun's fifteen children and grandchildren; a natural member of the District's original political élite, he was Vice-President of its general and primary assemblies during most of 1789 and early 1790, first assessor to the justice of the peace in 1790-1, elector in 1790, 1791, and 1792, and one of the founders in 1791 of the *Société des Jeunes Amis de la Liberté* on the rue du Bac, the major popular society of the Faubourg Saint-Germain. Lebrun was a Jacobin and he remained in the inner core of the Section's political élite until the Year III. In local social terms as well as in the depth of his political influence, he was the most prominent of those merchants and tradesmen who allied with ruined wig-makers, ex-heraldic painters, ex-dancing and fencing masters, and a range of lingering *valetaille*, not to combat the aristocracy of the Faubourg, most of whose members had emigrated well before 1793, but to struggle for political domination against bourgeois of the professions, especially the law and bureaucracies, who were attached to the constitutional liberalism of 1789-92. This alliance, temporarily victorious in 1793-Year II, was the reign of the *sans-culottes* in the Croix-Rouge. His Thermidorian persecutors recognized the qualities of personal and social mastery which assured J.-E.-A. Lebrun this influence once he had accepted the rôle of Jacobin justice of the peace, but in their language these qualities were refracted to emerge, in mingled accents of envy and hatred, as personal tyranny based on social demagogy. And Lebrun could reply to them from prison during the Year III:

> If, when they accuse me of having "duped" and "misled" my fellow citizens, my enemies are speaking of a politics inspired by love of freedom and respect for popular sovereignty, a politics dedicated to emancipating my fellow citizens from the prejudices and customs inculcated in them by the education for slavery which they received from the Old Régime, I admit, I did my best to "dupe" and "mislead" them![26]

The figure of Pierre-Henri Blandin is redolent of the rue des Lombards, of a lucrative and intricate wholesale commerce in oils and spices whose web of dependants and clients was spun from an ancient, physically constricted centre to ensnare a mass of retailers in the Halles and an entire, dense bourgeoisie of luxury purveyors on the rue du Faubourg Saint-Honore and in the Palais-Royal. He was born on the rue des Lombards, and into this commerce. Its prosperity allowed him to retire in the spring of 1792, at the age of forty-one, to become a full-time revolutionary executive and, from the

---

[26] A.N., F7 4774³, d. Lebrun; A.N., D III 254, *liasse* 3.

somewhat Olympian position of a local bourgeois magnate, even to embrace a full measure of political extremism in the Lombards' popular society and general assembly during the Year II. "Constantly, he ingratiated himself into that class which he called the *sans-culottes*, through his speeches and through his insulting references to those who are well-off", and Blandin had indeed exclaimed since the summer of 1793 that "an egoist, a royalist, a wealthy aristocrat, has no right to private property under a Republic". But the one hundred citizens who petitioned the Committee of General Security in Thermidor Year III for the release from prison of the retired wholesale merchant who had smoothly metamorphosed into a *sans-culotte* could also say of him: "Civil commissioner, deputy to the Commune, President, Vice-President and Secretary of the Section's primary assemblies, elector of the Section in 1790, 1791 and 1792, Treasurer of the Section and its justice of the peace for almost three years, he devoted himself constantly to public service".[27]

Pierre Chauvin in the Section Montreuil and Pierre-Edmé Imbault in the Section Ponceau were both personifications of success, pre-Revolutionary as well as Revolutionary, within the terms of their Quarters. The *père* Chauvin had been a member of the original permanent committee of the District Sainte-Marguérite in 1789-90, and an elector since 1790. In the summer of 1792 and at the age of sixty-five, he retired from the hat manufactory on the rue de Lappe where he employed an average of ten workers and which he passed on to his son Pierre-Noël, to become justice of the peace and to assume a full vocation of Jacobin leadership in the Section. Pierre-Edmé Imbault replaced a former barrister as justice of Ponceau in September 1793. He was a master fabric painter whose business association with his younger brother Denis-Pierre (a civil commissioner in 1793-Year II), in an embroidery manufacture where they employed an average of seven workers in 1790-1, was as characteristic of the productive world of the rue Saint-Denis as their political cohesion, brothers who were identical Jacobin militants, was characteristic of Revolutionary politics in Ponceau.[28]

Jean-Mathias Fontaine, an entrepreneur and wholesaler of gold-work, had occupied a brilliant position in the corporate structure of the Parisian bourgeoisie during the last years of the Old Régime, that of Judge-Consul of the great guild of goldsmiths, watch-makers

---

[27] A.N., F7 4602, d. Blandin; A.N., D III 253, *liasse* 16.
[28] On Chauvin, see A.N., D III 253, *liasse* 19 and A.N., F30 142, d. Chauvin. On the Imbaults, see A.N., D III 253, *liasse* 12, D III 256⁴, *liasse* 9, and F30 136, d. Imbault.

and jewellers, and during the early years of the Revolution he was a member of the original élite of the *Place Royale* (Section Fédérés), successively a member of the permanent committee and of the parish relief committee in 1789-90 and then police commissioner from the autumn of 1790 until his election as justice in August 1792. But Fontaine lacked the suppleness of Lebrun and Blandin; in 1792-3 he refused to choose the *sans-culotte* option which they, as well as Chauvin and Imbault, had chosen. In October 1793 the Section's revolutionary committee got him dismissed, imprisoned him as a "suspect", and pressured the general assembly into replacing him with their own candidate, Antoine Jabel, a coal merchant who had come to the *Place Royale* from Fressay (Haute-Sâone) only a few years before the Revolution.[29]

Florentin Phulpin in the Arcis and Mathias Hû in the Panthéon-Français were both middle-aged merchants, the first a native of Paris and the second of Armentières in the north, who were well, if not brilliantly, established in their Quarters in 1789, Phulpin in a wholesale thread commerce on the rue de la Verrerie and Hû as a wholesale grocer on the rue de Tournelle. Each was a virtual strong-man, *primus inter pares* among the revolutionary personnel of his Section in 1792-3 and until his political fall in the Year II, that of Hû in Pluviôse at the end of a bitter rivalry with the revolutionary commissioners of the Panthéon-Français, and that of Phulpin in Germinal through a brutal intervention of the Committee of Public Safety on the side of one of its minions who had contested Phulpin's power in the Arcis. Both had served a substantial apprenticeship to the power which they attained after August 1792 as justices and assembly leaders: Phulpin had fought in the assault on the Bastille, served on the permanent committee of his District in 1789-90 and, with Tallien and Dansart, he had been one of the founders in 1791 of the *Société fraternelle des Deux Sexes*, a major popular society closely linked with the Jacobin Club; Hû, who presided over the Section from the 9th through the 31st August 1792 when he was elected justice, had also taken arms on 13-14th July 1789 and served as a civil commissioner in 1790-1 and an elector in 1791-2.

Phulpin and Hû were both simultaneously local potentates and important emissaries of Paris Jacobinism. Phulpin, as President of the Arcis, largely organized the movement of "fraternization" through which several Sections, the Cordeliers Club, and the *Société des défenseurs de la Republique* weaned the newly arrived *fédéré* batallions of the provinces from the influence of the Girondins who

[29] A.N., D III 253, *liasse* 11.

had summoned them to Paris and won them as allies of the Paris
Jacobins in January 1793. During the first half of April he presided
over the metropolitan assembly which drafted the first general
demand for the purge of the Girondin deputies. And with a con-
summate arrogance, he could entitle the violently threatening address
which he read to the Convention on 2 June 1793, "Phulpin's ulti-
matum . . . accepted unanimously by the general assembly of the
Section Arcis for presentation to the National Convention", just as
on 25 February 1793, in the midst of the riots against grocers on the
rues de la Poterie, Tixeranderie and Verrerie, he had taken over the
responsibilities of both police commissioner and Section commander,
eclipsing both of these officials, to commandeer patrols, transform
crowds into queues and supervise the "tax". Mathias Hû presided
over the assembly of the Panthéon-Français at each moment of
crisis from the night of 9-10 August 1792 through September 1793.
When the Insurrectionary Commune decreed house searches for
"suspects" at the end of August 1792, Mathias Hû made the night
visits himself with the Section's rather timorous police commissioner
and had several persons arrested. Proud, domineering, brusque,
with a penchant for moralizing braggadocio, and yet highly competent
in the manipulation of their social inferiors, Florentin Phulpin and
Mathias Hû embodied much of the force of the mercantile bourgeoisie in Paris politics, as well as the vulnerability of this bourgeoisie,
its capacity to provoke the sort of violent hatreds among artisans,
bureaucrats and minor figures of the "liberal" professions which
finally destroyed these two justices.[30]

The world of the small atelier and shop was represented among the
justices of the peace of 1792-Year II not by obscure *sans-culottes*
who lived through militancy or were simply thrust into office by some
convulsive "popular movement", but by men with roots in their
Quarters and engaged in vital activities which conferred an identity
and possibilities for influence. Most of these men were "genuine
sans-culottes" in any political sense, and most were definitely of the
petty bourgeoisie. Collectively, this group of justices testified to the
versatility and dynamism of the late eighteenth-century Parisian
bourgeoisie at least as dramatically as did their more advantaged
colleagues such as Lebrun, Blandin, Chauvin or Hû.

[30] There are traces of Phulpin's rhetoric and career scattered throughout
nearly all the Parisian archives, but the principal sources are the following:
A.N., BB3 59, d. Phulpin; A.N., D III 253, *liasse* 23; A.N., F7 4774[13], d.
Phulpin; A.N., W 30, *liasse* 1704; Archives de la Préfecture de Police (cited
hereafter as A.P.P.) Aa 59, ff. 92-3. On Mathias Hû, see A.N., D III 254,
liasse 15 and A.N., F7 4745, d. Hû.

Three figures, Charles Balin in the Section Quinze-Vingts, Mathurin Bouin in the Marchés, and Augustin Duchesne in Popincourt, stand out in sharp relief within this group of justices, for they represented the political force and creativity of an authentically petty bourgeois world of the street atelier and shop in Revolutionary Paris. "I was poor before the Revolution, and I am still; my conscience is clean". And yet his was a rapidly qualified "poverty", for in the same letter to the Committee of General Security from prison during the Year III in which he boasted of his poverty, Charles Balin also proudly emphasized that he had been born and lived his entire life in the Faubourg Saint-Antoine, "where for over a century my family has lived and worked, with a spotless reputation". The son of a cabinet-maker, Charles Balin was a twenty-nine year old journeyman cabinet-maker in 1789, and worked with a furniture merchant at the "Marché aux Chevaux" until his election to the office of justice in September 1792. But in the evenings since 14 July 1789 and continuously after his election as justice he was of one of the Quinze-Vingts' Revolutionary chiefs, and in a style as rude and direct as the Faubourg itself:

> A powerful, sonorous voice allowed him to dominate the assemblies, which he frequently presided over. Author of all the petitions, member of all the deputations, all the illegal actions of the Section are in large part his work. Preaching the sovereignty of the people in order to intimidate and terrorize those who are respectable and well-off, his popularity was based on ruse; he flattered the poor so he could mobilize them against the rich.

The Thermidorians of the Quinze-Vingts knew what they were about in placing Balin at the head of their proscription lists, just as those of the Marchés did with Mathurin Bouin, of whom they said: "He is subtle, clever, adept at dissimulation, gifted with considerable natural intelligence and an extraordinary memory . . . an extremely dangerous man, the chief of the Jacobin cabal in the Section Marchés". Mathurin Bouin was as thoroughly of the Halles as Charles Balin was of the Faubourg Saint-Antoine. He was a young but fully mature man who had worked for several years as a stocking-weaver in the *Marché-des-Innocents* until he opened a small bonnet shop on the densely popular and commercial rue de la Chanvrerie; his wife, a former washerwoman, kept the shop after he gave himself fully to Revolutionary politics. Charles Balin and Mathurin Bouin were both "men of 10th August" who became Section chiefs through the Insurrection and after having served much the same political apprenticeship as *sociétaires* in 1789-92, Balin in the *Société des Vainqueurs de la Bastille* (of which he was a founding member) and Bouin in the *Société fraternelle des Halles*. Neither of them had held formal

Section office before the Insurrection and Bouin, at least, did not qualify for office under the censitary régime; in August 1792 they were both hoisted to power in the assemblies of their Sections and to the office of justice by friends, social analogues and fellow *sociétaires* in the Quinze-Vingts and Marchés. Both remained in power until the Year III.

Although he was one of the very few justices to represent his Section on the Insurrectionary Commune, the Commune of 1793 and that of the Year II, Charles Balin never really left the Faubourg Saint-Antoine where he was involved in orchestrating its participation in each of the *journées*. Mathurin Bouin, who was less violent, more intelligent and finely attuned to the nuances of general Parisian and national politics than the thoroughly "faubourien" Charles Balin, was given important missions to the provinces by the Committees of Government in 1793-Year II, missions which he carried out while retaining his office as justice until it was taken from him in Brumaire Year III.[31]

Augustin Duchesne — "one of the principal anarchists and sedition-mongers of the Faubourg Saint-Antoine and perhaps the most dangerous of the Section Popincourt" — was probably the most violent of the men who served as justices between September 1792 and Frimaire Year III, and as a justice of the peace he was a decidedly quixotic figure. By temperament and in style of action, Duchesne was an authentic *homme à poigne* who visibly exulted in crises, and from his origins as a café-keeper on the turbulent, savage rue de la Roquette to his imprisonment after the Insurrection of Prairial Year III he knew the euphoria of violence in all its forms in the pre-Revolutionary and Revolutionary Faubourg Saint-Antoine. A member of the *Société des Vainqueurs de la Bastille* like Charles Balin, he also fought in the assault on the Tuileries and was elected to the Insurrection Commune immediately after the battle. Duchesne was a revolutionary commissioner and, through his credit with the Cordeliers in the entourage of Bouchotte, he was employed in one of the offices of the Ministry of War when he was elected justice of the peace in September 1793. But he remained a man of the *journées* through Prairial Year III, a choice which earned him at least three prison terms in the Years III and IV.[32]

[31] On the career of Charles Balin, see A.N., D III 253, *liasse 24*, F7 4585, d. Balin, and F7 4635, d. Castille. On that of Mathurin Bouin, see A.N., D III 253, *liasse 17*, F7 4611, d. Bouin, and F7 4774⁴⁵, d. Michel.
[32] A.N., D III 253, *liasse 22*; A.P.P., Aa 266, ff. 228-38; Kare Tönnesson, *La défaite des Sans-culottes: Mouvement populaire et réaction bourgeoise en l'an III* (Paris and Oslo, 1959), pp. 140-1, 180-1, 208-9, 364.

None of the remaining artisan, merchant and related justices had the prominence of those already characterized, but in various ways, all had local, pre-Revolutionary roots and a social personality which had matured within the framework of their Quarters. Three of them were practically stereotypes in these terms: for several years before the Revolution as well as during its course, Jean-François Charpentier was a food tradesman at the *Gros-Caillou*, that sprawling maze of taverns, bordellos and cheap lodging houses at the social heart of the Section Invalides; François-Nicolas Therrin, justice of the Section Bon-Conseil, was a master enamel and porcelain painter on the rue Saint-Denis, in that zone of the Centre where most of this production was concentrated; Étienne Lambert-Becquet, justice of the Section Pont-Neuf, had been established as a master goldsmith on the place Dauphine for several years before the Revolution.[33] The others were all easily recognizable local figures, without being archetypical.[34]

The strongest social current feeding the recruitment of justices of the peace during this period was thoroughly local; its strength can be measured in the dominant presence of artisans, merchants and tradesmen and in their assertive identity as productive representatives of the Quarter. This current was strong enough to carry into this most intricate and exacting of Section offices men with little or no formal education and from the more obscure ranks of commerce, men such as Mathurin Bouin whose device was: "Even for the most important offices no more is needed than solid common sense, warm-heartedness and probity". All of them had acquired a further, civic identity and claim to office through militancy and gained an experience of formulas and administration through holding other

[33] A.N., D III 254, *liasse* 12 (Charpentier); A.N., F7 4775[27], d. Therrin; A.N., D III 256[1], *liasse* 9 (Lambert-Becquet).

[34] Simon Bourgoin was a middle-aged draughtsman who had lived and worked for six years on the rue des fossés Saint-Marcel before he became justice of the Section du Finistère in August 1792: A.N., D III 254, *liasse* 8; A.P.P., Aa 216, f. 453. Étienne Rivière, justice of Section Arsenal in 1792-Year II, had come to the rue Neuve Saint-Paul from his native Sainte-Honorine-la-Petite (Orne) in the early 1780s; during the years preceding the Revolution he had prospered there as a geometer and land-surveyor working with architects and building contractors in the Quarter: A.N., D III 253, *liasse* 1; F7 4774[94], d. Rivière. Antoine-Henri Colas was a retired goldsmith and engraver who had spent most of his life on the *Montagne Sainte-Geneviève* before he became justice of the Panthéon-Français in Floréal Year II: A.N., D III 254, *liasse* 15. Jean-Louis Treféon, who replaced J. Roulleau as justice of the Section Marais in Floréal Year II, entered the office not simply from the position of a revolutionary commissioner, but also from that of a fifty-two year old grocer who had been in business for over fifteen years on the rue de Poitou: A.N., D III 254, *liasse* 9.

Section offices or leading popular societies before they became justices, but their primary claim to office was local, non-professional, and in a sense pre-Revolutionary. It was the claim of the Quarter to grasp and hold entire responsibility for the Section.

*   *   *   *

Another distinct social current fed recruitment for the office of justice during this period, a current which was neither professional, flowing from "legal culture", nor tangibly local. It was the one which thrust into office the twenty-one men whose activities were neither productive nor commercial, but rather intellectual in the various ways which social theorists commonly describe as "tertiary" to the normal, daily life of a society, and which in a revolutionary situation can become quite vital and primary through providing those indispensable men whose vocation is to manipulate formulas, rules, rhetoric and ideas. They were all equipped with at least the rudiments of formal culture, and lived from certain skills of abstraction which could be adapted to various styles of action, and in a range of offices more or less indiscriminately throughout the City. But unlike the artisan, tradesmen and merchant justices, most of these various *clercs* had to adapt their skills to circumstances and acquire a local identity in order to live. For many of them, the office of justice was a hard-earned social promotion, a vocation, and a terminal achievement.

Certain of these men had adapted their skills of abstraction to the life and needs of their Quarters before 1789, and acquired a local status and formed a web of personal relations with those engaged in production and commerce which permitted them to move rather easily into positions of political responsibility. Henri-François Pelletier had been a mathematics tutor to the families of the Thermes-de-Julien for over two decades before the Revolution. A sixty-six year old patriarch and Jacobin, he became one of the Section's ideological tutors in 1792-Year II, a recurrent author of the resolutions and addresses of its general assembly and a propagandist of its popular society. Joachim Ceyrat had also tutored the children of his Quarter long before the Revolution and he moved into the office of justice of the Luxembourg from that of police commissioner, and from his secure position as one of the militants of the powerful *Société patriotique du Luxembourg*. In immediate, local terms, the career of Antoine Lamaignère in the Section Champs-Elysées was nearly identical to those of Pelletier and Ceyrat, with the rather superficial difference that Lamaignère, like his patrons among the dominant bourgeoisie of the Champs-Elysées, chose an anti-Jacobin politics. A native of Hainault, Lamaignère had been installed as a schoolmaster at Chaillot since 1770. He was intelligent and thoroughly familiar with the inhabitants of both Chaillot and the eastern portion of the Champs-Elysées, an outpost of the Faubourg Saint-Honoré, and his sensitivity to their will was rewarded by the offices of police commissioner, justice of the peace, and practically immovable president of the general assembly from 1790 to the Year III.[35]

Nicolas Baron in the Section Mail and Dominique Marmouzet in the Section Place Vendôme (Piques) both resembled Pelletier, Ceyrat and Lamaignère, beyond ideological differences and from the perspective of their relations with their Sections. Nicolas Baron was only thirty-four when he was elected justice in late August 1792, but he had been a notary's clerk for sixteen years, and for the past eight, chief clerk to a notary on the Place des Victoires. After having served as a civil commissioner in 1790-1, Baron was promoted, both socially and politically, by the Mail's bourgeoisie to the status of police commissioner and then to that of justice of the peace. Dominique Marmouzet, the only medical doctor among the justices of September 1792-Frimaire Year III, had lived and practised on the Place Vendôme since 1757; he became the Section's health officer in 1790, and Maxmilien Robespierre's personal physician shortly after the barrister from Arras settled in with the Duplays. A member of the Jacobin Club since early 1792, an elector of that year, a civil commissioner in 1792-3, and a revolutionary commissioner from the spring through the autumn of 1793, the elderly physician Marmouzet was respectably militant, and in Prairial Year II the Committee of Public Safety appointed him justice to replace the former priest Nicolas Mathieu, a de-christianizer who had violated the orthodoxy of Robespierre and his colleagues. But Marmouzet shared the tough, durable genius of the mature Parisian bourgeoisie, solidly rooted in its Quarters, a bourgeoisie which chose its régimes, or at least the terms and circumstances of its loyalty to them, maintained its integrity through betrayal at the right moments, and survived intact the falls of its temporary heroes, most of them national and thus "foreign", such as the barrister from Arras and his fellow provincials in the Committee of Public Safety who were ruthlessly

---

[35] On Pelletier, see A.N., D III 254, *liasse* 22, F7 4774⁶⁶, d. Pelletier, and W 80, *liasse* 3591. On Ceyrat, see A.N., D III 254, *liasses* 12 and 13. On Lamaignère, see A.N., D III 253, *liasse* 8, F7 4760, d. Lamaignère.

abandoned by the justice Marmouzet and the *Robespierriste* authorities of the Piques on 9-10 Thermidor Year II.[36]

Although they were also *clercs*, men who lived through intellectual skills, there was nothing secure or natural about the position in their Sections of most of the justices who had been career bureaucrats, of whom there were at least twelve among those of September 1792-Frimaire Year III. Most of these figures of the *cléraille* utterly depended on office, and had to adapt their skills to local circumstances after 1790 through and in the midst of Revolution. Until then, almost all of them had been foreign to the life of their Quarters and had merely resided there as individuals. As dependents of external institutions which were suppressed in 1790, they had suddenly to "naturalize" themselves and create a local identity through local Revolutionary service. For these ex-bureaucrats the stakes of success were often high, not simply a better salary as justice of the peace than the one received at some desk in the General Tax Farm or the chambers of the *Châtelet*, but also in the sort of aggressive prominence and influence which earned Melchior-Humbert Peligot, justice of the Section Réunion in 1793-Year II, the characterization "highly talented opportunist". The price of failure was equally high; when the office of justice was won exclusively through militancy in the Section, it could also be lost through new shifts in local power, and for minor ex-bureaucrats like François Thilly, justice of the Section Pont-Neuf in 1793-Year II, the result — disarming, confiscation of the precious *certificat de civisme*, and proscription — meant a "genuine civil death".

The same bureaucratic establishments of the Old Régime which provided candidates for the offices of justice of the peace and police commissioner also provided them for the membership of civil and revolutionary committees in 1792-Year II. And yet, in comparing the bureaucrats in these two categories of Section office, one is almost comparing two different generations of *cléraille*. The staffing of civil and revolutionary commissioners encompassed a large number of actual bureaucrats, of men, and there were many, who during the early years of the Revolution had made the transition from employment in some institution of the Old Régime to a desk or commission in an establishment created or reorganized by the Revolutionary régime, as well as men who had begun bureaucratic careers after 1790. Many of these actual bureaucrats kept their government jobs while serving on Section committees, even after this service was salaried early in

[36] On Nicolas Baron, see A.N., D III 253, *liasse* 13. On the career of Dominique Marmouzet, see A.N., D III 253, *liasse* 21 and F7* 2475.

the Year II.   But almost all the justices and police commissioners who came from the various Old Régime depots of *cléraille* were quite emphatically ex-bureaucrats, men whose careers had been ruptured in 1790 and who had begun in 1790-2 to move through the more modest salaried Section offices and various forms of militancy towards the two juiciest of local plums, the offices of justice of the peace and police commissioner.   These latter offices were terminal prizes for most of these ex-bureaucrats, and they gripped them very firmly.   For the minor bureaucrats, either former or actual, who were active members of revolutionary committees, this membership, particularly when it was adorned with militancy in a popular society or the Jacobin Club, was often a lever with which one could pry from the government of 1793-Year II a higher, more prestigious and remunerative bureaucratic officer or commission than the one previously or currently held.   In the cases of these men, service as a revolutionary commissioner was neither a rupture nor an "inversion", but a very real if devious expansion of a bureaucratic career.[37]   But among their bureaucrat colleagues in the offices of justice and police commissioner, the dominant social themes were precisely those of rupture and inversion.

There were only three figures among the bureaucrat justices of September 1792-Frimaire Year III whom these themes do not describe.   Two of them were not only striking exceptions to the social pattern offered by their colleagues, but also men whose careers were supreme examples of the richness and complexity of genuine leadership in Revolutionary Paris.   Pierre Isambert (Section Faubourg Saint-Denis) and Balthazard-Marie Laugier (Section Fontaine-de-Grenelle) came to the office of justice, to rôles of Section leadership, and to executive rôles in Jacobin Paris from quite different directions. For Pierre Isambert, fifty-five in 1792, these positions were at the same time a recognition of his success and personal capacity, and prestigious forms of active retirement chosen by him; in the life of Balthazard-Marie Laugier, who was thirty in 1792, they were important stages in a complex and brilliant administrative career whose curve had been ascending from its origin around 1780.

Isambert was thoroughly a bureaucrat of the Old Régime, but his career had not been stagnant and the man himself suffered from none of the ossifying rigidity that doomed those administrative structures

---

[37] The author is currently preparing a study of the careers of the men who served as police and revolutionary commissioners of the Sections, under the title: "The Personnel of Repression in Revolutionary Paris: Police, Revolutionary, and Surveillance, Commissioners, 1792-Year III".

which had employed him. He first sat at the copying desk in 1750, at the age of fourteen, in a provincial office of the Royal Domains, and at about the age of twenty he was promoted to the rank of ambulant inspector of royal possessions in Brittany. During the next ten years, much of which he spent on horseback or in shabby inns on the roads winding through the *bocage*, Isambert manoeuvred with competence in that genuinely feudal and wretchedly poverty-stricken world which, three decades later, provided Revolutionary France with its *chouannerie*; there, he worked among local gentry, major-domos of royal châteaux, magistrates of obscure bailiwicks, half-educated village notories and priests, share-cropping peasants whose condition was little more than that of serfs, and rural labourers, *gens de peine*, whose condition was even less. After mastering this charge, he made the substantial leap to Paris and a position in the royal *bureau des contentieux* for banks and finance in 1767. Pierre Isambert was adroit, he knew when and how to arrange the mutations in his career; in 1790, as his current office was on the verge of suppression, he rapidly moved into that of a first secretary and department chief in the Treasury, in that vast establishment whose denominating adjective was simply changed from "Royal" to "National" and whose structure and personnel were left intact by the Revolution. In a manner suggestive of J.-E.-A. Lebrun and Pierre Blandin, he simply retired from the Treasury in the summer of 1792 when he was simultaneously elected justice of the peace and a member of the General Council of the Paris Department. Isambert was a member of the first and last generations of Paris Jacobins; he joined the Club in 1790 and was still an active member in the beginning of the Year III. In 1792-Year II, he was both an executive of the Greater City and the undisputed Jacobin potentate of the Faubourg Saint-Denis.

Although he eclipsed it through personal qualities of intelligence, energy and administrative skill, the distance separating the ambulant inspector of royal domains in Brittany from the leader of the Faubourg Saint-Denis and the executive of the Paris Department was not so great as it may seem. The *sans-culottes* of the desolate Faubourg were a people far more rural than urban, a half-civilized population of labourers in vegetable farms, pastures and stock-pens, saltpetre refineries and stone quarries; the distance separating them from the wretched peasants and *gens de peine* of the west was itself continually eclipsed physically by immigration to the Faubourgs of the City. The "Parisianization" of Pierre Isambert was logically and brilliantly completed in the Faubourg Saint-Denis during the Revolution, but it had begun long before he first arrived in the City or on the rue du

faubourg Saint-Martin.   The physiognomies of rural and quasi-rural
greed, exploitation, labour and misery, the nuances of domination
and servitude in a community which lived through incessant struggle
with an obdurate soil and its raw products, the tension of existence
for landowners and particularly for those whose land made possible a
style of life adorned with some luxury, as well as for the covetous,
desperate landless who surrounded them, these were realities assimilated by Isambert during the ten years before he came to Paris, and
they were also the realities which surrounded him in the Faubourg
Saint-Denis.   For there also, life revolved around the conflicting
interests of power through ownership of land and survival through
manual labour; there, as in Brittany, both capital and the plights and
dodges of those who did not possess it were tangible and relatively
fixed.   These were both highly contentious terrains, and in both,
contention involved masses of people who were hopelessly uneducated.
The magic of the solemn, formal verb, of the fictions and formulas,
whether legal in substance or merely in guise, which can legitimate
desires, justify or refute claims, impose discipline, and even summon
forth the uniformed forces of physical repression, was probably
equally great in rural Brittany and in the Faubourg Saint-Denis.
At a higher but parallel level of abstraction, the same magic was as
vital in the labyrinths of the Treasury as it was in the subtle, tortuous
debates at the Jacobin Club or in the councils of administration of the
Greater City.   In the *bocage*, the ambulant inspector began to
acquire a command of this magic, a command which was nurtured
and expanded in the *bureau des contentieux* and Treasury, and
finally brought to something approaching perfection, in that dualism
which was the real source of Isambert's power in 1792-Year II, by
the Jacobin administrator of Greater Paris and the *sans-culotte*
justice of the Faubourg Saint-Denis.[38]

[38] A.N., D III 254, *liasse* 4; Flb II Seine, 18; F7 4747, d. Isambert.   Several
of the civil commissioners who had been Isambert's political subordinates in
the Section since 1792 were among those who composed the masterpieces of
vindictive denunciation which filled his dossier with the Committee of General
Security between Prairial and Fructidor Year III: "Justice of the peace,
president of the general assembly, civil commissioner, member of the
administration of the Department, juror of the Criminal Tribunal of 17th
August, founder and permanent president of the Popular Society . . . .   He is
regarded as the Robespierre of the Section du Nord, with the distinction of
having had the insolence to maintain his tyrannic empire for six months after
the fall of his master and model . . . .   Black-souled, hard-hearted, ungrateful,
cruel, he is accused of having tyrannized the Section for years, of having
accumulated offices in violation of the law, of having, through intrigue and
ruthlessness, monopolized elective offices which should have been distributed
among men who are just, enlightened and humane".

Pierre Isambert and Balthazard-Marie Laugier shared a common administrative intelligence and political careers which interlocked at the Jacobin Club and in the councils of the Paris Department in 1793-Year II, but the distance separating their respective Parisian environments, the points of local departure for their Revolutionary careers, was far greater than the physical space which lay between the Porte Saint-Denis and the Quai Voltaire.   There was very little of a bourgeoisie in the pre-Revolutionary and Revolutionary Faubourg Saint-Denis; after 1789-90, there was very little else in the Faubourg Saint-Germain.   Almost twenty per cent of the Faubourg Saint-Denis's population was officially indigent in 1794, as against a miniscule six per cent in the Section Fontaine-de-Grenelle.[39] Pierre Isambert's world on the savage fringes of Paris was fundamentally stable from the last decade of the Old Régime through the Revolutionary years, stable in its primitivism, in its peculiar internal tensions, and even in its protagonists, an eternal, swarming round of small-scale employers, penurious artisans, herdsmen, vegetable and dairy farmers, common labourers, beggars, *gens sans aveu*, many of whom easily slipped from the grange or the stone quarry into the nocturnal vocation of highwayman.   The social universe of Balthazard-Marie Laugier lay at the urban and urbane core of the City, but it was violently shaken by the Revolution, plunged into disequilibrium and flux by the emigration of most of the aristocracy which had been its social spine.

There is a Balzacian atmosphere to the life of Pierre Isambert, and that of Balthazard-Marie Laugier has strong traces of an inverse Julien Sorel.

> Doubtlessly, my impetuosity and enthusiasm contrast sharply with the indifference of those in whom Nature has not planted a hatred of kings and of tyranny . . . .   Is it not true that only the energy of the People has managed to rout the mercenary hordes which have dared to sully the soil of freedom? And for myself, I feel pride in being able to declare that all of my actions prove that I belong to this People enamoured of liberty!

This was indeed the self-aggrandizing *sans-culottisme* of a thirty-two year old *clerc*, but it was also a moment and a mode, those of 1793-Year II, in Laugier's brilliant passage from the private, involuted world of the *intendance* of an aristocratic family in the Faubourg Saint-Germain to completely public, exposed directorships of the Subsistence Commission of the Paris Department and the Commis-

---

[39] These figures are from Soboul, *op. cit.*, p. 1092.   On the historical development of the Faubourgs of the North and their socio-economic character at the end of the eighteenth century, see Michel Philiponneau, *La vie rurale de la banlieue parisienne. Étude de géographie humaine* (Paris, 1956).

sion of Agriculture and Trades.   The passage was accomplished in only four years.   It had distinct stages and forms of mediation, of which a tenure as justice of the Fontaine-de-Grenelle in 1792-3 was an important one, but the resilience of the man and the malleability of the environment caused them to be telescoped into a rapid, continuous ascent.

The environment was malleable because it was extremely fluid, and the man resilient because he understood it intimately.   When the aristocracy and upper bourgeoisie of the Faubourg Saint-Germain emigrated, an emigration largely accomplished before the Insurrection of 10th August, they did not simply leave a physical vacuum of massive, empty town houses and the dependent religious edifices abandoned by their *pieux*, but also a social vacuum.   The axes of life shifted from town houses and religious establishments to the commercial and modest residential zones — the rues de Lille, de Verneuil, du Bac, de Grenelle, Saint-Dominique, and the *Marché de Boulainvilliers* — which harboured a diffuse and disoriented population of tradesmen, merchants, luxury craftsmen and artisans, employees, notaries, small rentiers and ex-serving personnel, most of whom, in various ways and in varying degrees, had drawn sustenance from the formerly dominant aristocratic presence.   The Section Fontaine-de-Grenelle, in the most profound sense the product of this emigration, the result of the noble Faubourg's self-effacement, lacked any real social élite, and any genuine spine of leadership.

In the wake of the emigration, and particularly after the summer of 1792, these various groups of *roturiers* jostled among themselves for a power and status whose local meaning was quite ambiguous, in a strange competition whose shibboleths — "patriots" versus "aristocrats", *sans-culottes* versus "moderates" — came from the outside, from the same Parisian Revolution which grafted a rather artificial administrative framework and new forms of local authority on to the dislocated Faubourg.   There were indeed lingering elements of an upper bourgeoisie sympathetic to monarchy, and disparate groups, mostly among the liberal professions, who were attached to the Constitution of 1791 and fearful of further Revolutionary violence, but the Faubourg Saint-Germain had no laborious masses to introduce the brutal clarities of need and class conflict, and thus to give an immediate, flesh-and-blood reality to shibboleths which were otherwise little more than rhetorical weapons in rivalries within an indigenous bourgeoisie.   The only possible clarity in the politics of the Fontaine-de-Grenelle was both negative and external: it was provided after the summer of 1792 by Jacobinism, by the formulas and rhythms of participation in a Parisian and national front of opposition to the vengeful return of former masters and those still loyal to them. After 1791-2, the Fontaine-de-Grenelle had only one clear, cohesive élite, only one group which temporarily filled the void of domination left by the departure of the aristocracy and its social allies. This was the Jacobin or *sans-culotte* élite of 1793-Year II, a bizarre amalgam of ex-domestic servants, singing, fencing, riding, dancing and language masters, former scribes of magisterial families, ex-heraldic painters, small-scale tradesmen and obscure or unemployed luxury craftsmen. Of all those who had had a place on the social spectrum of the classical Faubourg, these men had suffered the most intense dislocation from the emigration of the aristocracy, but their condition was not simply one of abrupt and rather obvious desperation; it was also one of rare freedom, a brutally inadvertent and intense freedom to sponge away through militancy, propaganda and terror the vestiges of the aristocratic Faubourg and of their own collective past, to create the Revolutionary Section of the Fontaine-de-Grenelle and themselves as its élite. This spectacular inversion of authority in the Faubourg Saint-Germain fascinated contemporaries — including those among the future Thermidorian bourgeoisie of the Fontaine-de-Grenelle and the Croix-Rouge who had been its victims — and has worked subsequently on the imaginations of historians and novelists as one of the ultimate symbolic moments of the Revolution. Balthazard-Marie Laugier was one of its incarnations.

In his past as a dependant of the Faubourg's aristocracy, Laugier resembled most of his *sans-culotte* colleagues in the Fontaine-de-Grenelle's popular society and revolutionary committee, but the social resemblance was little more than formal. From the age of eighteen and for nearly ten years he had served as private secretary to the intendant of one of the Faubourg's great families. In the complex recesses of an *intendance* the young Laugier absorbed social cunning, gained the administrative skills of written and verbal manipulation, a practical knowledge of all the gradations in the world of the Faubourg Saint-Germain from the nobility to the artisans and tradesmen in the *Marché de Boulainvilliers*, and ultimately acquired the archly civilized urban guile which was not a quality of the valets, grooms, coachmen, wine-waiters, locksmiths, shoemakers and café-owners who became his political comrades. When the household collapsed with the emigration of its scions in 1790, the twenty-eight year old Laugier moved to an apartment near the fountain on the rue de Grenelle. A few months later, he was elected to the salaried offices of recording secretary to the justice of the peace and recording secretary of the general assembly. As a "patriot" and with several of his future Jacobin comrades, he was one of the founders in 1791 of the *Société des Amis-de-la-Loi* on the rue Saint-Dominique, and in the spring of 1792 he was admitted to the Jacobin Club. Through the Insurrection of 10th August, the artisans, tradesmen and former *valetaille* of the Faubourg gained an aggressive civic prominence in the Fontaine-de-Grenelle, and in September Laugier ascended to the office of justice and to his mature rôle as a local emissary of Jacobinism. There was a personal as well as an ideological resonance to Laugier's statement in the summer of 1793 that "the *journée* of 31st May and those of 1st-2nd June were the most superb of the Revolution". These were perhaps the most sophisticated *journées* of the Parisian Revolution; bloodless and crypto-legal, they succeeded through highly organized manipulation of lower-class energies by the Jacobin bourgeoisie, and Laugier, one of the Jacobin "Committee of Eleven" which met with the "Central Revolutionary Committee" from 31st May through 2nd June, was one of the manipulators. He was rewarded by the Montagnard Committee of Public Safety with concurrent directorships in the Subsistence Commission of Paris and the Commission of Agriculture and Trades, positions for which he resigned as justice of the peace.

Laugier had been a conscientious and quite political justice, and he never abandoned the Fontaine-de-Grenelle or completely extroverted his energies beyond the Faubourg; during the Year II he remained in close but discreet and informal association with the Section's *sans-culotte* chiefs. But the rhythm of his career was now essentially Parisian; he became justice through the victory of 10th August, and that of 31st May-2nd June admitted him to executive administration of the metropolis. Thus, and in that crucial summer of 1793, Laugier unlike his comrades in the Section was able to avoid the strictly local and terrorist path, to distance himself from that almost inexorable process which ensured those who applied laws of suspects during the Year II a collective persecution and imprisonment in the Year III. His source of power was no longer really local, nor was his vulnerability, and the cunning which had served the ex-private secretary also led the director of the Subsistence Commission to side with the Convention during the night of 9-10 Thermidor.

In the sessions of 20 and 30 Pluviôse Year III, when the Thermidorians of the Fontaine-de-Grenelle tried to engulf Laugier in their collective proscription of the Section's "ex-terrorists", he was able to deny having been a protagonist of the local terrorist régime of the Year II

> the very idea of being amalgamated with the partisans of that frightful régime of blood has caused me to suffer the equivalent of a century of indignation and bitterness during each of the last ten days .... Surely, the Terror which was suspended over me as it was over all reputable citizens prevented me from being the public defender of all those oppressed by that régime

and to justify his general Revolutionary career, his larger Jacobin militancy, by invoking the spectre of the aristocratic Faubourg, of the "intrigues of that caste which filled and infected our Section", a spectre which still haunted the civic bourgeoisie of the Fontaine-de-Grenelle during the Year III. In Prairial Year III, these same Thermidorians managed to sweep Laugier into prison along with most of his former comrades of 1792-3, but he was liberated soon after the other members of the Commission of Agriculture and Trades intervened with the Committee of General Security. By temperament and in action, Laugier was supple and realistic, not sanguine and dogmatic, and he lacked the self-defeating theatricality which usually marks the genuine adventurer. From the *intendance* in the noble Faubourg to the high commissions of the Revolutionary Government, his skill and career were consistent in their élitism, and the binding theme of Laugier's career after 1790 was less opportunism than highly sophisticated Jacobin orthodoxy.[40]

François Thilly, who was only twenty-five in 1792, was the youngest of the justices of 1792-Year II, and one of the most socially precarious. Like Isambert and Laugier, he had a bureaucratic position outside his Section, and did not have to depend for survival on the office of justice. Unlike them both, he lacked local roots, and in particular contrast to Laugier, his intense militancy in a very "brittle" Section, the Pont-Neuf, led him in the Year III to local ruin and the loss of his external bureaucratic possibilities. In 1785 and at the age of eighteen he came to Paris and the Pont-Neuf from his native Rheims, as clerk to an advocate of the *Parlement*. When the Court was suppressed in 1790, Thilly got a secretarial job in the offices of the mayor of Paris, at a salary of 1,800 *livres*, and remained there until the Year II, serving in the administrations of Bailly, Petion, Chambon and Pache.

[40] A.D.S., 2AZ 259; A.N., F7* 2509, f. 78; F7 4768, d. Laugier; B.N., Nouv. acq. franc., MS. 2446, fo. 182. See also J.–C. Goeury's admirable study of the population and social structure of the Fontaine-de-Grenelle, "Évolution démographique et sociale du faubourg Saint-Germain", in *Contributions à l'histoire démographique de la Révolution française*, Commission d'histoire économique et sociale de la Révolution française, Mémoires et Documents, xviii (Paris, 1965), pp. 25-60.

The Pont-Neuf was one of the wealthiest and most hermetic Quarters of Paris, a Quarter dominated by substantial artisan-merchants in goldwork, jewellery and watch-making, members of the legal profession, and prosperous rentiers.   In 1790-2 the Section was thoroughly monarchist in its collective politics and from the late summer of 1792 until the Year II it was a citadel of anti-*sans-culotte* conservatism.   François Thilly, whose place there was both recent and inferior, was one of the dissidents who gathered in the pro-Jacobin *Société populaire des Hommes Libres*; there, he formed friendships with the "patriot" goldsmiths, jewellers, opticians, watch-makers and luxury tradesmen who would control the Section in 1793-Year II.   This association bore fruit for Thilly outside the Pont-Neuf; because of it, in March 1793 he was promoted by Pache to a clerkship in the politically sensitive personnel office of the Municipal Police.   In early September 1793, and with the physical aid of *sans-culottes* from neighbouring Sections, the democrats of the Popular Society finally conquered the Pont-Neuf's assembly and administrative offices, purging and proscribing the conservatives who had dominated until then.   Thilly was one of the architects of this "regeneration", this grafting of the style and cadres of the Popular Society on to the civic corpus of the Section, and he was soon elected justice to replace the conservative Étienne Lambert-Becquet who fled the Pont-Neuf to hiding in the Section Marchés in order to avoid imprisonment.   At the end of September, he resigned his job at the Municipal Police, casting the die of his fortunes in the narrow circle of the Pont-Neuf.   Since early 1792, he had been the quasi-official ideologist of the *Société populaire des Hommes Libres*, the author of most of its addresses, petitions and correspondence with the Jacobins, Cordeliers and other Parisian societies.   After Vendémiaire Year II, the justice of the peace Thilly continued this activity, but now in the more august rôles of organizer and predicator of the Pont-Neuf's civic ceremonies and rituals.   The range of his predication during the Year II was fully Jacobin: celebrations of the immortality of "martyrs of liberty", exhortations to filial piety, productive labour, personal simplicity, and sanguine justifications of Terror in the Midi and the Vendée alternated with each other, and earned François Thilly the sobriquet "eulogist of the Terror" and vicious persecution during the Year III.

The Thermidorian reaction was rapid and hateful in the Pont-Neuf, and François Thilly was one of its most pathetic victims.   During the winter of the Year III, the Section's new masters literally hounded him from his office and residence, forcing him into "exile" in the

Section Halle-au-Blé. Two of his most determined persecutors had been his personal enemies and rivals in 1793. When, on 13 Germinal Year III, the Committee of General Security ordered Thilly's arrest, it was Étienne Lambert-Becquet who seized him in his rooms in the Halle-au-Blé and carried him off to prison; three weeks later, Antoine Daubenton, who had been Lambert-Bacquet's recording secretary in 1793 until he was dismissed by Thilly and imprisoned by the Pont-Neuf's revolutionary committee, was appointed to the office of justice by the Committee of Legislation. Unlike most of his revolutionary comrades, Thilly had no atelier or shop on the Place Dauphine or the Quai des Orfèvres to insulate him from political disaster; he also had no external resources, either political or financial, and the stigmata of his terrorist past and political imprisonment closed the doors of bureaucracies in the Years III and IV. In Messidor Year III he was provisionally liberated, without the return of his arms and *certificat de civisme*, and to forced residence in the Pont-Neuf.

> My present situation is even more miserable than the one which I endured in prison. There at least, I was serene in the knowledge of my innocence, I was harassed by no one, I was calm. Now, I am surrounded by suspicion and animosity, the inevitable results of being under surveillance. And this situation is ruining me both morally and physically; occupied all of life with office-work, I must enjoy confidence in order to make a living. This situation of surveillance, which prevents me from finding a job, is a genuine civil death.

The bitterness was real and poignant. In Brumaire Year II, François Thilly had designed and led that solemn procession of citizens of the Pont-Neuf, deputies from the Commune, and twelve Montagnards from the Convention which, marching in honour of Lepeletier de Saint-Fargeau and Marat, wound through the streets and along the quais of the Section to the freshly baptized Place de Thionville where he, simultaneously assembly president, justice of the peace and official predicator, delivered the final commemorative oration of the rite and proposed the first of the republican toasts which began the banquet. In Brumaire Year IV, he was unemployed and destitute, living an existence in which he and his family knew the humiliation of having to queue each morning for free bread and meat rations dispensed by the relief committee of the Section.[41]

The Revolutionary careers of the other nine bureaucrats were indeed shaped by the themes of rupture and inversion; they picked themselves up from various levels in the institutional debris of 1790,

[41] A.N., D III 254, *liasse* 16; A.N., F7 4775[28], d. Thilly; A.P.P., Aa 266, *liasse* Pont-Neuf; Bibliothèque historique de la Ville de Paris, MS. 745, fo. 153; B.N., Nouv. acq. franc., MS. 2713, fos. 2-298 (Minutes of the *Société populaire des Hommes Libres*, 1792-Year II).

adapted their skills and inverted their careers to begin the movement through minor Section offices and political militancy which led to the coveted reward and social redemption in the office of justice of the peace. Two of them had accumulated some modest bureaucratic seniority, and probably some personal savings, before 1790: J.-B. Lechevalier of the Faubourg-Montmartre had risen over the span of several years to the post of under-secretary in some unspecified Old Régime institution; Claude-Louis Bonenfant, who replaced Laugier as justice of the Fontaine-de-Grenelle, had been an under-secretary in the General Tax Farm for about ten years. The eldest of these men, Denis Boulanger who was sixty-one in 1792, had known almost forty years of respectable stagnation as a process-server of the *Châtelet*, from 1752 until the Court was suppressed in 1790, before he moved into office in the Section Oratoire. The others had been less successful or less securely placed, and found themselves in 1790-2 at the critical ages of maturity between thirty-five and forty-five, with careers which had been aborted. Clement Pinard, of the Section Poissonnière, had been employed only since the mid-1780s as a book-keeper in the General Tax Farm, and as for Melchior-Humbert of the Section Réunion, he could laconically summarize his pre-Revolutionary existence in the following phrase, "former book-keeper in several offices of finance", all of them suppressed in 1790. J. Roulleau of the Section Marais and J.-B. Fantin of the Section Tuileries had been simple recording clerks, the latter in the *prêvoté* of the Municipality. René Corbin was the most politically dynamic and socially precarious, if not desperate, of these men. He began in the early 1780s as a door-keeper and sergeant-at-arms of the *prêvoté* of the Faubourg du Roule, and after a few years rose to the modest charge of clerk and process-server of the Summary Court of Chaillot; when these jurisdictions were abolished in 1790-1, he remained in the Faubourg du Roule, but as a journeyman tailor.[42]

None of these men directly entered the office of justice of the peace. They ascended to it, by routes and stages where they served an apprenticeship to the solitary, highly individual responsibilities of justice of the peace or police commissioner — styles of action diametrically opposed to the anonymity and insulation of the bureaucrat — and where they also cultivated local friendships and political confidence. The process of adaptation was most rapid for J.-B.

[42] A.N., D III 253m *liasse* 10 (Lechevalier); A.N., D III 254, *liasse* 6 and F7 4607, d. Bonenfant (Bonenfant); A.N., D III 253, *liasse* 11 (Boulanger); A.N., D III 253, *liasse* 23 and F7 4710, d. Fossey (Pinard); A.N., D III 254, *liasse* 4 (Roulleau); A.N., D III 253, *liasse* 27 (Fantin); A.N., D III 253, *liasse* 20 (Dumeige).

Lechevalier, Claude-Louis Bonenfant and Denis Boulanger, each of whom had resided in his Quarter long before 1790 and had a certain social maturity. Lechevalier and Bonenfant had been members of the Jacobin Club since before 10 August 1792, and both had held substantial offices before they were elected justices: Lechevalier was an elector of the Faubourg-Montmartre in 1790, its police commissioner in 1791-2, and president of its assemblies in September and October 1792; Bonenfant was a member of the permanent committee of the Fontaine-de-Grenelle in 1790-1, one of its deputies to the Commune in 1791, and its police commissioner from September 1792 until he was elected justice in September 1793; Boulanger was elected police commissioner of the Oratoire within eight months of the abolition of its office at the *Châtelet*. But for J. Roulleau, J.-B. Fantin and Pierre Dumeige, the routes and stages were more humble: they led from the secretaryship of the permanent committee in 1790-1, an unsalaried, time-consuming but politically useful job, to the very modestly salaried posts of recording secretary to the police commissioner, followed by election to the office of justice after the Insurrection of 10th August.

This official, formal route was not the one travelled by René Corbin and Melchior-Humbert Peligot: their apprenticeship, acquisition of a political identity and of local knowledge, was more blatantly revolutionary, as *sociétaires*, and they entered the office through the victory of the local political faction to which they belonged. Neither had held Section office before the summer of 1792, and each was a "man of 10th August", but in a sense which corresponded to the revolutionary character of his Section in 1792 and afterwards. And their careers also exemplify the peculiar skills of survival and adaptation required of hundreds of other similar militants.

In 1791, the makeshift tailor and ex-clerk René Corbin was financially ineligible for office; in late August, 1792 he was elected justice of the Section Roule, replacing Nicolas Anquetil, a former private secretary to the Count of Artois. But in the Faubourg du Roule, this social devolution of authority was not confined to the office of justice; it encompassed the entire politics of the Section. Through the Insurrection of 10th August, the Section's monarchist élite, most of whose figures were wealthy members of the legal profession, rentiers, luxury purveyors and former royal magistrates who lived in the zone of the rue du faubourg Saint-Honoré, was abruptly supplanted by a prosaic, laborious and recent bourgeoisie which lived and worked in the western portion of the Section, beyond Saint-

Phillipe-du-Roule, beyond the stark frontiers of the great sewer and the *Chemin-Verte*, along the rue du faubourg du Roule and on the fringes of the *pépinière*. René Corbin was one of these *faubouriens* of the Roule and he ascended to local power with them, after having been second in command of the Section's companies in the assault on the Tuileries. This bloc of 10th August remained solid and consistently pro-Jacobin through 1793, and Corbin remained a prominent figure within it. But in the winter of the Year II the unity of the *sans-culotte* élite of the Roule began to fissure through a groundswell of lower-class opposition, expressed in the popular society, to the social conservatism of the revolutionary committee and the Montagnard Government behind it. At first, René Corbin and his recording secretary, Victor Gaudet, wavered, and then chose: they broke with their former comrades of the revolutionary committee in becoming spokesmen of this opposition in the Roule's popular society where at the end of Ventôse they moved that *certificats de civisme* be denied to all merchants and priests and that the government distribute fire-arms to all *sans-culottes*. Within three days of these motions, the revolutionary committee denounced them to the Committee of General Security, and on 8 Floréal the Committee had them both imprisoned as *hébertistes*. René Corbin had become justice of the peace through friendship and alliance with the Section's future revolutionary commissioners; his rupture with them in Ventôse Year II provoked his first imprisonment, and his earlier alliance with them determined his second, in Prairial Year III as a former terrorist.[43]

"A highly talented opportunist" was the tribute paid Melchior-Humbert Peligot by the Thermidorians of the Section Réunion. His fate in Prairial Year III was the same as that of Corbin, but his route to it was far more tortuous and intricate. The clarity of general politics in the Roule was reflected in the relative clarity of Corbin's career as a militant; this clarity was lacking in the Réunion, whose political anatomy was complex, and Melchior-Humbert Peligot was obliged to manoeuvre adroitly.

There was an extremely dense artisan and mercantile bourgeoisie in the Section Réunion, ranging from masses of small-scale, independent masters and shopkeepers who lived and worked in their ateliers and shops along the arterial rues Saint-Martin, Neuve Saint-Merry and Sainte-Avoye, to many wholesale merchants and manufacturers with large clienteles and work-forces. The zone was also thick with

---

[43] A.N., D III 253, *liasse* 25; A.N., F7 4653, d. Corbin; "Liste générale des citoyens actifs de la Section du Roule", MS. (July, 1790), F7 4718, d. Gaudet; A.N., F30 117; Soboul, *op. cit.*, pp. 857-8.

rentiers, office employees, and men of the law and liberal professions. The Section's political spectrum in 1792-3 was equally wide, moving from royalists and constitutional monarchists through the gradations of liberal and anti-*sans-culotte* feeling to more or less orthodox Jacobinism and a genuine, ultra-democrat left whose tendencies were insurrectionary and whose style was Cordelier. All of these currents, except the monarchist, were represented among the members of the *Société populaire des Amis-de-l'Égalité*, founded early in 1792, which grouped the "patriots" of the Réunion. Their cohesion was fragile, but it was maintained through struggle with monarchists, and with the Insurrection of 10th August the diverse members of the society gained control of the Section's offices and assembly. Melchior-Humbert Peligot, former book-keeper in several offices of finance, had inverted his career in 1792 through militancy with the Section's "patriots", and it was as an active member of the popular society that he was elected justice in September 1792. Politics in the Réunion were comparatively serene during the winter of 1792-3, in the absence of any general Parisian crisis which could crystallize local rivalries and transform them into conflicts, but in the spring the "patriots" of the Section and popular society split into factions and Peligot found himself walking a political tightrope.

The scission began in late March, and in reaction to external pressures; it unfolded in the classic pattern of the "regeneration" battles of that spring throughout Paris. On the 16th, the moderate group in the general assembly, in an address to the Convention, disassociated itself from "both the Right and the Left", and called for strong measures against the "anarchists" responsible for the obscure *putsch* attempt of 9-10th March. The resonance of the address was also internal, and amounted to something of a declaration of war: the Réunion had a tough, numerous and sanguine group of Cordelier militants, whose principal figures were Aristarque Didot, a former barrister's clerk, Louis-Antoine Noguès, who had no regular source of income in 1792-3, Rançon, a wine-shop keeper, Louvet-Dubois, a former gambler and, in 1793, an employee of the Municipal Police, Bistac, also employed in the Municipal Police, and, supporting them outside the Section, the long-standing Cordelier Étienne Michel, manufacturer of dyes, who represented the Section on the Commune in 1793-Year II. Determined to thrust the Réunion into the anti-Girondin movement, and in the process to wrench complete power from the hands of the more socially respectable and conservative bourgeoisie with whom they had co-existed, these *sans-culottes* of the Réunion counter-attacked. The author and orator of the address of 16th March, the merchant Grenier, was expelled from the popular society on the 21st; most of his supporters left the society in protest, and to the subsequent control of the *sans-culotte* faction. On the 26th, the *sans-culottes* gained temporary control of the general assembly and voted a violent address against the Girondins and their analogues in the Sections — "those moderates, egoists, and cowards". They were once more in a majority on 30th-31st March when the Cordelier militants were elected to form the surveillance committee of the Section. The Réunion's committee immediately overstepped its formal, legal boundaries to become the most aggressive revolutionary committee in the City in the spring of 1793: by mid-April, some fifty citizens of the Section, most of whom were prominent members of the anti-*sans-culotte* bourgeoisie, including Grenier and several others responsible for the address of 16th March, were disarmed as "suspects" and during the rest of the month the committee imperiously refused to justify this action to the general assembly. The reaction began in mid-April. On the 14th, a resurgent anti-*sans-culotte* majority in the assembly declared its full confidence in Grenier, and on the 29th voted him the *certificat de civisme* which he had requested. But on the 30th, the democrats got the assembly to resolve that it would "reconsider" its decision of the previous session, and Grenier deposited his certificate with the assembly until the final vote which was postponed until 3rd May. When this deliberation was begun on the 3rd, it was in an assembly packed by both factions, but presided over by the surgeon Jean-Nicolas Tilhard, a skilful and determined anti-*sans-culotte*, and with Grenier himself as its secretary; after two indecisive votes, the session dissolved into a general brawl.

Peligot's fate as justice of the peace depended on the issue of this conflict. In March and April he had been able to maintain a precarious and highly acrobatic neutrality, both in the popular society and in the uncertain general assembly over which he presided during the second half of April. Like most of the other ex-bureaucrat justices of the peace and police commissioners, he was socially marginal to the life of his Section and his insertion was political and tenuous; his dilemma in the spring of 1793 was more extreme than theirs because of the complexity and the intensity of this conflict in the Réunion, but it was not substantially different. The conflict had distinct social contours: the representative figures of the anti-*sans-culotte* group — the architect Jacques-Philippe Chassagnole, the merchant Grenier, the solicitors Jean-Joseph Coppéaux and Pierre Landais, the wholesale merchants Manus Palack, Jean Bosquet and

Jacques Merle — confronted a petty bourgeoisie and an artisan proletariat which was championed by men such as Didot, Louvet-Dubois, Noguès, Bistac, Rançon, or the shoemakers Dalizy, Humbert, Davranches and the fur-cutter Pierre Jard. Precisely because he was socially marginal, Peligot was suspended between these two groups but, as justice of the peace, he was faced with the imperative of winning the confidence of the one which would dominate. In the evening of 5th May, the Reunion's conservatives, strengthened and spiced by bands of enraged young men (or, in the Jacobin vocabulary, *muscadins*) who were threatened with conscription for the expedition to the Vendée, flooded the general assembly. They voted the suspension of the revolutionary committee and, late in the night, sent ten commissioners to seal its office and seize its papers. Neutrality was no longer possible for the justice of the peace Peligot.

This sort of internal, local conflict between *sans-culottes* and moderates, endemic to the Paris of 1793, was bloodless and hardly qualifies as the "larval civil war" alleged by Albert Soboul. It was rather a deadly serious, but highly urban and civilized ritual in which notions and appearances of legitimacy were even more important weapons than the fists, cudgels and chairs wielded by the protagonists in general assemblies, and this is why the ten commissioners of the sovereign general assembly of 5th May roused from their beds Peligot and the Section's police commissioner, both of whom represented judicial and executive authorities which could formally suspend the revolutionary committee in the name of the assembly. Aristarque Didot was then president of the committee and when this group, including Peligot, the police commissioner Charles-Antoine Martin and a small patrol of the Section force, arrived at his apartment on the rue Sainte-Avoye at three in the morning to notify him of the assembly's resolution, he levelled a sabre and pistol at them, shouting, "I know the swine who are responsible for this and that already eight revolutionary committees in Paris have been dissolved in the same way, but this manoeuvre will succeed only over my dead body", and then summoned Peligot to enter and confer with him. The deputation waited outside. Aristarque Didot was emphatic and Melchior-Humbert Peligot's political intuition was accurate; after an hour the justice of the peace came out to announce that he considered the mission of the commissioners to be illegal and that he would not accompany them. The police commissioner haplessly chose the other option, accompanied the commissioners to the office of the revolutionary committee, and posed the seals; three months later the general assembly dismissed him from office. And with the dawn of 6th May, Melchior-Humbert Peligot was a *sans-culotte*, accompanying Didot in mobilizing the other revolutionary commissioners and their ultimate supporter at the Commune, Étienne Michel. In the session of 7th May, the men of this faction, assisted by "fraternizing" deputations from the Sections Lombards and Bon-Conseil, annulled the resolution of 5th May. In mid-May, Peligot was elected by the assembly to the very sensitive "requisition committee" responsible for levying forced contributions and loans to equip the Section's contingent for the Vendée. His insertion within the local régime of 1793-Year II was now complete, and in the spring of the Year II he was able to remain aloof from the conflict between the revolutionary committee, now an instrument of government orthodoxy, and its renegade members, Aristarque Didot, Louvet-Dubois and Louis-Antoine Noguès, all *hébertistes* in the nomenclature of Germinal. But the political intuition of theSection's Thermidorians and the surveillance committee of the 7th *arrondissement* was as accurate as Peligot's had been on 6 May 1793, and their judgement inexorable: the "opportunist" Peligot was placed on each proscription list and in each denunciation of the ex-terrorists until he was finally dismissed and imprisoned in Prairial Year III.[44]

Finally, at an isolated extreme on the social spectrum of the Parisian justices of 1792-Year II, there was the one genuine *raté* and adventurer, Jean-Marie Martin of the Gravilliers. At the end of 1788 and at the age of thirty, he came to Paris and to furnished rooms at the *hôtel du Canada* on the rue Notre-Dame-de-Nazereth, armed with meagre funds and considerable ambition, leaving behind him a childhood and adolescence as the son of a prosperous landowning family at Marçigny (Saône-et-Loire) and several rather mysterious years as a putative notary at Lyons. Jean-Marie Martin's identity in Paris was collective, not individual, and his Revolutionary career

[44] A.N., D III 254, *liasse* 19; F7 4748, d. Jacob; B.N., Nouv. acq. franc., MS. 2704, fo. 55; Brit. Mus., F. 617 (25). The address of 16th March is in A.D.S., 1AZ 159², and that of the 26th in A.N., C 250, *liasse* 412, f. 31. On the expulsion of Grenier from the popular society, see A.N., F7* 2495, ff. 22 and 25. On the disarmings, see the minutes of the revolutionary committee in A.N., F7* 2494, ff. 4-5, 28-30. On the general assemblies of April, see A.N., W 11, *liasse* 529 and A.P.P., Aa 265, ff. 36-9. And on the confrontation of 5-6th May and its aftermath, see A.N., W 11, *liasse* 529 and F7 4677, d. Didot. The exemplary *sans-culotte* Aristarque Didot, who once more brandished pistol and sabre in Ventôse Year II when his former comrades of the revolutionary committee came to arrest him as an *hébertiste*, was a native of Saint-Firmin (Oise) and a member of one of the great publishing families of late eighteenth-century, and then nineteenth-century, Paris — the Firmin-Didots. See the baptismal records in A.N., F7 4677, d. Didot and A.N., F30 151, d. Didot (Firmin).

was a mirror-image of the fortunes of Jacobinism in the Gravilliers. His naturalization as a Parisian occurred between 1789 and 1792 in the *Société populaire de la rue du Vertbois*, through militancy there with Léonard Bourdon, Germain Truchon and Jacques Roux, against the legal District and Section of the censitary régime, dominated by an exclusive and wealthy monarchist bourgeoisie. Through the patronage of Léonard Bourdon and Germain Truchon, he was admitted to the Jacobin Club in the spring of 1792, and during the night of 9-10 August the Section's assembly chose the three of them to represent the Gravilliers on the Insurrectionary Commune. At the end of August, he was elected justice of the peace, replacing the wealthy monarchist barrister Jean-Baptiste Jossier. As an assiduous member of the Jacobin Club and a political justice of the peace, Martin was eligible for Montagnard patronage and for several months during the Year II he balanced his tenure as justice with a lucrative commission in the Ministry of War; within the Gravilliers he was one of the forces of orthodoxy, with Léonard Bourdon, the revolutionary commissioners and the leaders of the popular society, which proscribed Jacques Roux and silenced his partisans in Brumaire Year II.

The depth of moral commitment behind Jean-Marie Martin's loyalty to Jacobinism is difficult to gauge, and in his case the question is almost misplaced. This provincial immigrant of 1788 was so thoroughly a product of Jacobin Paris and through it had so totally defined himself in the Gravilliers that in the spring of the Year III he had no choice but to join in desperation the insurrectionary movement of 12 Germinal and in the hope of saving Léonard Bourdon and the remaining Montagnards in the Convention. This was followed by the inevitable dismissal from office and imprisonment.[45]

The themes of rupture, adaptation and ultimate fragility which illuminate the careers of the justices who had been bureaucrats also illuminate that of Jean-Marie Martin. In another and larger sense, that of the extraordinary versatility of Paris Jacobinism, a versatility in recruitment and sources of allegiance which defies any reduction to the "upper levels of the petty bourgeoisie", the figure of Jean-Marie Martin completes this social tableau of the office of justice of the peace in 1792-Year II, a tableau begun with images of the urban patriarchs J.-E.-A. Lebrun, Pierre Chauvin and Pierre Blandin.

*   *   *   *

[45] A.N., D III 253, *liasse* 12; F7 4774[37], d. Martin.

Through the "regenerations" and purges of Section élites between the summer of 1792 and the spring of the Year II several *bureaux de paix* witnessed dramatic, if temporary, displacements of authority from wealthy to modestly respectable or even to rather penurious justices, displacements of social class whose most striking instances were perhaps those from the former advocate of the *Châtelet*, Nicolas Herbault, to the ex-stocking weaver, Mathurin Bouin, from the former advocate of the Royal Council, Sanson Duperron, to the porcelain painter, François Therrin, from the former secretary to the count of Artois, Nicolas Anquetil, to the ex-process-server and journeyman tailor, René Corbin. These were not singular shifts, but rather incidences of collective fall and rise, of the seizure of Section institutions by new social and political clans, and most occurred in the aftermath of the Insurrection of 10th August, with the displacement of monarchists by "patriots" and not in 1793-Year II when the *sans-culottes* defeated the "moderates" and "aristocrats". But the over-arching pattern of social recruitment for the office of justice in 1792-Year II was respectable, rather prosaic, and in certain respects even predictable, despite the variety of the pre-Revolutionary and Revolutionary currents which flowed into the staffing of the office during this period. Almost all the justices of September 1792-Frimaire Year II were mature, recognizable figures in the landscape of Parisian life at the end of the century.

Equally, in political terms there were few genuinely "new men" among the justices of this period. At least forty-five of the sixty-five men who held the office during these years had held one or more formal Section office before their election to that of justice of the peace; of the remaining twenty, at least five had been officers of popular societies, and another five, members of the General Council of the Insurrectionary Commune. Fully twenty-five of these men had served as civil commissioners for periods of from eight to eighteen months before their election as justices, and five had served as revolutionary commissioners. Internal promotion, from within the *bureaux de paix*, was slight in 1792-Year II; only five former assessors and three former recording secretaries became justices during this period. And yet fifteen of the justices of 1792-Year II had been police commissioners of their Sections, an office in which they had served a definite apprenticeship to the solitude and individual responsibility of the justice of the peace, as well as to the very wide, somewhat ambiguous, and potentially dangerous range of his competence. Of the forty men who entered the office in late August and early September 1792, at least twenty-three had held office in their Sections during the censitary régime, and at least thirteen of them had been members of permanent committees in 1789-90.   And of the seventeen *sans-culotte* justices of 1793-Year II, twelve had held Section offices, most of them substantial, before their election.   Five of these *sans-culottes* had indeed entered the office of justice from that of revolutionary commissioner, but another five had also been civil commissioners during the censitary régime.

Beyond the ideological differences between them and despite the clanging abruptness with which many entered the office of justice of the peace, in the wake of "regeneration" upheavals and purges, the justices of 1792-Year II were almost to a man, not meteoric products of political crises, but varied figures within a bourgeoisie of the pre-Revolutionary and Revolutionary years who, and from at least the inception of the Revolution, had matured to the office of justice of the peace.   The one genuine new man, the one figure who in no way possessed an identity or local claim to office was François Cousin, the utterly faceless and, one suspects, obedient clerk in the Central Post Office who was appropriately chosen by the Committee of Public Safety to replace Florentin Phulpin as justice of the Arcis in Prairial Year II.

The succeeding generation of Parisian justices, that of the Years III to V, await its historian.   But one can perhaps glimpse its social contours in the replacement of the ex-scribe François Thilly by the solicitor Antoine Daubenton, of the career-less immigrant Jean-Marie Martin by the barrister Joachim Letellier, of the packing-case manufacturer Louis Bocquéaux by the ex-advocate Boucry de Saint-Venant.

In the Section Halle-au-Blé at least, the re-establishment of institutional order, of a socially rigid order reminiscent of the censitary régime of 1789-92, required that the last traces of the "anarchic" phase of 1793-Year II, a phase of relative social expansion and experimentation, be wiped from the *bureau de paix*.   And this was done in a manner highly suggestive of the mentality which infused the institutions of Directorial Paris.   The former advocate Boucry de Saint-Venant returned to the Section shortly after the fall of Robespierre and his colleagues, and from ten months' imprisonment by the revolutionary committee of the Halle-au-Blé.   In Prairial Year III the Legislation Committee appointed him justice of the peace to replace the *sans-culotte* Louis Bocquéaux, who had been imprisoned as a former terrorist and dismissed as justice.   Saint-Venant inherited Bocquéaux's process-server, Coquillard, a young ex-sales clerk and former member of the popular society of the Section who depended for his existence on the meagre salary of this office.   Sometime during the Year IV, Saint-Venant dismissed Coquillard and appointed to replace him a man with no political past who had been a professional process-server since 1773.   In protest at this action, the assessors began a prolonged "strike" which paralysed the *bureau de paix* of the Section.   Saint-Venant pleaded his case to the government and argued, from various decrees of the Constituent Assembly, that although justices could choose their process-servers they could not do so indiscriminately, and that those chosen must be *huissiers* by profession[46]   But the edge of Boucry de Saint-Venant's argument was not legalistic: it was nakedly social.   To assert that all citizens, whatever their occupations, are eligible for the office of process-server in a *bureau de paix* — and, by a facile extension, for any office including that of justice — "is to deny the very basis of social order, to cut its essential integuments; to argue the contrary is to express nostalgia for that time of disorder and anarchy when society was shaken to its foundations, when the reigning idea was that all offices are open and appropriate to every citizen . . . that savage, barbarous pretention"!

[46] *Mémoire au Corps Legislatif* (Paris, l'an IV), Brit. Mus., F. 570 (17). See also A.N., D III 253, *liasse* 14; F7* 2484; F30 123, d. Bocquéaux.

8. The Condition of the Poor in Revolutionary Bordeaux

ALAN FORREST

THE PROBLEMS WHICH THE QUESTION OF POVERTY POSES FOR THE historian of eighteenth-century France are — as Olwen Hufton has demonstrated in her most humane and illuminating discussion of begging and vagrancy[1] — in large measure problems of identification and definition. For poverty, the continual struggle to afford the bare essentials necessary to keep oneself and one's family alive, was the accustomed norm for vast sections of French society. A sudden crisis in the domestic economy, like the illness of a breadwinner, could bring the whole family to the brink of destitution, as could a particularly bad harvest, a sudden rise in food prices, or a failure to find even casual employment. Or again, an extra mouth to feed, whether through the arrival of another child or the need to look after an ailing relative, could tip the delicate balance between poverty (the customary state of perhaps one-third of French families in the eighteenth century) and utter destitution, the inability to fend for oneself and the humiliation of being reduced to begging, to the charity of men and women less unfortunate than oneself, if one were to succeed in keeping body and soul together. Before the outbreak of the Revolution little attempt was made to organize poor relief in any comprehensive, all-embracing way. Legislation by the central government was not seen as a universal panacea until after 1789. And though most towns and cities did make some attempt to deal with the perpetual problem of the destitute, largely through the establishment of municipal *bureaux de charité*, poverty remained largely a domestic issue for the individual family. Relief could be sought from friends and relatives, especially where, as in many country areas, families were strongly cohesive social units and communities were small and often closely-knit. Only if this failed would the indigent appeal for outside support — by begging at the farmhouse door, by turning to the Church for aid in times of distress, or by appealing to the local *bureau de charité*. Except in years of crisis

[1] O. Hufton, "Begging, Vagrancy, Vagabondage and the Law: an aspect of the problem of poverty in eighteenth-century France", *European Studies Rev.*, ii (1972). For a detailed local study of eighteenth-century poor relief, see J.-P. Gutton, *La société et les pauvres: l'exemple de la généralité de Lyon, 1534-1789* (Paris, 1970).

when famine threatened, the easing of poverty remained very much a local problem, one which neither the central government nor the regional estates or *parlements* considered as lying within their strictly-defined spheres of activity.

With the coming of the Revolution, however, the organization of poor relief ceased to be regarded as a purely localized activity, and the central government came to see poverty as a national scandal for which national solutions would have to be devised. Voluntary charity — the solution which had, albeit inadequately, sought to ease the burdens of the poor throughout the previous decades — was now rejected as inappropriate to so grave a social problem, while the very idea of charity, of the paternalistic sense of do-gooding which the term implied, seemed repulsive to many of the Revolutionary leaders. After 1790 the clergy, who had in many areas of France been the very pivot of the voluntary system, were stripped of their special position of influence in society. The abolition of feudalism incurred a marked reduction in the sense of responsibility, however patronizing, which the rich and noble had felt towards the more unfortunate members of their local communities. French social relationships were revolutionized, and the subsequent upheaval had severe repercussions in the field of charity and poor relief: the general sense of insecurity among the rich, the emigration of large numbers of noble families, the new and enduring hatred and bitterness between classes engendered by the social legislation of the years after 1789, all had the effect of reducing the amount of voluntary charity that was available to the poor. Voluntarism, it could be claimed with some justice, was no longer adequate to the needs of a situation in which, particularly after the outbreak of the war, the poor were becoming even more numerous and the funds available even more lamentably inadequate.

It is greatly to the credit of the Revolutionary governments that they were so profoundly concerned by the challenge of popular misery. Their awareness and diligence, indeed, provide striking proof of the new sense of social responsibility which had most surely been awakened by the Revolution, a sense of responsibility that clearly underlies much of the social legislation of the various assemblies in Paris. The right of every individual to work, for instance, was regarded as quite fundamental; it had ceased to be merely the intellectual plaything of philosophic and masonic societies. Thus the Constituent Assembly in 1790 set up a *Comité de Mendicité* which was responsible for assistance payments to the indigent, for payments to various towns for the upkeep of hospitals, and for the answering of individual petitions. The *Comité* was most methodical and assiduous in its work, collecting information from the provinces and drawing up specialized and often most lucidly-argued reports on the problems and difficulties that arose. In particular, it was recognized that work must be provided for all able-bodied men, and that unemployment was the root cause of much of the misery and degradation that assailed the people of France. The *Comité's* was a most notable contribution both in terms of research and of assistance, attempting to rationalize the work being done by local authorities throughout the country as they struggled to cope with the ever-mounting cost of relieving poverty.[2]

The establishment of this committee was, however, no more than one step among many; in all, Ferdinand Dreyfus has noted, the Legislative passed fifty-six decrees embodying measures to ease poverty. And under the Convention assistance became even more highly centralized. Measures of 1793, for instance, accepted the principle of state aid to the poor as "a national debt", organizing charitable *agences de secours*, dividing the available resources among the departments of France according to need, and assuming responsibility for orphaned and abandoned children.[3]

With the intentions of the legislators few would quarrel. But certain questions remain to be answered, questions that were seldom seriously considered by either the *Comité de Mendicité* itself or by the various committees nominated by the Convention to help solve the social problems posed by indigence and misery. The measures taken look impressive. Millions of *livres* were distributed to local authorities, clubs and hospitals; statistics were assiduously collected and mulled over by the administrators in Paris, and their findings dutifully embodied in resonant, clearly-formulated decrees. But how relevant were these measures to the needs of the poor themselves? To what extent did they succeed in their expressed aim of "destroying" mendicity and vagrancy? How much of the money actually reached the intended beneficiaries, and to what extent was its value diminished by other requirements of Revolutionary government? All these questions are in a sense functions of one of the themes most basic to any study of Revolutionary government: the relations between the centre and the periphery, between Paris and the provinces, between the administrators and the people. It is a theme

[2] C. Bloch and A. Tuetey, *Procès-verbaux et rapports du Comité de Mendicité de la Constituante, 1790-91* (Paris, 1911).
[3] F. Dreyfus, *L'assistance sous la Législative et la Convention, 1791-95* (Paris, 1905), esp. pp. 16, 64-5.

that has received surprisingly little attention from historians of the period, despite a general acceptance of its importance.[4]   The field of poor relief is one which goes far to throw this problem into high relief, illustrating both the strengths and weaknesses of centralization. For this was a field of activity to which the authorities devoted a large amount of attention and very considerable resources.   And yet, as I hope to demonstrate, they failed, in part at least because of the cumbersome bureaucratic apparatus they devised and of the manifest importance of local circumstances which they overlooked.

*   *   *   *

Nowhere was the question of poor relief more rigorously institutionalized than in the great urban centres which had grown so dramatically in population in the course of the century.   For the purposes of this paper, I shall examine the case of one such city, Bordeaux, a town which had in the sixty years before the outbreak of the Revolution achieved unparalleled wealth and commercial success.   The lure of wealth and employment had attracted large numbers of immigrant workers, both from the immediate hinterland and from further afield — from Poitou, the Limousin, the Auvergne — young men, often poor and unskilled, who had come in search of employment in the docks and markets and workshops of the city. These immigrants more than doubled Bordeaux's population in the course of the eighteenth century as they swarmed into the new, sprawling suburbs *(faubourgs)* that were hastily thrown up on the low-lying, rather marshy land beyond the old city walls.   It was here, in the dark alleys of the Faubourg Saint-Seurin and the closely-packed backstreets of the Faubourg Saint-Julien, that poverty was most widespread and assistance most desperately needed in the Revolutionary years.

For Bordeaux's prosperity, based almost exclusively on wine exports and colonial commerce, was to prove brittle and vulnerable. The high returns that could be obtained from fitting out ships for the Caribbean made the Bordeaux merchant community more than usually conservative and unimaginative in their business dealings. For this reason there was little diversification and the entire economy of the city became dangerously closely tied to the continued buoyancy of colonial trade.   With the Revolutionary wars and the blockade this

[4] See however, R. C. Cobb, *The Police and the People* (Oxford, 1970), for a most illuminating insight into the lives of the poor in these years; also his more recent *Reactions to the French Revolution* (Oxford, 1972).

somewhat fragile prosperity collapsed, and the city found itself facing a slump that engulfed not only the port itself but all those ancillary industries that were dependent on it, like the ropeworks and sugar refineries, the glassworks and shipyards. Profit margins were slashed, unemployment rose dramatically, and misery became widespread in the popular quarters of the city.

The social consequences of this sudden reversal in Bordeaux's economic fortunes make painful reading. General Brune, reporting on the condition of the people in September 1793 after the city had been forced to surrender to his besieging army, described to the Committee of Public Safety how long queues were forming outside bakers' shops, waiting patiently, without a murmur of complaint, for their ration of poor-quality black bread at eighteen *sous* per pound.[5] And Tustet, pointing in 1794 to the hardships that his fellow-citizens were suffering in the cause of the Revolution, spoke of men and women dying of hunger and fatigue in the streets, and emphasized that both the Bordelais themselves and the people from the neighbouring *communes* had suffered terribly. There was, he claimed, a period when there was not even enough meat to make soup for the sick and wounded in the hospitals; while in the rural areas of the Gironde many went without bread for twenty days at a time and were even reduced to eating the grass intended as fodder for animals.[6] Such accounts, however exaggerated, do help to illustrate the essential inadequacy of the increasingly doctrinaire solutions of the legislators in Paris to the task of eliminating harsh, grinding poverty from the garrets and lodging-houses of the Bordeaux *faubourgs*.

Many of the people living in these districts were desperately poor, eking out a miserable existence in conditions of great squalor and overcrowding. It was here that assistance was most desperately needed, not least by the numerous widows and women deserted by their husbands who were left with families to raise on their quite derisory earnings. In the popular areas of the city, indeed, it was generally accepted that the womenfolk had an important part to play in the domestic economy; most took a job to bring in an additional income. It was they who provided the vast majority of the domestic service in the city; this gave employment to some five thousand

---

[5] Archives de la Guerre (Vincennes), B⁴8, "Correspondance des Armées des Pyrénées", letter from Brune to the Committee of Public Safety, 29 Sept. 1793.
[6] Archives Municipales de Bordeaux (hereafter Arch. Mun. Bordeaux), 18/25, Tustet, *Tableau des évènements qui ont eu lieu à Bordeaux depuis la Révolution de Quatre-vingt-neuf jusqu'à ce jour* (Bordeaux, 1794), p. 37.

women, particularly, it would seem , to the many girls who had come to Bordeaux from the country districts of the South-West to find work.[7] For the rest, most had hard manual jobs, as cleaners and laundresses, seamstresses and washerwomen, saleswomen and stall-keepers in the *faubourgs*.[8]

Others again kept lodging-houses *(chambres garnies)* for the many immigrant workers, single men who had come to Bordeaux in search of employment. It was here that the utterly destitute might find shelter, in the cheap, dank, miserable rooms let out by the night that were to be found, for instance, along the rue du Pont Long. The case of Jean Lanusse, a clerk forced by 1793 to seek agricultural labouring in the country areas, illustrates the depths of poverty to which men could sink in the Revolutionary years. Lanusse was forty-four, a native of the *commune* of Beautiran in the Gironde, of no fixed address, and dependent for his very existence on casual labour. On the day on which he was arrested for wandering around at night without his *carte de section*, that invaluable proof of both identity and civic virtue, he had been labouring at Saint-Médard-en-Jalles, and was hunting for a room in the rue du Pont Long after a meal with a woman in the Bacalan, to whom, he says, he had taken some fish by way of payment.[9] For the very poor, for men like Lanusse, the *chambre garnie* provided the only alternative to sleeping in the open.

Even more typical of the popular areas was the little backstreet bar or *cabaret*, often kept as a second source of income by the workers of the *faubourg* or by their wives. Philibert Dodille, for instance, was an *aubergiste-cafetier* who ran, with his wife, a small café in the rue Beauvais. He told the *Comité de Surveillance* in evidence that his clientele were for the most part artisans, plasterers and harness-makers *(des plâtriers et des selliers)*, who whiled away their time drinking coffee and playing dominos or the occasional game of cards.[10] Then, as now, such cafés were the very centre of social life in working-class districts. In Saint-Seurin such enterprises were both more numerous and more lucrative, for, with many of the wealthy middle classes living on the edge of the *faubourg*, the district had come to acquire a well-deserved reputation as a social centre for the playboys of the city. Here, as in the Chartrons, the income of the poor could often

---

[7] J.-P. Poussou, "Les structures démographiques et sociales", in F.-G. Pariset (ed.), *Bordeaux au dix-huitième siècle* (Bordeaux, 1968).
[8] Archives Départementales Gironde (hereafter A.D.G.), C2794, *capitation* roll for the Faubourg Saint-Seurin in 1786; also Arch. Mun. Bordeaux, K11.
[9] A.D.G., 13L25, Dossier Jean Lanusse.
[10] A.D.G., 13L22, Dossier Philibert Dodille.

be supplemented by the work of the barmaid (*cabaretière*) and the prostitute (*fille de joie*).

As in most seaports, the rôle of the prostitute in Bordeaux society was a not insignificant one; the *capitation* roll of 1784 lists some one hundred and fifty girls earning a living from this source in Saint-Seurin alone.[11] To the respectable bourgeois of the town, they were a source of embarrassment and irritation that on occasions came close to prudery. Henry Blanchard, for instance, a military *aide-de-camp*, wrote indignantly to the Municipal Council in 1790 to complain about prostitutes stridently selling their wares and fighting noisily outside his house. He begged the Council to take immediate action to control their activities, pointing out contemptuously that they were being allowed to "infest" the area and bring it into disrepute by soliciting for custom in doorways and insulting any respectable residents who might pass by.[12] To the city health authorities, moreover, prostitution posed a serious problem — as circumstantial evidence one could cite the statistics given about the inmates of the *Dépôt de Mendicité* (poorhouse) in *Pluviôse* Year III (the only month for which these are available): of a total of 137 individuals listed, one hundred are women, and no fewer than ninety-two are noted as suffering from venereal disease.[13] And throughout the Revolutionary period we have several indications that venereal disease was causing havoc among men in the *Garde Bordelaise* and the military battalions of the South-West: one outraged report of January 1793 tells how two soldiers of the eighth Battalion, after intensive hospital treatment, were discovered on the very night of their release in bed with prostitutes in Bordeaux and were promptly clapped in prison.[14]

In the Year II the *Comité de Surveillance*, turning to the problem of prostitution, urged that all prostitutes be forbidden to ply their trade and be put instead to useful work, sewing camping equipment and knitting articles of clothing for the troops on the frontiers. For, argued the Committee, not only did they lead "an indolent and scandalous life", but they also did irreparable harm to the military effort. National interest was invoked to support the demands of moral puritanism, the Committee pointing out that young soldiers were being corrupted and infected by these women, and that they were dying in hospital beds when they could and should have been fighting

[11] J.-P. Poussou, *op. cit.*, p. 366. Poussou goes on to argue that there must have been a similar number of prostitutes working in the bars of the Chartrons.
[12] Arch. Mun. Bordeaux, I7, "Police Locale", letter dated 31 July 1790.
[13] A.D.G., 4L134, "Dépôt de Mendicité", document listing the inmates of the *Dépôt* for *Pluviôse* Year III.
[14] Arch. Mun. Bordeaux, H40, "Hôpitaux militaires", document I.

for the cause of France and the Revolution.[15]   Again the solution proposed was one of harsher penalties and constant surveillance. But if for the military authorities prostitution was a source of trouble and irritation, for the poor of the *faubourgs* it was no more than an integral part of the economics of everyday life.

As in Paris, the social conscience of Bordeaux towards the needs of the poor was awakened by the Revolution; their plight was discussed and money raised on an unprecedented scale.   Especially prominent in social work and poor relief were the two rival political clubs of the city, the socially-conservative *Amis de la Liberté et de l'Egalité* and the Jacobin *Club National*.   The sums of money distributed had by 1793 risen to very considerable proportions.   The *Amis*, for instance, claimed on 1 June of that year to be handing out two thousand *livres* per month and complained that the tasks they faced were far too great for the funds at their disposal.   They pointed out that they were currently making payments to some three hundred women living in acute hardship, to say nothing of the numerous volunteers for the armies who asked for help on the grounds that they had lost their wallets, or who needed money for the journey to rejoin their companies, or who had pregnant wives to support or were unable to pay the rent.[16]   Such appeals were listened to with patience and understanding.   As for the *Club National*, it proved most energetic in raising funds to help the deserving poor, the good citizen who had fallen on evil times through no fault of his own and who petitioned the Club for aid to save him from starvation.   Of the Clubists' good intentions one has no doubts, but it does at times seem as though their concern was not so much for poverty as such, as for poverty tempered by Revolutionary virtue: widows of men killed in action, fathers of families left with children to support, these are given a special degree of consideration.   And although there is no direct proof that anyone was actually deprived of aid because of his lack of *civisme*, nevertheless it is highly symptomatic that urgent pleas for assistance were almost always accompanied by accounts of the applicant's unassailable *sans-culotte* virtue.   These petitions also serve to reveal the depths of misery of the *bas peuple*.   Some, like that asking for a deputation to be sent urgently to see the state of poverty into which the petitioner has fallen, are poignant indeed; it ends in a wild crescendo of misery, "in the name of humanity",

[15] Arch. Mun. Bordeaux, I2, "Police Locale", letter of 16 *Messidor* Year II from the *Comité de Surveillance* to the *Municipalité*.
[16] A.D.G., 12L18, "Amis de la Liberté", letter of 1 June 1793 from the Society's *comité des secours*.

scrawled in a semi-literate hand. Many indicate a feeling of shame and bitterness mingling with a deeply-engrained pride, a pride which makes them reluctant to ask for charity and resentful that they have been reduced to doing so.[17]

At the Sectional level, too, funds were distributed to the needy by the *comités des secours*, and much time was spent discussing the problems posed by the existence and increasing urgency of poverty. Many demanded and implemented a subscription or a levy on the rich as the most immediate solution. The poorer Sections, not unnaturally, championed the cause of a central agency to collect and distribute funds; in this plea can be detected not only self-interest on their part, but also, I think, something of the basic egalitarian ideal of "from each according to his abilities, to each according to his needs". But among the richer, more merchant-dominated Sections, the welcome given to such schemes was a cautious one indeed. Section 19 (*du Bon Accord*) welcomed ideas for public works, includ-ing the draining of Bordeaux's marshes to provide extra land for agriculture; but on the question of paying for these schemes, it turned down any idea of a fixed imposition on the grounds that this would undermine the social function of voluntary charity. The merchants of *Bon Accord* clearly saw the moral value of giving freely to their less fortunate fellows as the primary benefit to be derived from charity: the tone of their deliberations on the subject shows that they were more concerned with the satisfaction they might obtain from giving than with the very real human need which they might be helping to alleviate.[18] And that most conservative of all Bordeaux's Sections, *Simoneau*, went still further. It also welcomed these suggestions, provided that the money was not to be raised by any progressive rate calculated on rents, arguing that financial and social inequalities were necessary and desirable for the prosperity of trade and industry and lay at the base of all human relations in society; for the maintenance of inequality the Section declared itself perfectly prepared to tolerate poverty as "a sad but necessary consequence" and to regard poor relief as a debt to be borne by society.[19]

In the event, the Sections decided in July 1793 to take collective action to solve the problems of the city's poor, and a central *bureau* and Sectional committees were duly elected. These committees were to play a major part in helping to alleviate some of the most patent cases of suffering; their work was thorough and painstaking, with

[17] A.D.G., 12L28, "Club National", documents concerning poor relief.
[18] A.D.G., 12L10, Section 19, minute of 9 May 1793.
[19] A.D.G., 12L3, Section 5, minute of 10 May 1793.

commissaires considering requests for aid and investigating the circumstances of applicants for charity. Here the poor did gain from the Revolution; for there can be no doubt that the Sectional committees were far more efficient than the former parishes in relieving misery. The very distribution of parishes in Bordeaux before 1790 illustrates clearly how out of touch the Church authorities were with the needs of the *faubourgs* and how singularly ill-equipped they were to deal with the problem of poor relief, which was, of course, most serious in these very quarters.[20]

But perhaps the new concern for the welfare of the poor is most tellingly illustrated by the relentless campaigning of Clochard, an architect in Section 1, the *Section des sans-culottes*. His detailed scheme, published in pamphlet form in 1793, did much to bring both the problem and possible solutions to the problem before the city authorities, and to open the issue to public debate. He was a most skilled propagandist and — as he was to show in the Year II when, as a member of the Municipal Council, he was given responsibility for the problem of indigence — an able and ambitious administrator. In his pamphlet he shows how best the available finances could be used.[21] He begins by classifying paupers, distinguishing between, on the one hand, the blind and crippled, infirm and aged, and, on the other, those who can but will not work, the thieves and vagabonds, the lazy and the drunkards. Again, he seeks to cater for orphans and abandoned children, and those children whose parents are too poor to feed and care for them. For the aged and infirm — those who in Victorian England were to become known in Poor Law jargon as "the deserving poor" — the degree of freedom is rigorously circumscribed. In the institutions (*enclos*) that were to be provided under his scheme, the eating, living, and sleeping amenities were to be adequate, never comfortable. The food ration was to include soup and vegetables, with five ounces of meat on every other day; clothing and bedding were to be provided and strictly regulated, while the men should be made to do light, non-industrial work, and the women laundering, sewing and cleaning to keep the building in order.

Much more severe was the régime he recommended for able-bodied beggars. For them, as he himself made clear in Year IV, the primary purpose of confinement was that of "correction", since he considered

---

[20] The contrast is striking between parishes with only fifteen hundred or two thousand parishioners in the older area of the city centre and the new suburban parishes, which often contained between ten and twenty thousand.

[21] A.D.G., 4L134, Clochard, *Observations utiles au sujet des secours et des établissements que la mendicité rend nécessaires* (printed brochure, 18 Jan. 1793).

beggars to be utterly "incorrigible" as long as they continued to roam the highways and city streets. He therefore intended to impose discipline on their lives and convert them to social *mores* more acceptable to the majority of their fellow-citizens.[22] They should be put to work, in cleaning up the harbour or sweeping the streets, or in providing manual labour for public works schemes organized by the municipal authorities. Only when they obtained a job in a private firm would they be allowed to leave the *enclos*, and should they subsequently be caught begging yet again, they should be brought back and confined to the institution "for all time". Poor and abandoned children, declares Clochard, ought to be given a basic instruction in reading and writing up to the age of twelve, when they should become self-sufficient, either as agricultural labourers on the land or as apprentices placed with master-craftsmen. Again, as in the *enclos* for the aged and indigent paupers, discipline was to be severe, mealtimes strictly observed, leisure very closely limited and supervised. The overall impression is one of regulation and inspection, of a régime which alleviated the physical hardships of poverty but which emphasized and may even have increased the psychological cruelty. Clochard's ideas were not strikingly original; they owed much to the prevailing orthodoxies of the eighteenth century. And they were dominated, like so much Jacobin thinking on poverty, by a burning desire for justice — that severe, puritanical justice of the self-righteous that has no place for compassion, no understanding of human dignity.

The Revolution was, indeed, particularly unsympathetic to beggars, who were persistently and systematically persecuted from the *Grande Peur* of 1789 onwards. To the *Montagnards* they were a constant irritant, men who refused to conform and fulfil a useful social function. The Convention's law of 24 *Vendémaire* Year II was to make it quite clear that beggars ought to be repatriated to their *commune* of origin, while *maisons de répression* (prisons) should be opened in the main town of every department, in which habitual beggars should be obliged to serve periods of detention.[23] And Clochard, in pressing the details of his plan on the Municipal Council, went out of his way to stress that it could effectively "put an end to mendicity" in Bordeaux and the surrounding area — this, as much as alleviating the sufferings of the poor, was its declared intention. Nor was this harsh attitude to beggars confined to those of a Jacobin persuasion; the same intolerance

---

[22] Arch. Mun. Bordeaux. Q4, letter of Clochard to *Municipalité du Sud*, 12 *Messidor* Year IV.

[23] Details of this law are given in F. Dreyfus, *op. cit.*, pp. 65-8.

is to be found among the expressed views of several of the more conservative Sections of the city. From Section 10 (*de la Concorde*), for instance, came a complaint about the large number of beggars who had come into Bordeaux from outside, "who are more harmful than they are useful to the city".[24] And Section 19 (*du Bon Accord*) asked the city authorities in March 1793 to take steps to end an abuse that had arisen, whereby men had been roaming the streets, claiming that they had enrolled in the armies of the Republic and demanding money, knocking on every door and insulting and threatening those who refused to make any contribution.[25] To the prosperous middle classes, beggars were social undesirables who should be arrested or moved on; to the rabid *Montagnards* they were a social curse inviting radical, authoritarian reform.

But they were also individuals to whom the Revolution brought not comfort but harrying by the police and *Garde Nationale*, especially, it would seem, in the frenzied early months of 1790, when police files contain full records of those imprisoned as mendicants.[26] The majority were men, though there were some women among them. Most were young, aged between seventeen and twenty-five, with trades or work when they could find it — as gardeners, dockers, joiners, carpenters and weavers. Of the seventy-one arrested in February, March, and April 1790, the three most vigorous months of police activity, twenty-four gave their occupation as sailors, often with the fleet at Blaye or Libourne, who were reduced to begging when they were paid off or when the fleet was in port. Surprisingly few — only two in this sample — were agricultural workers. The women generally gave their profession as seamstresses, laundresses, cooks and domestic servants — the standard tasks performed by women of the working classes. Very few of those arrested came from Bordeaux itself; a large number had come to the city from the rural areas of the South-West to find bread and work, while others claimed to have come from the Limousin or Poitou, or from as far as Brittany, Provence and Lorraine. In other words, in a large number of cases, the beggars were really following the thousands of other workers who, in the course of the century, had chosen to move to Bordeaux to make their fortune. In their interrogations all insisted that their reason for begging was unemployment; again and again, they replied that they were unable to find work and had to beg in order to stay alive.

[24] A.D.G., 12L6, Section 10, minute of 22 Aug. 1793.

[25] Arch. Mun. Bordeaux, D103, "Conseil Municipal", minute of 26 March 1793.

[26] A.D.G., 4L134, dossier on those imprisoned for begging in February, March and April 1790.

They were, in short, not villains or agents of counterrevolution or subversion, but simple men desperately seeking an escape from misery and hunger.

Nor did hospitals and charitable institutions derive any benefits from Revolutionary legislation; rather, they were badly prejudiced by the side-effects of the two-pronged attack on feudalism and the Church. The abolition of feudal dues, indeed, served to deprive the hospitals of Bordeaux of a substantial part of their annual revenue, and this at a time when the number of patients was steadily rising through the admission of sick and wounded men from the armies in the Pyrenees and the strain on hospital facilities and finances was becoming proportionately more unbearable. For the many religious charitable institutions of the region had been largely dependent for income on feudal *rentes*; the authorities calculated in 1791 that the total loss to these *maisons de charité* in rents alone as a result of reforming measures was 188,862 *livres*, and that figure is certainly well on the low side, being based on a combination of official returns made thirty years previously in 1764 and the declarations of the houses themselves, almost always unwillingly given for fear of confiscation and hence widely underestimated. A further 39,868 *livres* in declared *rentes* were lost by the four religious educational endowments in the city, the *Frères des Ecoles Chrétiennes* and three orders of nuns, the *Ursulines*, the *Religieuses de Notre-Dame* and the *Religieuses de la Merci*.[27] The plight of the chief hospital of the city, the *Hôpital Saint-André*, is not untypical. In 1792 the hospital authorities complained bitterly that through the loss of privileges and dues their income had been cut by more than half — they had lost 55,023 *livres* of their old revenues and were left with only 45,127 *livres* to pay their annual expenses — yet, in the meantime, the number of patients had risen far beyond the capacity of the building to an average of 492 in 1790, 440 in 1791, and more than 500 in 1792.[28] To balance their budget each year proved quite impossible, even with regular payments from the Municipal Council, which was forced to step in to prevent the closure of the hospital. Thus the deficit carried forward from 1791 stood at 17,480 *livres*, that of 1792 at 62,951 *livres*, and by 1793 it had soared to 111,596 *livres*, in each case after subtracting a sizable and growing municipal subsidy made necessary by inflationary pressures.[29]

[27] A.D.G., 4L133, "Hôpitaux et hospices", lists of losses suffered by various Bordeaux charitable institutions as a result of the Revolution.

[28] A.D.G., 4L133, MS. *mémoire* of 1792, entitled "Etat des Hôpitaux de la Commune de Bordeaux".

[29] Arch. Mun. Bordeaux, Q8, table of revenues and expenses of the *Hôpital Saint-André* for 1791, 1792 and 1793; the finances of other Bordeaux hospitals are dealt with in *liasse* Q6.

The other hospitals and charities in the city were suffering similar financial setbacks. Nor were their embarrassments and troubles purely monetary. The hospital services were dependent for their very existence during the Ancien Régime on the religious orders, and even the Revolutionary governments in Paris realized that exceptions from expulsion and persecution would have to be made for those religious engaged on charitable work. In Saint-André, for instance, the staff included twenty-seven sisters (*soeurs grises*) whose services were retained throughout the Revolution. Their very indispensability gave them an entrenched position and a strong bargaining counter with the authorities, to such an extent that a plan to dismiss the three priests who acted as almoners at the hospital had to be dropped in the face of a unanimous threat by the sisters to withdraw their labour.[30]   In Bazas, where the nursing sisters were dismissed, the quality of hospital services was seriously undermined, and it was accepted, even by the Municipal Council, that the political decision to appoint lay nurses would inevitably cause some suffering to the patients.[31]   As for education, the *Frères des Ecoles Chrétiennes* were dismissed in 1791 on the grounds that they constituted a threat to the Republic and primary teaching was entrusted to new, lay teachers; Simone Dalby claims in her article on education in Bordeaux during the Revolution that standards were high and results excellent. But her optimism was not universally endorsed. In April 1793, indeed, *Beaurepaire*, one of the Sections more alive to social issues, is found complaining about the conduct of these new masters, alleging that they were neglecting their duties to the extent that they were giving the children less than two hours' instruction per day, while many children were spending entire weeks without reading a word or repeating a single lesson.[32]   Such shortcomings in hospital and educational provision could not but further worsen the lot of the poor and underprivileged.

The advent of war also hit the poor disproportionately hard. It disrupted the city's economic pattern and caused widespread

---

[30] A.D.G., 4L7, District of Bordeaux, minutes of 23 and 24 Apr. 1793. It is explained that the almoners, as priests, ought to have been expelled from France within a fortnight of the Decree of 26 August 1792. The District was, however, determined at all costs to retain the services of the sisters, and such was the "consternation" among them when the almoners were arrested by order of the *Comité de Sûreté Générale* that the District voted to set them free in an attempt to restore calm.

[31] Archives Municipales de Bazas, reg. 7, minutes of 21 and 23 Oct. 1793.

[32] Arch. Mun. Bordeaux, D103, letter from Section 22 dated 17 Apr. 1793; S. Dalby, "L'instruction publique à Bordeaux pendant la Révolution", *Revue historique de Bordeaux*, xxix-xxx (1936-7), p. 160.

unemployment and hardship. Imports as well as exports were affected, and the corn supplies on which the citizens were so totally dependent often failed to arrive. In the summer of 1793, with Bordeaux in revolt against the Convention, an army was sent to besiege the city and starve it into surrender. The speed of their success is a token of the vulnerability of the Bordelais through food shortage. Then, and through much of 1794 and 1795, it was the poor who shouldered the burden; their anger and resentment were only increased by the sight of grain and other foodstuffs being shipped off to feed the armies on the frontier or the fleet at Blaye while they remained inadequately fed. In August of 1793, at the very height of the provisioning crisis in the city, *représentants-du-peuple* Leyris and Chaudron-Rousseau decreed that grain be supplied by all the departments of the South-West to feed the armies of the Pyrenees. In all, a total of eighty thousand quintals was demanded for each of the two armies, the quota for the *Armée des Pyrénées occidentales* having to come from the six departments of the Gers, Landes, Gironde, Dordogne, Lot-et-Garonne and Basses-Pyrénées. The Gironde alone, in spite of its grain deficiency, had to supply ten thousand quintals.[33] At all times, military requisitions had to have priority, an important aspect of the much larger overall problem of food supply and bread prices.

More directly, the war affected the lives of the people through the requisitioning of men for service on the frontiers, or for the Vendée. Many families were thus deprived of their breadwinner, and though in principle relief was available,[34] in practice money was constantly falling in short supply, and the wives, widows, and children of soldiers were not infrequently lumped together with the indigent, the provision of military equipment, and the purchase of grain supplies in the regular sectional appeals to their members for urgently-needed funds. The mortality rate in war was high and the Government never tired of repeating its requisition demands. In the spring of 1793, for instance, it was declared policy to raise the strength of the Army to 502,800 men, of which the Gironde had to find a contribution of

[33] Archives Nationales (hereafter A.N.), AFii261, dossier 2203, decree on the requisitioning of grain, 20 Aug. 1793.
[34] A.N., AFii81, "Hospices et secours", rates of pension and indemnity decreed by the Convention of 26 November 1792 and 4 May 1793. These measures laid down statutory rates for the wives and dependants of those fighting on the frontiers, and higher rates of benefit for the wives and dependents of the men who died in the Republican armies. Wives, children up to the age of twelve, children over the age of twelve should they be ill or incapacitated and hence unable to work, and fathers and mothers either over sixty or too ill to work were entitled by law to fixed benefits.

2,832.[35]   The response in Bordeaux was good, the Sections vying
with one another to show their patriotism, and the city's requisition
was over-subscribed.[36]   But an examination of the inscriptions of
these volunteers shows clearly that it was not the sons of the
professional classes who were dashing to fight for France.   They
were tradesmen and manual workers, masons and ironworkers, shoemakers and porters, carpenters and hairdressers.

That this should be so in predominantly working-class areas is
hardly to be wondered at, though the high proportion of those
recruited who were immigrants to the city is noteworthy.[37]   What is
really revealing is the requisition list of one of the wealthy merchant
sectors, *Brutus*, situated in the very heart of the business area of the
port.   The Section proudly boasted thirty-seven recruits whom it
had equipped for war.   All whose occupation is recorded were
manual workers and journeymen artisans (only in five cases is no
information given about the occupation of the recruit); and of these no
fewer than twelve were shoemakers and ten unskilled labourers
(*portefaix*).   Only one is listed as being born in Bordeaux; the rest
were young workers, in from the country and almost all living in
chambres garnies in the city. Many had come from other parts of France
— three from Brittany, two from the Cantal, one each from the Limousin, the Périgord, Besançon and Toulon, and no fewer than eight from
the Auvergne. Though some were resident in the Section, the majority
were not, and there are several addresses in areas as far removed as
Saint-Seurin and the new *faubourgs*. A number of them, moreover, had
clearly been recruited by their employers, like two labourers signed on
at the same time and working in the same glassworks.[38]   Other recruitment lists reflect the same trends. Of the fifteen men inscribed by the
Section de l'Egalité, that merchant-dominated part of the inner Chartrons and the area round the *Jardin Public*, all were manual workers,
only three were able to sign their names, and not one was a native of the
city of Bordeaux.   Here, too, the fact that three of the men inscribed

[35] A.D.G., 3L259, "Guerre et recrutement", decree of 24 Feb. 1793 to raise
the strength of the armies to 502,800 men.
[36] A.N., AFii261, dossier 2199, report of *représentants-en-mission* from the
Armée des Pyrénées Occidentales, 14 Apr. 1793.
[37] Arch. Mun. Bordeaux, I63, Section 16, list of 23 volunteers for the *levée
en masse*, 20-22 Mar. 1793; A.D.G., 12L10, Section 22, list of 33 volunteers for
the *levée en masse*, 20-23 Mar. 1793.
[38] Arch. Mun. Bordeaux, H3, "Affaires militaires", recruitment slips for the
armies of men from Section 7 (*Brutus*).   The slips were all registered at the
Mairie of Bordeaux on 30 March 1793, each being countersigned by Mayor
Saige and the *secrétaire-greffier*, Basseterre.

were tradesmen (*cloutiers*) in the same workshop, would suggest that
their employer, one Pacquier, was at least giving some degree of encouragement.[39]   Similarly in Section 17 (*Michel Lepeletier*), three of
those recruited, all young men from the Auvergne, were living in the
same lodgings, with a shoemaker in the Place du Palais.[40]   It was men
such as these, young and often unskilled, frequently living in conditions
of the utmost misery and degradation, lacking roots in the community
and the sense of security that such roots might bring, who could be
persuaded to respond to the call to arms in the spring of 1793.

Those who remained faced shortages and high prices, at least until
the *Montagnard* period of control (from October 1793 until
thermidor), when the *maximum* was introduced to curb the free
market in a wide range of commodities.   But for much of the
Revolution, the poor suffered severe shortages of the very goods they
needed most, and with the *maximum* rationing was introduced which
equally served to keep consumption low.   For long periods soap was
virtually unobtainable; in the Year II a mission was to be organized
to go to Marseille, the centre of the soap industry, for emergency
supplies.[41]   And an acute shortage of firewood was a chronic source
of popular distress.   In a long and interesting letter to the
représentant-du-peuple, Ysabeau, in *Fructidor* Year II, a seventy-two-
year-old "véritable sans-culotte de la Section Francklin", Magnouac
père, asked that steps be taken to end the free-for-all in marketing
wood and to set up wood stores on the model of those in Paris and
other cities.   Only in this way, he argued, could distribution be
made on an equitable basis; what was happening was that the rich
were stockpiling while prices were low and accumulating a year's
supplies at once, whereas the poor were the victims of unscrupulous
merchants who bought stocks on board ship in the roads and speculated on popular misery to maximize profits.[42]   He was not exaggerating, for the Sectional minutes of 1793 indicated widespread
discontent with the arrant speculation and extortion of wood-
merchants.   The fear was well-established that cold, as much as
hunger, could enflame popular feeling and give rise to disturbances
in the streets.

But by far the greatest source of alarm in the Revolutionary years

[39] A.D.G., 12L2, Section 4, "Inscription pour l'enrolement des volontaires",
list opened 20 Mar. 1793.
[40] A.D.G., 12L9, Section 17, list of volunteers in minute of 23 Mar. 1793.
[41] A.D.G., 3L206, "Département de la Gironde — subsistances".
[42] A.N., F⁷4560, dossier 3 (Gironde), letter of Jean Magnouac *père* to Ysabeau,
28 *Fructidor* Year II.

was the virtually perpetual fear of a shortage of bread, the staple item in the diet of the poor. It was a natural enough fear — in the last years of the Ancien Régime there had been several bad harvests, and 1773 saw fairly serious bread riots in Bordeaux. A series of bad harvests in the Revolutionary years themselves could only add immediacy to fears so widespread as to constitute a constant and nightmarish part of the French popular mentality. For the citizens and the inhabitants of the surrounding area alike were totally dependent on the Bordeaux bread market, a market which needed to supply some sixteen hundred bushels of grain per day, twelve hundred of them for the requirements of Bordeaux alone.[43] In the summer of 1793, the situation was particularly grave; if the supplies of wheat in magazines and warehouses stood at 26,828 bushels on 1 June, they had fallen to only 1,015 bushels by 17 August, supplemented by only a further 1,155 bushels of ground flour. The consumption figures issued weekly during these summer months indicate a considerable enforced switch from wheat-flour to less appreciated grains or flour mixtures, including the common use of barley, rye, beans, and maize.[44]

So great was the belief that the city was on the point of experiencing not only shortage but actual famine and starvation that proposals for alternatives to grain were put forward and eagerly listened to. At moments of particular alarm, for instance, rice was distributed among the *comités des subsistances* of the poorer Sections.[45] And in April 1793, Section 2 (*des Amis de la Paix*) ordered the printing of the proposal of one of its members, which — though natural enough today — seems to have caused a considerable stir at the time, that the Department should offer bounties or premiums for the growing of potatoes in the Gironde. The pamphlet pointed out that grain imports not only cost France large sums of money every year and were a steady drain on the national resources, but also that in time of war and disruption they were not reliable. Potatoes, on the other

---

[43] Arch. Mun. Bordeaux, D103, letter to the Minister of the Interior on food supplies, 26 Mar. 1793.

[44] A.D.G., 4L68, "Subsistances", contains the weekly returns on the state of grain supplies in the Bordeaux granaries, including those for 1793.

[45] A.D.G., 12L12, documents of the *Comité des Subsistances* of the Sections of Bordeaux. On 11 September 1793, for instance, it was agreed to sell off limited quantities of rice to the individual Sections, on condition that that rice was resold in the sections at cost price. Also A.D.G., 12L9, Section 18: on 14 August the Section agrees on measures to provide each family within its area that is in receipt of the bread indemnity from the *Municipalité* with two pounds of rice per person at a price of ten *sols* per *livre* instead of the cost price of 13 *sols*.

hand, while saving foreign currency, could be mixed with grain to produce a most wholesome and nourishing bread, and their use would have the beneficial effect of reducing corn prices.[46] Nevertheless, there is no evidence of enthusiasm among the people; in matters of diet the poor of Bordeaux were as conservative as any, and Sectional concern about shortages took the form of demands for greater surveillance, more rigid controls, harsh punishments for hoarders and speculators, equality of distribution, and uniformity of quality. Just about the most radical solution proposed, indeed, was to come from the *Société Populaire* of the tiny *commune* of Moupon in the District of Mussidan in the Dordogne, which suggested in *Frimaire* Year II that the only way to avoid starvation was to tear up the vines and sow grain in their place.[47] Such solutions reflect faithfully the desperate proportions assumed by the problem of provisioning.

Throughout the period the municipal authorities were most active in their efforts to purchase grain from the various regions with a surplus that had come to be the traditional areas of supply. *Commissaires*, provided with money to spend and letters explaining the urgency of their missions, were sent out to other departments to make grain purchases and arrange for their transportation to the city. These tended to concentrate on the rich agrarian areas to the north of the Garonne; thus the mission sent out in April 1793 was instructed to visit the Charente and Charente Inférieure, the Loire Inférieure and Mayenne, the Deux-Sèvres, and, in the last resort, the Vendée.[48] But the results of these missions proved totally inadequate, and the authorities were often left complaining querulously about the interference with grain convoys that went unpunished and the wilful attacks on carts bound for Bordeaux by the hungry peasantry of rural areas. In July 1793, for instance, the *Garde Nationale* had to intervene to protect food convoys for the city which were being attacked and pillaged near Barsac.[49] Section after Section reaffirmed its undying faith in the principle of the free circulation of goods within the Republic; but by the summer of 1793, with the city in open revolt

[46] A.D.G., 3L204, "Département de la Gironde, subsistances". This contains a printed pamphlet which includes a speech entitled "Mémoire sur les patates ou pommes de terre, et l'utilité d'en encourager la culture". The pamphlet was read to Section 2 on 29 April 1793.

[47] A.D.G., 2L7, correspondence of the *représentants-du-peuple en mission*, 5 *Frimaire* Year II.

[48] Arch. Mun. Bordeaux, D143, instructions to *commissaires* Laplace and Saurès, 4 Apr. 1793.

[49] In *Frimaire* Year II, moreover, the *Armée Révolutionnaire* had to be specially instructed to ensure the free circulation of grain in country areas; decree of Ysabeau and Tallien, 8 *Frimaire* Year II, A.D.G., 2L1.

against the Convention, it became the patriotic duty of every department and every *commune* that remained loyal to the *Montagne* to prevent grain supplies from reaching the beleaguered citizens — then the desperation of a hungry peasantry became legalized into responsible civic consciousness.

Principle, however, varied greatly with convenience, and these same Sections were by no means unanimous on the desirability of allowing free circulation when it was a question of the unimpeded export through the port of shiploads of corn for the West Indies.   On this issue opinion, along with vested interests, was divided.   The complaints of the hungry and threats of serious disorder outside bakers' shops were sufficient to move certain sections to demand that grain exports be banned, and more especially that any neutral ship entering the port in ballast be compelled to leave in the same state.[50] Indeed, in a rowdy meeting of Section 18 (*du Dix-août*), one of the office-bearers, Bardon, himself in trade as an agent for a large overseas shipping company, was bitterly attacked on straight class lines for suggesting that grain exports be allowed on United States ships, as they had served the colonial trade well and provisioned the colonists; Bardon was accused of putting the interests of traders before those of the poor.[51]   Nor was he alone in this stand, for it is clear from their arguments that many of the Sections feared the effects on the commerce of the port more than the threat to law and order posed by widespread hunger.   In September 1793 all the Sections of the city jointly complained to the Convention of the quite disastrous effect on trade of the prohibition placed on the export of essential foodstuffs. They argued that far from reducing the degree of hardship, the restrictions merely prevented the export of surpluses of wine, salt, and brandy, further slowed down the port's economic activity, and actually worsened the bread crisis by reducing grain imports.[52]

Scarcity was, however, only one aspect of the problem.   Even when grain was available and had been ground into flour (and Bordeaux's mills, at Bacalan, were widely believed to be inadequate for the needs of the population), the quality of the bread served to the poor in the Revolutionary period gave rise to constant and bitter complaints. That many of these complaints were justified there can be little doubt, as witnessed by the black, putrified pieces of bread produced as exhibits by the irate citizens of a number of the less wealthy Sections.   The anger

---

[50] Sections 4, 10 and 15, for instance, all demand that ships entering the port in ballast should be forced to leave without a cargo; A.D.G., 12L2, 12L6, 12L9.

[51] A.D.G., 12L9, Section 18, minute of 6 Aug. 1793.

[52] A.D.G., 12L12, letter of the sections of Bordeaux to the Convention, 3 Sept. 1793.

of the poor became directed, not unnaturally, against bakers, who would seem to have few rivals in the pages of popular demonology; again and again they were denounced as hoarders of grain (*accapareurs*), as speculators and profiteers at the expense of the poor. The unequal distribution of bakeries in the city — in the whole of Section 11, for instance, there were only one *boulanger* (baker) and one *canolier* (unregulated, small-scale baker) — could only add to the very real fears of famine in many quarters.[53] The very status of the *canolier*, indeed, would seem to have been largely intended to avoid the fairly rigid restrictions placed on bakers by the Municipal Council, an abuse against which the radical *Section de la Liberté* had protested bitterly, pointing out that they formed a privileged class who were still able to sell bread freely without being subject to any controls on either price or weight. The Section went on to demand that all bakers be supervised by the police and compelled to bake only three standard qualities of bread.[54]

In the summer of 1793 a number of cases of deliberate fraud by bakers came to light, generally cases of bread sold underweight or falsely described. On 16 August, for instance, one Montaubon was fined one hundred *livres* for selling as good-quality bread two inferior loaves made of rye and twelve ounces underweight; and eight days later Raimbault, a baker in the Chartrons, was fined one hundred and fifty *livres* and sentenced to a week's imprisonment for selling substandard bread which had not even been properly cooked.[55] But though there were such cases of fraud by bakers in the Revolutionary years, in most cases bad-quality loaves stemmed directly from low-grade flour supplied by the city itself, or from flour which had stood too long or rotted in the holds of ships and which was responsible for mouldy bread.[56] For there can have been few bakers as corrupt as a miller from Tauriac in the District of Bourg, Marie Gombaud, and her son, Jean, who were sentenced to death by the *Commission Militaire* for having committed the dreadful crime of mixing into the

[53] A.D.G., 12L7, Section 11, minute of 21 Aug. 1793.

[54] A.D.G., 12L10, Section 21, minute of 11 Mar. 1793.

[55] Arch. Mun. Bordeaux, I83, "Tribunal de la Police Municipale", 1791 — Year VI. The actual charge reads as follows: *pour avoir vendu pour du pain cô du pain très-brun, mal manipulé, chargé de grosses matières, n'étant pas cuit, et sans même être marqué.*

[56] The use of black, infected, putrified flour by bakers in the Bacalan, for instance, led Section I to fear the spread of illness and epidemics. On 18 June 1793, members of the Section found three bakers working bushels of lumpy, infected grain which, they all claimed, had been supplied by the *Comité des Subsistances* of the *Municipalité* at a cost of fifty *livres* per bushel plus the costs of transportation; A.D.G., 12L1, Section 1, minute of 18 June.

flour cinders and other ingredients capable of poisoning their fellow-citizens.[57]   More generally, the baker, especially in popular districts, was in a most unenviable position, a petty capitalist often living among the very people he exploited, constantly blamed for shortages, frequently denounced and perpetually supervised for hoarding stocks, speculating in grain and flour, and selling underweight or poor-quality bread.

As the Revolution progressed, the baker became more and more the butt of popular discontent, a discontent that could so easily turn first into rumour, then into a firm denunciation to the local authorities. From 1792 there were regular demands for greater and greater surveillance of bakers and further controls of their freedom of manoeuvre — in a time of shortage, uniformity was the order of the day.   In each Section a committee was formed to ensure that uniform standards were maintained; cards were issued to each citizen entitling him to a stipulated quantity of bread each day, a quantity carefully estimated as being sufficient to his needs.   The hours during which sales could be made were laid down, and *commissaires* would inspect bread and ensure against disturbances. And the quality of the bread itself was very closely checked.   At the beginning of 1793 there were still three main qualities, dependent on the degree of whiteness or the ratio of pure wheat-flour in the ingredients — the most expensive, *le pain choine*, was considerably dearer than *le pain cô*, and almost twice the price of the ordinary *pain brun* that was eaten by the greater part of the population.[58]   But as the shortage grew, the Sections became more and more adamant in their demands that there should be one standard quality: the politics of *égalité* could so easily become sadly close to the politics of pure envy. It was therefore decided that one quality only should be baked, and that the manipulation of the dough as well as the selling of the loaves should be supervised to ensure that no-one was given preferential treatment.

As the bread shortage grew worse, this was the principal victory that the poor were to win: the Revolution had given them the right to demand a fair share, to insist that the whole community should share

[57] A.D.G., 14L20, Dossier Marie Gombaud.
[58] Arch. Mun. Bordeaux, F 36, "Boulangers".   Such were the complaints about fraud by bakers that on 24 April the *Municipalité* decreed that, as from the next day, *boulangers* and *canoliers* alike would be authorized to charge only the following prices for the three standard qualities of bread:

le pain choine ....8 *sous* 6 *deniers*
le pain cô ....6 *sous* 10 *deniers*
le pain brun ....4 *sous* 6 *deniers*

in their sacrifice. But even here they were cheated, for if the bread market was strictly controlled, little could be done to control the private dealings of individuals. In this connection, the memoirs of a local painter, Pierre Lacour, are of the greatest interest. He writes of his childhood in Bordeaux, in a bourgeois household in the rue du Palais Gallien, and recalls that the bread shortage became so severe that his highly respectable father, an artist and miniature painter, would, once a fortnight or so, bake bread for the family in the oven in their kitchen. They would grind the wheat or barley in two large coffee-mills, sifting it carefully to have a flour that was reasonably fine. But, he explains, the baking had to be done late at night, around eleven o'clock, and only on such nights as there was no guard at the gate of the *Grand Séminaire* opposite; for they lived in that most Jacobin of Sections, *Francklin*, and the danger of detection was always considerable. If someone, or more particularly some late patrol, had passed the house, the smell of hot bread would certainly have betrayed them, which would have led to his father's arrest and condemnation as a hoarder of grain.[59]

But though the supply and quality of bread were burning issues, it was the question of price which, in the last analysis, caused the most serious disturbances outside bakers' shops and which on one occasion — on 8 March 1793 — caused a bread riot in the city. The sheer non-availability of grain was accepted comparatively passively; Sectional demands for the confiscation of cargoes bound for the Islands, for the seizure of the stocks reserved for the use of the Navy, or for the compulsory purchase of cargoes on board ship in the roads were the nearest the city came to violence on that score. On the other hand, and not unreasonably, the belief that they were starving while corn supplies existed in the city, whether in the hands of bakers, or of hoarders, or merely of those with the money to pay for them, raised the political temperature of the *faubourgs* to flashpoint: it is not for nothing that grain-hoarding was regarded during the Terror as one of the gravest of Revolutionary crimes, while profiteering — the crime of *négociantisme* that was a speciality of Revolutionary government in the South-West — also led to very substantial fines and occasionally to death sentences.[60]

Throughout the Revolutionary period the authorities recognized the essential threat to public order posed by high and rising prices for

[59] Bibl. Mun. Bordeaux, MS. 1603, Pierre Lacour, "Notes et souvenirs d'un artiste octogenaire", p. 33.
[60] A.D.G., 14L, "Commission Militaire".

bread, and, as a result, for most of the period bread prices were subsidized to keep them artificially low.   Indeed, the need for a
municipal subsidy to bakers had been recognized even before the
outbreak of the Revolution, and the price of bread remained below
that of grain from the introduction of the indemnity by the *jurade*
in 1787 until its abolition by a financially-embarrassed Municipal
Council in March 1793.[61]   Throughout the summer months of that
year the free market was allowed to operate, but the Sections did
receive grants from the city authorities to pay to the indigent.   With
the introduction of the *maximum* in October, the price of a loaf was
pegged at three *sols*, perhaps a quarter of its real market price.   And
when after *thermidor* the *maximum* was abolished, the galloping
inflation of 1795 and 1796 pushed prices up to quite extortionate
levels.   By June 1795 the price of bread had reached five *livres* a
pound, but there were around sixty thousand people inscribed on the
registers of the indigent getting their half-pound ration at grossly
subsidized rates.   Meanwhile the price for the non-indigent continued
to lurch upwards in wild, uncontrollable jerks and bounds: bread cost
thirty *livres* per pound by December 1795, fifty *livres* by the beginning
of February 1796, and seventy *livres* by the end of that month.[62]
But for the poor the important point was that throughout they were
sold their ration of bread at subsidized rates; that the city faced a
deficit of quite frightening proportions by 1796 did not affect their
living standards.   What did, and what in doing so caused great alarm
in the popular Sections of Bordeaux, was the decision of March 1793
to end the indemnity to which they had become accustomed and on
which they had so much come to depend.   As an instance of popular
alarm and panic, the events of that month justify a closer examination.

The bread indemnity had had the effect of sheltering the consumer,
and particularly the poor, from the effects of severe fluctuations in
corn prices.   For even in the early years of the Revolution, before the
full effects of the inflation of the *assignats* came to be felt, seasonal
price fluctuations could reach considerable proportions.   Thus the
price of a bushel of wheat varied between approximately 14 *livres* 2 *sols*
and 17 *livres* 1 *sol* in 1788, between 17 *livres* 13 *sols* and 20 *livres* 4 *sols*

[61] A.N., M669, report of Roullet, *procureur-général-syndic* of the Department,
to the Minister of the Interior on the bread riot in Bordeaux on 8 March 1793.

[62] P. Bécamps, "La question des grains et de la boulangerie à Bordeaux, de
1793 à 1796", *Actes du 83e Congrès des Sociétés Savants-Aix/Marseille, 1958*
(Paris, 1959), p. 270; J. Benzacar, *Le pain à Bordeaux au dix-huitième siècle*
(Bordeaux, 1905), pp. 52 ff.

in 1789, and between 16 *livres* 1 *sol* and 21 *livres* 12 *sols* in 1790.[63]
Prices generally reached their peak around June and July when the
previous year's stocks were running low and the new harvest was not
yet ready. But by 1793 the summer price increase was much
steeper, as the effects of shortage and the war came to be felt; wheat
which had cost 19 *livres* 10 *sols* in January of that year was fetching
31 *livres* 13 *sols* by 1 May for one hundred pounds weight — and
a bushel cost forty-two *livres* on the market at Castelnau, or twice the
Bordeaux figure for 1790.[64] Such huge rises added so greatly to the
cost of the city's bread indemnity as to make the Council reconsider
its whole policy; in his report to the Minister of the Interior, Roullet,
the *procureur-général-syndic* of the Department, explained that the
subsidy in March 1793 was running at the quite unprecedented
level of twenty *deniers* per pound of bread, and that its effect was to
add a further two million *livres* to the city's colossal debt every year.[65]
This cost had been largely met by raising loans among the richer
citizens. A loan of 600,000 *livres* in January 1793 was over-
subscribed, but such was the prohibitive cost of the scheme that in
February the target had to be raised to 1,200,000 *livres*.[66]

Opinion against the indemnity began to gain wide support,
especially among the middle classes. Section 9 (*des Loix*) took the
initiative as early as 21 February in urging its immediate
suppression.[67] And on 7 March Section 24 (*de la Fraternité*), a Section
that was to hit out virulently against the introduction of the *maximum*
later in the year, passed a motion quite blatantly proposing a return

[63] A.D.G., 4L68, "Relevé du prix commun du boisseau froment, depuis et
compris le mois de juin 1791". The statistics for 1789-1791 give some idea
of the degree of seasonal fluctuation in market prices: all figures are in *livres,
sols, deniers*.

	1789	1790	1791
January	17.13. 8	20. 7. 6	16. 0. 5
February	17.16. 1	20. 4. 5	16. 2.10
March	18. 0.10	19. 8.11	15.18. 6
April	18.16. 8	20. 2. 6	15.11.10
May	19.12. 7	20.18. 0	13. 9. 2
June	19.14. 7	21.12. 3	14. 2. 6
July	20. 4. 6	16.17. 5	
August	19.16.10	16. 2. 0	
September	19. 0.10	16. 7. 8	
October	19. 4. 2	16. 6. 6	
November	19.16. 7	16. 6. 3	
December	19.14. 8	16. 1.11	

[64] A.D.G., 4L67, lists of market prices for grain at Bordeaux and Castelnau,
1793.   [65] A.N., M669, report of Roullet.
[66] Arch. Mun. Bordeaux, D102, minute of 10 Feb. 1793.
[67] Arch. Mun. Bordeaux, D102, minute of 21 Feb. 1793.

to free market conditions in bread, thereby favouring the interests
of the rich, by arguing that a rich man should have the right to obtain
bread according to his means (as opposed, one must assume, to his
needs) and that those selling bread on the port and in the markets
should be obliged to distribute it "pound for pound to the first cus-
tomers who came to buy it".[68]   Weight was added to such criticisms
by the fact that the indemnity was paid only to bakers inside the city,
while the people of the country areas had to pay market prices for corn
that had frequently been bought in the market in Bordeaux itself.
As a result, there were constant complaints that people from the rural
areas were coming into the city to buy subsidized bread, while bakers
in the District who received no subsidy were clamouring for similar
concessions and were in some cases refusing to continue baking.   To
the District, in short, the indemnity had become an acute embarrassment, "an abuse incompatible with true [revolutionary] principles".[69]

These arguments, and especially a genuine alarm lest the indemnity
bankrupt the city, were powerful in persuading the municipal
authorities to end it on 6 March.   From the following day prices
jumped to new levels: in particular, the *pain brun* of the poorer classes
rose by one-third from two *sols* nine *deniers* per pound to three *sols*
six *deniers*.   And this was only the start of a spiralling trend, with new
rises being announced from day to day.   By 24 April the price of *pain
brun* already stood at four *sols* six *deniers* per pound.[70]

It must not be thought, however, that the poor were expected to
pay these inflated prices, for it is clear that such a policy would have
resulted in widespread famine conditions in the more industrial areas
of the city.   On the contrary, the indemnity to bakers was merely
replaced by another indemnity paid to the Sections for distribution
among their members — in short, universal welfare benefits gave
way to means-tested welfare payments.   A minute in the city's
financial records makes it clear that between its introduction in March
and its replacement by the *maximum* in September, this scheme cost
close on four hundred thousand *livres*.[71]   In addition, the agitation
caused by the change-over induced a number of employers to increase

---

[68] Arch. Mun. Bordeaux, 165, Section 24, minute of 7 Mar. 1793.   On
21 June the Section was to condemn the idea of a *maximum* on grain as being
harmful to provisioning and hence to public order; A.D.G., 12Lii.

[69] Arch. Mun. Bordeaux, D102.   The complaint of the District was noted
during the debate on the indemnity on 6 March 1793.

[70] Arch. Mun. Bordeaux, D103, entry for 24 Apr. 1793.

[71] Arch. Mun. Bordeaux, L4, "Finances municipales", document 15, dated
18 Sept. 1793.   The total sum paid out to the Sections between March and
September 1793 for the cost of the bread indemnity was 395,548 *livres* 12 *sols*
11 *deniers*.

wages to cover the rise in the cost of living; more than a hundred workers in the Navy stores in the Bacalan, for instance, received an extra five *sous* for each day's work, and the Municipal Council itself openly suggested that such wage increases might provide a viable way of saving the city from bankruptcy.[72].   But, as is so often the case in discussing popular movements, what is important is not so much the real effect on living standards as what people imagined these effects to be.   The result was the outbreak of popular hysteria that culminated in a bread riot on 8 March.

To the Girondin deputy, Boyer-Fonfrède, this disturbance was the work of agitators, of "brigands", whom, he told the Convention, he suspected of being in league with "le comité contre-révolutionnaire de Paris".[73]   But this facile dismissal of the very real anxieties of the people is far less informative about the riot than about Fonfrède's arrogant isolation from the poor and his readiness to turn any incident to his own political advantage.   Roullet's account of the scene to the Minister is both more detailed and more instructive.[74]   The men, he claims, were passive; it was the women who gathered in large numbers and hustled towards the Town Hall, breaking all the windows, throwing stones at the National Guardsmen, and endangering the life of their general.   The troops fired back, killing one of the women; the rest of the crowd scattered, and, claims Roullet, there was no trouble on the ensuing days.   On the contrary, the new bread prices were paid without any disturbance.   As for the criminal elements (*malveillants*) who were inevitably accused of fomenting trouble, there were allegations of crowd manipulation by men dressed in women's clothing, inspired by the anarchistic faction in Paris, as the Bordelais were wont to describe the *Commune* and the *Montagnards*.   In the event, we do hear later in the month of two men from Libourne arrested on charges of stirring up discontent on the day of the riot.[75]   And Mayor Saige, in analysing the social composition of the crowd, was to congratulate himself and Bordeaux on the fact that no honest workman had taken part in the incident and that even the poor, "the least enlightened social class", had not been open to seduction by political agitators.   The women who took part, he adds with evident satisfaction, were the most ignorant of all, being predominantly beggars (*mendiantes*) and those who performed the most menial tasks in the markets. If Saige is to be believed, even the *regratières*, those poor women who resold market produce in the outer suburbs, would have no part in it.[76]

[72] Arch. Mun. Bordeaux, D102, minute of 7 Mar. 1793.
[73] *Le Moniteur*, 14 Mar. 1793.   [74] A.N., M669.
[75] Arch. Mun. Bordeaux, D103, minute of 27 Mar. 1793.
[76] Arch. Mun. Bordeaux, D102, minute of 8 Mar. 1793.

In matters of food supply and pricing policy, the conclusion is inescapable that the Revolution brought a new paternalism, a new and unprecedented degree of economic intervention which helped alleviate the misery of the poor and shield them against the most cruel of the economic forces of the 1790s.   Yet many of these forces had been unleashed by the Revolution itself.   By the summer of 1793 some form of price control, of *maximum*, was necessary in Bordeaux, in part at least because the widespread lack of confidence in *assignats* had already led to an inflationary spiral that in the case of many workers greatly exceeded the rate of wage increases and thus actually reduced their purchasing power.   For between November 1792 and July 1793 the real value of the paper currency had tumbled progressively from sixty-nine per cent to a mere twenty-seven per cent of its face value in coin, the lowest point it was to sink to until November 1794, when rapid inflation once again set in.[77]   Wages did rise steeply: in the District of Bazas, for instance, the daily rate for a carpenter increased from one *livre* ten *sous* in 1790 to ten *livres* in *Ventôse* Year III, while an unskilled manual worker, like a *portefaix*, who had earned two *livres* ten *sous* in 1790 was taking home around nine *livres* five years later.   Essential commodity prices, however, soared much more dramatically over the same period.   A quintal of wheat which had cost fifteen *livres* eighteen *sous* in 1790 was by 1795 commanding as much as 220 *livres*, and the price of soap had risen one hundred-fold, from fifteen *sous* per pound to fifteen *livres*.[78]

Other direct results of Revolutionary policies had, as we have seen, actually proved detrimental to the welfare of the poor.   The

[77] A.D.G., Fonds Bigot, 8J714, "Finances, monnaies".   The following figures give the equivalent value in coin of one hundred *livres* in *assignats* for the period up till December 1794.   They are taken from the more comprehensive *Tableau des valeurs successives du papier-monnaie dans le Département de la Gironde, 1791-an IV*, published in Bordeaux in the Year IV:

	1791	1792	1793	1794
January	89½	67	55	41¾
February	89¾	59¼	53¾	43
March	89¾	58½	53½	37½
April	89	61¾	47	37½
May	83¾	57¼	44¾	35¼
June	82¾	59½	37	31½
July	84¼	61½	27	35½
August	81¼	61	28½	32½
September	81¾	66½	32	30¼
October	·81¾	66½	30¼	27¾
November	79½	69	41¼	26¼
December	73¾	65½	51¾	28½

[78] A.D.G., 5L22, District of Bazas, "Tableau du coût de la vie et des salaires dans le District de Bazas", 28 *Ventôse* Year III.

from the Army in Italy.[85]   Or again, in towns like Le Havre, the increasing use of the local *dépôt de mendicité* to house hardened criminals led to still greater human degradation for the inmates; in one instance, at Bourges, men serving ten-year sentences were transferred there by the Revolutionary authorities.[86]   But everywhere it is clear that the treatment of the poor is marked by two dominant trends.   In the first place the old tradition of voluntarism was being replaced by centralized state control.   And in the second place the legislation that was passed was rarely put into effect at local level, partly because the legislators were ignorant of local circumstances and traditional practice but more particularly because, quite simply, inflation, the British blockade and the cost of waging a European war all served to deprive the various administrations of the money they required if they were to bring to fruition their ambitious plans for social reform.   The experience of Bordeaux illustrates graphically the problems which faced both the poor and the legislators, problems stemming from rapid urbanization as well as those created by the Revolution itself. In spite of the good intentions displayed on all sides, it is a striking instance of one of the more conspicuous failures of Revolutionary government.

[85] Archives Départementales Rhône, 1L903-904, "Hôpitaux militaires".
[86] Archives Départementales Cher, L565, "Dépôt de Mendicité".

9. *Resistance to the Revolution in Western France**

HARVEY MITCHELL

ALTHOUGH STRICTLY SPEAKING RESISTANCE TO THE REVOLUTION IN
the western parts of France did not cease completely until 1815, the
last important outburst came in 1799 so that the present study will
not deal with events after that year. And while I am aware of the
risks involved, notably those of swallowing regional differences in
a general account, I believe there is value in drawing examples from
the west as a whole, if only because the points I want to make are
derived from the observations of men scattered throughout the
region.

The revolutionary authorities developed a certain attitude towards
the civil war which coloured their view of the struggle and indeed
often sharpened its intensity instead of easing it. Yet whatever their
perceptions of it were, they were committed to ending the resistance.
This was their primary goal. So demanding was it that they more or
less stumbled on the fact that they had to understand the deeper
causes of the conflict before they could expect to gain the confidence
of the insurgents and end the war. This, in turn, meant reintegrating
the resistants into the new régime, either by trying to persuade them
through various degrees of coercion to accept the revolutionary
innovations, or by recognizing and making some allowance for the
satisfaction of their needs. We might call this process experiencing
the enemy and coming to terms with him. Quite obviously this
approach will yield some information, however imperfect, about the
mental world of the insurgents.

Those who sought to direct and control the resistance to the
republican authorities — I am referring to the counter-revolutionary
élites, the opposite numbers of the revolutionary élites — tried to keep
it alive by exploiting, militarily, whether by traditional or guerrilla
warfare, and by means of propaganda warfare, the various sources of
insurgent dissatisfaction. Directly or implicitly, this meant assessing
their discontent, the better to make use of them, and again this involved
the use of degrees of coercion. In contra-distinction to the efforts of
the republican authorities, we might call this process experiencing

* This article is a somewhat different version of a paper that was presented on
23 March 1972 at the annual meeting of The Society for French Historical
Studies.

one's supposed supporters and coming to terms with them. And because this process was also an attempt to understand them, it should similarly furnish information about them.[1]

There seems to be some merit therefore in analysing these evaluations by the competing élites of the nature of the conflict and thereby of the mentality of the insurgents. In the case of each, however, it is significant that they laboured under certain preconceptions which they either consciously or unconsciously concealed from themselves. Both the republican and royalist élites, by adopting a ritualistic and formalized vocabulary to describe and analyse a highly complex situation, were incapable at times of seeing things as they were. Yet in dealing with the problem either of ending the resistance or perpetuating it, they could not but take into account facts about the situation which they found clashed with their own more comfortable version of it. It was not always a straightforward matter of looking only at those facts that confirmed previously held views. What we might term "unpleasant" facts continually intruded themselves upon the consciousness of the élites on both sides. The growing awareness of the complexity of the struggle improved the level of contemporary perceptions, and can thus be of some value to the historian who is seeking to establish the impact of revolutionary change and war on peasant and artisan mentalities.

Anyone who has the slightest acquaintance with contemporary accounts of the civil war in the Vendée and of *chouannerie* is forcibly struck by the charge of religious fanaticism with which the rebels were branded. When confronted with the first signs of peasant fractiousness, a great many revolutionary administrators reported how difficult it was to dispel centuries-old ingrained habits of deference towards the priests, of the persistence of superstition in far-off settlements, of the near impossibility of negating these modes of thought, of how ineffective appeared to them the measures they were contemplating and adopting to bring the benefit of reason and efficient government to these benighted and backward peoples. Soon, also, as the will of the peasants stiffened, the prescriptions offered by the new cantonal, municipal and departmental governing élites were escalating into demands for wholesale and forcible conversion to the new order; and, when the areas of disaffection finally exploded in near-total civil war to be followed, year by year, by *chouan* massacres

---

[1] Cf. Marcel Faucheux's remarks: "When one wishes to understand the Vendée, the truth must often be sought from the enemy himself" see "Le cas de la Vendée militaire", in *Occupants-Occupés, 1792-1815* (Actes du colloque qui s'est tenu à Bruxelles, les 29 et 30 janvier 1968; Brussels, 1969), p. 325.

and depredations of all kinds, the call from many responsible quarters was for the deportation of a whole people[2] given over to the preservation, as it was put, of Gothic barbarism.

Understandably the Year II was a time when full-scale hostilities, panic and the reactions of vengefulness which it induced obliterated cool and intelligent appraisal; the reports of administrators and of the military tend to dull the senses by their endless reiteration of formula responses and solutions. Such was not always the case, especially in the period before and following the most intense warfare. There were discerning individuals who were able to catch a glimpse of some of the problems of greatest concern to the peoples of the insurgent areas, even if they found themselves helpless to deal with them. What impressed those in authority was the split between urban and rural life, the distinctions between the nature of life in town and country. To them they ascribed the chief causes for the reception on the one hand and the rejection on the other of the innovations for which they were responsible. As townsmen they believed they possessed an undeniable and paternalistic right to bring the benefits of revolutionary change to the countryside, an extension as some of them saw it of the various schemes for improvement that were being discussed before the Revolution by some of the more enlightened professionals and administrators of the crown.

Dr. Gallot's[3] career as a medical man in the region of Saint-Brieuc before the Revolution was duplicated by others. The interest shown

---

[2] See, for example, the advice given the Convention by Mazade and Garnier de Saintes on 12-13 June 1793: "This war is hardly an ordinary war; it is a war of chicanery. Fearlessness must be shaped by the imaginative uses of deception. We must at one and the same time set traps, conceal our procedures, turn the very difficulties of the region against the enemy, have reliable spies at any price; and to ensure success, we must, as fast as we move through rebel country, *burn the mills, remove men, women and children, and locate them in the interior of the Republic.* For it is these women, these old people, these children, who are causing us the most harm, either because they are themselves supplying the enemy army, or because, under the pretext of selling their produce, they come into our midst to ascertain our movements and our strength. We should tell you, *you will bring this region under control only by deporting the present generation to different parts of France and resettling it with new men*". Ch.-L. Chassin, *La Vendée patriote (1793-1800)*, 4 vols. (Paris, 1893-5), ii, p. 74. The italics are Chassin's.

[3] See Louis Merle, *La vie et les oeuvres du Dr. Jean-Gabriel Gallot (1774-1794)* (Poitiers, 1962), for an illustration of the interest displayed by one professional in the problems of the countryside. See also the views of Guillemau, a member of the Directory of the District of Niort, who wrote: "There is a great deal of ignorance in our countryside and it cannot be otherwise, since there is little education and trade. The result is, Sir, that the persons who are stimulating the country folk to make efforts to improve their situation are not given any hearing at all, or, what is worse, are immediately

in the last years of the old régime in the health of the population opened the eyes of administrators to actual conditions.   The Revolution is, in this respect as in others, no break with the past.   When the Revolution came, the chronic problems that had been engaging the attention of the crown's servants remained as intense as ever, if not more so under the impact of war.   Like the medical men of the old régime whose records are now being studied, but lacking their intimate knowledge of life in the countryside, the agents of the revolutionary administration believed that the removal of seigneurial dues, tithes and royal taxes would by itself lighten the major sources of economic deprivation.   They often expressed compassion for this large impoverished part of humanity, yet they also shared with their predecessors a distaste for peasant filth and brutalization, and an exasperation with peasant distrust of any external advice aimed at improving their lot.   Their accounts are indeed strongly reminiscent of those that have come down to us from the physicians who, as good men of the Enlightenment, fought a stubborn obscurantism in the countryside.   The revolutionaries belong to this lineage of men, eager to bring order, salubrity, and the advantages of science to masses of people victimized by murderous illnesses, magical beliefs and practices, and an obsolete morality.[4]   They were confident that the various committees established by the Constituent Assembly to propose measures to combat poverty, unemployment, mendicity and poor health, or to increase agricultural production, revive and

---

suspected of seeking to abuse them.   On the 15th of this month, being recruitment *commissaire*, whatever gentleness I employed, I found [myself] the victim of the ease with which the ignorant people are frightened by everything that does not emanate from the sphere of their ordinary ideas, and I really saw, as Rousseau says, that men are evil only because they are ignorant" (21 Aug. 1792). Archives nationales (hereafter A.N.), F[IC] III Vendée 7.

[4] On the significance of the work of the Royal Society of Medicine, the records of which are now being studied, see Jean-Pierre Peter, "Une enquête de la Société Royale de Médecine (1774-1794): Malades et maladies à la fin du XVIIIe siècle", *Annales. E.S.C.*, xxii (1967), pp. 711-51; "Médecine, épidémies, et société en France à la fin du XVIIIe siècle d'après les archives de l'Académie de Médecine", *Bulletin de la société d'histoire moderne*, 14th ser., no. 14 (1970), pp. 2-9; "Les mots et les objets de la maladie.   Remarques sur les épidémies et la médecine dans la société française de la fin du XVIIIe siècle", *Revue historique*, ccxlvi (1971), pp. 13-38.   The work of Peter and his colleagues is outstanding for the way in which it is illuminating the abrasive shock the two worlds of town and country experienced when they collided with each other's views of the larger meanings of life.   Keith Baker discusses some aspects of the crown's efforts to use science as an instrument of social amelioration in his "Politics and Social Science in Eighteenth-Century France: The Société de 1789", in J. F. Bosher (ed.), *French Government and Society 1500-1850. Essays in Memory of Alfred Cobban* (London, 1973), pp. 208-30.

stimulate local industry, would in time rescue peasant communities from backwardness, lethargy and isolation. They knew from the rural *cahiers* that such questions were crucial. What they, and of course others, did not expect was the deep fissure created by the Constituent Assembly's religious legislation, the reactions to which became the centre of their preoccupations.

It was during the attempts to enforce the decrees establishing the Constitutional Church that the image of the non-juring clergy in a rural setting, not far removed from an atmosphere of superstition, became for local élites the reason for the accumulation of frustration and rage. Did this evaluation impede a more subtle assessment of the nature of religiosity and its connections with other questions which found expression in demonstrations of religious feelings? Were contemporaries able to see the links between the anti-revolutionary rôle they attributed to the refractory *curés* and the functions they exercised in rural communities, quite apart from whether or not the priests took the lead in questioning, ridiculing and opposing the new measures? In short, was the image of the *curé* the simple one of an active agent working on a pliant population? Not quite. Both before and after the fiercest fighting, while recognizing the organizing powers of the non-conforming priests — and how persistent a theme this was — observers in positions of authority were able to detect some of the intricate criss-crossings in the rural community's structural web.

For example, they seemed to be aware of geographical isolation as a factor in inducing intense loyalty to traditional mores and practices. The following bit of eighteenth-century sociological analysis from the register of the Directory in the Loire-Atlantique (Inférieure) Department furnishes an account of the roots of popular resistance to the new authorities in the early summer of 1792:

> The place called Saint-Joachim is better known by its name of Brières, [and] contains a considerable extent of marshy terrain from which peat is cut. Almost always in flood, this locality is divided into villages separated by channels of sea water cutting its way into the salty marshes, access to which is known only to the local people. This makes access to this region very difficult. These people make up isolated, half-organized communities composed of eight or ten very large families; the result is that almost all of them have the same name, and they are obliged to use nicknames to mark themselves off from the others; they have little contact with their neighbours, and think of the rest of mankind as foreigners .... The ignorance and simple-mindedness of the Brières people, accustomed to seeing their former nobles as fearsome masters and their priests as infallible, and who put their faith solely in those people who are intent on deceiving them, have forced them to become the victims of guile and enticement.[5]

[5] A.N., F⁷3681⁶ Loire-Inférieure.

In Finistère, the commissioner of the Department's Executive Directory some five years later referred to the tenacity of habit which ensured strong attachment to traditional religious practices. But here in Finistère, he added, thereby establishing a connection between geographically remote areas and survivals of magic and superstition, the inhabitants:

> have a strong belief in miracles, listen with eager foolishness to accounts of happenings which appear to them to lie outside the usual laws of nature, and the shrewd man who has learned how to win their confidence is able before long to convince them that the hand of God is ready to lay hold of them with symbols of this sort.[6]

Conscientious civil servants were having to encounter a range of human experience which made little or no sense in the world of science and the faith in progress that gave meaning to their own lives. Primitive catholicism, they were beginning to see, was not simply catholicism of an unsophisticated and illiterate kind. It was much more than that. In fact, any understanding of rural mentalities demanded some acknowledgement of the power of beliefs and practices, which were derived not only from the teachings of the church, but from those that were older and more deeply embedded. In the case of illness and death, peasant communities relied on incantations, home remedies, witches, sorcerors, as well as pilgrimages to the shrines of their favourite "curative" saints. The rural parish priest perhaps understood better than his urban counterpart the close connection in the peasant mind between catholic practices and the pre-Christian forms; and he was likely to make use of existing credulity to strengthen his ties with his parishioners. The countryside was the locus in which popular culture fed on a view of man determined by forces over which he had no power — the astrological, the elemental, the occult, the world of spirit and of animism.[7] To the

---

[6] Quimper, 21 Ventôse Year VI: A.N., F^{IC} III Finistère 9. On the persistence of pre-Christian beliefs and practices, see Jean Delumeau, *Le catholicisme entre Luther et Voltaire* (Paris, 1971). Two additional studies provide further illustrations of how shallow the roots of Christian belief were in many areas of the west: Jean Meyer, *La noblesse bretonne au XVIIIe siècle*, 2 vols. (Paris, 1966), and Fr. Lebrun, *Les hommes et la mort en Anjou aux XVIIe et XVIIIe siècles* (Paris-The Hague, 1971). Lebrun's work is brilliant and original.

[7] See Jean Delumeau's remarks in his paper presented at the 1972 meeting of The Society for French Historical Studies, "Ignorance religieuse et mentalité magique sous l'ancien régime": "For large numbers of people, religion made up for the shortcomings of science and technology. It was concretely useful since it held sickness and death at bay, protected crops, [and] produced fine harvests". In view of recent studies by Delumeau, Lebrun, *op. cit.*, and Peter, *op. cit.*, it would appear that Robert Mandrou, *De la culture populaire aux XVIIe et XVIIIe siècles* (Paris, 1964), offers a more convincing

town-dweller, nurtured in a milieu which put far more stress on calculation, scientific conceptualization, and a commitment to the successful coercion of nature, the other milieu which operated on such different premises was mysterious, repugnant, and totally hostile.

Ignorance, lassitude, credulity, primitive religion, a strong spirit of localism, remoteness from the main routes of commerce: do these alone explain rural opposition to the Revolution and its works? No, according to a prefect in the Vendée who tried to get to the root of the matter in 1805, and whose observations recall the categories of religious belief devised by Pierre-François Hacquet, the Montfortain who has left a record of his missions in the west over a thirty-nine-year period ending in 1779.[8] Like Hacquet, the Vendée prefect was groping towards a formulation of a few crude sociological notions. Hacquet had noted the lack of religious fervour in the plains regions of the west in contrast to the devout, docile and generous-minded *bocage*, calling attention to the impact of a market economy as an explanation of the differences in attitudes. The prefect in the Vendée saw only that the *bocage* and western marshlands of the Department had resisted while the plains areas and southern marshlands had no difficulty in accepting the constitutional priests. Why? Simply because, as he put it, the people in the latter region were:

> less responsive than those in the *Bocage*, not capable of the same exalted feelings. Lacking the capacity of true conviction, they were [content] to be resigned. They fell in with this change rather from [feelings] of indifference than from attachment to the Revolution.[9]

The people in the plains were certainly not "much more enlightened than those of the *bocage*". Their make-up, it was implied, was somehow different. Both the missionary and the prefect were making an attempt to relate economics, geography and mentality.

account of popular culture than does Geneviève Bollème in her *Les almanachs populaires aux XVII et XVIIIe siècles* (Paris-The Hague, 1969). Bollème's conclusions that the old astrology and mythical tales were yielding to science and a more modern view of history do not square with the evidence, at least in the countryside. For an assessment of their work which did not take account of Peter's or Lebrun's, see Robert Darnton, "In Search of the Enlightenment: Recent Attempts to Create a Social History of Ideas", *Jl. of Modern History*, xliii (1971), pp. 113-32.

[8] Pierre-François Hacquet, *Mémoire des missions des Montfortains dans l'Ouest (1740-1779)*, ed. Louis Pérouas (Fontenay-le-Comte, 1964).

[9] Statistique du département de la Vendée, 12 Vendémiaire Year XIV: A.N., F20269 Vendée. Pierre Chaunu's description of religion in the Mauges as "the mystical *bocage* of the Mauges" uses a vocabulary of similar lineage. See his article, "Une histoire religieuse sérielle. A propos du diocèse de La Rochelle (1648-1724) et sur quelques exemples Normands", *Revue d'histoire moderne et contemporaine*, xii (1965), pp. 5-34, esp. p. 14.

Investigators and administrators were, however, much less concerned with those areas of the west in which the traditional ties of religion were being weakened than with those in which they appeared to be tenacious. From their earliest observations, we come upon the conviction time and time again that religion and ignorance were inseparable, and that the presence in rural parishes of priests hostile to the new régime ensured a continuing threat to it. Remove them, it was proposed, and these docile, incredulous peasants would be won over.[10] Yet even when deportation and other coercive measures had thinned the ranks of the non-juring clergy, resistance continued. The reason for its persistence, it was concluded, was the incomplete purge of the countryside. The locals were concealing and protecting the priests who were thus free to carry on their subversion with impunity, perpetually feeding the resentments and fears of their parishioners.

To many contemporaries the time-honoured patterns of life were breaking down because of the formidable weapons at the command of the non-juring priests and their allies. What was less clear to the new governing élites, at least before large-scale revolt erupted, was that the small parishes of the west, by expressing such passionate, and by their lights irrational, opposition to the new legislation were not so much the "prisoners" of fulminating priests as men and women for whom the fabric of personal relationships depended on the preservation of a host of rituals that were an integral and concrete part of their lives. And what angered and terrified them was the imposition of new regulations administered by individuals whose motives they questioned. This eluded the minds of the new authorities for some time. After all, they reasoned, what possible difference could the introduction of the conforming clergy have on the religious life of thousands of parishes so long as the sequence and meaning of various religious ceremonies remained unaltered. Perhaps they were able to appreciate the consequences of their invasion of parish customs only after the event, when at the end of their patience they authorized a speedy end both to the dilatory acceptance of the juring priests and the more aggresive forms of resistance to them. It was then that local populations banded together to articulate their views on the matter, promising obedience to the laws — the flouting of which they attributed, in a reversal of the official charges made against themselves, to Jacobin trouble-makers — if and only if they were permitted to retain their old priests and worship as always — rights, they claimed,

[10] For one example, see: les commissaires du roi au département du Morbihan to De Lessart, 4 June 1791: A.N., F⁷3682[18] Morbihan.

that were enshrined by the laws of the state.[11]   Or they met to record
in ringing tones, as in the parish of La Chapelle Erbrée in the Department of Ile-et-Vilaine, their fears at the prospect of losing their *curé*:

> [It] would cause the worst possible damage considering the need for [holding]
> divine service and for [our] meetings at our churches on feast-days and
> Sundays. [These are] the only times during which the people can be
> instructed in those matters which are of special concern to them and to the
> public welfare; moreover it [would have the effect of] endangering the
> salvation both of the new-born and of the sick.   It [would] deprive individuals
> of the right they have in uniting themselves in marriage and in that way not
> infrequently expose them to incalculable ruin . . . .[12]

When, finally, the civil war broke out in earnest, the thought that
the major centres of resistance had been accumulating a series of
grievances over two or three years and that perhaps they had some
foundation in the violation not only of the immemorial links of a
complex religious setting, but in the frustration of material improvement which the Revolution had promised, began to make some
impression on the agents of the revolutionary régime.   Even before
1793 some observers were able to pick out the various causes of the
mounting disorder, to articulate how religious, social and economic
questions created the realities of life for large sections of a neglected
and misunderstood region.   These men believed that ignorance,
backwardness and religion were mutually reinforcing, but they came
to realize that the eradication of the first two would not mechanically
follow from the suppression of the third.   The idea that material
improvement held one of the keys to the religious question, but that
it could make little headway by ignoring the religious integrity of the
parish, was thus an advance over the propensity to think that
"fanaticism" demanded a frontal attack.

There is impressive evidence of this cast of mind.   At Bangor and
Locmaria on Belle-Ile, and at Quiberon, the priests were reported as
being the only individuals capable of administering local affairs.
There the opposition to the new taxes was, along with the onerous
and inequitable *afféagements*, a potential source of ferment.[13]   So
determined was the resentment against the new taxes that the women

[11] Pétition remise aux administrateurs du directoire du district d'Evron au
nom des communes de Chammes, Nuillé, Châtres, Livet, St.-Leger, after
2 Apr. 1792: A.N., F⁷3682¹⁰ Mayenne.

[12] Conseil de La Chapelle Erbrée, 3 Aug. 1792: A.N., F⁷3679¹ Ile-et-Vilaine.
For other instances, see the remarks of Yves Tupin, mayor of Bruz, district of
Bain, Ile-et-Vilaine, 28 Feb. 1792: A.N., F¹⁹430; and the address of the
municipality, notables and other inhabitants of the parish of Laignelet (Ile-et-
Vilaine), 28 Nov. 1791: Archives départementales, Ile-et-Vilaine, L438.
For the latter citation I am indebted to Donald Sutherland.

[13] See, les commissaires du roi au département du Morbihan to De Lessart,
23 Aug. 1791: A.N., F⁷3682¹⁸ Morbihan.

of Ile-D'Yeu demanded their abolition and the restoration of "the old ways, that is to say . . . the former administration", which meant exemption from taxes — adding for good measure that their parish required the services of two *vicaires*, as in the past.[14]

The deterioration of conditions wrought by the war and administrative decisions did not escape the attention of observers at a town like Vannes. There the contrasts with Nantes, where industry was flourishing, was striking. The prohibition of grain exports from Vannes had virtually shut down the little port. In addition, the economic life of the town had been severely affected by the closure of the sixteen convents, the flight of the nobility, and the curtailment of the Presidial courts. In the countryside near Vannes, and indeed throughout large areas of Brittany, ignorance, routine and inertia were responsible for the perpetuation of incredible poverty, which could be combatted only by a policy of encouraging further land reclamation (*défrichements*) that had been started in a small way near the town.[15]

Pretty much the same advice reached Paris from the Directory of the Department of Mayenne. The unimpeded export of grain for Brittany was pushing prices up and occasioning fear of "popular commotions". "Let the Convention", the proposal ran, "decree aid to the disabled poor, funds to employ the able-bodied poor in *ateliers de charité*, and we can assure you that the public peace will not be disturbed in our Department".[16]

"Let us relieve the lot of the poor", pleaded yet another official at Vitré (Ile-et-Vilaine) in mid-April after the fighting in the neighbouring departments had begun:

let us procure work for them, let us establish primary schools, let us offer for everyone a wise law, the justice of and the need for which is easily felt and we will thwart the schemes of malicious individuals. Unfortunately fanaticism is deep-rooted in this district, we must not confront it directly [for fear of] shedding too much blood. Let us educate, let us be persuasive, and we will bring everyone round.[17]

---

[14] 2 Jan. 1792: A.N., F⁷3695¹ Vendée.
[15] Compte rendu au citoyen Roland, 17 Oct. 1792: A.N., F¹ᶜ III Morbihan 11.
[16] Administrators of the Directory of the Department of Mayenne to Roland, 27 Jan. 1793: A.N., F¹ᶜ III Mayenne 8.
[17] 14 Apr. 1793: A.N., AA58, plaquette 2, dossier 1537. See also the *procès-verbal* of the meeting of the "Amis de la liberté et de l'égalité" at Fontenay-le-Peuple, 3 Apr. 1793: "The Society, profoundly distressed by the misfortunes which fanaticism has heaped on these regions; certain that public instruction is the most successful [weapon] against these infernal machinations [favours] the establishment of patriotic clubs in the Department of the Vendée [because] public instruction is the Hercules under which this reviving hydra will perish": cited in Chassin, *op. cit.*, i, p. 50.

Was this advice so very different from the grievances listed by expectant peoples throughout many departments of the west in anticipation of the Estates General's deliberations? Was it not indeed identical in tone, apart from the repudiation of the institutions of the *ancien régime*, to the complaints of the popular society of Chigné in the Maine-et-Loire, where by September's end during the first year of the rebellion its violence and slaughter stimulated a search for a solution conducive to well-being, at least as seen from the level of rural life? There is ample support for the general feeling in large parts of the insurgent areas that republican troops had, under poor leadership and general licence, aggravated rather than assuaged the rancour of local populations by wholesale and indiscriminate atrocities, in contrast, as Philippeaux, the conventional from the Sarthe observed, with the royalist soldiers who were fighting "as authentic *sans-culottes*, without bounty, without pay, with a morsel of bad bread as their total nourishment . . .".[18]   The Chigné popular society also accused the authorities of prolonging the war and thus exposing innocent people to butchery, and of calling up their sons who were needed in the fields.[19]

The point is that, perhaps with few exceptions, the peasant and artisan rebels shared with their opposite numbers who did not take up arms a general dislike for the most arbitrary social and economic features of the new régime, personified by men who were impatient with and insensitive to people living in social structures that did not fit their vision of a centralized political régime with the capacity to enforce compliance with values stressing work, sobriety and reasonable common sense — the essence of bourgeois culture. The rebellious populations were almost exclusively concerned with the preservation of community relationships and were prepared to welcome only such changes as were necessary to end their fiscal burdens, reduce the level of poverty, improve communications for the more efficient sale of their products, ensure employment, and above all, restore the *curé* to his traditional functions — which meant for them not only the care of their souls and their well-being, but the rudiments of education for their children. The pre-Revolutionary *cahiers* from future resisting or compliant communities, whether from the future Vendée *militaire* or *chouan* country, reveal the depth of these concerns, however much the impact of an older commercial nexus, as in the Saumurois or parts of the Sarthe, discloses a rather differing hierarchy of grievances, the

[18] See Albert Philippon, "La première commission militaire, dite commission Sénar, 22 juin-17 juillet 1793", *Bulletin de la société archéologique de Touraine*, xxix (1944), p. 103.
[19] Popular society of Chigné to the minister of the Interior, 30 Sept. 1793: A.N., F^{IC} III Maine-et-Loire 10.

chief distinction being the greater significance of the *curé* in parishes less touched by a market economy.[20]   For many of them life was so precarious from one year to the next that the rôle of the *curé* in the community and, indeed, in the parish economy was seen as indispensable. From the *cahiers* and the complaints of the post-1789 period the overwhelming impression is of populations utterly at a loss to comprehend why the benefits they had anticipated had not materialized; that instead, the burdens they had shouldered, while changing their form, had really not been eased — indeed, had become or appeared even more onerous, especially since the *curé*, who had previously acted as intermediary with the authorities, had often helped them out in bad times, and had also done not a little to assist the poor in the parish, was suddenly and inexplicably removed.[21]

As the war continued without let-up, as entire areas came to resemble a country under occupation, officials in all ranks increasingly came to see that the "moral economy" (to use Andrew Ure's phrase) with which they had to deal demanded tacit if not open recognition of the central rôle of the *curé* in it and vigorous measures to reduce the level of poverty.   They also came to realize that the demoralized state of the inhabitants under conditions of war, chronic lawlessness and ineffectual occupation was only the acute culmination of prolonged periods of deprivation, momentarily relieved by the hopes of amelioration which they believed would be the result of the political

[20] On the contrasting responses of different areas in the west to the Revolution, see the important studies by Charles Tilly, *The Vendée* (Cambridge, Mass., 1964).   See especially, on the points made here, *ibid.*, p. 112, and Paul Bois, *Paysans de l'ouest: Des structures économiques et sociales aux options politiques depuis l'époque révolutionnaire dans la Sarthe* (Le Mans, 1960), esp. pp. 616-17, 658.   For an assessment of these works, as well as that of Marcel Faucheux, *L'insurrection vendéenne de 1793: Aspects économiques et sociaux* (Paris, 1964), see Harvey Mitchell, "The Vendée and Counterrevolution: A Review Essay", *French Historical Studies*, v (1968), pp. 406-29.

[21] See Faucheux, *L'insurrection vendéenne . . .* , pp. 89-91.   If it was not quite the same in the sénéchaussées and communities of Niort and Saint-Maixent in the Department of Deux-Sèvres, where the parish *cahiers* demanded a respectable income for the *curés* who would thus possess sufficient revenues to care for the poor, the priests were clearly seen as the key figures in a tenuous economy overwhelmed, as the *cahier* of the small parish of Saint-Liguaire reveals, by "the old people, the widows, the orphans, in a word, all the poor". See Léonce Cathelineau, *Cahiers de doléances des sénéchaussées de Niort et de Saint-Maixent et des communautés et corporations de Niort et de Saint-Maixent* (Niort, 1912), p. 49.   Nor were the peasant parishioners blind to the manifold duties and responsibilities of their *curés*, as is obvious from the *cahier* of a peasant community in lower Poitou: "Our good shepherd, our respectable *curé* who instructs us, lightens our burdens, and, day and night, administers to us the consolations of religion, who often comes to wipe our tears away, has hardly enough to live on".   See H. Couturier, *La préparation des Etats-généraux de 1789 en Poitou* (Poitiers, 1909), p. 312.

decisions of the agents of the Revolution, both close to home and in far-off Paris. How to end their hostility and to restore some semblance of normal conditions widened the perceptions of administrators, both civil and military, forced them to enlarge their perspective of the struggle, to engage in the difficult task of understanding the relationship between past and present grievances. The best of them were far from content to continue mouthing the shop-soiled diatribes against priests; and even those who did usually looked for additional explanations for the overt aggression or resigned sullenness of the insurgents.

The impressions gained from the reports of administrators working in distant parts of the west that had experienced full-scale war and the lesser devastations of *chouannerie* suggest that nothing short of an exceptional policy was necessary first to placate the fears and eventually to gain the confidence of the rebels. One illusion some were quick to dispel. The presumed bonds of sentiment or respect uniting the peasants and their former seigneurs had been grossly exaggerated. What appeared to outsiders as a union of effort and will in the countryside was really the superior organizing abilities of *chouan* chieftains, who did so by exploiting fears of conscription, by promising payment in hard coin rather than in *assignats*, by threatening the families of the men they needed to enlarge their bands to support them with volunteers, supplies and food, or simply by offering them the choice between their benevolence in areas under their control in return for compliance, and the alternative of real or imagined impositions by republican officials. As one of the latter pointed out from Dinan in the Côtes-du-Nord:

> The peasant is as tired of the government of these gentlemen [the *chouans*] as they are of the tyrannical government of 1794. While he was mutilated in the name of the Republic, he called on the *chouans* to defend him. Harassed and crushed by the latter, his hope is for a government that will protect him . . . . It is still true that the [people in the] countryside fear the restoration of the seigneurial power as much as they do the Terror; [and it is also true] that they are very wretched and that gentle measures, judiciously devised, would easily [restore] good feeling. Violent measures will only make things worse . . . . [22]

[22] The remainder of the analysis bears notice: "But let the government display all its power in this region, let it show a large enough military force, let it re-establish distributive justice which will make the guilty of all parties retreat in fright; let it [enforce] respect for security and property; let it demonstrate its protective powers everywhere and let it be prepared to overlook previous mistakes and the population will support it and attach itself to it . . . . This can be the consequence only of the continuance of a good system of government and of people accustoming themselves to it (for which time is necessary)". [?] to Rupéron, juge de tribunal de la Nation à Paris, 25 Nivôse Year IV: A.N., F⁷3669¹.

From this one may see at once both the peasant fears inspired by the possibility of a restored seigneurial system and the peculiar dynamics of irregular warfare. This was true also during the more organized period of the fighting in the Vendée. From Montaigu, one of the earliest centres of the uprising in the Vendée Department, Grigau, brigadier-general and chief of general headquarters, firmly denied the existence of deep attachment between peasants and their erstwhile seigneurs.[23]

The horrors of the war remained the most enduring memory of people caught up in a struggle the dimensions and duration of which they could scarcely conceive. They longed for any régime which would bestow its protection over them and respond positively to their most basic material needs. Those responsible for administering these devastated regions could not but gain additional insights into the lives of the communities requiring assistance to restore their economic foundations, renew, albeit according to the new orthodoxy, the shattered links of their social structures, and recreate within them an assured and unchallenged place for the priest. Hoche, into whose hands the responsibility of ensuring the success of pacification had been thrust, saw fairly clearly the reciprocal nature of all three. Like Dumouriez before him, Hoche was far from complacent about the outcome. Unlike Dumouriez, however, Hoche had a much greater reservoir of troops to police the area — 100,000 men were enrolled in the Armée de L'Ouest by 1796. The success of the pacification, he was well aware, rested on force, intelligent administration, and religious toleration. The hostility to the Patriots (the supporters of the Revolution) he saw through the eyes of the rebels, as the triumph of a new breed of men whose avidity for and easy acquisition of land had been so blatant and whose contempt for religion, the priests and the memories of a traditional past, so open, that the antagonisms engendered thereby would not disappear for some time to come. It was therefore necessary:

[23] The latter were, he declared: "... wretched, ignorant men who raised themselves over the other Vendeans only because of their ferocious, bloody character. They were divisional chiefs in Charette's army; they were brave and knowledgeable in the tactics employed by the brigands, but [with what] revolting barbarism; all those who are now liking and appreciating peace in this region, the refugees who are returning in crowds and rebuilding their dwellings will take flight if such men return to the interior of the *bocage*. You will see there the chevaliers Debruc, petty nobles from upper Poitou as detested by their peasants under the old régime as they have been under their command during the civil war; they are ignorant, immoral, cruel. The country where they were divisional chiefs detests and abhors them": Grigau to Merlin, 23 Messidor Year IV: A.N., BB[18]481, D. 7637.

to have the region administered by its former inhabitants, and even by royalists who would have made their peace with the Republic voluntarily. The feelings of the population are hostile to the revolutionary principle . . . . Inspire the Vendeans with confidence by [adopting] measures that might even be a bit counter-revolutionary; play upon their religious ideas; [be ready] to make concessions to their monarchical fanaticism, and most particularly give in to their excessive desires, common to all of them, not to lose sight of their close attachment to their village . . . . The Vendée is an exceptional region: it must therefore be allowed to administer itself by means of exceptional laws.[24]

Others equally close to the problems also urged a policy of exception and stressed, more than did Hoche, the need to adopt measures conducive to economic reconstruction, even entailing a full or partial exemption from taxes, requisitions and conscription, not only because these were seen as having led in the past to the accumulation of resentment, but because only such steps would convince this devastated section of France that the authorities were at last willing to recognize its peculiar needs, which were anterior to the Revolution. Taxes, it was pointed out, would impose such heavy burdens on the peasants that in order to meet them they would be forced to sell their draught animals without which they could not cultivate their holdings.[25]

[24] Hoche to the Directory, quoted in J. Crétineau-Joly, *Histoire de la Vendée militaire*, 2nd edn. (Paris, n.d.), ii, p. 532.   In another letter, Hoche wrote on 9 March 1796: "I have told the Directory twenty times that, if religious toleration is not permitted, the hope of [establishing] peace in these regions will have to be given up.   The last inhabitant, desperate to enter heaven, will [willingly] invite death defending the man who he believes will open the doors for him. Once [the focus is removed] from the priests, there will be neither priest nor war; if they are prosecuted as one, we will be assured of war and priests for the next thousand years".   Cited in J.-J. M. Savary, *Guerres des Vendéens et des Chouans*, 6 vols. (Paris, 1824-7), vi, p. 216.

[25] See the observations of Gautier, commandant of the battalion of the reserve at Saint-Philbert-de-Grandlieu, Loire-Atlantique, to Bénézech, 26 Germinal Year IV.   As "an old military man" who had spent twenty-five months in the Vendée he had, he wrote, travelled through the countryside speaking to the people who almost to a man complained that the continued imposition of taxes and other demands was a vicious circle from which they could not be rescued.   Gautier's advice was: "not to demand from the peoples of these devastated regions any kind of contribution, [especially from] those who would need relief.   And yet demands are made of them and they feel threatened; a *métayer* who at one time worked five ploughs and had sixty cattle has found himself reduced to four oxen with which he worked as much land as he could. He has been asked to pay taxes, he has been forced to sell two of these oxen to pay the taxes, and half of these lands which he had prepared for seed will be returned to waste": A.N., F^{1C} III Loire-Inférieure 10.   See also, for another example of the same dilemma, the assessment of the situation in the Vendée Department by the commissaire of its Executive Directory at Fontenay-le-Peuple, 23 Pluviôse Year IV: "All possible order", he recommended, "should be observed in the requisition of grain and beasts so as not to deprive the cultivators of the grain which is indispensable for their own subsistence and to leave them at least the cattle which they require to cultivate their land": A.N., F^{7}7104.

The close relationship between the practice of religion and the economic needs of the occupied territories was seen as a constant feature, at any rate so long as blindness to the importance of the first and incapacity to deal with the second persisted. The *Annales de la Religion*, founded by the constitutional bishops in Paris in 1795, in which the condition of the church in the west was discussed, was fully alive to the first. Its criticism of the "counter-fanaticism" that had been practised by administrators and reinforced by that of the de-Christianizers, was unsparing. It was possible, so its contributors argued, to reconcile religion and republicanism, even in the Vendée, provided that one made the best of the opportunities presented by the relaxation of the punitive features that had curtailed the free exercise of religion. By these means, they counted on an increasing number of orthodox priests to end their presumed or actual support of the *chouans*.[26]

Was their condemnation of the occupying régime in the west justified? In many respects, the answer must be yes. Some administrators on the spot continued to develop the theme of what might be aptly called "relaxation of the laws", after the period of limited official toleration was terminated in September 1797 and religious persecution was revived. As an instance, the commissaire in the Department of the Vendée acknowledged the presence of forty-two refractories in twenty cantons, but discounted their power to do mischief in view of his conviction that their influence had declined and would further diminish, given "time, education and the wisdom of administrators".[27] The clear implication is that an indiscriminate and uniform application of the anti-religious laws would revive and intensify hostile sentiments against the régime.[28]

Beyond such exhortations to make allowances for the religious preferences of "ignorant" folk who "are not yet ripe for the Revolution",[29] lay the vastly complex terrain of economic deprivation. Its elimination was seen as the prerequisite to the breaching of a closed world where unquestioning patterns of deference rested on foundations of poverty and stagnant economic conditions. It may be that in some areas officials were too quick to associate the two in the fear that failure to improve economic prospects would continue to throw entire sections of the population into the receptive hands of the

[26] See the issues of 27 June, 15 Aug. and 5 Dec. 1795.
[27] Commissaire of the Executive Directory at the Central Administration of the Department of the Vendée at Fontenay-le-Peuple, 24 Vendémiaire Year V: A.N., F⁷3695¹ Vendée.
[28] So wrote the commissaire in the Mayenne Department on 8 Prairial Year VI and 19 Brumaire Year VII: A.N., F¹ᶜ III Mayenne 8.
[29] *Ibid.*

chouans who, they believed — more than the evidence justifies — were promising economic relief and the restoration of the orthodox church. While this must have been true in some instances, what cannot be overlooked is that the thinking on this question, whatever its lack of comprehensiveness, was hardly devoid of an appreciation of a more generous perspective by means of which the problems of the rebel areas in the last years of the Directory were seen as having their origins in the period before 1789.[30]

Gradually the enormity of the problems in these devastated regions ensured a sympathetic response. Moreover, surveys of conditions came increasingly to bear the authenticity of minute attention to practical detail and to the more elusive psychic longings of populations that had survived the pressures of total commitment to preserve their identity. Make no mistake, warned an official in the Maine-et-Loire canton of Montfaucon, love of the fatherland and respect for its laws means little or nothing to people whose thoughts are entirely centred on restoring some semblance of continuity to their lives, by linking their hopes for a better future with their memories of the pre-revolutionary past. The wars had left their mark. A people who had at one time been good-natured, frank, loyal and without affectation, had become defiant, withdrawn and vindictive, in short, were exhibiting all the symptoms of a prolonged illness whose cure demanded unique understanding to rescue them from the emotional turbulence that was wrecking their lives. Economic renewal and education were the best insurance against poverty and ignorance.[31]

The administrator was overstating his case in one particular. The

---

[30] Even if, as at Loudéac in the Côtes-du-Nord, the municipal administrators despaired of dealing with the enormous army of weavers thrown out of work by the closing of the markets for Breton linens — since the start of the war there were 800 of them — the tasks confronting them were more than doubled by the presence of an almost equal number of "deserving poor" for whom relief had never been available in an area where the soil had long resisted the best efforts of agricultural improvers and where in 1797 the number of deaths was double the number of births. Thus, as for "the class of indigents (and unfortunately they form the vast majority of our population), they are totally in despair; they want their priests": the administrators of the commune of Loudéac to the minister of the Interior, 20 Vendémiaire Year V: A.N., F^{IC} III Côtes-du-Nord 12.

[31] The difficulties were immense: the wages of day-labourers were one third above those of 1790, chiefly because of population decline; the hands of land-owners whose resources were insufficient to cultivate all their holdings, let alone extend them, were consequently tied; while the problems were compounded first by arrears of from four to five years in rents from tenant farmers and second by chronic food shortages and high prices. The vicious circle had to be broken; but how, and at whose expense, was clearly beyond the competence of the Directory's commissaire at Montfaucon. Girard to the minister of the Interior, 18 Vendémiaire Year V: A.N., F^{9}310.

presumed docility of the rural inhabitants of the west, the mildness of the Angevin people, to name only one area in western France, are hardly to be credited from what we know of the environment of violence which permeated their lives, a violence which could erupt on the slightest pretext and was stimulated by the spectacle of public executions, the criminal activities of smugglers, the roughness of the boatmen on the Loire, murder on the roads, and the brutal treatment of women and children.   The violence of the *chouannerie* cannot be viewed as a new phenomenon, the distinct product of the civil war. Its roots are to be found in the patterns of criminality of the pre-revolutionary west, where the most macabre forms of punishment were carried over into the post-1789 period by men accustomed to the sight of excessive brutality and ready to perpetuate torture and murder as acceptable and salutary.   Moreover, familiarity with the omnipresence of death due to natural causes could not but mitigate the impact of death from violent causes.[32]

Two years later, in the waning days of the Directory, the economic situation had not changed significantly, according to Chapelain, an administrator who cast his eye over the disaffected areas in a report destined for the government's consideration.   In the countryside, the key to the economic rehabilitation of the landowners lay in two kinds of concessions.   To ensure the loyalty of the proprietors, whose major goal was the guarantee and increase of their incomes, the government had to desist from conscripting their sons and from a too rigorous collection of taxes.   Indeed, unless the burden of taxes were sufficiently lightened, the prospect of economic recovery remained dismal not only for these better-off sections of the rural community, but impossible for the incomparably disadvantaged

[32] On the nature of crime in Anjou, see Lebrun, *op. cit.*, pp. 418-19.   The growing interest in the nature of criminality can be gauged by the appearance of a number of studies in recent years.   Richard Cobb's highly individual treatment of crime in the pre-revolutionary and revolutionary periods can be tasted in *The Police and the People: French Popular Protest 1789-1820* (Oxford, 1970) and *Reactions to the French Revolution* (London, 1972).   Olwen Hufton's article, "Begging, Vagrancy, Vagabondage and the Law: An Aspect of the Problem of Poverty in Eighteenth Century France", *European Studies Review*, ii (1972), is excellent for its classification of the poor and how the law dealt with them.   A number of historians (*une équipe*) have published preliminary findings of their investigations into crime in various towns and cities of eighteenth-century France.   They can be sampled in *Crimes et criminalité en France sous l'ancien régime, 17ᵉ-18ᵉ siècles* (Paris, 1971): the contributors are A. Abbiateci, F. Billacois, Y. Bongert, N. Castan, Y. Castan and P. Petrovich.   See also T. J. A. Le Goff and D. M. G. Sutherland, "The Revolution and the Rural Community in Eighteenth-Century Brittany", *Past and Present*, no. 62 (Feb. 1974), originally read at the 1972 meeting of The Society for French Historical Studies and now reprinted as chapter 2 of this volume.

métayers and day-labourers, whose capacity for bare survival demanded a policy of tax restraints. Chapelain was suggesting, no more and no less, that measures for the amelioration of the *métayers'* conditions should be the government's central concern. Should it fail to support their independent existence, the entire edifice of agricultural income, wages and taxes would crumble. If the government were willing to reduce the scale of taxation by the amounts contributed by *métayers* for the army's subsistence in 1796 and 1797, and if the government further ended the tax inequities as between neighbouring communes — a continuing source of hostility — the entire economic picture would change for the better. Production would increase to the benefit of the landowners as well as of the *métayers*; a reservoir of income would be consolidated and a tax basis created; the wages of day-labourers could be stabilized and thus the threat of future rebellion removed.[33]

A view that complements and rounds off that offered by Chapelain is to be found in a study of the economy of the Loire-Inférieure, published in the Year XII. It is, as nearly as I can make out, applicable to other parts of the insurgent areas. There, in succinct fashion, the author noted peasant hostility towards the *noblesse* dating from before 1789, their expectations of economic improvement under the new régime, their resentment of the bourgeoisie who had adopted the "manner of seigneurs", their hatred of the new taxes and of military service, their banding together under non-noble leaders, their opposition to the new political structures in the municipalities and districts, and their attachment to the restoration of the monarchy as a last resort.[34] Perhaps the last word in this section ought to be General Watrin's. For him the *chouan* marauders were expressing a revolt against the social order: they wanted "neither religion, nor the king, but the destruction of all the landowners who had been having it good for long enough".[35] Like the rural *sans-culottes*, these inveterate opponents of the Patriots focused their hatred on the same

---

[33] Chapelain's observations were sent to the minister of the Police on 5 Brumaire Year VII: A.N., F⁷3695¹. See also, the views of the president of the municipal administration of the canton of Ferté-Bernard in the Sarthe sent to the minister of the Interior, 24 Nivôse Year VIII: A.N., F⁷3687⁷. Unless something were done, he wrote, to alleviate poverty, check mendicity, bring prices down and revive industry, *chouannerie* would continue to spread and gain recruits from among those who would be driven to it from sheer economic desperation.

[34] *Recherches économiques et statistiques sur le département de la Loire-Inférieure. Annuaire de l'an XI* (Nantes, Year XII), pp. 443-7.

[35] Cited in Marcel Reinhard, *Le département de la Sarthe sous le régime directorial* (Saint-Brieuc, 1936), p. 72.

groups in rural France, *les gros* — those who accepted bourgeois values and needed public order to defend them against the dispossessed.

II

The perceptions of counter-revolutionary élites also underwent change during the course of the insurrection, especially when it was contained after its greatest advances. Until then, there appeared to be no compelling need to question or challenge the prevailing view that the insurgents were fighting on behalf of the monarchy and religion. Allusions to the monarchy became more frequent and more studied only when the prospects of rebel success began to diminish, but those who sought to persuade the doubtful were themselves far from convinced that the Bourbons possessed the authority to move and unite masses of peasants and artisans; and their reservations, it should be added, explain the negative tone of royalist propaganda, stressing as it did the shortcomings of the Revolution rather than any of the positive advantages of a restoration.

Some merely noted the absence of enthusiasm for and the indifference to the monarchy, the result perhaps of a feeling of remoteness from the power and magic which were once attached to the sacerdotal qualities of kingship. Others, like Loaisel who had been a confederate of de la Rouërie, tried to distinguish — without more than *a priori* reasoning — between urban hostility and presumed rural belief that the restoration of the orthodox church was inseparably linked with the fortunes of the crown.[36]

The baron de Nantiat attempted a more explicit analysis of the distressing absence of royalist sentiment which he believed could be reversed by a policy of active propagandizing in the countryside. Except in the Vendée and among some of the *chouans* in the neighbourhood of Nantes, he had found that the country people were much more greatly moved by hatred against the Republic than by loyalty to the king. The Republic had become for them a symbol of suffering. If they inclined towards the *ancien régime*, they did so only because any other form of government was beyond their experiences. Yet the concept of royalty was, in his opinion, too metaphysical. He also observed that the person of the monarch was no longer invested with reality for most people. Nothing, he concluded, was being done to endow either the crown or its living

[36] Aperçu de l'état de la Bretagne by Loaisel, 10 Oct. 1796: Public Record Office, H.O. 69/31.

representative with those attributes from which the people could derive a sense of meaningfulness in their lives.[37]   Of even greater practical difficulty, according to an unnamed observer who had undertaken a tour of Normandy in or about 1795, were the unmistakable expressions of fear of a restoration under Louis XVIII, who was being depicted by republican authorities as an angry king, returning like a punitive father to affirm his authority and to chastise his errant and disobedient children.[38]   What was most disturbing was the realization that the monarchy by itself no longer possessed the force to attract devotion from any significant part of the population.   On the one hand, it was associated with a régime of privileges, the living examples of which were the *émigrés* who were almost universally suspected of harbouring fantasies of restoring their powers to their full vigour; while, on the other hand, no vital connections were seen between the monarchy and the religious sensibilities of the people who were presumably sacrificing themselves for it.   The royalist commission of lower Maine, for example, was bitter in its denunciation of the priesthood for fostering belief in the dissolubility of the ties between altar and throne and noted that people were ready to obey any political régime that permitted the free exercise of their religion.[39]

It was in consequence of perceiving that the monarchy could never be the focal point of opposition to the Revolution that the leadership of the counter-revolution, whether in France or in Britain, was forced to look behind their myth-making to grasp the fact that discontent was real, that it expressed itself through means of existing social structures, that it had a religious component, and that the structure of authority appropriate to deal with it was not necessarily predetermined by tradition unless it could answer needs.[40]   In other words, the idea

[37] Observations sur l'opinion régnante en France, et sur la ville de Nantes en particulier, July 1795: British Museum, Windham Papers, Add. MS. 37860, fo. 53 v.

[38] Aperçu de mes observations sur la Normandie notamment sur la partie que j'ai parcourue [1795?]: *ibid.*, fo. 66.

[39] AZA (président du bureau central de l'arrondissement du Bas Maine) to de Chalus, 10 July 1797: Brit. Mus., Puisaye Papers, Add. MS. 8009, fos. 8–9.

[40] The desperate appeal of one of Puisaye's confederates, Grimaudière, is a good example of the feeling of loss and disappointment: "... As the French people have now forgotten the good fortune of having a king, and only aspire to enjoy the advantages of a peaceful and moderate government, it would be valuable to know [the nature of] the laws which our worthy sovereign expects to bestow upon them ...": Grimaudière to Puisaye, ? Oct. 1796: Brit. Mus., Puisaye Papers, Add. MS. 8017, fo. 41 v.   See also the views conveyed to Puisaye by de Chalus of the commission intermédiaire des Etats de Bretagne à Rennes: "Even the royalist who is most devoted to the king did not clearly grasp whether he was fighting for the king or for a faction.... And why

that the pre-1789 forms of government would by themselves ma
things right again was seen to be a fallacious premise. Even if tl
earliest allusions to the restoration promised the return to the
"ancient" forms of authority minus the abuses, without, however,
specifying them, the painful task of trying to slough off preconceptions
came only under the stress of failure to shape the resistance to the
Revolution.

A fair amount of attention was devoted to economic dissatisfaction,
the presumption always being that the split between town and
country, between bourgeois and peasant, was one of the basic
antagonisms threatening the Revolution. Virtually every survey of
economic conditions stressed the point that the bourgeoisie were the
despoilers of the old régime, that their material stake in the Revolution was highest. Blind rejection of their gains did not always follow.
Rather, as some of the more clear-sighted counter-revolutionaries
appreciated, potential support for a restoration — "a mitigated
monarchical government" — from *propriétaires*, merchants and
cultivateurs was not out of the question if such a government
sanctioned the burial of "the feudal system and honorific rights".[41]
Consolidation of these material advantages, particularly those achieved
through the purchase of church and *émigré* property, was seen as the
condition of venturing into the unknown terrain of political change.
The problem, though it was never explored fully, was how to nurture
the political sentiments that would accommodate the economic
security of the most literate and self-confident groups in French
society. Yet could they be acted upon when they were the natural
targets of punitive counter-revolutionary action or the focal point of
émigré antagonism and hatred? Or even in the earliest phases of the
civil war, when in the zones occupied by the rebel armies the
provisional authorities set up by the rebel generals did all they could
to erase every vestige of the Revolution?

The illusion that the peasantry were eager for the return of their
former masters and the traditional network of social and economic
dependency was hard to shatter. The investment in the theory of
overwhelming economic hardship — so many of the observers
expatiated on this theme, as did Windham at the War Office,[42] and

should that be — because no one appeared at the right moment to second him;
all who did showed only the mailed fist" (? May 1797): Brit. Mus., Puisaye
Papers, Add. MS. 8077, fo. 11 v.
[41] Réflexions du sieur Loaisel sur la situation actuelle de la France, au retour
d'un voyage qu'il vient d'y faire, 21 Sept. 1795: Pub. Rec. Off., H.O. 69/29.
[42] See William Windham's notes, *passim.*, in Brit. Mus., Windham Papers,
Add. MS. 37903.

others who wrote on the devastating effects of *assignat* inflation[43] — supported the postulate that sheer economic desperation in the countryside and, by impulse, to the towns, would fortify opposition to the Republic, particularly as the burden of new taxes and forced loans was increased.[44]   But not all were so convinced, for first-hand evidence of peasant wishes revealed a rather different picture. Indeed, whatever resentments were festering in the countryside against the purchasers of land and their protectors in the local revolutionary structures of government, they had no real desire to welcome into their old accustomed places of authority and prestige a group of men whose links with them bore few traces of affection or economic well-being.

In part the dynamics of the fighting were responsible for the distancing between the rank and file rebels and those who sought to forge them into units acting in a concerted way.   But if the lack of organization in the rebel armies was the primary concern of the élites who believed that therein lay the chief cause of the fragmentation of rebel resistance, their dismay inadvertently revealed horror at the prospect of peasants escaping their control.   By freely helping themselves to the *biens nationaux*, the former domains of the crown, and *émigré* property, which they looked upon as the legitimate conquest of war, they would, it was feared, satisfy their most immediate needs, create unimaginable chaos, and deliver a stunning blow to the long-term hopes of reversing the Republic.[45]   As the comte de Moustier put it, a year after the rebellion began, the people of the Vendée had been quick to distinguish between their true plebeian leaders and the *seigneurs émigrés* whom they did not want to see in their midst.   "What effect would the proprietors produce among their vassals", he asked, "if they were suddenly returned to them?   Popular indignation against them and the desire to get rid of them".[46]

In that rather remarkable collection of letters written and received

---

[43] Cf. d'Andigné's beliefs as expressed in his *Mémoires*, 2 vols. (Paris, 1900-1), i., pp. 145-6.

[44] See, as an illustration, the predictions of Leveneur de la Roche, 10 Jan. 1796: Brit. Mus., Puisaye Papers, Add. MS. 8022, fo. 17.   He spoke of organizing resistance in the countryside against the imposition of taxes by hindering the movement of grain to the towns.   Cf. also, de Cresolles to Puisaye, 21 Jan. 1796: *ibid.*, fo. 278 v.

[45] See the anonymous memoir in: Brit. Mus., Windham Papers, Add. MS. 37861, fo. 127 v.

[46] Comte de Moustier's memorandum, 19 Apr. 1794: Brit. Mus., Windham Papers, Add. MS. 37855, fo. 215.

by royalist chiefs, intercepted and printed by the Directory in the Year VII,[47] there is considerable evidence in support of Moustier's opinions. The collection reflects the worries, hopes and illusions of *émigrés* whose chief thought was to salvage what remained of their property, exact former seigneurial dues, and ensure the loyalty of their former tenants. The desire to obtain positions of authority in the rebel armies is also expressed complacently and naïvely. Both are striking examples of the blindness of men who rarely questioned the possibility of regaining their pre-eminence. That some of them thought that they would be able to reconstitute some of their holdings — and indeed did — is proof that this expectation rather than loyalty to any other part of the *ancien régime* was their chief consideration. But those portions of the correspondence dealing with the resentments of the local leaders against the pretensions of the *émigrés* are, I think, even more impressive proof of popular rejection of a social hierarchy that had been barely accepted in the years before 1789,[48] as well as of undisguised peasant hostility to the renewal of a discredited landholding system. True, the correspondence also contains reports of peasant eagerness to welcome their seigneurs as deliverers, but these are suspect at worst, or isolated examples at best, in light of the overwhelming evidence to the contrary.

What emerges from my findings on this aspect of the insurrection confirms what has been known for some time. The rebellion was a manifestation of popular discontent. If it was a resistance against those bourgeois who had been made newly secure by their acquisition of national property, it was not at the same time a movement favouring the reclamation by the dominant representatives of the previous social and economic structures of their former privileges and property. The *chouan* uses of *émigré* and national property, were not, as so many *émigrés* hoped, proof that it was being held in trust for them, but rather illustrated a widely held popular belief that it belonged properly to the rebels who were risking their lives against the Republic. They saw themselves as the authentic opponents of the Revolution in contrast to the sybarites who were waiting in the wings to rob them of their labours. There were, as we know, bands of false *chouans* who terrorized the countryside, exploiting the appeals to the old order to cloak their criminal activities. The literature agrees on the variegated

[47] *Correspondance secrète de Charette, Stofflet, Puisaye, Cormatin, d'Autichamp, Bernier, Frotté, Scépeaux, Botherel, etc.* (Paris, Year VII; copy in Brit. Mus.).
[48] See particularly, Charles, officier Vendéen, to Stofflet, 10 Dec. 1795, and d'Autichamp to d'Autichamp, 28 Mar. 1796: *ibid.*, pp. 51-72, 200.

social composition of the *chouan* bands — deserters, former salt tax collectors, returning volunteers, criminals, as well as domestics, weavers, and peasants of all degrees — so that it is easy to see how observers on both sides of the struggle could conclude that the chaos was the work of marginal social elements.   But, in the minds of many royalist élites, desperately clinging to some mental structure that would give meaning to the disorder that was assailing them, the false *chouans* soon became the term they applied indiscriminately to all the *chouans*; and it was to the *chouans'* stubborn resistance to the possibility of having the warfare organized under returning *émigrés* and their intention to hold on to their gains that the royalists partly ascribed the continuing failure of the counter-revolution.   Contrary to the expectations of those who tried to harness it, the insurrection was taking its own course.   The documents attest to the bitterness of many that such a state of affairs was injurious to the cause and should consequently be ended, and the warnings of a few that it had to be met with understanding.   Even the most biased observers among the royalists could not deny the independent origins of the rebellion, its apparent spontaneity, the creation of its own élites, its suspicions of external pressures, and its particularism — in other words, its commitment to a kind of primitive equality that found its earliest expression in the democratic structure of the provisional rebel councils in the towns and *bourgs* they had captured, a movement that was, in the view of those who wanted to impose a structure more in keeping with past practices, "incompatible with the true principles of monarchical government".[49]   Indeed, the former commandant of the *maréchaussée* of Poitou, de Solérac, in happy anticipation of the restoration, proposed in mid-1794 the creation of a special police corps to re-establish order in the rebel territories to forestall, as he said, the peasants from taking the law into their own hands and dictating to the nobility.[50]

[49] Savary, *op. cit.*, iv, p. 446.   See also the *Mémoire politique et historique des insurrections de l'Ouest.   Par un officier qui a été chargé d'une partie des opérations relatives au rétablissement de la tranquillité intérieure* (Paris, n.d.; copy in Brit. Mus.).   The author, who had been active in the pacification, could not avoid the conclusion that: "It is a remarkable thing, this picture of primitive equality offered by the very enemies of social equality; there one sees boldness and courage take hold of men and affairs.   It is not in family archives, but rather by means of his personal abilities, that the rebel finds his resourcefulness" (p. 16).

[50] De Solérac's memorandum, 24 May 1794: Brit. Mus., Windham Papers, Add. MS. 37856, fo. 13.   See T. J. A. Le Goff and D. M. G. Sutherland, *op. cit.* They point out that the Breton *maréchaussée* was the only permanent source of order in an area known for its turbulence.   Since criminal statistics for Poitou are not available, it is difficult to compare it with Brittany.   But it would be

A popular insurrection without proper organization, taking its own direction, and opposed to the grafting on to it of the goals of a class of men who had discredited themselves by flight, could hardly commend itself to those who had to devise means to counteract the centrifugal forces at work in the rebellion without alienating them at the same time. The dilemma was not faced squarely, despite the insistence of many observers that the perennial expectations of massive risings in defence of the old verities were founded on misconceptions. Instead old plans were rehashed; the old illusions were dusted off; and the stubborn facts were disregarded. No better example of this can be offered than the fact that, when they realized how the religious sources of discontent were no longer operating to their benefit after 1795, they denounced those members of the clergy who were making their peace with the authorities and tried to get the clerical hierarchy to intervene in the quite mistaken belief that the refractory clergy had actively initiated and could again initiate the aggressive resistance of their parishioners. Like most of their revolutionary counterparts the royalist leadership took for granted the religious origins of the rebellion, in fact ascribed to them the chief reasons for it without, however, examining the components of religiosity at the popular peasant level. They did not question the power of religious practices and customs to shape peasant mentality and always distinguished it from the corrosive forces of secularism in the towns. In short, they lumped together religion and the innocence of rural life, and equated them with loyalty to the traditions of monarchical government.

That way of thinking was put to a severe test when, in response to the policy of quasi-toleration, members of the clergy in France began to show signs of making some accommodation with the republican authorities. The point was that if the clergy — and if we are to believe the reports of the royalists, a fairly large number of them were involved — continued to take advantage of the decrees favouring the liberty of religious exercise, their tacit or open acknowledgement of the new religious legislation would be seen by their parishioners as a justification for abandoning the monarchy and the *noblesse* and ending all resistance to the Revolution.[51] The dangers of such a

surprising if the local attitudes towards crime in Poitou in the pre-revolutionary period were radically different from those in Brittany. In any case, de Solérac must have had them in mind when drawing up his memorandum, and equated the freedom that peasants felt they had to vent their hostility against the nobility with crime.

[51] Report on a mission to France by Loaisel and the comte de Trémic, 28 June 1795: Pub. Rec. Off., H.O. 69/29. Gavard, the president of the secret royalist central bureau of the arrondissement of lower Maine, who served as

development were thought so great that twelve *émigré* bishops assembled in London to denounce the *prêtres soumissionnaires* (the priests who had agreed to the tests of civic submission according to the decrees of 28-9 September 1795), to state categorically that this was contrary to their submission to the principles of the monarchy, and to urge priests to "exercise the cult of Religion as had the very first Christians, in secret, . . . [and] in the midst of all the risks and dangers . . . and denunciations, [to be dependent] on the hospitality of the faithful, [with the expectation of suffering the full vigour of the penalties] of banishment, imprisonment and even of death . . .".[52] The injunction was apparently not heeded.   Evidence of clerical compliance with the new religious policies continued to disturb local royalists who reported that priests were cautioning the faithful to return to peaceful pursuits.[53]   At the same time, they appealed for guidance and proposed that a firm statement from the hierarchy was essential to prevent what was seen by at least one observer as the beginning of a new schism.[54]   Lacking such intervention, the further risk of presbyterianism, the greatest source of heresy in the church, would proceed unchecked.   Attacks on the hierarchy from within the church — "the Christian catholic religion is a religious monarchical [species] of government" — would consecrate the end of monarchical government in the civilian sphere itself.   Without the reaffirmation of the principle of the traditional hierarchical structure of the church, especially at a time when the civil power had separated church and state and accorded freedom of religion to all cults, the episcopacy would give way to the supremacy of the simple priesthood and the monarchy would lose its greatest source of support.[55]

intermediary between Puisaye and the abbé Bernier, put it this way: "The priests can [use] their influence not only on religious, but on political, matters . . . .   It would be useful if on crossing over from England again, they would be instructed in the necessity of convincing all those whom they can influence that they could have the religion of their fathers restored only if, as a preliminary, they did their utmost to restore Louis XVIII . . . .   A good many priests were already not finding the submission a bad thing".   Gavard to de Chalus, 10 July 1797: Brit. Mus., Puisaye Papers, Add. MS. 8009, fo. 8 v.

[52] Sentiments unanimes de douze évêques réunis à Londres et plusieurs fois assemblés pour délibérer sur le présent objet, 2 Sept. 1796: Brit. Mus., Puisaye Papers, Add. MS. 8012, fo. 81 r-v.

[53] See St. Victor to Puisaye, 9 Feb. 1796: Brit. Mus., Puisaye Papers, Add. MS. 8020, fo. 65 r-v.

[54] Charles de la Crochais to Puisaye, 7 Sept. 1797: Brit. Mus., Puisaye Papers, Add. MS. 8022, fo. 204.

[55] Unidentified letter [1797 ?]: Brit. Mus., Puisaye Papers, Add. MS. 8007, fos. 28-9.

With the resumption of religious persecution after Fructidor, the royalists breathed a little more easily, but not much more so. Excuses were even found for the submissive priests: some had acted out of fear; others had been misled; still others had believed that they were serving the interests of religion and the monarchy by acceding to the decrees of the Republic.[56] The imputation that the priests could have done more and could be more actively engaged in the struggle was challenged by a priest. The abbé le Made, who had been sent in September 1796 by the *émigré* Bishop of Tréguier to Brittany to observe the response of local priests to the new religious decrees, reported at the close of the period of religious liberty that nothing ought to be expected from this persecuted band of men, imprisoned in the towns, massacred in the countryside, forced to live in secrecy, but that rôle of hallowed martyrdom which they were assuming so unquestionably and so heroically. To draw attention to themselves would merely decimate their ranks and be a disservice to the cause.[57]

These assurances of clerical devotion to the monarchy could not conceal the profound changes that had taken place in the ranks of the priesthood since the proclamation of the Civil Constitution. The lack of clerical unity on relations between the church and the republican form of government became acute after 1795, with some bishops advising submission and others counselling the contrary. It was plain to even the most intransigent royalists that the church was not necessarily the unassailable arm of the counter-revolution. It was also painfully clear that even those priests who had the undivided loyalties of their parishioners in resisting the Revolution did not always identify themselves with pre-revolutionary forms of political authority and social privilege, and in fact were as hostile to the upper clergy as were those of their colleagues in other parts of France, as well as in their own, who had taken the oath to the Civil Constitution of the Clergy as a way of expressing their opposition to the hierarchy.

[56] Comte de Chalus to Leveneur de la Roche, 7 Dec. 1797: Brit. Mus., Puisaye Papers, Add. MS. 8022, fo. 52 v.
[57] Abbé le Made to Puisaye, 29 Oct. 1797: Brit. Mus., Puisaye Papers, Add. MS. 7999, fo. 75.

III

From this survey it is clear that there is a common thread binding together the observations and perceptions of the adversaries who were struggling to force into submission a people whose resistance, it should be stressed once again, was directed in almost equal measure against both.   The fact is that the élites, revolutionary and counter-revolutionary, were in a very real sense witnessing a foreign country, a region of France most of whose people could not be fitted easily into structures that valued the newer patterns and sources of authority and obedience, nor forced to resume deference to the institutions that had not served them well.   Apart from the central rôle of the *curé*, the latter had lost most if not all of their vitality.   The displaced élites demonstrated the hollowness of their pretensions by their futile fantasies of restoring a mythic past — mythic because so many of them had already before the Revolution been dislodged from their positions of power by townsmen, however unwelcome they were. The difference is that the counter-revolutionary élites were desperate to re-establish control according to precepts and practices that evoked little response, while their antagonists wanted to impose a new set of controls and had a slightly better chance of doing so, if only because they showed signs of appreciating more fully, though imperfectly, some of the authentic needs of these people.   The Revolution was, it hardly needs repeating, chiefly a centralizing and modernizing development, centred in the towns; its consequences were most traumatic in the countryside, either because it favoured a relatively small number of well-to-do peasants, or because it denied to the much larger numbers of the disadvantaged some of the most obvious economic benefits of its innovations.   Only the shock of massive resistance brought some of the contours of the mutual feelings of alienation out into the open.   If cold incomprehension led to brutality, it was not by any means the constant or dominant reaction of the revolutionary generation.   Like the bureaucrats, the upper ranks of the clergy, and the medical administrators and practitioners who had served the crown, the men who succeeded them were able to discern dimly the dynamics of a society that responded to older rhythms and to accord it some degree of sympathetic understanding, while never giving up their prior commitment to a newer, perhaps even harsher vision of the world.

IV

The sources for my study are not very different from those exploited by historians for many years. By themselves they tell us only indirectly about how the great mass of the insurgents felt and why they acted or reacted as they did. The attempt to penetrate the mental world of the peasants by a judicious interpretation of the interrogation records of the military commissions in occupied territory, while throwing some light on the problem, is also ultimately frustrating. In this, the conjectural part of my study, I should like to suggest the kinds of questions that may contribute to our understanding of what lay behind the external meanings of religious observance in the insurgent areas.

One fact is indisputable: during a hundred years or so, from about the middle 1600s to roughly the middle 1700s, the western parts of France were areas of intense missionary work the object of which was to impose conformity of religious observance, reduce the vestiges of popular rites grounded in superstition and magic, and neutralize the impact of protestantism. It was then that standard forms of the catechism were introduced, the mystic significance of the sacraments exalted, the practice of easy confession proscribed, and, under the guidance of the Jesuits, priests were trained in seminaries to deal with the practical requirements of the confessional and the sermon. Yet the residue of this great spurt of energy was not the same everywhere, for it was in the plains areas that the churches were poor, while in the *bocage* catholic piety multiplied local sanctuaries, *confréries*, priests and pilgrimages. Montfortain missionary activity in the middle part of the eighteenth century deepened the contrasts between the two areas, though the catholic revival had its limits and variations even in the Mauges.[58]

Its impact, moreover, was limited throughout the west. The catholic offensive in the earlier part of the century failed to maintain its energy in the few decades before the Revolution. The decline in the number of *confréries*, absenteeism, and the difficulty of recruiting for the priesthood attest to a diminution of clerical vitality. Perhaps the revival was most permanent in the relationship between a small group of clergy and the better-off social strata which constituted a small élite far removed from the great mass of country folk for whom piety and superstition, faith and credulousness, were inseparable.[59]

[58] The single most impressive study on the catholic revival in the west is: Louis Pérouas, *Le Diocèse de La Rochelle de 1648 à 1724. Sociologie et pastorale* (Paris, 1964). [59] Lebrun, *op. cit.*, p. 414.

Popular beliefs lived on side by side with the teachings and doctrines of the church; the peasants saw no contradiction between them; nor is there any reason to doubt their devotion to Christianity because of their attachment to magic and superstition.[60] The country *curé* surely understood this more easily than his urban counterpart.

One of the striking facts in the revival, while it lasted, was the near exclusion of Jansenist influences. Dealing with this question is not easy. It has been suggested that the areas of Jansenist diffusion during the eighteenth century were the major areas of anti-clericalism in the nineteenth century.[61] This view has some support in a recent study of the parish clergy in the diocese of Reims at the end of the old régime, where the social distance between *curé* and parishioner was fortified by the rigour of Jansenist seminary education which stressed morality and religious conformity rather than authentic religious experience.[62] But whether it was the rigid commands of religious obedience, or the uses of the confessional and sermon by Jansenist priests ever ready to threaten their erring followers with damnation, that alienated many of the faithful in Reims remains an open question. In Reims the truly observant, that is to say, the truly pious, especially women, were probably a minority responding to an equally small number of demanding clergy. It may also be that the absence of deep Christian feeling in a diocese like Reims[63] or in the plains areas of the west had much to do with a failure of imagination on the part of the priests, a failure, that is, to examine their own preconceptions formed in the seminaries and to deal with the needs of those they professed to serve at a time when the older forms of community

[60] Mircea Eliade says this very well: "It could even be said that a part of the popular religion of pre-Christian Europe survived, either camouflaged or transformed, in the feasts of the church calendar and in the cult of the Saints. For more than ten centuries the church was obliged to fight the continual influx of 'pagan elements' — that is, elements belonging to the cosmic religion — into Christian practices and legends .... The religious experience peculiar to the rural populations was nourished by what could be called a 'cosmic Christianity'. In other words, the peasants of Europe understood Christianity as a cosmic liturgy .... It is clear that this popular Christianity has kept alive certain categories of mythical thought even down to our day". See his article, "Survivals and Camouflages of Myths", *Diogenes*, xli (1963), pp. 1-25, esp. pp. 8-10.
[61] Theodore Zeldin, "The Conflict of Moralities", in *Conflicts in French Society. Anti-Clericalism, Education and Morals in the Nineteenth Century* (London, 1970), pp. 13-50.
[62] Dominique Julia, "Le Clergé paroissal du diocèse de Reims à la fin de l'ancien régime", *Etudes Ardenaisses*, lv (1968), pp. 41-66.
[63] Cf. M.-L. Fracart's study of Niort, in which she writes, "There is no need to be astonished by the deep religious ignorance in this period, despite the external Christian practices of the largest number of people": *La fin de l'ancien régime à Niort* (Paris, 1956), p. 79.

cohesion were being altered by changing economic conditions and a more sceptical frame of mind. In other regions in which the quality of life was more or less impervious to such changes, neither the faithful nor their priests suffered the same doubts or anguish, and continued to be bound together, as always, loosely and unquestioningly.

The anxieties the peasants did experience were the product of the Revolution. What they had thought of as normal, what they had learned to accept, what they knew they could expect, were now being put to some severe tests. The midwife, for example, was an important person in the parish, who was blessed by the *curé* before beginning her work, and therefore had, so to speak, a delegation of power from him, including the right of baptism in the event that the child was not likely to survive. In the small peasant communities, she practised without the benefit of any professional instruction. The attempt to improve the standards of midwifery in Anjou through a series of courses in the dozen or so years before the Revolution made scarcely any impression in the Angevin countryside where, even when qualified women were available, the peasants preferred to call on the older, uninstructed midwives.[64] With the arrival of the constitutional priests, there can be no doubt that it was these midwives who encouraged village mothers to seek out their non-conforming priests rather than run the risk of improper baptism. This was one of the most overt acts of defiance against the new church, reports of which came in from places as separated as Vannes in the Morbihan and the bourg of Saint-Georges-du-Puy-de-la-Garde in the Mauges.[65] It was perhaps this active opposition to the constitutional priesthood that led to the decree by the Maine-et-Loire Department in July 1794 inviting women to enrol in a course in midwifery at public expense to counteract the "rash and thoughtless intrigues of the majority of midwives".[66] Although it is equally likely that the decree's parentage

[64] Lebrun, *op. cit.*, p. 229, n. 125.

[65] Les commissaires du roi au département du Morbihan, Vannes, 4 June 1791 (A.N., F⁷3682¹⁸): "Also the people no longer dare to bring their infants to the church for baptism, and, in dread of that terrible excommunication, hand them over unbaptized to wet-nurses and without taking any precautions [in case of disputes] regarding their birth and civil status. More than thirty have been sent into the countryside in this way these past few days. The midwives have banded together to stop taking the infants to church, or to accompany those women to church upon recovering from their confinement. Yesterday a woman in the town who went to the church by herself was mocked and almost booed by the people". See also Tilly, *op. cit.*, p. 253.

[66] See the decree of the department of Maine-et-Loire, 24 July 1794 (6 Thermidor Year II), in *Affiches d'Angers*, 30 July 1794 (12 Thermidor Year II). On this journal's influence in the last years of the old régime, see François

owed as much to the far from successful efforts in the 1770s and 1780s to train women, the departmental authorities were probably trying to achieve the twin goals of neutralizing both the recalcitrant older generation of midwives who were in league with the refractories and the refractories themselves.   It must be remembered that many pre-revolutionary *curés*, either through ignorance, lack of funds, or avarice had refused to send women for training in midwifery.

We are aware, too, of the desertion from the households of the constitutional clergy of domestic servants who fled in terror from the prospect of attending to the needs of men presumed to be, in some cases, the emissaries of the devil, in others, the infectious agents, so it was said, of protestantism.   These were normal occurrences in the Vendée and in *chouan* country, and were observed incredulously by revolutionary administrators and by the new constitutional priests.

It would also be interesting to speculate on the implications of the stories that may have been circulated about these juring clergy leaving their callings and marrying to see how far it would be possible to understand the mind of a peasant for whom such an act was tanta-mount to the release of sexual energies, barely tolerated for the layman except for purposes of procreation, and totally forbidden for priests who were thought of as the guardians of traditional sexual morality.   The monastic establishments in southern Anjou had been bitterly resented in the Val-Saumurois, and though the Mauges, a centre of fervent counter-revolution, had fewer of them, many of the monks, eager to renounce their vows, transferred their allegiance to the constitutional church, joined the revolutionary administrations, or even married,[67] so strengthening the image of a perfidious and self-aggrandizing group of men, not unlike the protestant clergy of popular myth.   When, therefore, the constitutional priests were reviled as protestants — and we ought not to forget that the near-eradication of protestantism was of relatively recent date — was it the fear that a marrying protestant clergy would, as in the past, pollute the community and so provoke divine anger, that stirred the community to action?   If this was so, what greater certainty of damnation could there have been than the marriage sacrament performed by a priest who would desecrate it by his own thoughts and potential deeds sanctioned by blasphemous politicians and libidinous clergy?   Did echoes of the campaign against clerical celibacy published in

Lebrun's article, "Une source de l'histoire sociale: La presse provinciale à la fin de l'ancien régime. Les 'Affiches d'Angers' (1773-1789)", *Le Mouvement social*, xl (1962), pp. 56-73.
    [67] Tilly, *op. cit.*, p. 229.

L'Observateur Provincial at Angers in December 1790 reach the countryside, and with what effect?[68] A royalist almanac of 1795, which circulated in Normandy, Brittany, Poitou, Maine, Perche and Anjou, depicts a young girl who had been married by a constitutional priest being devoured in the flames of hell.[69] So tenacious were these fears that even those young people who had been married by the new priests took care to regularize their unions, as we know from the activities of priests who emerged from hiding after 1795.[70]

However scanty the information on such questions, it is worth raising them. Historians, in their reconstruction of peasant communities, have looked at their socio-economic axes, relying either on a meticulous combing of the sources or on applying the newer sociological models to them. They have also begun, particularly in France, the immensely difficult task of reconstructing the demographic structures of urban and semi-urban communities. They can now point to the perceptible changes in fertility and the increasingly widespread practice of *coitus interruptus* as the most probable means of limiting the size of families. Associated with these inquiries into contraceptive practices is the question of illegitimacy. In the future insurgent areas where the rate of illegitimacy was very low,[71] can any

[68] See John McManners, *French Ecclesiastical Society under the Ancien Regime. A Study of Angers in the Eighteenth Century* (Manchester, 1960), p. 272. In her study of priests leaving the church, Sister M.-L. Fracart draws our attention to the marriage of priests even before they renounced the ecclesiastical state and notes that this did not shock certain areas of Deux-Sèvres where protestanism had taken strong root before the Revocation of the Edict of Nantes. See her article, "Les déprêtisations dans le département des Deux-Sèvres", *Actes du 89 Congrès national des sociétés savantes, Lyon 1964*. (Section d'histoire moderne et contemporaine, i; Paris, 1964), pp. 183-205.
[69] Bernard Plongeron, "Regards sur l'historiographie religieuse de la Révolution", part ii, "La déchristianisation", *Annales historiques de la Révolution française*, xxxviii (1968), p. 156.
[70] See the figures cited in H. Maisonneuve, "Recherches sur la sociologie religieuse de la Vendée", *Mélanges de Science religieuse*, 11th year (1954), p. 103. For a fuller study, see Paul Longuet, "Une source pour l'étude de l'activité sacerdotale des prêtres réfractaires dans le Calvados: Les actes des baptêmes et des mariages clandestins", *Annales historiques de la Révolution française*, xl (1970), pp. 329-45.
[71] On the low proportion of illegitimate births in Brittany and Anjou (from 1740 to 1789 it averaged 0·824%), see Yves Blayo and Louis Henry, "Données démographiques sur la Bretagne et l'Anjou de 1740 à 1829", *Annales de démographie historique* (1967), p. 106. This figure is somewhat higher than in Languedoc where it was 0·5%: Emmanuel Le Roy Ladurie, *Les paysans du Languedoc*, 2 vols. (Paris, 1966), i, p. 644. It is Henry who makes the connection between premarital sex and illegitimacy in, "L'apport des témoinages et de la statistique", in Hélène Bergues (*et al.*), *La prévention des naissances dans la famille. Ses origines dans les temps modernes* (Paris, 1960), p. 386. J.-L. Flandrin questions whether the connection can be made so confidently. The assumption

connections between priestly injunctions and prevailing sexual morality be established? We do not know how local populations were instructed.[72] Nor do we know whether, if a greater openness in questions of sexual morality was beginning to be expressed — as may have been the case with the appearance in Normandy in 1782 of Père Féline's *Catéchisme des gens mariés* (even though it was almost immediately suppressed by the hierarchy) — such directness in fact responded to the practices of people who in any case may have thought *coitus interruptus* an offence against the fertility of the earth.[73] It is in the light of such questions that I would like to offer my concluding reflections.

What gave cohesiveness to the traditional rural communities were not only ties of an economic and social kind, but those of a sexual nature which were equally compelling if only because they energized the entire structure of authority and hierarchy. In such communities, sexual repression was unquestioned,[74] indeed reinforced both by religious sanctions and by the need to exclude alternative forms of sexuality that threatened to upset or challenge the maintenance of social stability. Any profoundly qualitative shift from the traditional methods, at both the conscious and unconscious levels, of dealing with sexual relationships could only be viewed as alarming, disturbing and destructive. Hostility to change in the social, economic and religious realms was underpinned by fears of greater sexual freedom which was

is that the illegitimacy rate was low because of the long period of sexual inhibition before marriage. Flandrin suggests that *coitus interruptus* was judged by the church and generally by the populace more severely within marriage than outside it, implying therefore that the practice was more common before marriage. Thus in his view low illegitimacy rates need not be connected with traditional sexual morality. Surely, however, this form of contraception in or outside marriage would have required enormous self-control to account for the low illegitimacy rates. See his article, "Contraception, mariage et relations amoureuses dans l'Occident chrétien", *Annales. E.S.C.*, xxiv (1969), pp. 1,370-90. For André Burguière's critique of Flandrin, see his article "De Malthus à Max Weber: le mariage tardif et l'esprit d'entreprise", *Annales. E.S.C.*, xxvii (1972), pp. 1,128-38. Among other things, Burguière asks, if men and women experimented with contraception before marriage, would they not continue to do so in marriage?

[72] Alfred Sauvy suggests that the examination of church archives may divulge whether or not the hierarchy gave precise instructions to confessors on contraceptive practices: see his "Essai d'une vue ensemble", in Bergues, *op. cit.*, p. 390.

[73] For this, see Ferdinand Lundberg and Marinya F. Farnham, *Modern Women, The Lost Sex* (New York, 1947), p. 253.

[74] Edward Shorter raises the question of sexual morality in the period before and after the spread of industrialism in his, "Illegitimacy, Sexual Revolution, and Social Change in Modern Europe", *Jl. of Interdisciplinary History*, ii (1972), pp. 237-64.

instinctively felt to be the consequence of innovation in the other, more obvious, more tangible, spheres of human activity. Hence such threatened communities moved even more closely in on themselves and sought out their priests, the figures of moral authority, to protect them through a reaffirmation of the sacral nature of their deepest and most intimate personal and social commitments.

What I am suggesting is that the violence in western France will remain elusive unless historians give more attention to these matters. There are clues scattered here and there. As yet they are far from possessing the full reality of concrete events. For example, if I may refer once again to Jansenism, it is known that at the moment of confession Jansenist priests set themselves against leniency and imposed burdensome and irksome forms of penance. Jansenist insistence on the connections between sexuality, concupiscence and original sin was unrelentingly pursued in confession, as proved by Ligouri's campaign in the mid-eighteenth century to have confessors refrain from questioning their parishioners on deviation from prescribed sexual practices. "The hards were not all Jansenists, but all the Jansenists were hard".[75] In the *bocage*, however, the moral scrutiny of the priest was apparently not so crushing, if only because he could not be permanently present in areas of scattered settlement:

> He [the *curé*] could not maintain close control over what happened on the farms or in the distant hamlets, whereas in the bourg, or, elsewhere in France, in concentrated villages, his surveillance . . . has sometimes seemed tyrannical and has encouraged distrust and the beginnings of an anti-clericalism which had no *raison d'être* in the *bocage*.[76]

It would be tempting to conclude that, because of the lack of close control, departures from prevailing patterns of sexual morality were allowed greater scope. In fact this seems not to have been the case, if the illegitimacy rate is an accurate indicator of premarital sexual morality. In western France, as we have seen, the rate was low and its forms differed, it has been suggested, as between the *bocage* and open-field communities. In the former, young servant-girls were sexually exploited by their masters; in the latter, premarital intercourse took place among people of the same age.[77] What this could

---

[75] See John T. Noonan jr., *Contraception. A History of Its Treatment by the Catholic Theologians and Canonists* (Cambridge, Mass., 1965), p. 317. Since Ligouri's views did not command widespread acceptance until the next century, it is difficult to assess the extent of his influence in France during the second half of the eighteenth century. On the Jansenist penetration of Ireland, cf. K. H. Connell, *Irish Peasant Society. Four Historical Essays* (Oxford, 1968).

[76] Bois, *op. cit.*, p. 614.

[77] Pierre Chaunu, *La civilisation de l'Europe classique* (Paris, 1970), pp. 196-7.

mean is that in the *bocage* young people took fewer risks or rarely dreamt of taking any, and that conformity to prevailing sexual morality was sufficiently internalized to obviate the constant reinforcement of priestly intervention. In a sense, then, it is entirely conceivable that compliance with and loyalty to existing sexual mores was strongest among individuals who were not harassed by inquisitorial priests; that where confession was used so repressively it placed an intolerable burden on individuals who were already repressed, and who consequently found it difficult to live with the strain of rejecting the fantasies evoked thereby. If this is the case, confession may not always have insured against pre-nuptial pregnancy, but rather have produced the opposite result.[78]   Indeed, the sparing or limited use of the confessional for these purposes could have acted as a more effective deterrent against the freer expressions of sexuality.

The rôle of the *curé* in the *bocage* was distinctive at the levels of life we have previously examined but in the domain of intimate matters he seems not to have been an oppressive presence. He was trusted precisely because of his discretion. His displacement by new men, *les "intrus"*, who, it was feared, would not respect the more or less tacit agreement to desist from probing too deeply into sexual matters, surely contributed powerfully to peasant support for him. He was not the tyrannical or fanatical priest of revolutionary propaganda. Under the stress of violence he did become so. His easy tolerance in all matters was probably the reason for the community's attachment to him. That tolerance, as we have seen, also extended to the survival and acceptance of pre-Christian religious practices which flourished in close connection with the demands of a harsher Christian orthodoxy, neither one displacing the other, but rather nourishing and being nourished by each other. The peculiar complex of beliefs and practices that gave vitality to these isolated *bocage* communities provoked what seemed to outsiders an excessive and hysterical reaction. Within the mental framework of these communities on the other hand, the violent response was a reasonable barrier of defence against changes that imperilled their very existence.

The Revolution was seen by these rebellious peoples as a total attack upon the visible and invisible ties that gave their lives a sense of order and reality. Their commitment to the preservation of their

---

[78] Keith Thomas in his study of English society in an earlier period has wisely left the question of the nature of the relationship open. See his *Religion and the Decline of Magic. Studies in Popular Beliefs in Sixteenth and Seventeenth Century England* (London, 1971), p. 156.

society had been challenged before the Revolution.   They had had some foretaste of the world outside the confines of their collectivity as missionaries moved in to impose religious conformity, as medical men came in to offer strange and inappropriate remedies, as agents of the crown attempted to rationalize administrative procedures, as urban bourgeois began to buy up land in the countryside.   With the Revolution, not only was the new government obtrusive; its agents were multiplying.   They were everywhere, prying, questioning, recording; they were abrupt in manner; and above all, strange and different, invested with powers which could be used less intermittently and more efficiently on behalf of a world centred on the demands of predatory townspeople.   It was from the towns that the threat to established forms came.   It was from the towns that the new priests came, without, it was believed, the instinctive understanding or the easy tolerance which had shaped life for generations.   The new priests were, as were the new administrators, seen as the instruments of a powerful external authority, intent on disturbing and erasing the old patterns, on invading all aspects of life, including the most intimate.   The violent struggle to maintain the present meant keeping the external world out, and continuing to do what had always been done.   It also meant preserving the means of keeping to themselves those aspects of their lives which they always had been able to conceal.   For these people, the maintenance of community meant the need to keep secret those matters that ought to be kept secret. The Revolution was an assault on such a view and it was met by the violent acts of desperate men and women.

10. *The White Terror of 1815 in the Department of the Gard: Counter-Revolution, Continuity and the Individual*

GWYNN LEWIS

IT IS ONLY IN THE RELATIVELY RECENT PAST THAT THE SOCIAL AND economic approach to French Revolutionary studies, inherited from Albert Mathiez and Georges Lefebvre, has been employed to analyse the significance of counter-revolutionary movements. The work of Charles Tilly and Paul Bois on the counter-revolution in the west of France added a new, although still incomplete, dimension to the history of the Vendée.[1] The history of the counter-revolution in the south-east of France — the former provinces of Languedoc and Provence — remains largely unexplored, although there is every indication that the time when the term "counter-revolution" was practically synonymous with "the Vendée" has now ended.[2] If one accepts that the Revolution, even in its "heroic" phase, did not end in 1795 with the collapse of the *sans-culotte* movement in Paris and that those who fought ostensibly for "Church and King" are as worthy of the attention of historians as those who fought for Robespierre and the Republic (*sans-culottes* in Paris and catholic royalists in the Gard were, after all, often fighting the same 'bourgeois" enemy), then the importance of events in the south-east becomes clear. Certainly in the department of the Gard, as in many regions of the west of France, it was the impact of capitalism and urbanization, with all that this entailed for traditional modes of economic and social behaviour, that induced so many catholic royalists to oppose the Revolution.

It was to be in the department of the Gard that the most widespread

---

[1] Charles Tilly, *The Vendée* (Cambridge, Mass., 1964); Paul Bois, *Paysans de l'ouest* (Paris, 1960). [See also additional note, p. 313 below.]

[2] One of the best, and most recent, exceptions to the above statement is the work of J. N. Hood, "The Riots in Nimes in 1790 and the Origins of a Popular Counter-Revolutionary Movement" (Princeton University Ph.D. thesis, 1968). M. Agulhon, *La vie sociale en Provence au lendemain de la Révolution* (Paris, 1970) and R. C. Cobb, *Police and the People* (Oxford, 1970) both contain original and interesting observations on the counter-revolution in the south-east. M. Sonenscher and B. Fitzpatrick of the University of Warwick are preparing Ph.D. theses based on the same region.

and most violent manifestations of counter-revolutionary activity were to occur. The first "popular" counter-revolutionary movement in France, which culminated in a bloody collision between catholics and protestants in the city of Nimes, was based in the Gard. The successive *camps de Jalès*, undoubtedly the most significant conter-revolutionary threat before the outbreak of the Vendée, were organized in the neighbouring department of the Ardéche and were closely associated with events in the Gard. The White Terror of 1795 and the subsequent prolonged period of brigandage from 1796 to 1802, which affected the whole of the south-east, were again particularly severe in this department. Finally, the last link in this chain of bloodshed and violence, the White Terror of 1815, was forged in this same region of Lower Languedoc. It is hardly surprising that in 1820 the latest in a long line of despairing and bewildered prefects complained that he had been given "the most disgusting administrative position in the entire kingdom".

Why should the Revolution have provoked such prolonged and bitter discord in this region of France? It is possible that the influence of climate and temperament should be entered into any historical equation. However, the importance to be attached to such factors is difficult to estimate, while blood flowed as freely and almost as frequently in the west of France where neither climate nor character can convincingly be described as latin! Of far greater significance was the presence of a large protestant minority in the department: one-third of the total population was of the calvinist faith. It was in the city of Nimes (again, one-third of its forty thousand inhabitants was protestant) and in the *arrondissements* of Uzès and Alais to the north and west that the counter-revolution was to recruit its most faithful adherents. Centuries of conflict, mutual fear and hatred, dating back to the latter half of the sixteenth century when those of the calvinist faith first made their home in Nimes and the Cévennes mountains, continuing through the Wars of Religion, the Revocation of the Edict of Nantes by Louis XIV and the protracted *guerre des Camisards*[3] at the beginning of the eighteenth century, had produced deep divisions between the inhabitants of this region.[4]

The eighteenth century, for the vocal minority a century of reason

[3] For an account of the installation and consolidation of protestantism in two villages in the south-east see T. Sheppard, *Lourmarin in the Eighteenth Century* (Baltimore, 1971), and P. Higgonnet, *Pont de Montvert: Social Structure and Politics in a French Village* (Cambridge, Mass., 1971).

[4] J. N. Hood, "Protestant-Catholic Relations and the Roots of the First Popular Counter-Revolutionary Movement in France", *Jl. of Modern History*, xliii (1971).

and toleration, began and ended in the south-east with open warfare between the two religious communities. The *guerre des Camisards*, which originated in the inhospitable mountainous areas to the north of the Gard and which lasted, with decreasing severity, from 1702 to 1710, was primarily a reaction by the poorer members of the protestant community to the burnings, hangings and deportations which characterized Louis XIV's attempt to force catholicism down the reluctant throats of the calvinists. The reaction of the latter equalled in ferocity the repressive measures of the State. In the mythology of French protestantism the *guerre des Camisards* takes its place in the proud tradition of résistance to an intolerant catholic State; for the catholics it provides further evidence of protestant treachery and rebellion. Although it can be argued that the Enlightenment had reduced the temperature of the debate, one can, on the eve of the Revolution, still point to the existence of two fairly well-defined and mutually antagonistic communities. As purely confessional and theological difference became less evident so the political aspirations of the protestant community increased, evoking a corresponding fear from the largely catholic administration. The edict of Toleration in 1787 did little to improve the situation: indeed, it may have aggravated it.[5] It was to be the Revolution, however, which, by decentralizing the administration and relating wealth more closely to political power, was to offer the powerful protestant élite an opportunity of seizing control of the department.

The antagonism caused by differences of religious faith had been aggravated during the eighteenth century by economic factors. Although, both in the towns and the countryside, the majority of protestants suffered the privations and miseries associated with years of bad harvests and economic depression with their catholic neighbours, the real wealth of the department was concentrated in the hands of a small minority of protestant merchants, bankers and manufacturers. Protestant bankers helped to finance princes of the blood as well as the Monarchy itself;[6] protestant silk and textile merchants had established links with European, Near-Eastern and American countries.[7] In economic terms, protestantism was any-

[5] Hood, "The Riots in Nimes . . .", p. 158.

[6] G. Chaussinard-Nogaret, *Les Financiers de Languedoc au dix-huitième siècle* (Paris, 1970), pp. 12-18.

[7] Jean Méjean, complaining to the Minister of Justice about the treatment he received during the Terror of 1815, pointed out that he "was one of the most respected *négociants* in the whole of Languedoc"; he had "built up, in the town of Ganges, a commercial venture which involved trading with Spain, Russia and the two Americas": Archives Nationales (hereafter A.N.), BB. 18 327, 6 Feb. 1817.

thing but parochial.   Nimes was second only to Lyons in the manufacture and distribution of silk and ancillary textile goods.   The
small town of Beaucaire was the venue for one of the most famous
international trading fairs of the ancien régime.   The rearing of
silk-worms and the reeling of the raw material provided employment
for thousands of peasants, particularly in the mountainous regions
of the Cévennes and Gardonnenque.   The link between protestant
workers and protestant employers was strengthened in the eighteenth
century as the merchants (*négociants*) sought cheap labour outside
the towns and cities where guild restrictions were still in force.[8]
When, in 1790, thousands of protestant peasants marched down
from the hills around Nimes to support their urban brethren in the
struggle against catholic royalism they were bearing historic witness
not only to the existence of strong religious, but also economic, affil-
iations.   Sociological distinctions in the Gard on the eve of the
Revolution can be explained not by any crude application of the much-
quoted "town versus countryside" antagonism but by the religious
and economic life of its inhabitants.[9]

Although the protestants in the south-east had been integrating
themselves into civic and political life throughout the latter half of the
eighteenth century, the Revolution offered them unique possibilities
of exploiting their economic and social supremacy.   Political labels
were adopted to pursue a struggle for power which had been only too
evident in the decades immediately preceding the Revolution.   By
1790 the department was divided between catholic royalists represen-
ing clerical and landed interests, supported by small merchants and
traders, and protestant *patriotes* representing the more dynamic values
of a commercial and manufacturing élite.   The conflict between the
extremists of both factions led to the *bagarre* of Nimes in June of the
same year.   In the previous December the National Assembly had
decreed that new municipalities should replace the *ad hoc* assemblies
which had been organized at the beginning of the Revolution.   The
protestants were asked if they would accept one-third of the places
on the new council.   They refused, claiming that their wealth

[8] Replying in February 1779 to complaints from the guilds in Nimes of
preferential treatment for workers in the countryside, the merchants denied that
any wage differential was involved.   It was simply that workers in the countryside were "more sober and more careful in their labours": Archives du Gard
(hereafter A G.), IV E 23, *mémoire* to the Intendant of Languedoc.

[9] In 1815, in the town of Vauvert, a catholic woman was severely beaten by
her catholic neighbours "because she had, in her time, accepted work from the
protestants (fait le commerce des grenouilles)": A.G., M/6 167, mayor of
Vauvert to sub-prefect of Uzès

qualified them for at least half the seats. Disappointed in the municipal elections, the protestants began to form pressure-groups in order to secure a more favourable position in the departmental elections.[10] This struggle for political power, exacerbated so far as the catholics were concerned by the attack on the monasteries and church property in general, produced an extremely tense situation. The composition of the National Guard faithfully reflected the existence of two mutually hostile factions. Preparations for the departmental elections in June 1790 precipitated the violent conflict which was to have profound consequences for the subsequent history of the Revolution in the Gard.

For three days, the city of Nimes witnessed scenes of bloodshed and devastation which recalled the horrors of the Wars of Religion. After provocations by extremists amongst the catholic section of the National Guard, the protestant *légionnaires*, assisted in the latter stages by their co-religionists from the hills surrounding the city, indulged in a frenzy of killing and devastation which left more than three hundred catholic royalists dead and many more wounded.[11] The so-called *bagarre de Nimes* was to condition much of the character and intensity of the counter-revolution in the south-east. It enabled the leadership to isolate protestantism as its principal enemy, to exploit the traditional fear of the catholic majority.[12] Its immediate consequence was to give the protestants a controlling influence in the administrative and political life of the Gard. Although their fortunes fluctuated in the 1790s, particularly during the Terror when the craftsman and artisan section of the population pursued its own grievances against the wealthy merchant and manufacturer, the protestants succeeded in maintaining their supremacy throughout the period of the Directory and the Napoleonic Empire.

[10] Hood, "The Riots in Nimes...", p. 11.

[11] The catholic version of these events supports a figure of over a thousand killed: Dom Devic and Dom Vaissète, *Histoire général du Languedoc* (Toulouse, 1846), vol. x, p. 727. B. Poland, *French Protestantism and the French Revolution* (Princeton, 1957), p. 132 and Hood, *op. cit.*, p. 1, both agree on a figure of 300.

[12] The comte de Saillans, organizer of the *camp de Jalès* in the department of the Ardèche, stated in 1792: "We have noticed with what sheer audacity, with what diabolical cunning, the protestant sect in the Midi rules tyrannically... dominating the administrative posts they have usurped, controlling the armed forces and directing them towards the realization of its objective which is none other than the destruction of the catholic religion and the Monarchy": A.G., L, 416, "proclamation du comte de Saillans". Exploiting the memory of the *bagarre de Nimes*, Saillans exhorted the Catholic National Guards to "cast their eyes over the tragic accounts of the massacre of the king's faithful Guards perpetrated at Nimes against your own brothers... strangled, hacked to pieces, burnt alive, hung from hooks... their bodies left unburied for dogs to devour": *ibid.*, "déclaration aux Gardes nationales du camp de Jalès", 1972.

However, the Revolution, with its frequent shifts of political power, never permitted the deep wound inflicted by the *bagarre* to heal. From 1790 to 1793 the "protestant ascendancy" was challenged by various counter-revolutionary movements, the most significant being the *camp de Jalès* situated in the neighbouring department of the Ardèche. After the fall of Robespierre in 1794 marauding bands of catholic royalist brigands continued the struggle well into the reign of Napoleon, bringing the south-east at times to the verge of administrative anarchy.[13] The imposition of law and order which accompanied the advent of Napoleon Bonaparte, and particularly the religious settlement with the Papacy, in 1802, temporarily destroyed any expectation of catholic royalist revenge. It was Napoleon who reorganized the Protestant Church, granting to the *notables* the same control of religious life that they already enjoyed in the social and political sphere.[14] A contemporary observer of the White Terror in 1815, sympathetic to the protestant cause, was obliged to admit that: "Under Napoleon, the Protestants, by virtue of their wealth had acquired a powerful influence in the department . . . they made little effort to conceal the fact that they preferred members of their own faith".[15]

The return of the Bourbon Monarchy in 1814 produced no significant transfer of power in the Gard, a fact which exasperated many émigrés who had served "Church and King" faithfully throughout the difficult years of the Revolution. Louis XVIII, under pressure from the Allied Powers, was anxious not to disturb the uneasy calm which followed the collapse of the Napoleonic Empire; hence his refusal to indulge in widespread purges of administrative personnel. Nonetheless, the protestants were clearly apprehensive concerning the possibility of a return to the "bad old days" of the ancien régime. The theme of continuity is well illustrated in a letter dated 14 May 1814 in which the prefect of the Gard wrote: "There is considerable animosity in this department. It arises from the profound rivalry which exists between the two religious sects. The catholics are convinced that they have everything to gain; the protestants that they have lost everything . . .".[16] The fear on the part of the protestants was given more substance by the activities of extreme catholic royalists, or *ultraroyalists* as they were now known. Royalist groups had been organizing in the Gard

---

[13] Cobb., *Police and the People*, pp. 142-3.
[14] D. Robert, *Les Eglises Réformées en France* (Paris, 1961), pp. 112-16.
[15] L. de Péret, *Causes et précis des troubles dans le département du Gard en 1815 et 1816* (Paris, 1819).   [16] A.N., F⁷ 9049, to the Minister of Police.

long before the fall of Napoleon.   During the First Restoration, they
expanded their activities, provoking disturbances, threatening
revenge, seeking to overthrow "the settlement of 1790".   On 24 June
1814, the prefect informed the Minister of Police that "the *ultras* are
occupying their time in preparing a report on everything that
happened during the *bagarre* of 1790.   They hope to name every
living person involved, to omit nothing which might rekindle the
flames of past hatred".[17]   Their declared aim was "to remove the
protestants from every office and to revenge themselves, if only by
humiliation, for the wrongs which they atribute to this sect".[18]

Napoleon's brief and — for the protestants — disastrous return
from Elba in March 1815 gave the *ultras* an opportunity of exploiting
the resultant administrative and political chaos to their own advantage.
Many protestants, disturbed by the resurgence of extreme royalism
during the First Restoration, had been more than eager to place the
welcome-home notice for Napoleon in their windows.   The duc
d'Angoulême was given the unenviable task of rallying catholic royalist
support in the Midi against "the Usurper", but lacking the confidence
of the regular army, which remained attached to the memory of
Napoleon's great exploits, resistance proved to be brief and feeble.[19]
Thousands of catholic peasants, however, had answered the appeal of
the duc d'Angoulême.   Organized into volunteer battalions called
miquelets they were now forced to return to their homes defeated and
humiliated.   In one or two instances they were subjected to attacks
from protestant villagers, the worst incident taking place in Arpaillarques where four *miquelets* were despatched with pitchforks and
scythes.[20]   Towards the end of June 1815, the news of Napoleon's
defeat at Waterloo began to circulate in the Midi.   The rapid cycle
of revolution and reaction, so characteristic of the early years of the
Revolution, so potent a force in creating a desire for revenge, was to
contribute in no small measure to the severity of the White Terror
in the Gard.   In the small town of Beaucaire, situated on the river
Rhône, the *miquelets* regrouped; isolated detachments of Bonapartists

---

[17] *Ibid.*
[18] *Ibid.*, Latour Maubourg to the Minister of Police, 8 June 1814.
[19] H. Houssaye, *1815* (Paris, 1905), i, p. 419.·
[20] *Ibid.*, i, pp. 431-2.   Royalist accounts of the Arpaillarques affair state that
twenty *miquelets* were killed: A. de Beauchamp, *Histoire des campagnes de 1814
et 1815* (Paris, 1817), i, pp. 517-8.   It is, however, unusual that, although
statements appear to have been taken from most of the *miquelets* involved (see
A.G., M/6, "correspondence de la commissaire-général de la police", nos. 392,
397, 400, 407, 408 and 411), not one of them could give the names of any of their
companions who had been killed, apart from those of Fournier and Calvet.

troops were eventually forced to surrender. Just after four o'clock in the afternoon of 17 July 1815 the advance companies of *miquelets* entered Nimes. Their first action was to massacre a small detachment of about two hundred Bonapartist soldiers stranded in the *casernes* of Nimes.[21] The White Terror of 1815 had begun.

The Terror was to affect the whole of the South of France with varying degrees of intensity.[22] In every region, however, the reign of terror exercised by the *ultras* would have been impossible without the connivance of the authorities. The strength and influence of ultraroyalism completely paralysed the action of justice, not only in the summer months of 1815, but throughout the early years of the Bourbon Restoration.[23] From the focal point in Toulouse where the duc d'Angoulême continued to use the extraordinary powers vested in him during the Hundred Days and where a separate administration functioned under the guidance of the baron de Vitrolles and the marquis de Villeneuve, the influence of the *ultras* passed from the *commissaires extraordinaires* to prefects, sub-prefects, military commanders, mayors, municipal councillors and, in particular, the National Guard and the Judiciary.[24] So far as violence against property and persons was concerned, however, the Gard was to suffer far more severely than any other department.

It was by no means coincidental that, as in 1790, the worst excesses of the Terror were committed during the departmental elections which took place in August. On 19 August, the night before the elections, at least fifteen protestants were killed in Nimes, five of them hacked to death with sabres.[25] As a result of this violence only a minority of protestants qualified to vote dared to appear at the sessions of the electoral assembly, which resulted in the nomination of four

[21] When asked by the Minister of Police for details of the massacre, the *procureur du roi* in Nimes replied that he thought it would be unwise to throw too much light on the incident since it might provoke further trouble! A.N., BB3/154, 30 Aug. 1815 and A.G., M/6 168.

[22] See D. Resnick, *The White Terror and the Political Reaction after Waterloo* (Cambridge, Mass., 1966); E. Daudet, *La Terreur blanche*, 2nd edn. (Paris, 1906); Houssaye, *op. cit.*

[23] G. Lewis, "La Terreur blanche et l'application de la loi Decazes dans le département du Gard: 1815-1817", *Annales Historiques de la Révolution Française*, xxxvi (1964).

[24] Houssaye, *op. cit.*, iii, p. 551.

[25] A.G., M/6 337, no. 269. At the subsequent trial of two terrorists accused of these murders, the counsel defending the widow of one of their victims stated: "At ten o'clock in the evening of 19 August a number of men knocked on her door. Her husband got up, went to the door and was immediately dragged outside by men armed with sabres . . . this was the last time that she saw her husband": A.N., BB 18 Ic 19, dossier 422.

leading *ultras,* all implicated in the organization of the Terror.[26]   However, following the massacre of the Bonapartist troops on 17 July, assassinations, pillaging and the devastation of property had become a matter of daily routine in the Gard. On 1 August, twelve victims were accounted for, the majority shot on their own doorsteps.   In almost every case these killings were carried out by former *miquelets* dressed in the uniform of the National Guard.[27]   In the town of Uzès, on 4 August, twenty houses belonging to protestants were either partially or wholly destroyed and nine protestants killed, again by men dressed as National Guards.[28]   On the same day, the leading terrorist in Uzès, *Quatretaillons,* marched into the prison, dragged out six men and shot them in the public square under the eyes of the municipal authorities.[29]   Altogether, excluding the massacre of the troops and the killing of over sixty protestant peasants near the town of Ners by Austrian troops, about a hundred protestants were killed in the White Terror of 1815.   Thousands of protestants fled the department temporarily; hundreds more were imprisoned, in some instances for well over a year.[30]

[26] The four deputies elected to the *Chambre Introuvable* in Paris were the marquis de Calvières, temporary prefect of the Gard during part of the Terror, the duc de Bernis, one of the *commissaires extraordinaires* appointed by the duc d'Angoulême, Trinquelaque D'Uzès, one of the leading figures in the counter-revolution at the beginning of the Revolution, and the comte de Voqué, nominated *Inspecteur-général des Gardes Nationales* in the department.   In 1817, after the dismissal of the *ultra* prefect d'Arbaud Jouques, a close friend of the king's favourite the duc de Decazes was chosen to succeed him.   His first task was to prepare a report on the White Terror of 1815 in which, referring to the four deputies, he wrote: "I know more than enough about what happened [in 1815] to formulate the conviction that these excesses must be attributed not to the indifference but to the active will of these leaders": A.N., F⁷ 9051, Feb. 1817. This is confirmed by a report sent to the British Ambassador by a government agent, Colonel Ross, despatched to the Midi in 1815 to learn the precise situation: "the four ultraroyalist deputies are suspected of having precipitated and encouraged the whole business", Pub. Rec. Off., F/O 120, no. 234, 14 Dec. 1815.

[27] A.N., F⁷ 9657, *commissaire-général* to the Minister of Police, 14 Aug. 1815.

[28] A.G., M/6 22, sub-prefect of Uzès to the prefect, 21 Aug. 1815.

[29] In a report submitted to the government in 1817 it was stated that "more than four hundred houses in the city [of Nimes] and the surrounding countryside have been sacked or pillaged, more than twelve hundred people have either been attacked or maltreated, more than three hundred assassinated"; A.N., F⁷ 9054, 1 Mar. 1817.   A study of the relevant documents, A.G., M/6 337, reports of the *commissaire-général de la police,* A.N., F⁷ 9049, *procureur-général* to the Minister of Police, A.N., BB. 18 154, reports to the Minister of Justice etc., suggests that the figure of three hundred is too high, unless it includes the troops killed by the *miquelets* on 18 July.

[30] On 25 November 1815, Decazes's secret agent in the Gard, Eymard, reported that "since the troubles began the city (of Nimes) has lost 2,500 men, 1,500 silk-workers, 600 farm-workers or artisans and 400 persons belonging to the families of merchants and landowners": A.N., F⁷ 9049.

The theme of continuity is emphasized in the adoption of revolutionary institutions and terminology by the *ultras* in the pursuit of a counter-revolutionary programme. During the First Restoration in 1814, the mayor of Nimes pointed out that "*les séditieux* are organizing another Terror . . . the most odious forms of Jacobinism are borrowed, the most infamous songs and slogans which recall the time of the popular clubs".[31] There was, no doubt, a touch of macabre mockery in this calculated imitation, but it is clear that the *ultras* had learned to use the institutions of the Revolution to their own advantage. In 1790 it had been the protestant legions of the National Guard which had been primarily responsible for launching the *bagarre de Nimes*; in 1815 it was to be the catholics who exploited the Guard for their own purposes.[32] The victims of the White Terror in 1815 alleged that there was "a kind of Revolutionary Tribunal which passes sentences and executes them".[33] On 1 August, certain detachments of the National Guard "had formed a plan to invade the prisons and massacre all the detainees".[34]

This conscious attempt to exploit the past in order to create an atmosphere of terror and fear was taken a stage further. Protestants were subjected to threats of "a new Saint Bartholomew".[35] It was on the eve of the anniversary of the massacre of Saint Bartholomew that a detachment of royalist *chasseurs* was sent to the Gardonnenque provoking panic measures of self-defence on the part of hundreds of protestant peasants for whom the memory of the *dragonnades* of the eighteenth century was all too recent. On 24 August, a battalion of Austrian troops was moved into the region to quell the "rebellion". After a brief encounter the Austrians retired, leaving over sixty dead on the battlefield. They took several prisoners back to Nimes, three of whom were publicly shot before a crowd estimated at about thirty thousand.[36] One of the most revealing consequences of the Terror from the standpoint of the collective memory of the protestant community was the "conversion" of scores of protestants, generally

[31] A.N., F⁷ 9049, to the Minister of Police, 7 Oct. 1814.
[32] When the central government eventually felt strong enough to disband the National Gard in the department, the prefect wrote: "They may not know it in Paris, but everyone in the Gard is fully aware that the killing, pillaging and devastation committed in Nimes and the surrounding countryside in 1815 was almost exclusively the work of individuals wearing the uniform of the National Gard": A.N., F⁷ 9051, 24 Aug. 1818 to the Minister of Police.
[33] A.N., F⁷ 9049, anonymous letter to the Minister of Police, 12 Aug. 1815.
[34] A.G., M/6 337, no. 160, reports to the Minister of Police.
[35] A.G., M/6 337, no. 160, *commissaire-général* to the Minister of Police, 2 Aug. 1815.
[36] *Ibid.*, no. 268, also *Arch. des Affaires Etrangères, Mémoires et Documents*, supplement 691, no. 263, report of the comte de Stahremberg.

from the poorer sections of the population, to the catholic faith.   On 30 December 1815, a protestant pastor in Nimes wrote to a friend: "I have seen, on several occasions, dozens of these unfortunate people going to mass where they rebaptize them as if they were Jews or pagans . . .".[37]   Clearly the tradition of over a century of intolerance and persecution weighed more heavily upon the minds of many ordinary protestants than the philosophizing of the Enlightenment and the Revolution.

Again, as in 1790, the catholic royalists who composed the rank and file of the terrorists were drawn from the poorest section of the population.   During the First Restoration, army commanders had observed that practically all the rioters who had provoked the authorities and frightened the protestant community were either agricultural labourers or unemployed artisans:[38] one observer described them as "the vilest members of the populace".[39]   During the summer of 1815, the high percentage of unemployment made it easier to recruit catholic workers, either for the National Guard or for the irregular companies led by *Trestaillons* in Nimes and *Quatretaillons* in Uzès.[40] As James Hood has pointed out in his analysis of the *bagarre de Nimes* in 1790, the working class, particularly in times of crisis, could be divided along socio-religious lines, their primary allegiance being to their employers upon whom they depended, either for work or for charity, during a period of economic recession.[41]   This was no less true in 1815.   The economy of the Gard was divided between wealthy protestant manufacturers and traders, employing, mainly but not exclusively, people of their own faith in Nimes and in the Cévennes, and

an infinity of commercial traders of the second rank, much inferior to the former by their fortune, but equally noteworthy for their industry and activity: these are the Catholics.   Each of these classes has under its direction and, to all intents and purposes, under its orders, a great number of

[37] A.G., M/6 333, "listes des Protestantes qui ont fait abjuration pour entrer dans l'église catholique": Archives consistoriales de Nimes, B 53[24], letters of Oliver Desmons.

[38] A.N., F[7] 9049, *chef de l'état-major* to the Minister of Police, 10 Aug. 1814: "We have yet to discover one important figure participating in these demonstrations.   The crowds are exclusively composed of *la classe ouvrière*, many of whom are women".

[39] *Notes intended as Material for a Memoir on the Affairs of the Protestants of the Department of the Gard* (London, 1816), p. 10.

[40] A detailed study of textile production figures for the Gard from 1812-20 makes it clear that certain leading sectors of the economy in the Gard were virtually at a standstill after the spring of 1815; see "Etat de statistiques des fabriques et manufactures", A.N., F[11] 1575.

[41] Hood, "The Riots in Nimes . . .", p. 117-26.

workers, each one protected and assisted by his *co-religionaires*. This results in an identification of interests and principles between the protestants and the catholics.[42]

The two leading terrorists in the Gard, responsible for the great majority of crimes committed in 1815, were both agricultural workers. Jacques Dupont, known to his accomplices and victims alike as *Trestaillons* (supposedly after his practice of cutting his victims into three pieces), was a *travailleur de terre* "completely uneducated and without any means of subsistence". It was alleged that the personal motivation behind his terrorist activities was the fact that "his father had been killed by Protestants during the *bagarre de Nimes* along with nine hundred other catholics".[43] It is interesting that Vidocq, the arch-criminal who became one of the founders of the *Sûreté nationale*, wrote in his colourful memoirs that *Trestaillons* was the last of the *chauffeurs*, the brigands of the ancien régime who occasionally laid out their victims on burning beds of straw.[44] At least one of the victims of the White Terror in 1815 was burned alive.[45] In Uzès, *Trestaillons's* crimes were duplicated by Jacques Graffand (in honour of his mentor he called himself *Quatretaillons!*). Graffand had also risen from the ranks of the unemployed. His devotion to the royalist cause provoked him into one last desperate gamble on behalf of the Bourbons when, after the July Revolution of 1830, he led an abortive counter-revolution in the Gard on behalf of Charles X.[46]

It is not, however, with the White Terror of 1815 itself that we are principally concerned but with the continuity of counter-revolution and the socio-economic and religious antagonisms which provided catholic royalism with such widespread support. A study of the case-histories of some of the victors and victims of "1815" enables us to probe more deeply into the essential nature of the struggle in the Gard.

[42] C. Durand, *Marseilles, Nimes et ses environs* (Paris, 1818), part III, p. 57. This is precisely the point made in 1790 by its leading counter-revolutionary figure in the Gard, François Froment: "At Nimes, the protestants . . . have formed a secret organization to force catholic merchants out of business. They have succeeded so well that catholics can never expand their commercial activities beyond a certain stage": A.G., Fonds légals, F. Froment, "Charles Sincère à Pierre Romain", pp. 3-4.

[43] A.N., F⁷ 9657, prefect to Decazes, 25 Sept. 1816.

[44] F. E. Vidocq, *Mémoires* (London, 1829), iv, p. 256: "the last exploits [of the *chauffeurs*] had for their theatre the South of France, principally the environs of Nimes, Marseilles and Montpellier during the dictatorship of Monsieur Trestaillons".

[45] D'Arbaud Jouques (prefect of the Gard during the Terror), *Troubles et agitations du département du Gard en 1815 et sa réfutation* (Paris, 1818), pp. 97-8.

[46] A.G., M/6 273, *commandant de la gendarmerie du Gard* to prefect, 30 Dec. 1830.

The outstanding figure in the history of catholic royalism in the south-east of France is François Froment of Nimes. For over twenty-five years, whether as the organizer of royalist movements in the Gard at the beginning of the Revolution, or as an émigré in the service of Louis XVIII for whom he carried out missions in Spain, Russia and England, Froment personifies both the continuity and the links which united the Church with rural society in the Gard. In 1775, his father, Pierre Froment had been appointed *greffier* of the municipality of Nimes; François acted as his deputy. Their responsibilities included the apportionment of taxation levied on the landed and the commercial interests in the region of Nimes. The latter faction, led by wealthy protestant merchants, many of whom were suffering from the trade slump of the late 1770s,[47] accused the Froments of favouring the landed interests at their expense. After a protracted and bitter struggle Pierre Froment was finally forced to leave the department in 1784, accused, by the protestants, of various acts of financial mismanagement. His son never forgot the disgrace heaped upon his family, sympathizing entirely with the anonymous catholic author who wrote in May 1785 that the aim of the protestants "has been and still is to place people of their own religion at the head of the city".[48] Thus the struggle for power in the Gard, which forms such a constant theme throughout the Revolution, was first formulated under the ancien régime.

Emphasizing the close relationship between clerical and landed interests at the end of the eighteenth century, François Froment was appointed *receveur des revenus du clergé* for the rich cathedral chapter of Nimes: the family were even offered accommodation in the bishop's palace. It was a disagreement over the occupation of the bishop's palace by the protestants which was to be the immediate cause of the *bagarre de Nimes* in 1790. Motivated by the unfortunate events of 1784 and his personal interest as a receiver of clerical dues, Froment not unnaturally opposed the Revolution from the outset. In November 1789, he helped to organize a meeting of catholic nobility in Toulouse, subsequently joining the official ranks of the counter-revolution by becoming an agent of the comte d'Artois, based quite

---

[47] The closure of the Spanish and colonial markets due to the protectionist policies introduced by the Spanish court proved to be a severe blow to the stocking and hat-making industries in the Gard. In February 1790 the guild of stocking-makers informed the government that it could not pay the interest due on its capital debts, "owing to the complete inactivity in which the stocking industry finds itself since the prohibitive edicts passed by the Court of Spain": A.G., sous-série IV E, *corporation d'Arts et métiers, mémoire* to Necker, 21 Feb. 1780.

[48] Hood, "The Riots in Nimes . . .", p. 147.

conveniently at Turin.[49]   In Nimes, it was Froment who openly challenged the threatened domination of the department by the protestants.   In a series of inflammatory pamphlets and petitions he succeeded in raising the temperature of the political debate in the Gard, contributing in no small degree to the tragic events of June 1790.[50]   Defeated as his father had been before him, but at infinitely greater cost, Froment managed to escape the massacre of his fellow catholics and begin a career which was to span the entire period of the Revolution and Napoleonic Empire, culminating in the White Terror of 1815.[51]

A police report for 1797 informs us that "everything which happens in the Midi can be traced back to the original source of the trouble: M. Froment of Nimes . . . a man of great energy, flexible, artful, audacious, a man capable of conceiving and implementing a plan".[52] Froment remained in the service of Louis XVIII throughout the Napoleonic period, returning to France with the Bourbons in 1814. In July of the same year, the inhabitants of Jalès — the foyer of counter-revolution in the Midi from 1790 to 1793 — sent a deputation to pay their respects to Louis XVIII.   One of their first actions was to contact Froment and ask him to join them.

> Since the *camp de Jalès* had only been organized to assist the catholic royalists I had commanded [during the *bagarre de Nimes* of 1790], I greeted this proposition gladly [Froment wrote in his memoirs] but, convinced at the time *that the Revolution was not over* [underlined in the original] . . . I invited the deputation to ask everyone whom they knew in Paris to join us and decided upon M. le comte de Vogüé to address the meeting.

The comte de Vogüé was subsequently to be chosen as *Inspecteur-général* of the National Guards and elected as a deputy to the *Chambre Introuvable* in 1815.   It was Froment who laid down the blueprint for the White Terror of 1815; "a general surveillance of all the enemies of the State and the King; the National Guard

[49] See the manuscript copy of Froment's memoirs, compiled in 1815 at Bordeaux, which is deposited in the departmental archives at Nimes, "Recueil des écrits relatifs à la Révolution Française".   Unfortunately the pages are not numbered.

[50] "Charles Sincère à Pierre Romain"; "Déclaration et pétition des catholiques de Nimes", A.G., L. 1975.   In the former pamphlet, Froment suggests that the Edict of Toleration of 1787 "only attracted to France the scum of foreign protestants" (p. 12).   Despite the experience of the Revocation of the Edict of Nantes, Froment was quite convinced that the forced emigration of protestants "far from being detrimental, would be extremely advantageous to the State" (p. 18).

[51] Writing in 1815 and referring to his feelings before the *bagarre* of 1790, Froment stated: "Then as now, I was convinced of this truth — that one cannot defeat a strong passion, but by an even stronger one and that religious zeal alone could stifle the desire for republicanism": "Recueil des écrits . . .".

[52] A.N., F⁷ 6260, dossier 5183.

commanded by its sympathizers; and a *levée en masse* prepared secretly and ready to act upon the orders of royalist secret societies".[53]

The thread of continuity which links the career of a man like Froment to the events of 1815 can be duplicated in the case of Charles Trinquelaque. The history of the Trinquelaque family also illustrates the clash between the landed and the commercial interests in the Gard at the end of the eighteenth century. Like the Froment family in Nimes, the Trinquelaque's associated themselves in the Uzès region with the attack on protestantism and the industrial values associated with it. Also like the Froment's, the family was to suffer personally as a result of the Revolution, emphasizing the conjuncture of career interests and certain socio-economic attitudes which, independent of pressures exerted by the polarization of the two religious communities in the Gard, helps to explain the political options chosen by individuals in a revolutionary situation.

Trinquelaque *père* held the position of *syndic* for the *Assiette du diocèse d'Uzès*, the body responsible under the ancien régime for the collection of taxes and the distribution of funds in the Uzès region. In 1782, Trinquelaque's son was appointed to his father's place.[54] The impact of the early industrial revolution in the north-west of the department, a region of textile-workers, small-owners, share-croppers, charcoal and lime-burners, was to provoke several pre-revolutionary disturbances. Froment, in his propaganda pamphlets, constantly refers to the exploitation by protestant merchants of the rural population in the Gard. They are accused of forcing producers of raw silk to sell at ridiculously low prices; they buy large quantities of grain at harvest time, sell a little at low prices on the open market to force the small farmer to part with his surplus crop at equally low prices, then, a few months later, push the price up so that the small-

---

[53] "Recueil des écrits . . .". Froment's involvement in the preparation of the Terror in the Gard is substantiated, not only by his own admissions, but also by reports reaching the Ministry of Police. On 17 June 1814, the Minister was informed that "M. Froment, an émigré in the service of the comte d'Artois, and a lawyer named Boyer are, through their correspondence, responsible for the trouble in Nimes": A.N., F⁷ 9049. It is extremely interesting to note that, after the excesses of the White Terror in 1815, the Court disowned Froment. See "Recueil des écrits . . .", second note to the comte de Blacas (Louis XVIII's favourite), 7 Oct. 1815: "Do you deny that not only did you reject my plan (see (2) above) but that you also employed various agents and intriguers to divide and crush the royalist party that I have organized over twenty-five years, which by the purity of its principles and the exaltation of its zeal was able to activate royalism throughout the kingdom". Froment might well have echoed Wolsey's cry "Put not your trust in Princes!".

[54] E. Bardon, *L'exploitation du bassin houillier d'Alais* (Nimes, 1898), p. 255.

owners and share-croppers, who have now exhausted their reserves, are obliged to borrow money in order to purchase food, "thus reducing small farmers (*cultivateurs*) and workers (*ouvriers*) to a state of abject misery".[55] There is no question that this kind of speculation and exploitation did operate in the Gard: it was a most important factor in the outbreak of the *révolte des masques armées*, the serious peasant *jacquerie* which affected the Gard/Ardèche region in the winter of 1783.[56] It was to be in this same region that the counter-revolution was to recruit so many of its followers; place-names like Uzès, Bagnols, Barjac, and Laudun recur persistently as focal points of conflict from 1790 to 1815.

The Trinquelaque family had established themselves as the protectors and *patrons* of this deprived rural population. In 1779, Trinquelaque's son had denounced the activities of a Norman entrepreneur called Tubeuf who was endeavouring, against what appeared at times to be insurmountable odds, to concentrate the scores of small coal-mines which pock-marked this area of the Gard, destined to become one of the most productive coal-fields in France in the nineteenth century.[57] In April 1780, Trinquelaque, in a classic, almost *sans-culotte* expression of anti-industrial values, demanded that these mines be kept for individuals who only worked them in order to supplement their meagre earnings as farmers or rural artisans, adding that "these mines would be more productive if left to a number of small-owners than concentrated in the hands of a single individual".[58]

In the history of the counter-revolution in the Gard, Charles Trinquelaque occupies a position second only to that of François Froment of Nimes. It was Trinquelaque who organized the disturbances in the Uzès region in the spring of 1791, as a result of which several catholics lost their lives. The pattern of the disturbances bore a remarkable similarity to the events leading up to the *bagarre de Nimes*, although the consequences were far less tragic.[59] A denunciation of the *comité de surveillance d'Uzès* in 1794 describes him as "a scoundrel

[55] Froment, "Charles Sincère à Pierre Romain", pp. 7-8.
[56] J. Regné, *Les Prodromes de la Révolution dans l'Ardèche et le Gard* (Largentière, 1916).
[57] Bardon, *op. cit.*, p. 155.
[58] *Ibid.*, pp. 191-2.
[59] In an official report sent to the National Assembly it was pointed out "that the trouble in Nimes occurred at the same time as the administrative councils of the department were being formed. ... It is remarkable that the recent disturbances in Uzès and Saint Ambroix preceded by only a few days the electoral assembly convened to appoint a bishop for the department": A.G., L. 413, "precis historique des événements qui se sont passés dans les departements de l'Ardèche et du Gard dépuis février 1791 jusqu'au 28e du même mois".

who has done everything in his power to torment the *patriotes*".[60]
Having survived the Revolution, mainly in exile, Trinquelaque
returned to the Gard before the advent of Napoleon in order to
continue his legal career, eventually being appointed *conseilleur à la
Cour Impériale de Nimes.* By 1815, he was in a powerful position to
restore, not only the fortunes of catholic royalism, but those of his
own family and friends. Chosen as one of the four ultraroyalist
deputies to represent the Gard, Trinquelaque's ambition finally
secured him a position as an under-secretary in the Ministry of Justice
in Paris. His involvement in the actual events of the White Terror
in 1815 is well-documented. In an official report on the Terror
compiled in 1817 it was stated that Trinquelaque and a fellow émigré
named Baron, "are known to have fomented and encouraged the
assassinations and pillaging committed by the Catholic Royalists
during the months which followed 8 July 1815".[61]

Through the influence of men like Trinquelaque, the *ultras*
succeeded in placing men of their own conviction in key posts
throughout the department. Charles Vidal had filled the post of
procureur to the municipality of Nimes in 1790. A denunciation of
the *comité révolutionnaire de Nimes* in 1794 describes him as "one of
the leading figures behind the *bagarre* of 1790".[62] In 1815 Vidal
was given the post of *commissaire-général de la police* and it was under
the umbrella of impunity with which he covered the activities of
royalist terrorists that most of the crimes of the Terror were
committed.[63] Trinquelaque's friend Baron appears to have played
no major rôle in the events of 1790, although he also thought it
expedient to leave the Gard until after 1795. Baron held a similar
position as *conseilleur à la cour Impériale* under Napoleon. Towards
the end of the Empire, Baron decided to cement the religious, social
and professional bond which united him to Trinquelaque by marrying
off his daughter to the latter's son. During the First Restoration
Baron was kept busy organizing petitions to Louis XVIII requesting
the king to recall the Jesuits and restore "an Absolute and Catholic
Monarchy".[64] A member of the royalist society of Nimes, related to

[60] A.G., L. 1198, "opérations du comité révolutionnaire", I Prairial Year II.
[61] A.N., F⁷ 9051, Savagnes to Decazes, 18 Apr. 1817.
[62] A.G., L. 1198, "opérations du comité révolutionnaire de Nimes".
[63] In October 1815, the government sent General Lagarde to Nimes in order
to assist in the restoration of order, a mission which he carried out only too
energetically, until he was shot a few weeks later! Before the attempt on his
life he explained to the Minister of Police that "every time I receive information
from M. Vidal it is based upon the most absurd untruths". A.N., F⁷ 9049,
"renseignments sur M. Vidal".
[64] A.N., F⁷ 9049, prefect to the Minister of Police, 28 Feb. 1815.

the influential Trinquelaque family by marriage, Baron was in an excellent position to complement Vidal's work as *commissaire-général de la police*. The one important judicial official in the Gard who attempted to keep some semblance of justice alive during the Terror, Cavalier, informed the government in November 1815 that "Trinquelaque's son and M. Baron . . . are extremely angry with the government for keeping me in power". Apparently Trinquelaque wanted Cavalier's post of *procureur-général* for his own son! "You may judge" concluded Cavalier, "into what excesses the mania for high office can lead people in these parts".[65] In January 1816 Cavalier was indeed forced out of office.

The case of Alexis Lavondès, one of the intermediaries between the leading *ultras* and the catholic population, emphasizes one of the most significant trends in the social and economic history of the Gard — the depression of the independent craftsman and small merchant class by the wealthy protestant *négociants* and merchant-manufacturers (*marchand-fabricans*). The persistent attempt to eliminate craftsmen and the guilds which protected them can be traced throughout the last decades of the eighteenth century.[66] Froment had exploited the consequences of this development in 1790.[67] Henri Rivoire in his economic study of the Gard notes that the number of *marchand-fabriquans* and *maître-ouvriers* fell rapidly during the Napoleonic period.[68] Alexis Lavondès, à born agitator with a distinguished revolutionary pedigree, provides an individual example of the collapse

[65] A.N., BB[18] 327, to the Minister of Justice, 25 Nov. 1815.

[66] This development can be most clearly detected in the stocking industry. In the early eighteenth century the industry could be divided into three groups: *marchand faisant fabriquer*, the merchant who provided workers with the raw material and organized the sale and distribution of the finished products; *fabriquant*, actually engaged in the production of textile goods and working for himself; *ouvrier travaillant à façon*, skilled and unskilled workers who were completely dependent for their living on the merchants. Throughout the latter half of the century the first group were doing everything in their power to amalgamate the first and second groups and to deprive the third of any separate identity and privileges. According to the wealthy silk merchants, the creation of just two classes "bosses" and "workers" would mean that the craftsmen working for them "would show more interest in getting work and *une docilité* which is too often lacking. Once relieved of the fear of competition [between different craftsmen] they would pay more attention to their work, and would follow more precisely the instructions of the *fabriquans*". In pursuance of this policy of creating a textile proletariat the merchants endeavoured to abolish all apprentice schemes and qualifications for becoming a master craftsman. The latter saw their fate quite clearly: "All you seek to offer us is the humiliating and everlasting status of an ordinary worker". A.N., F[12] 780, letter of *marchand-fabriquants* to the Intendant, 28 Feb. 1783; *ibid.*, mémoire of *maître-ouvriers*, n.d.

[67] See p. 297, note 42.

[68] H. Rivoire, *Statisque du Gard* (Nimes, 1842), ii, p. 24.

of this social group.   In 1796, Lavondès was in business and secure
enough to challenge one of the wealthier protestants in the department
named Teste.[69]   In 1814, we find him in dire financial straights, in
the words of the prefect, "a mad, bankrupt merchant, exploiting
circumstances and the support he enjoys amongst *le peuple* to frighten
off his creditors".   Lavondès did indeed become one of the principal
recruiting-officers for the ultraroyalist cause in the Midi.[70]   Such
cases can be multiplied: that of Fajon, *marchand drapier*, a prominent
member of the royalist society of Nimes, "who has affected the most
exaggerated form of ultraroyalism in order to secure employment".[71]
In 1817, when the new prefect was attempting (with little success) to
win "moderates" away from the *ultra* secret societies in the department, he tried an appeal to their social pride by pointing out "that it
was rather dishonourable for them to be implicated with bankrupt
merchants".[72]

Through the activities and dedication of men like Froment,
Trinquelaque, Vidal and Baron, assisted by the comte de Vogué,
the marquis de Calvières and the duc de Bernis, all (with the
exception of Froment) local notables, often related by marriage, the
majority implicated in the struggle against protestantism before and
during the Revolution,[73] the *ultras* succeeded in wresting power from
the protestants and in maintaining that power throughout the
Restoration.   They could rely on the support of the poorer catholic
merchants and master-craftsmen, threatened with failure by the
economic success of the wealthy protestant élite and the economic
depression which occurred during the last years of the Napoleonic
Empire.[74]   This group in turn was instrumental in attracting popular
support for the counter-revolutionary programme.

[69] See p. 306.
[70] A.N., F⁷ 9049, to the Minister of Police, 17 June 1814.
[71] *Ibid.*, F⁷ 9051, 19 Dec. 1817.
[72] *Ibid.*
[73] The duc de Bernis was a wealthy landowner with property in the Lozère
and the Gard yielding a revenue of over 40,000 francs a year.   The marquis de
Calvières was born in Nimes; a former officer in the *régiment de Chartres*, he had
acquired part of his wealth by marrying de Bernis's sister, just as Baron had
benefited from his daughter's marriage to Trinquelaque's son. A.G. M/6
176, "registre de la statistique personelle de l'arrondissement de Nimes",
1812: the *provincialism* of the counter-revolution in the south-east is, in part,
to be explained by the fear of a separate protestant state in the Midi.   As Vidal
explained to the Minister of Police: the protestants in the Cévennes and
Gardonnenque "never cease plotting and only await a favourable opportunity
to re-introduce their federal system . . . they invoke the ghost of Napoleon
simply to cause trouble and thus seize the power they have just lost in Nimes and
throughout the department".   A.G., M/6 337, no. 372.
[74] See J. Vidalenc, "La vie économique des départements méditerranéens
pendant l'Empire", *Revue d'histoire moderne et contemporaine*, i (1954).

A study of the victims of the reaction in 1815 confirms the importance of *la longue durée* in analysing the true character of the counter-revolution in the south-east. Clearly one cannot ignore the *fact* of the Revolution, the politicization of the socio-economic and economic grievances nurtured by catholic royalists, in explaining why some protestants and not others found themselves the target of murder gangs in 1815: protestants like Jean Paris, commander of the protestant detachment of the National Guard which defended the bishop's palace during the *bagarre* of 1790;[75] Jean Bonijoli, a leading figure in the *comité révolutionnaire de Nimes* who only escaped death in 1815 by hiding with friends in the Cévennes (his mother and his aunt were disembowelled by six men, dressed, as always, as National Guardsmen);[76] and Alexander Fabre, "one of the most infamous revolutionaries in this department", who was imprisoned for almost eighteen months.[77] The desire for revenge in the Gard fitted very neatly into the general programme of political reaction pursued by the *ultras* in the south of France.[78]

However, the protestants marked down by the assassins (*égorgeurs*) of both the first White Terror of 1795 and the second Terror of 1815 had provoked the hatred of catholic royalists not simply as protestants, nor even as office-holders during the Terror or the Hundred Days, but as lawyers (*notaires*), landowners, merchants and purchasers of National Lands. More than ninety country-houses belonging to wealthy protestants were demolished during the first few weeks of the Terror.[79] Decazes's secret agent in the Midi emphasized that this destruction was by no means indiscriminate. The terrorists knew their men, "a list had been prepared in advance . . . it included the names of the richest Protestants".[80] In the case-histories of some of the victims of this attack we can glimpse something of the socio-economic conflicts which provide the essential backcloth to the Terror. We can understand more fully the mentality and motivation of the terrorists, trace the origins of private feuds within a single town or commune, in some cases, within the same household.

[75] A.N., F⁷ 9049, prefect to Decazes, 2 Aug. 1816; F. Froment, "Anniversaire du massacre des Catholiques de Nimes" (Nimes, 1791), p. 27.
[76] A.G., M/6 172, *commissaire-général de la police* to the *procureur du roi*, 20 Aug. 1815.
[77] A.N., F⁷ 9053, prefect to Decazes, 10 Aug. 1816. For more cases of this kind, see Lewis, "La Terreur blanche et l'application de la loi Decazes dans le Gard: 1815-1817".
[78] Resnick, *The White Terror*, p. 116.
[79] *Ibid.*, p. 51.
[80] A.N., F⁷ 9050, MSS. Eymard, "observations sur la situation présente de quatre contrées du Midi de la France".

The cases of Antoine Teste and Charles Dutour, two men hated by the majority of catholics in the town of Bagnols, provide good examples of this kind of antagonism.[81]   Antoine Teste represented, so far as the great majority of tenant farmers and share-croppers were concerned, everything they most hated — a protestant, a substantial landowner, a mine-owner, a *notaire* and a dedicated supporter of the Revolution. Little wonder that the ancien régime lawyer was a far more hated figure than the *seigneur*, possessing as he did a powerful combination of legal and financial expertise.   In the words of Teste's bitterest enemy: "We know him as an *avocat*, a *notaire*, always the plague of his clients, attracting the most evilly-disposed persons and the most unsavoury cases".   He had defended rapacious millers, made money by administering the wills of rich widows and (the worst crime of all!) had assumed responsibility for dealing with grain hoarding (*commissaire des accaparements*) during the Terror in which capacity "he had sold the goods and lands of émigrés at the price fixed by the Maximum to his henchmen, he had requisitioned carts and horses and forced non-juring priests into hiding",[82] an indictment of the successful ancien réigme *notable*, precisely the kind of man against whom the *masques armées* had vented their fury during the winter of 1783 in exactly the same region.   It is possible to appreciate from such cases how the Teste's of the Gard exploited the Revolution in order to consolidate their economic and social position.

Charles Dutour, "another crooked ancien régime *notaire*",[83] was a close associate of Antoine Teste.   He lived in the small commune of Laudun destined to be the scene of one of the most appalling crimes committed by the catholic royalist brigands of the Bagnols region.[84]

---

[81] Commenting on a collective denunciation of the two men by the inhabitants of St. Etienne des Forts in 1796, the *commissaire du Directoire exécutif* explained that "the motives [for the denunciation] are to be found in the hatred and personal animosity which exists between the commune and these two individuals . . . both men are loathed here": A.N., BB[18] 316, to the Minister of Justice, 24 Germinal Year IV.   Bagnols was almost exclusively catholic. Under the July Monarchy there were only twenty-three protestants living in the town out of a total population of 4,932.   Rivoire, *op. cit.*, pp. 437-45.

[82] A.N., BB[18] 316, *adjoint* of the mayor of Bagnols to représentant Poujols, Floréal Year IV.   Ode was recognized as one of the chief protectors and accomplices of the murder gangs operating in this region.   See *ibid.*, 317, "rapport sur les assassinations commis dans le département du Gard", n.d.

[83] *Ibid.*, BB[18] 316, *op. cit.*

[84] On the night of 15-16 Brumaire Year V, twelve members of a single household, including a child of two and a woman of seventy, were found in the same house, all with their throats cut.   The murder gang responsible was led by Dominique Allier, an ex-curé and close friend of François Froment.   See the report of the *accusateur public* to the Minister of Justice, A.N., BB[18] 318, 20 Brumaire Year V.

Both men had held important administrative or judicial posts during the Terror. It was alleged that Teste had been an accomplice of Courbis, the infamous mayor of Nimes during the Terror, and had carried out punitive missions to Beaucaire (like Bagnols a focal point of counter-revolutionary activity throughout our period). On one such mission Teste had dismissed the entire municipality and arrested thirty people "who were guillotined the same day in Nimes".[85] Dutour had served as an officer of the National Guard in 1790 and had also made many enemies during the Terror.[86] The legacy of bitterness left by the Terror, the personal animosities created, were masked to some extent during the first years of the Directory as the various factions fought out their battles in the electoral arena. In 1796, Dutour, accompanied by yet another *notaire* from the Bagnols region named Chambon, led a force of six hundred protestant National Guards (allegedly shouting "Vive Robespierre") on Bagnols in order to compel the royalist authorities to resign.[87] It was as a result of such activities (the habits of the Terror died hard) that catholic officials like Ode, the mayor's deputy in Bagnols, and Miellon, the *juge de paix* of Roquemaure and a personal enemy of Charles Dutour, eventually joined catholic royalist murder gangs (*égorgeurs du Midi*).[88]

The notairial trinity of Teste, Dutour and Chambon were made to pay dearly for their arrogance and — in the eyes of the catholics — their abuse of power. From 1795 to 1802 Teste was forced periodically to pack his bags and flee to Avignon, leaving his property to be ravaged by catholic royalist brigands.[89] Dutour's property was also the target for continual raids by these same gangs.[90] Joseph Chambon, who became mayor of Alais for a short period during the Napoleonic Empire, narrowly escaped with his life during the White Terror of 1815 when a crowd of catholics marched

[85] *Ibid.*, BB[18] 316, Ode to Poujols, *op. cit.*

[86] Dutour was imprisoned after Thermidor, but released by the *représentant en mission*, Fréron, and rewarded with the position of *commissaire provisoire* in the *tribunel correctionnel d'Uzès*: *ibid.*, Dutour to the Minister of Justice, I Frimaire Year V.

[87] *Ibid. juge de paix* of Bagnols, 15 Germinal Year IV.

[88] *Ibid.*, BB[18] 320, president of the municipal administration of Bagnols to the Minister of Finance, 6 Frimaire Year IV.

[89] On 10 Frimaire Year IV, Teste complained to the Minister of Justice that "catholic royalists, directed and encouraged by the *juge de paix* [Miellon] and accompanied by the Mayor of Bagnol's deputy [Ode] have pillaged my crops, devastated my property, uprooted my vines and those of my share-croppers": A.N., BB[18] 316.

[90] *Ibid.*, BB[18] 319, *commissaire du pouvoir exécutif de Beaucaire* to the Minister of Justice, 6 Floréal Year VI.

on his house "determined to kill father and son and burn down their property". The lives of the two men were only saved by the intervention of the *commissaire de police* who decided to keep the elder Chambon in prison for several months "for his own safety".[91]

Another protestant landowner and, prior to the Revolution, one of the most influential and wealthy industrialists in the department, was Jean Méjean, originally a silk-manufacturer from the town of Ganges.[92] He had retired early in the Revolution, but in order to keep himself active had purchased a small iron-ore mine. In 1791 he had taken advantage of the sale of National Lands and acquired the château and lands of the St. Julien estate, an acquisition which, in his own words, brought him nothing but trouble. Like Teste, he became one of the principal targets for the catholic royalist brigands during the Directory: in the winter of 1799, "six brigands, their faces blackened, entered the house and accused him of having bought National Lands". They killed one of his servants, destroyed part of the house and stole a considerable sum of money.[93] In 1815, his right to own the château he had bought in 1791 was still being contested. It was once again a catholic merchant, named Darvieux, acting on behalf of the original owner of the property, who exploited the Terror of 1815, forcing Méjean to leave the department. In a subsequent letter to the Minister of Justice, Méjean explained that Darvieux, "in order to please his *patronne* and serve his own interests, had affected an exaggerated form of *ultraroyalism*".[94] By 1817, as a result of twenty years of litigation, the destruction of his property and the economic circumstances of the late Napoleonic period, Méjean was forced into bankruptcy.[95]

The complexity of the political struggle in the Gard, the theme of personal animosity and revenge is well illustrated in the long conflict between François Boissier, a catholic, and Antoine Roux, a protestant, both living in the town of Vauvert. Before the Revolution, Boissier had been a *practicien*, dabbling in minor legal affairs. His family, however, had played a leading rôle in municipal affairs for decades. In 1797, Antoine Roux compiled a long dossier on the alleged crimes of his arch-enemy, noting that "if [Boissier] was not always successful in causing trouble in the countryside around Vauvert, he can hardly deny that he was the cause of several personal feuds".[96] It is clear

---

[91] *Ibid.*, BB[18] 327, *commandant d'armes* in Alais, 28 Mar. 1816.

[92] *Ibid.*, *affaire de M. Méjean*, 6 Feb. 1817.

[93] *Ibid.*, BB[18] 321, *commissaire du pouvoir exécutif* to the Minister of Justice, 2 Nivôse Year VII.

[94] *Ibid.*, BB[18] 327, Méjean to the Minister of Justice, 12 Apr. 1816: *ultraroyalism* underlined in the original.

[95] *Ibid.*, prefect of the Hérault to the Minister of Justice, Feb. 1817.

[96] *Ibid.*, BB[18] 318, "mémoire contre le citoyen F. Boissier", Germinal Year V.

that, in origin, it was the difference of religious faith and, more particularly, the struggle for power on a local level rather than conflicting social or political views which separated the two men. At each successive stage of the Revolution we find Roux and Boissier in open conflict. Before the Revolution, Roux had been responsible for the administration of the estates of Boissy d'Anglas, a prominent protestant *notable* and future deputy. In 1789, Boissier had been chosen as mayor of Vauvert and in that capacity had propagated some fairly radical solutions to the land problem in the Gard, "actively encouraging the local population [of Vauvert] to seize communal lands and even the lands of the monastery of Franquevaux" (a very different attitude from that of dedicated counter-revolutionaries like François Froment). He had also supplanted Roux as the administrator of part of d'Anglas's property, but (according to Roux) had been forced to resign as a result of his bad management and his refusal to pay his creditors.

By 1793 Roux had taken over from Boissier as mayor of Vauvert, while his old rival had become an extreme jacobin, "L'émule de Robespierre". It is obvious however that Roux himself had espoused the jacobin cause since it was the latter who was imprisoned after Thermidor, discovering (to his alleged astonishment) upon his release in 1795 that Boissier had left his jacobin phase behind him and was "now sporting very different colours", those of catholic royalism.[97] Clearly, in the case of men like Boissier, political labels were relatively unimportant. Until the Napoleonic period, whether on the "Left" or the "Right", as an extreme jacobin or an extreme catholic royalist, Boissier had concentrated his fire upon the big landowners and industrialists, the protestant establishment in the Gard.[98] It is necessary to distinguish between the dedicated counter-revolutionary like Froment or Trinquelaque, who were implicated in power politics on a national scale, and those, particularly amongst the poorer sections of the population, who exploited the Revolution in its early stages to be only disillusioned with its results, joining the ranks of the catholic royalists after 1795.[99]

[97] *Ibid.*
[98] *Ibid.*, "mémoire justificatif de F. Boissier", n.d.
[99] General Lagarde expressed part of the truth when he wrote to the government in December 1815: "There is widespread misunderstanding about the Midi: it is believed that the *bas peuple* are devoted royalists. In fact, this class is synonymous with the *sans-culottes* of the Revolution, only too eager to seize upon the slightest pretext for pillaging and assassination": A.N., F⁷ 9049, General Lagarde to the Minister of Police, 17 Dec. 1815. It was alleged that the terrorist who shot Lagarde in November 1815 had been "a faithful supporter of the Terror who had participated in the pillage of Lyons [after the insurrection of 1793]".

One of the most interesting and instructive cases in emphasizing the character and continuity of the counter-revolution in the Gard is the remarkable history of the protestant Lanteiris-Lazelle family, living near the town of Générac in the small commune of Chamborigaud. Their conflict with the catholic Labastide family dates back to the year 1770 when Victor André Lanteiris had been awarded damages of 30,000 francs by the parlement of Toulouse against the Labastides following a bitter quarrel over a will. Over thirty years later Lanteiris wrote that this legal victory "has made me the inveterate enemy of the present mayor [Labastide, a former noble]".[100] As "one of the wealthiest landowners in the commune",[101] Lanteiris was an elector, a former mayor and *administrateur du district d'Alais* during the Terror.[102] His nephew, Charles, had been imprisoned for about two years after Thermidor as a result of his revolutionary zeal.[103] In 1797, Victor Lanteiris informed the authorities that his wife, a catholic, had been trying to poison him for over seven months, first with emetics, then with chestnut soup and finally with adulterated wine! According to her estranged husband she had been led astray "by the fanatical and royalist party [Chamborigaud was almost entirely catholic in composition] aided and abetted by the refractory priest". Whether or not it was simply his wife's indifferent cooking which had induced Lanteiris's gastric problems, or more probably, village gossip at a time when mixed marriages were at a discount, the wife herself left home to find refuge with — of all people — his old enemy Labastide.[104] About five years later, after yet another quarrel over the disposition of property belonging to Lanteiris's estranged wife, the body of Labastide was found in the courtyard of his home: he had been savagely murdered.[105] Public opinion indicted Lanteiris and his nephew Charles, but, although arrested and brought to trial, they were found innocent of the crime. Nonetheless, probably to appease the anger of the catholic villagers (more than five hundred

[100] *Ibid.*, BB[18] 323, letter of Victor Lanteiris to the *Grande Juge*, 29 Germinal Year XI.

[101] *Ibid.*, *adjoint* of Chamborigaud to the Minister of Justice, n.d. See also the letter of Lanteiris's nephew to the prefect of the Gard, 17 Floréal Year XI, in which he described his uncle as "the highest tax-payer in the commune".

[102] *Ibid.*, BB[18] 316, Charles Lanteiris to the Council of 500, 16 Frimaire Year IV.

[103] *Ibid.*, Minister of Police to the Minister of Justice, 2 Germinal Year IV.

[104] *Ibid.*, "mémoire par le citoyen Victor Lanteiris", Prairial Year IV.

[105] In his defence Lanteiris claimed that the Labastide family had been persecuting him for years, this case being "the ultimate act of ill-will by a family whose hatred had brought about the ruin of my own": *ibid.*, Lanteiris to the *Grand Juge*, 29 Germinal Year XI.

of them turned out for Labastide's funeral) Lanteiris *père* was kept in prison for almost a year.[106]

"This hatred, the consequence of long-standing rivalry, sustained by differing political and religious views and exacerbated by recent events led almost inevitably to such acts of vengeance".[107] This comment by a judicial official in the Gard may be taken as a commentary on so many of the cases associated with the White Terror of 1815. The final act of the Lanteiris drama was to be played out at the height of the Terror when Charles Lanteiris was forced to evade the attentions of *Trestaillons* and his band and take refuge in the Cévennes hills. Eventually tracked down, Lanteiris was arrested and detained under the provisions of the *loi Decazes* in the catholic commune of St. Gilles, "living in the most miserable conditions, frequently with insufficient bread to eat".[108]

That the counter-revolutionary movement in the Gard should have manifested itself so early and sustained itself over such a long period is hardly surprising. It has become almost a cliché to claim that any given region in France is in some way unique or peculiar. However, when one considers the tradition of religious hatred and fear, the existence of two mutually suspicious, if not always overtly hostile, communities, the early but perceptible impact of the industrial revolution, then the Gard does indeed offer many distinctive features. Under the ancien régime, the catholics had been accustomed to consider their religion as a reasonably safe bastion against the encroachments of a wealthy protestant élite. The Revolution altered the situation quite dramatically by giving the latter the opportunity of seizing power. This struggle for office, which antedates the Revolution, is essential to an understanding of the counter-revolution in the Gard. The catholic church, landowners and smaller merchants, increasingly on the defensive as a result of political, intellectual and economic change, ultimately defeated in the *bagarre de Nimes*, sought to gain their revenge, initially, after Thermidor when "émigrés and returning deportees sought to control everything. Their relatives, friends, sympathisers, even assassins began to occupy every office".[109] Disappointed in their expectations, particularly after the *coup* of Fructidor Year V, catholic royalists resorted to "political brigandage" in an attempt to destroy the

[106] *Ibid., commissaire du tribunel criminel du Gard*, n.d.
[107] *Ibid.*
[108] A.G., M/6 173a, sub-prefect of Alais to the prefect of the Gard, 23 July 1816.
[109] A.N., BB[18] 316, "dénonciation de 200 patriotes du Midi", 25 Frimaire Year IV.

administrative life of the department, a task they accomplished with a remarkable degree of success until thwarted, yet again, by the advent of Napoleon Bonaparte.   As we have seen, these same royalists, "their relatives, friends and sympathisers" began during the First Restoration of 1814 to implement a programme of reaction whose origins can be traced back to the counter-revolutionary movements of 1789-92.   In an electoral régime, with the wealthy protestants holding most of the ballot-slips, it was only through Terror that the catholics could regain control of the department.

Clearly economic distress helped to create the necessary climate in which historic loyalties could be exploited by leaders like Froment. We need hardly be reminded of the destructive force of religious hatred and bigotry, exploiting genuine social and economic grievances, in our own age.   In a pre-industrial society in which personal and religious bonds between landowner and day-labourer, merchant and textile worker, were much closer it is not difficult to appreciate the part played by religion in helping polarize political opinions in the Gard.[110] There was very little evidence of working-class solidarity between catholic and protestant workers in 1790 or in 1815.   The atomization of the labour-force, scattered throughout the department, made it so much easier for employers to exercise influence and control over their employees.   If we look at the labour-force employed by seventeen of the richest silk and cotton manufacturers in the Gard towards the end of the Napoleonic period, we find that of 2,262 workers employed only 242 were engaged in workshops.[111]   It was, therefore, socio-religious, not class, antagonisms which explain the widespread degree of popular support which the counter-revolution enjoyed in the Gard.

The events of 1815, however, must also be analysed within the context of historic and traditional rivalries, of the jealousy which existed between towns with ancient traditions like Uzès, Beaucaire and Nimes, of the personal and collective feuds which existed between two communes, occasionally in terms of the human drama played out within the same family.   Every régime of terror provides peculiar opportunities for private vengeance, the settling of old scores: the White Terror of 1815 was no exception to this historic rule.   We are also dealing with a rather brutal society.   The Revolution has inured people to the sight and smell of blood: the Rhône competes with the Loire as the river most favoured by terrorists for the disposal of human evidence.[112]

[110] Rivoire, *Statistique du Gard*, ii, p. 24, makes the point that the structure of industry did not undergo any important technological change until after 1816, and the introduction of the Jacquard loom.
[111] A.N., F¹² 937, prefect to the Minister of the Interior, 6 Sept. 1810.
[112] Cobb, *Police and the People*, pp. 131-50.

The severity and duration of the struggle in the Gard also explains, in contrast to what occurred in the neighbouring department of the Var where the White Terrorists of 1815 were gradually transformed into the Red Terrorists of 1848,[113] "the intensity of confessional differences which, under the Third Republic, even submerged economic factors". As late as 1877, protestant cantons to the west of Nimes were the only ones to vote Republican by large majorities; catholic cantons voted, almost to a man, for the royalist candidates.[114] If the causes of the White Terror of 1815 must be sought long before the Revolution of 1789, the consequences of this prolonged struggle for power profoundly affected the history of the Gard, and indeed the history of protestantism in France, throughout the nineteenth century.

ADDITION TO NOTE I, 1976

For an evaluation of these works see H. Mitchell, "The Vendée and the counter-revolution: a review essay", *French Historical Studies*, v (1967-9). For more recent research on the impact of the Revolution on western France see T. J. A. Le Goff and D. M. G. Sutherland, "The Revolution and the Rural Community in Eighteenth-Century Brittany", reprinted as chapter 2 of this volume, and H. Mitchell, "Resistance to the Revolution in Western France", reprinted as chapter 9 above.

[113] M. Agulhon, *La République au village* (Paris, 1970), pp. 17-18.
[114] S. Schram, *Protestantism and Politics in France* (Alençon, 1954), pp. 67-8.

Index

Académie Française, 54, 57, 58, 59, 61, 63, 71, 73, 85
Acigné, 48
Aisne, 137
Aix, 106
Alais, 307, 310
Albigeois, 24
Ambon, 33
Amiens, 94
Angers, 94, 154, 281
Anjou, 265, 279, 280, 281
Annales: Économies, Sociétés, Civilisations, 1
Anquetil, Nicolas, 207, 214
Aquinas, 152
Arcis, 173, 188, 189, 215
Ardèche, 287, 301
Ardennes, 139
Aretino, 77
Argentré, 49
Ariès, Philippe, 145
Arles, 109
Armentières, 188
army, the, 2n, 17–18, 19, 27, 107–8, 119–20, 127n., 223, 231–3, 245, 246–7, 250, 261, 293, 294
Arnaud, abbé, 55, 56, 62
Arras, 91, 194
Assembly, Constituent, 42–4, 124, 134, 135, 169, 175, 178, 216, 218, 251, 252
Assembly, Legislative, 47, 158, 219
Assembly, National, 91, 121, 128, 289
assignats, 135, 141, 157, 261, 270
Athis, curé d', 151
Aubert, 58
Audouin, 75
Aulard, Alphonse, 21 and n., 22, 165
Aunis, 133
Austria, 158, 294, 295
Auvergne, 220, 232, 233
Avignon, 307

Babeuf, 130
Bagnols, 301, 306, 307
Bailly, Sylvain, 175, 203
Balin, Charles, 190, 191
Balzac, 62, 76

Bardon, 236
Barère, 100
Barjac, 301
Baron, 302, 303, 304
Baron, Nicolas, 194
Barsac, 235
Bartholomew, Saint (massacre), 295
Basses-Alpes, 231
Bayeux, 91, 152, 154, 157, 162, 163
Bayreuth, margrave of, 57
Beaucaire, 289, 292, 307, 312
Beaumarchais, 65
Beauménil, Mme., 75
Beauvais, Beauvaisis, 22, 90
Beauvau, prince de, 56, 58
Beauvau, princesse de, 56
Bédée, 36
Belle-Ile, 256
Bergerac, 158
Bernardin de St. Pierre, 58
Bernis, Cardinal de, 6
Bernis, duc de, 304
Berry, 126
Besançon, 157, 158, 163, 232
Betton, 35, 39
bishops, 14–15
Bistac, 209, 211
Blanchard, Henry, 223
Blandin, Pierre-Henri, 186–7, 188, 189, 197, 213
Blin de Sainmore, 58
Blois, Ordinance of, 94
Bocquéaux, Louis, 215
Boileau, 103
Bois, Paul, 41, 286
Boisgelin, archbishop, 62
Boissier, François, 308, 309
Boissy d'Anglas, 309
Bon-Conseil, 179, 192, 212
Bondy, 173
Bonenfant, Claude-Louis, 206, 207
Bonijoli, Jean, 305
Bonnecombe, 156
Bordeaux, 91, 106, 121, 133, 138; parlement of, 16; 1780 arrêt of, 17; condition of the poor in, chapter 8 *passim*
Bort (near Clermont), 151

Bosquet, Jean, 210
Botot, François-Marie, 180
Bouchotte, 191
Boucry de Saint-Venant, 215, 216
Bouin, Mathurin, 173, 174, 190, 191,
    192, 214
Boulainvilliers, 3, 11
Boulainvilliers, marché de, 200, 201
Boulanger, Dennis, 206, 207
Bouloiseau, Marc, 143
Bourdon, Léonard, 213
Bourg-des-Comptes, 35
Bourgogne, duc de, 10
Bouyoux, Pierre, 138
Boyer-Fonfrède, 243
Bréal, 49
Brienne, 6, 13
Brières, 252
Brissot, 70, 71, 83, 84, 85
Brittany, 25, chapter 2 passim; 127,
    134, 139, 150, 196, 197, 198, 228,
    232, 257, 281
Broglie, duc de, 144, 145
Brune, General, 221
Bruz, 39
Buffon, 55, 64
Buquet, Jean-Antoine, 180
Burgundy, 24, 120, 123, 139; northern,
    134

Cadoudal, Georges, 40
Caen, 162
cahiers de doléances, 21 and n., 25–6,
    43, 252, 258
Cailhava, 55, 58
Calonne, 58, 66, 81, 126
Calvados, 165
Calvières, marquis de, 304
Camisards, 287, 288
Cantal, 232
Caraccioli, 59
Carcassonne, 146
Carra, 60, 67, 70, 77, 81, 84
Castelnau, 241
Castries, 6
Cavalier, 303
Cévennes, the, 287, 289, 296, 305,
    311
Ceyrat, Joachim, 173, 175, 193
Chaise Dieu, 154
Chalons, 157, 158
Chambon, 203

Chambon (notaire), 307, 308
Chamborigaud, 310
Chambre introuvable, 299
Chamfort, 55, 58, 62, 85
Champcenetz, 67
Champ de Mars, 175
Champs-Elysées (section), 193–4
Chapelain, 265, 266
Charente, 235
Charente Inférieure, 235
Charles X, 297
Charpentier, Jean-François, 192
Chassagnole, Jacques-Philippe, 210
Chastellux, marquis de, 56, 62
Chateaubriand, 134
Châteaudun, 90
Châtelet, 180, 184, 195, 206, 207,
    214
Chaudron-Rousseau, 231
Chaulnes, duc de, 94
Chauvin, Pierre, 187, 188, 189, 213
Chénier, 75
Chépy, Nicolas, 180
Chigné, 258
Choiseul, 6, 13, 56, 57
Choiseul, Stainville, 137
chouan, chouannerie, 30, 40, 42, 47, 50,
    51, 197, 249, 258, 260, 263–4, 265,
    266, 267, 271, 272, 280
church, the French, 14–15, 18–19; in
    Brittany, 32; and Revolution, 45,
    47
Cicero, 104
Cité (section), 180, 183
clergy, 45, 46, 47, 48, 49, 50, 62, 164–6,
    226, 246, 252 ff., 298
Clermont-Ferrand, 91, 158
Clochard, 226–8
Cobb, Richard, 1n., 51
Cobban, Alfred, 21 and n., 25n.,
    88–90, 132–3, 147
Coicy, Mme. de, 150–1
Coigny, duc de, 57
Colbert, 10, 71
Colin, Antoine, 171
Collot d'Herbois, 67, 85, 91
Colmar, 94
Combourg, 134
Committee of General Security, 203,
    205, 208
Committee of Public Safety, 91, 188,
    194, 202, 215, 221

Commune, the, 205, 207, 209, 212, 213, 214, 243
Condillac, 64
Condorcet, 85
Conti, 6
Convention, the, 91, 157, 202, 205, 236, 243, 257
Coppéaux, Jean-Joseph, 210
Coquillard, 215, 216
Corbin, René, 206, 207, 207, 214
Cordeliers, the, 191, 204, 209, 210
Côte, d'Or, 136, 137, 158
Côtes-du-Nord, 260
Counter-revolution, 30, 41–2, 246, chapter 9 passim, chapter 10 passim
Courbis, 307
Court de Gébelin, 73
Cousin, François, 215
Coutances, 166
Coyer, abbé, 19
Crébillon fils, 66
Crime, 30–1, 33–40, 150–4, 237–9, 265, 310–11
Croix-Rouge (Paris), 185, 186, 201
Cubières, 55, 58

D'Aguessau, 118
d'Aguillon, duc, 6, 8, 13, 57, 80
Dalby, Simone, 230
d'Alembert, 54, 56, 57, 61, 62, 63, 64, 67
d'Angoulême, duc, 292, 293
Dalizy, 211
Danton, 180
Danycan, 115
d'Arc, chevalier, 12, 18, 19, 123
d'Artois, comte, 18, 139, 207, 214, 298
Darvieux, 308
Daubenton, Antoine, 205, 215
Dauphiné, 126
Davranches, 211
Decazes, 305; loi Decazes, 311
Defarge, Citoyenne, 159, 165
Delacroix, 75
De la Frezeliére, Mlle., 137
De la Rivière, Étienne, 179
de la Rouërie, 267
De La Tour du Pin, marquise, 134
Delille, 55, 62
Delisle de Salles, 60
de Nantiat, baron, 267

Depont des Granges, 140
derogation, 5, 18, 28, 120
Des Essarts, 58, 76
Desmoulins, Camille, 67, 84, 180
de Solérac, 272
Desrosiers, 184
Deux-Sèvres, 235
d'Havré, duc, 142
d'Holbach, 55, 63
d'Houdetot, 55
Diderot, 56, 63, 64, 69
Didot, Aristarque, 209, 211, 212
Dijon, 22, 139, 154, 157
Dinan, 260
Directory, the, 86, 130, 138, 169, 215, 264, 265, 271, 290, 307
Dodille, Philibert, 222
Dôle, 91
domaine congéable, 43
Domat, 102
Dorat, 55
Dordogne, 158, 231, 235
d'Ormesson, 76
Doubs, 136
Dournel, J.-B., 181
Doyle, William, 105, 106
Dreyfus, Ferdinand, 219
Du Barry, Mme., 80, 82
Dubois, 14
Duchesne, Augustin, 190, 191
Ducis, 59
Duclos, 56, 62, 63, 67, 69
Dumeige, Pierre, 207
Dumont de Sainte-Croix, 60
Dumouriez, 261
Dupaty, 106
Duperron, Sanson, 179, 214
Dupont, Jacques, 297
Duport du Tertre, 75
Duras, maréchal de, 62
Dutour, Charles, 306, 307

economic crisis, 124, 156, 159–61, 230 ff., 269–70
education, 230
Elba, 292
elections, 44–5, 124–9, 290, 293, 312
Elven, 35, 38, 39
emigration (noble), 135–9, 141–3, 200, 268, 269, 270–5, 311–12
Empire, the, 169, 290, 299, 303, 304, 307, 309, 312

Escherolles, Mme. des, 136, 139, 146
Estate, Third, 91, 108, 109, 124–9
Estates (provincial), 8, 31–2
Estates-General, 10, 91, 124–6, 258
Eure, 137

Fabre, Alexandre, 305
Fabre d'Eglantine, 60, 67, 76, 85
Fajon, 304
Fantin, J.-B., 206, 207
Fariau, Fréderic, 184
Faucheux, Marcel, 42
Fayel, J., 181
Fédérés (section), 188
Féline, Père, 282
Fénélon, 11
feudistes, 20–6
Finistère, 179, 253
Fitz-James, duc de, 8
Flavin, 156
Fleurigné, 50, 51
Fleury, 6
Fontaine, Jean-Mathias, 187, 188
Fontaine-de-Grenelle, 174, 196, 199,
    200, 201, 202, 203, 206, 207
Fontenelle, 56
Ford, Franklin, 15
Fougeray, 34
Fougères, 30
Franquevaux, 309
Fréron, 76
Fressay, 188
Froment, François, 298, 299, 300,
    301, 303, 304, 309, 312
Froment, Pierre, 298, 299, 300
Furet, François, 1n., 4, 89

Gahard, 45
Gaillard, 62
Gain, André, 136–7, 139n., 142, 145
Gallot, Dr. Jean-Gabriel, 250–1
Ganges, 308
Garat, 55, 58
Gard, chapter 10 passim
Garnier, J. J., 68
Gaudet, Victor, 208
Gavot, Charles, 184
Genérac, 310
Geoffrin, Mme., 55, 56
Gerbier, P. J. B., 53
Gers, the, 231
Gironde, the, 137, 138, 222, 231, 234

Girondins, Girondist, 86, 91, 188–9,
    209–10
Gluck, 87
Gombaud, Marie, 237–8
Gorsas, 60, 67, 75, 84
governors, provincial, 6, 7, 8 and n., 10
Graffand, Jacques, 297
Grammont, duchesse de, 56
Grand-Champ, 38
Gravilliers, the, 173, 179, 212–13
Greer, Donald, 135, 136
Grégoire, Henri, 53, 86
Grenier, 210
Grenoble, 106, 111
Grigau, 261
Gruder, Vivian, 4
Guard, National, 42, 44, 45, 46, 47, 48,
    176 (of Paris), 228, 235, 243, 290,
    293, 294, 295, 296, 299, 305, 307,
    308

Hacquet, Pierre-François, 254
Halle-au-Blé (section), 205, 215
Halles (section), 183
Haute-Garonne, 137, 235
Hébert, 84, 86
Hébertistes, 157, 208
Hérault de Seychelles, 91
Herbault, Nicolas-Alexandre, 179, 214
Hoche, 261
Hood, James, 296
hospitals, 229 ff
Hû, Mathias, 173, 188, 189
Hufton, Olwen, 2, 218
Humbert, 211

Ile-d'Yeu, 257
Ille-et-Vilaine, 137, 256, 257
Imbault, Pierre-Edmé, 187, 188
intendants, 4, 7, 8, 10, 11, 14, 44, 95,
    105, 108, 116, 201
Invalides (section), 184, 192
Isambert, Pierre, 196–9, 203

Jabel, Antoine, 188
Jacobins, 86–7, 130, 165, 166, 174,
    180, 181, 186, 187, 188, 193, 194,
    196, 197, 198, 199, 200, 201, 202,
    204, 208, 209, 211, 213, 224, 227,
    239, 255
Jalès, camps de, 287, 291, 299
Jansenism, 105, 278, 283

Jard, Pierre, 211
Jaurès, 88, 95
Jesuit, 31, 277, 302
Jews, 296
Jossier, Jean-Baptiste, 179, 213
Jura, 137
justices of the peace, chapter 7 *passim*

Keralio, 58

Labastide family, 310
La Blanchèrie, 73
La Bruyère, 103
La Chapelle Erbrée, 256
La Chapelle-Janson, 49
Lacombe, Claire, 148
Lacour, Pierre, 239
La Harpe, 55, 57, 58, 62, 64, 72, 76, 85
Laignelot, 104
Lamaignère, Antoine, 193–4
Lambert-Becquet, Étienne, 192, 204, 205
Lamoignon, 114
Landais, Pierre, 210
Landéan, 50
Landes, the, 231
Languedoc, 286, 287
Lanjuinais, 86
Lanteiris-Lazelle family, 310
Lanusse, Jean, 222
Lardy, Sylvain, 181
Larevellière-Lépeaux, 94
La Rochelle, 140
Latreille, André, 164
La Tremouille, 137
Laudun, 301, 306
Laugier, Balthazard-Marie, 174, 196, 199, 201–3, 206
Laval, 150
Lavondès, Alexis, 303, 304
La Vrillière, duc, 79
Law, 110
Lebrun, J.-E.-A., 185–6, 188, 189, 197, 213
Le Chapelier, 125
Le Chevalier, J.-B., 206, 207
Lefevbre, Georges, 137, 286
Lefrançois, Claude, 180
Légier, Nicolas-Vincent, 179
Le Goff, Tim, 2
Le Havre, 90
Le Made, abbé, 275

Le Mans, 93, 133
Lemierre, 58, 62
Le Peletier de Saint-Fargeau, 205
Le Puy, 154, 161, 166
Le Sage, 69
Lespinasse, Mlle de, 55
Lessore, J. B., 181
Letellier, Joachim, 215
Letellier, Pierre-Nicolas, 173
Leyris, 231
Libourne, 243
Ligouri, 283
Limousin, 220, 228, 232
Lindet, Robert, 122
Linguet, 68, 73
Livy, 104
Loaisel, 267
Loire, 265, 312
Loire-Inférieure, 146, 235, 252, 266
Lombards, the, 173, 186–7, 212
Loménie de Brienne, 62, 126
London, 274
Lons-le-Saulnier, 158
Lorraine, 228
Lot-et-Garonne, 231
Loudun, 122
Louis XIV, 3, 5, 6, 7, 8, 9, 10, 11, 13, 14, 15, 17, 28, 80, 101, 102, 105, 110, 287, 288
Louis XV, 14, 64, 80
Louis XVI, 4, 5, 13, 14, 15, 20, 21, 22, 23, 25, 27, 28, 65, 105
Louis XVII, 51
Louis XVIII, 268, 291, 298, 299, 302
Louis-Philippe, 97
Loustalot, 84
Louvet, 84
Louvet-Dubois, 209, 211, 212
Louvois, 7
Louvre (section), 180, 181
Loyseau, 102
Luxembourg (section), 173, 175, 193
Lyons, 157, 246, 289

Mably, 64
Macon, 158
Madrid, 142
Magnouac, 233
Mail (section), 194
Maine, 150, 268, 281
Maine-et-Loire, 258, 264, 279
Mallet du Pan, 66, 127–8

Manuel, 67, 75, 83, 84, 85, 176
Marais (section), 177, 184, 206
Marat, 70, 75, 77, 84, 85, 159, 205
Marchais, Mme. de, 56
Marchés, the, 173, 179, 185, 190, 204
Marçigny, 212
maréchaussée, 30–1, 34–5, 37, 46
Maret, 84
Marie Antoinette, 148
Marion, Marcel, 138
Marmontel, 55, 58, 61, 62, 64, 72, 84
Marmouzet, Dominique, 194, 195
Marseille, 90, 233, 246
Martin, Charles-Antoine, 211
Martin, Jean-Marie, 173, 212–13, 215
Marxism, 88
Masannay, 161
Massé, Pierre, 141
Mathieu, Nicolas, 177, 194
Mathiez, 165, 286
Mauges, the, 277, 279, 280
Maunoir, Father, 31, 47
Maupeou, 8, 10, 80, 81, 121
Maurepas, Mme. de, 57
Maury, 55, 72
Mayenne, 235, 257
Médoc, 137
Méjean, Jean, 308
Mende, 156
Mercier, L.-S., 30, 60, 66, 67, 68, 75, 84, 123
Merle, Jacques, 211
Metz, 151
Meuse, 136
Michel, Étienne, 209, 212
Miellon, 307
Mirabeau, marquis de, 12, 19, 74, 91
Molière, 76
Molière-et-Lafontaine, 180
—monarchy (and royalists), chapter 1 passim, 80, 266, 267–9, 273–5, 286, 288, 291, 296, 297, 298, 299, 304, 305, 309, 311, 312
Montagne Sainte-Geneviève, 183
Montaigu, 261
Montauban, 90
Montaubon (baker), 237
Montautour, 34
Montesquieu, 3, 11–12, 55, 64
Montfaucon, 264
Montmorency-Laval, 137

Montpellier, 154
Montreuil, 187
Morande, Charles Thévenau de, 74, 78–82
Morbihan, 279
Morellet, 55, 58, 72, 84
Mornet, Daniel, 123
Moustier, comte de, 270, 271
Mouvel, 76
Mussidan, 235

Nancy, 106
Nantes, 125, 246, 257, 267
Nantes, edict of, 287
Napoleon, 130, 140, 291, 292, 299, 302, 312
navy, the, 17–18, 228, 239
Necker, 14, 32, 57, 114, 126, 150
Necker, Mme., 55, 57
Ners, 294
Newton, 77
Nîmes, 287, 289, 290, 293, 295, 296, 297, 298, 299, 300, 301, 302, 304, 305, 307, 311, 312, 313
Nivernais, 139
Nivernais, duc de, 57, 58
Noguès, Louis-Antoine, 209, 211, 212
Nord, department of the, 23, 137
Normandy, 94, 145, 161, 268, 281, 282

Ode, 307
Oratoire (section), 206, 207
Orléans, 152, 157
Orléans, Duke of, 6, 137

Pache, 203, 204
Pacquier, 233
Palack, Manus, 210
Panckoucke, 56
Panis, 76
Panthéon-Français, 173, 181, 188, 189
Paris, 55, 65, 66, 67, 68, 69, 91, 117, 137, 141, 143, 161, 163, 167 ff., 224, 230, 243, 246, 260
Paris, Jean, 305
parlements, 8, 9, 10, 11, 12, 16–17, 18, 30, 44, 106, 108, 110–12, 114–16, 118, 119, 121, 126, 135, 138, 218
parlement of Paris, 9, 16, 100, 106, 116, 117, 124, 179, 203
Patris, Pierre-Étienne, 180

peasants, 4, 23–5, 32, 43–5, 46, 123, 129, 134, 140–2, 146, 157, 235–6, 249 ff., 300, 301
Peligot, Melchior-Humbert, 195, 206, 207–12
Pelletier, Henri-François, 193
Perche, 281
Périgord, 232
Pétion, 176, 203
Phulpin, Florentin, 173, 174, 188, 189, 215
Piccini, 87
Piis, 58
Pinard, Clement, 206
Piques (section), 177, 195
Place Vendôme (section), 194
Plaudren, 35, 37, 45
Plescop, 35
Ploeren, 45
Ploermel, 47
Pointard, Charles, 181
Poissonnière, 206
Poitiers, 139
Poitou, 220, 228, 272, 281
Polignac, 144
Polignac (family), 94
Poligné, 35
Ponceau, 180, 187
Pontarlier, 158
Pont-Neuf, 179, 192, 195, 203–5
Pont-Scorff, 37
poor, the, 42, 44, 45, 91–2, 149 ff., 217 ff., 257; poor nobility, 18 ff., 119–20, 251, 309
Popincourt, 184, 190, 191
population, rise of, 112–13
Port en Bessin, 159
Postes (section), 179
Pourvoyeur, 159
Prévost, 69
prostitution, 151, 223
Protestants, 280, 287 ff.
Provence, 24, 125–6, 228, 286
Prudhomme, 75, 84
Prugnon, 178
Pyrennees, 146

Quercy, 134
Quiberon, 256
Quinze-Vingts (section), 190

Raimbault, 237

Rameau, 70
Rançon, 209, 211
Raynal, abbé, 55
Regency, the, 9, 11, 24
Rennes, 30, 35, 46, 110, 111, 125; parlement of, 17, 106
Restif de la Bretonne, 67, 151
Restoration, the, 135, 145, 291, 292, 293, 296, 302, 304, 312
Réunion (section), 195, 206, 208–12
Rheims, 203, 278
Rhône, river, 292, 312
Rhuys, 39
Richelieu, 108; vineyards of Richelieu family, 137
Richeprey, 150
Richet, Denis, 89
Rivarol, 60, 67, 72, 85
Rivoire, Henri, 303
Roanne, 91
Robespierre, 163, 194, 215, 286, 291, 307, 309
Rochefort, princesse de, 59
Rodez, 150, 156
Rohan, cardinal de, and diamond necklace affair, 83
Rohan, comte de, 54
Roland, Mme., 148
Romillé, 36
Roquemaure, 307
Roucher, 55
Rouen, 154, 162, 163, 246
Rouergue, 150
Roule (section), 207, 208
Roulleau, J., 177, 206, 207
Roullet, 241, 243
Roure, comte de, 142
Rousseau, 56, 64, 83, 86, 87
Rousselet, Jacques-Charles, 185
Roux, Antoine, 308, 309
Roux, Jacques, 213
Rulhière, 55, 62

Saige, mayor, 243
Saint-Brieuc, 250
Saint-Denis (section), 183, 196, 197, 199
Saint-Didier, 45
Saint-Georges-du-Puy-de-la-Garde, 279
Saint-Gildas-de-Rhuys, 33
Saint Gilles, 311

Saint-Joachim, 252
Saint-Lambert, 58
Saint-Malo, 115, 125
Sainte-Marguérite (district), 187
Saint-Médard-en-Jalles, 222
Saint-Mendé, comte de, 140
Saint-Patrice, 165
Saint-Seurin, 222, 223, 232
Saint-Simon, 3, 6, 11, 102
Saint Vincent de Paul, 162
Saintonge, 133, 134, 137, 140
Sallust, 104
sans-culottes, 50, 53, 86, 92, 148, 160,
    167, 173, 177, 181, 186, 187, 197,
    198, 200, 201, 202, 204, 208, 210,
    211, 212, 214, 215, 224, 233, 258,
    286
Santerre, 176
Sarthe, 137, 139, 258
Sartine, 14
Saulx-Tavanes, Duchy of, 23n., 24,
    139
Saumurois, 258
Saurin, 56, 59
Saurin, Mme., 55, 59
Ségur, ordinance, 17, 19, 27, 106, 108,
    120
Seine, 164
Séné, 34, 38
Sens, 137, 139
sexual practices, 281 ff.
Sieyès, abbé, 128
Soboul, Albert, 1n., 3n., 4n., 11n., 12,
    20n., 88, 167
Sorel, Julien, 199
Soulavie, abbé, 60
sports, 39–40
state, rôle of in Ancien Régime, 2,
    29 ff, 40–1, 44, 52, 101, 121; rôle
    under Revolution, 44 ff., 217 ff.,
    258 ff.
Suard, Jean-Baptiste-Antoine, 54, 55,
    56, 57, 61, 64, 65, 70, 84
Suard, Mme., 55, 56, 57, 65
Sutherland, Donald, 2

Tacitus, 104
Taine, 85
Tarbes, 158
Target, 55
Tauriac, 237
taxation, 9–10; and parlements, 23–6;

and papier timbre revolt 1675, 31;
    taxes, 31–2, 33–4, 40, 43, 93, 95n.
    25, 98, 116, 135, 251, 265–6, 298
Taylor, G. V., 89–90
Temple (section), 180, 191
Terray, 6, 80
Terror, the, 168, 204, 239; the White
    Terror, chapter 10 passim., 306,
    307, 310
Tessé, Mme. de, 56
Teste, Antoine, 304, 306, 307, 308
Théâtre-Français, 180
Therrin, François-Nicolas, 192, 214
Thilly, François, 195, 203–5, 215
Thomas, 55, 62, 64, 72
Thorillon, Antoine-Joseph, 179
Thouret, 169–70
Thuillier, Claude-Louis, 180
Tilhard, Jean-Nicolas, 210
Tilly, Charles, 42, 286
Tocqueville, 29, 72, 146
Toleration, edict of, 288
Toulon, 232
Toulouse, 90, 106, 110, 133, 138, 142,
    143, 144, 154, 163, 293, 298, 310;
    nobility of, 23–4
Tours, 151, 163
Treffléan, 38, 39
Tréguier, bishop of, 275
Trevor-Roper, H. R., 100–1
Trinquelaque, Charles, 300, 301, 302,
    303, 304, 309
Troyes, 152, 162
Truchon, Germain, 213
Tubeuf, 301
Tuileries, 180, 191, 206
Turgot, 121
Turin, 299
Tustet, 221

ultras, 292, 294, 295, 304
United States, 236
Ure, Andrew, 259
Uzès, 287, 294, 296, 297, 300, 301, 312

Val-Saumurois, 280
Vannes, 30, 33, 35, 44, 45, 46, 47,
    257, 279
Var, 313
Varennes, 142, 180
Varin, Pierre, 184
Vauvert, 308, 309